# CALL OF DUTY MODERN WARFARE 2

## CONTENTS

W9-CMZ-914

# INTRODUCTION

## WELCOME BACK, SOLDIER

If you're a returning fan of *Call of Duty 4: Modern Warfare*, we know you've been waiting for this game with a great deal of anticipation—we have too! Fear not, it's everything you could have hoped for and more.

This guide takes you through all aspects of the game, from the single-player campaign to the multiplayer. We hope it enhances your enjoyment, so dig in!

There are a lot of subtle tweaks to the gameplay, from the netcode that powers multiplayer, to fine tuning the various weapons in the game. Here are just a *few* of the key new features that'll get your blood pumping...

## NEW WEAPONS

Many new weapons have been added to the game, including a few that show up only in the multiplayer.

Of particular note are the new attachments, including several new types of optical scope, as well as the new Thermal Scope, which provides an infrared view of the battlefield ideal for picking out targets in rough terrain.

The new Heartbeat Sensor gives you a short-range human 'radar' that periodically sweeps the area around you for living targets. It's great for stealthy operations or finding targets in dense urban terrain.

It's now possible to have *two* attachments on a weapon. So, for example, you can find weapons in the campaign that have grips and scopes at the same time, and you can create similar loadouts in multiplayer!

The under barrel shotgun attachment gives you another option to take in place of the grenade launcher. It gives medium-range assault rifles extra punch for close-range combat.

## NEW TOOLS

New secondary items have been added, including a laser designator in the single-player campaign that lets you direct the fire of a Stryker!

There are also new Semtex sticky grenades that pack a serious punch—strong enough to take out an BTR in one blast.

An extremely cool new weapon is the Predator Drone control rig, which allows you to rain guided air-to-ground missiles down on your opposition!

A new CQC-style of handgun allows you to carry your combat knife in the ready position while using your sidearm. This allows much faster stabs, giving you a strong secondary tool for close-range assassination.

Riot Shields provide a new defensive option, providing near immunity to small arms fire in your frontal arc. You cannot fire while you hold the shield and, as you get hit, the viewable area becomes obstructed with cracks as bullets impact the shield. Riot Shields work very well in cooperative play, with one player drawing fire and another taking down exposed hostiles.

The ability to dual-wield guns is another new addition. Several small firearms can be used twin-fisted, including the Mini-Uzi and G18 machine pistol. Dual weapons have poor accuracy at long range due to your inability to scope, not to mention that a shooter's accuracy naturally suffers wielding two weapons. However, dual-wielding is superior for laying down a sheer wall of fire at close range. You can also get very long bursts of fire by shooting first with one hand, then continuing to fire with the second hand while the first gun reloads.

# NEW MODES

Special Ops has been added to the game as a new third mode. It's a cooperative mission mode that allows you and a friend to play various scenarios from portions of the campaign, parts of *Call of Duty 4: Modern Warfare*, and some entirely new battles.

Multiplayer has added *many* new modes and options. Check the multiplayer section of this guide for details. There are new Perks, new secondary weapon options, new Killstreak and Deathstreak rewards, and much more.

# IN THIS GUIDE

## CAMPAIGN WALKTHROUGH

The main campaign walkthrough takes you through all 18 missions of the story. The campaign consists of three Acts, with five, six, and seven missions, respectively.

## A SPOILER-LIGHT WALKTHROUGH

We've made every possible effort to avoid spoiling any major story elements. While certain aspects of the game simply have to be shown to provide any sort of guidance, whenever possible, we've obscured or hidden references to key events in the game.

Consequently, you can use the walkthrough without fear that we'll ruin any major surprises that Infinity Ward has prepared for you!

CAMPAIGN BASICS

CAMPAIGN WALKTHROUGH

SPECIAL OPS MISSIONS

MULTIPLAYER BRIEFING

MULTIPLAYER WARFARE

TACTICAL

CLANS

INTEL CHARTS

SATELLITE INTEL

ACHIEVEMENTS

## SPECIAL OPS

This guide's Special Ops chapter provides coverage for all 23 of the cooperative missions, along with tips for clearing the more difficult missions on Veteran difficulty.

All Spec Ops missions can be played cooperatively with a friend, but there are two that can be played *only* with a partner. Playing with a buddy is a ton of fun, so we recommend bringing a friend along even on the missions that don't require two players!

Spec Ops missions are divided into Alpha, Bravo, Charlie, Delta, and Echo classifications, with progressively more difficult challenges in the later tiers. You earn mission stars for completing Spec Ops missions, and unlocking new challenges requires a certain number of mission stars.

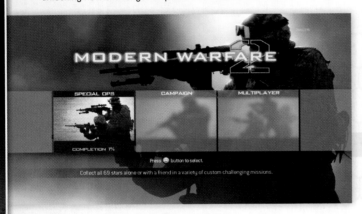

## MULTIPLAYER

Multiplayer is a huge part of the *Modern Warfare* experience. Consequently, we've devoted a large section of the guide to all the multiplayer details, including charts covering unlockable and customizable features and items, detailed maps of every multiplayer level, plenty of advice for customizing your character class loadouts, and expert tactics for excelling in all aspects of multiplayer action.

## BLACK OPS

We've provided a list of all the Achievements and Trophies you can acquire, as well as the locations of all of the Intel hidden throughout the campaign.

## COMBAT

We aren't going to rehash the manual or the in-game tutorial, but a few fundamental concepts will help you get through all of the single-player and co-op content in the game. Keep in mind that multiplayer combat is *very* different from single-player, so hit this guide's multiplayer chapters when you're ready to hop online.

### READ THE USER MANUAL

This chapter is intended as a *supplement* to the user manual that comes with your copy of *Call of Duty: Modern Warfare 2*, not a *replacement* for it. We intentionally avoid rehashing content that's already in the user manual, except when it's necessary for explaining other concepts. The discussions in this chapter assume that you have read and understand the user manual, and that you've played the in-game tutorial.

## WEAPONRY

One of your first considerations in every mission is your gear. You're always given a basic loadout of weaponry for any particular mission, but you can swap out either (or both) of your starting weapons at any time. You may *need* to switch because you're running low on ammo. You may *want* to switch because you've found a different weapon that you favor. Or you may *have* to switch because you need a specific tool to deal with a specific threat.

In multiplayer, your weapon choices are intensely personal and have a heavy impact on your effectiveness in varying combat scenarios. In single-player, weaponry tends to fall into broader categories, where a certain class of weaponry is useful in a wider range of situations.

### BULLET PENETRATION

Be sure to use bullet penetration to your advantage whenever possible. This allows you to take out enemies hiding behind corners or thin walls. This is especially important on harder difficulty settings. Assault rifles and sniper rifles boast particularly good bullet penetration.

### ▶ ASSAULT RIFLES

Assault rifles are your bread and butter weapon for much of the campaign. They have good accuracy at medium range, where a lot of in-game combat takes place, and they are reasonably effective at long range. Up close, you can still use them in a pinch, as a burst of full auto takes down most any opponent.

Assault rifles work well with a Red Dot, Holographic, or MARS sight for medium-range work, with an ACOG giving you a bit more accuracy at longer range.

A grenade launcher attachment gives you anti-vehicle capability, while a shotgun attachment gives you more close-range punch.

## SUBMACHINE GUNS

SMGs are ideal for close- to medium-range combat, particularly room-to-room fighting, where their excellent accuracy and high rate of fire makes them perfectly suited to CQC engagements.

With a proper sight, they can be reasonably effective at medium range, but they are somewhat less useful for longer-range engagements.

## SHOTGUNS

Shotguns are powerhouse close-range weapons, taking out nearly any nearby enemy in a single shot. Several varieties of shotgun appear in the campaign and Spec Ops missions, with the automatic variety trading longevity for sheer rate of fire.

Be careful with the automatic shotguns. Burning your clip on one or two enemies is a good way to end up dead when their friends show up.

Shotguns *can* take down foes at slightly longer ranges. They simply aren't well suited to it, and are poor at hitting enemies behind hard cover.

Shotguns are also notable in that they are good for taking down enemies carrying Riot Shields, challenging foes that appear at several points in the game.

## HANDGUNS

Handguns are secondary weapons of last resort for most of the campaign and Spec Ops missions. They have a smaller clip size, shorter range, and with one exception, no automatic fire. Some handguns can be used CQC-style with your knife at the ready, allowing faster stabbing attacks against close-range enemies.

Using a handgun over other weapon types is generally not recommended in the campaign or Spec Ops. The two main benefits of using a handgun—faster movement speed and quicker weapon switching—are generally more useful in multiplayer matches.

## SNIPER RIFLES

Sniper rifles are fairly rare in the single-player campaign, and somewhat more common in the various Spec Ops missions. They provide extreme long-range accuracy, and are ideal for picking off most opposition well before it becomes a threat.

In most cases where you *can* pick up a sniper rifle in single-player, you should do so. Use it until any long-range threats are eliminated, and then swap it out for another weapon.

## HEAVY WEAPONS

Heavy weapons include anti-vehicle explosives, such as the RPG-7, AT4, Stinger, and on occasion, the Javelin. These weapons are crucial for eliminating armored threats to you and your squad throughout the campaign and Spec Ops.

In most cases, you can grab such a weapon, use it to take down the vehicle, and then swap out for a different weapon immediately. We always warn you ahead of time when you're dealing with vehicular threats, so you don't need to lug one around for an extended length of time.

You can also find heavy machineguns, which are very useful during missions in which you face intense infantry resistance.

Heavy machineguns have huge clip sizes. With careful burst fire, they are nearly as accurate as assault rifles at mid and long range. Whenever possible, resist the urge to fire on full-auto; heavy machineguns have strong recoil, and your accuracy falls immediately.

# SECONDARY WEAPONS

Choosing your secondary weapon is largely a matter of personal preference. As a rule of thumb, you should take a second weapon to deal with a specific threat during the mission: a sniper rifle for long-range combat, shotgun for CQC, or explosives for vehicles.

If there is no specific threat, you can bring along a second weapon with an alternate type of sight for a different range band, or a favored Attachment, such as a Heartbeat Sensor or Grenade Launcher.

Silenced weapons are usually used in primary/secondary pairs—on most missions where you have the option to use a silenced weapon, you need to be stealthy for most or all of its duration.

## ) SPECIAL WEAPONS

### GRENADES

Grenades are useful during *all* missions, and you should use them frequently. You can find new grenades on fallen opponents and occasionally in weapon caches during missions. Ammo caches that resupply you also refill your grenade loadout.

On most missions, you are given four Frag Grenades and four Flash Grenades. A few provide you with four Semtex sticky grenades.

Frag Grenades taste best when you "cook" them by holding the grenade for a few seconds before you thow it. With practice, a skilled throw can detonate in midair above a target behind cover.

However, even when you throw them "cold," you can flush enemies out of cover. They either have to move, or they get hit by the blast. Either result is positive for you, as it reduces incoming fire and gives you a chance to take down the enemies that move.

Flash Grenades detonate instantly on impact. They blind and stagger nearby enemies. This is a *very* powerful tool. You can use them to suppress enemies when you take an unacceptable level of incoming fire, or when you need to clear a room and you're certain enemies are inside.

Semtex is mostly useful for taking out vehicles in the absence of an explosive weapon, but they can be used as makeshift Frag Grenades if necessary.

## EXPLOSIVES

Claymores and C4 are standard issue in some missions. They're useful in a defensive firefight. You can use both of these explosives to "wall off" a flanking advance to your position, giving you protection from enemies that may catch you unawares.

Claymores are generally better suited for this role than C4, as they work automatically. C4 is usually better as a trap, placed in a position where you can see it and trigger its detonation.

Remember that, even with a different weapon out, you can detonate C4 by double tapping the Reload button—you don't need to have the detonator in hand. (The PC version does not have this feature.)

This allows you to place C4 near a likely target area—an explosive fuel container or a vehicle, for example—take cover, and then blow the C4 when enemies move near it. The resulting explosion is usually enough to down an entire hostile squad.

Remember also that you can shoot C4 and Claymores to detonate them. In the campaign, enemies *will* do so, especially on higher difficulty levels, so watch where you place them!

## ATTACHMENTS

Both the underslung grenade launcher and shotgun attachments are quite useful, particularly the Grenade Launcher. The Grenade Launcher can take out hostile clusters, destroy light vehicles, detonate nearby explosives, and, with a well aimed shot, even helicopters!

You often start a mission with a very large load of grenades. Be sure to use them—they can make difficult firefights considerably easier.

The shotgun attachment gives you some flexibility in your weapon loadout, as you can use an assault rifle with a shotgun attached and a second weapon that is more specialized, such as a sniper rifle or anti-vehicle explosive.

## SPECIAL TOOLS

On a few missions, you're given very special equipment, in the form of night vision goggles or a laser designator. In both cases, their use is straightforward and simple. Use night vision goggles if you want better vision in a darkened portion of the mission, and you use the laser designator to direct friendly fire during two special missions.

## SIGHTING

Shouldering gun and using the integral iron sights or attached scope is a fundamental mechanic in *Call of Duty: Modern Warfare 2*, and it's vital for long-range accuracy throughout the game. Additionally, sighting has a special function that works only in the campaign: your view to "snaps" to the nearest enemy in view (this does *not* work in multiplayer).

Use this ability heavily, as it allows you to acquire a new target instantly. With just a few short bursts, you can quickly take down the next target. Only enemies well hidden behind heavy cover resist this technique.

For those enemies, you must aim down the barrel or scope and line up the shot more accurately. Pick off an exposed limb or head when they go for a shot. Note that your crosshair has a slight 'drag' over enemies. You can use this to pick out enemies hiding in heavy brush or otherwise difficult to spot behind cover.

## COVER

Cover is vital to survival in the *Modern Warfare* series. Almost anything you can put between you and incoming bullets works as cover: a tree, a rock, a wall, a vehicle, doesn't matter.

Note that there is no inherent "cover bonus." You don't take less damage while in cover—you simply get hit less.

If you're in a firefight, you should always reload while you're behind cover. Moving between cover when you're under fire can also lower the heat, as enemies take a moment to reacquire you as a target when you shift locations.

Your health automatically regenerates after you take damage if you aren't hit for a few seconds. So, ducking behind solid cover and healing is very important during intense firefights. This is especially true on Veteran difficulty, where accurate enemy fire and lower health make any exposure dangerous.

Remember that you can shoot through light cover with higher-caliber weaponry. This works both for and against you, depending on whether you or your enemy is the one getting shredded behind light cover. When you have a high-powered weapon and your target is behind a flimsy wooden board or a door, shoot him straight through the cover!

Always try to keep cover between you and the bulk of hostile forces. Prioritize enemies in large groups that have elevation or are moving toward your flank. As long as you have reliable cover, enemies directly in front should be your last targets, as they have a much harder time damaging you.

## WHERE TO?

That's enough training. If you need more, consult the game's user manual, try out the in-game tutorial, and practice. It's time to dive into the game! You're free to begin anywhere you wish, as you can start with the campaign, the Special Ops missions, or jump right into multiplayer.

Stay frosty on the battlefield, be alert for foot mobiles, Oscar Mike to your position, and have fun!

# ACT 1

*"War is the greatest plague that can affect humanity; it destroys religion, it destroys states, it destroys families. Any scourge is preferable to it."*

**—Martin Luther**

# ACT 1

**RANGER**

OPERATIVE: PFC. JOSEPH ALLEN, RANGERS

OPFOR: NONE

LOCATION: CAMP PHOENIX, AFGHANISTAN MILITARY BASE

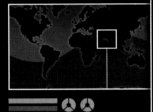

INTEL: 1

OBJECTIVE: TRAIN LOCAL MILITARY FORCES

---

**INITIAL LOADOUT**

**M4A1**

---

MISSION 01:

# S.S.D.D

## TRAIN THE LOCAL FORCES

Your mission begins in the dusty hills of Afghanistan, during a live-fire training exercise, demonstrating Ranger shooting techniques to the native military.

This mission is a simple tutorial, but don't miss the Intel! It gives you a chance to become acclimated—or re-acclimated—to the controls.

## ❯ ENGAGEMENT 1

Your first task is simply to spray bullets at the targets from the hip, in order to demonstrate the technique's inaccuracy.

After that, you can pick off the targets properly by crouching, sighting down the barrel, and firing aimed shots.

Shoot targets while firing from the hip.

**LEGEND**

1 ENGAGEMENT

i 1 INTEL

## TARGET SNAP

Remember that in single-player, unlike multiplayer, pressing the iron sights button causes your crosshair to snap instantly to the nearest hostile target.

With practice, this allows you to cycle quickly between multiple enemies, neutralizing them in short order.

This does *not* work in multiplayer, so don't get too comfortable.

If you find the target snap uncomfortable, you can disable it in the Options menu.

After the aiming demo, you are called on to fire through a wooden board to a target, and then to toss a grenade at multiple targets.

## SOFT COVER

Shooting through soft cover is a useful technique in many levels, as enemies take cover behind objects that aren't entirely impenetrable.

Any gun can shoot through very light materials, but larger-caliber weapons are especially suited to penetrate cover, and some can even shoot directly through walls.

If you know an enemy is behind a piece of cover, don't hesitate to fire a few shots directly *at* the cover. You change weapons a lot during the campaign, and some of the time your weapon can penetrate the cover and dispatch the target, saving you the trouble of waiting and carefully aiming for an exposed target.

# SHOW OFF YOUR SKILLS IN THE PIT

Once you're done with the preceding exercise, you can leave the training area and make your way over to The Pit, a live-fire training ground that's more suitable for testing your skills.

## GRENADIER

Grenades are powerful and useful tools. Though you are usually limited to a handful of Flash and Frag Grenades for any given mission, even a single grenade can be helpful.

Thrown at large groups or in confined spaces, a single grenade can disable or kill multiple targets.

Even if a Frag Grenade fails to score a kill, flushing your enemies out of cover can work just as well.

Flash Grenades are particularly helpful for clearing rooms and disabling very large enemy groups. Thrown ahead of you into a room, they can daze opponents, giving you the time you need to penetrate and eliminate any hostiles.

## ❯ ENGAGEMENT 2

Over at The Pit, Corporal Dunn instructs you to pick up a sidearm, a Desert Eagle in this case. Practice swapping between your primary weapon and your sidearm.

After that, you can then choose a weapon from the available options: SCAR-H Foregrip, MP5K Holographic, ACR Holographic, or M9. Test each of them for feel before you move on, and take whichever one you favor.

## WEAPON SWAP

Switching from your primary weapon to a pistol is always faster than reloading. However, because it's possible to carry two non-pistol weapons simultaneously, remember that switching from one assault rifle to another isn't necessarily faster.

However, in cases where you carry one weapon and a sidearm (typically at the start of many missions), don't hesitate to switch and quickly fire if you run out of ammo and still have a hostile target at close to medium range. Doing so can finish off an enemy before he gets a chance to harm you.

When you're ready, Dunn informs you that General Shepherd is watching your training in The Pit. He's recruiting soldiers for a special operation. Show him what you've got!

The entrance to the training grounds is just past the Corporal. The training run is a simple live-fire exercise. Run through the grounds, shooting down hostile targets while avoiding any of the civilian targets.

You must clear the hostile targets in each area before you move to the next.

At the halfway mark, you *must* kill the target with a knife attack. This teaches you an important technique. If you ever get jumped at pointblank range, knifing is always an instant kill against your opponent. Plus, it's fast and requires no ammunition.

Once you reach the end of the training grounds, you receive a grade based on your speed and number of civilians hit. In turn, this yields a recommended difficulty level for the single-player campaign.

If you are completely new to the *Call of Duty: Modern Warfare* series, we strongly recommend you play on Recruit difficulty. However, if you're a returning veteran, Regular difficulty provides a low-stress, high-intensity game. We don't recommend Hardened or Veteran difficulty for your first campaign playthrough, unless you *really* enjoy struggling against nasty opposition.

For completionists, we recommend playing through on Regular or Recruit to gather Intel, and then tackling Hardened or Veteran once you're familiar with the encounters.

### ACHIEVEMENT / TROPHY
### PIT BOSS

To earn the Pit Boss Achievement/Trophy, finish The Pit with a final time under 30 seconds.

## ROLL OUT!

Clearing the training makes a larger number of weapons accessible at the entrance. You can pick a new gun and retry the training as often as you like. You can pick from the M9 Pistol, ACR, Holographic, SCAR-H Foregrip, Desert Eagle, and MP5K Holographic.

### ON-THE-FLY DIFFICULTY

Remember that, while you're on a mission, you can always change its difficulty setting!

If you've chosen a higher difficulty level and you find one mission or area too frustrating, you can always lower the difficulty and come back later from the mission select to try again.

ENGAGEMENT 3

When you're finished with the training area, head back up the steps to exit. When you do, you arrive at a chaotic scene. Military trucks arrive, ferrying wounded from the front lines, and you're called out on an incursion into a nearby city. The first proper mission of the game begins.

### ACHIEVEMENT / TROPHY
### BACK IN THE SADDLE

You receive the Back in the Saddle Achievement/Trophy for completing this mission.

**RANGER**

OPERATOR: PFC. JOSEPH
ALLEN, RANGERS

OPFOR: MILITANTS

LOCATION: THE RED ZONE,
AFGHANISTAN

INTEL: 2

OBJECTIVE: CLEAR
MILITANT FORCES FROM
THE CITY

### INITIAL LOADOUT

**M4A1 Grenadier w/Holographic**

**M9**

**4x Flash Grenade**

**4x Frag Grenade**

**10x Grenade Launcher**

MISSION 02:

# TEAM PLAYER

## WELCOME TO THE SUCK

Your first real combat mission begins with a bang, as you awaken staggered from a blast. A front line General pulls you to your feet and orders you into the fray—Rangers lead the way!

Quickly take position at the river bank, and crouch before you look around to take stock of your situation.

Your squad has engaged in a firefight with a large group of militants on the river's opposite side. A destroyed section of bridge has halted your company's advance into the city.

## ⟩ ENGAGEMENT ① 1

Friendly Ranger troops are situated on this side of the river, along with some light armor providing support fire. The problem is a gap in the nearby bridge, just to your left.

You have to hold the position and drive off the militants to allow the bridge layer to successfully span the bridge's gap.

Use this opportunity to practice your aim in a live combat situation. Remember that you can quickly snap from target to target by tapping the Iron Sights button.

As long as you stay crouched behind the embankment, you should take little fire from the militants, giving you time to line up shots and get a feel for your weapons.

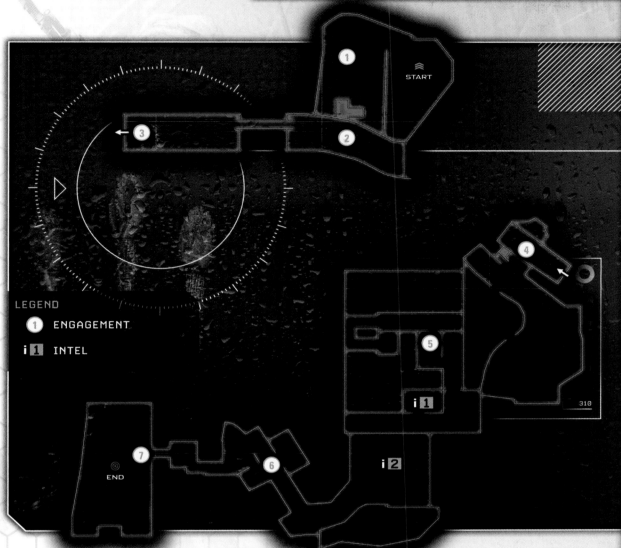

LEGEND

1 ENGAGEMENT

i 1 INTEL

After you exchange
fire with the
militants on the
opposite bank, a
new threat arises. A
technical rolls up on
the bridge gap and
unloads a squad of
militants, including
several with RPGs.
Concentrate your
fire on the bridge
gap to neutral-
ize them. If you
aim well, a single
launched grenade
can remove most of
the threat immediately.

## GRENADE LAUNCHER

This is also a good opportunity to practice using
your Grenade Launcher. In many single-player
campaign missions, you possess a large load
of grenades, much more than you can carry in
multiplayer matches.

In this case, you're loaded for bear with 10
grenades in your under-slung M203. Make good use
of them by blasting any clustered enemy groups
that you see.

Get a feel for the weapon's range. Try deliberately
aiming low or high to see how the arc of fire changes.
Later in the game, delivering spot-on launched
grenades can make certain situations
considerably easier.

# JOIN THE CONVOY

Once they are cleared out, the militants lose their taste for the fight, and you can begin to move out.

## ) ENGAGEMENT 2

Once the militants begin to fall back, proceed up the stairs to the bridge and wait for your Humvee to roll up. Then hop in the back. Don't run in front of it—you can get squashed!

Before the convoy sets out, an airstrike is called in to take down a nearby building filled with militants. You get to watch the show. Sit tight and watch for the airstrike to demolish the building on the other side of the river. Then man your turret as the convoy begins to roll.

## ) ENGAGEMENT 3

### ON THE GUN

The next section has you manning a mounted turret on your Humvee as the convoy rolls through the streets. Once you get clearance to open up, don't feel shy about holding the trigger—there's no ammo limit, and you can't overheat!

The convoy enters the narrow streets of the city ahead, and your team is warned that you are *not* permitted to open fire without orders.

This becomes particularly unnerving when the convoy passes several militants standing brazenly in the open on a balcony, but without any weapons in sight.

Worse, if you keep a close eye out on the alleys that you pass, you occasionally catch a glimpse of hostiles with RPGs darting through the shadows.

However, this doesn't last, as the sounds of gunfire ring out ahead. Your Humvee pulls up to an abandoned school. Militants run along the rooftop in plain view, armed and firing at the convoy.

Open up with the turret, taking down as many as you can. The convoy soon takes excessively heavy fire, and your driver is given the order to get you out of there!

You're quickly driven into the narrow alleys near the school. Be sure to watch the path ahead of you. You pass technicals with mounted machineguns—they can kill you if you don't take them out first!

The other militants on the rooftops and streets are less of a concern, so just keep an eye out for the machineguns and hold on.

## SO MUCH FOR YOUR RIDE

Partway through, your Humvee is forced to ram through a technical in an alley to break free. While this clears your path, an RPG fired from a nearby rooftop soon hits your vehicle.

The blast staggers and dazes your squad, but you don't have time to fully recover. Quickly sprint into the nearby building and take cover—you don't want to be exposed out in the street.

## ) ENGAGEMENT 4

Once you're inside, take a moment to recover. Then take stock of the situation.

The destruction of your ride has left you on the bottom floor of a building that is not filled with friendlies!

There are hostile militants on the second floor, and you have to clear them out.

### FLASHBANGS

On many missions, you're equipped with several flashbang grenades, and they are extremely useful in room-to-room combat.

Simply toss one into an un-cleared room where you have confirmed hostile presence. Then quickly blitz the room while the hostiles inside are staggered and blinded by the blast.

Flashbangs can also work well out in the open when you fight large enemy groups. A single well-placed toss can incapacitate a large number of foes, in some cases more than a frag grenade would kill.

Toss a flashbang up to the second floor, then head up the stairs and take down the few militants up there.

## SCHOOL'S IN SESSION

When the building is clear, you receive a distress call from friendly troops pinned down by fire from the school building. Your wild ride through the nearby alleys managed to put you across from that location.

Your squad is to advance into the school and clear it of enemy presence. Move out of your current building, onto the street, and quickly sprint across the school grounds to reach the front entrance.

# ) ENGAGEMENT 5

Be careful as you move into the school. The wide hallway you confront as you enter the school leads to a staircase at the end, and militants wait for you in cover.

A schoolroom harboring another target is off to your right. You may wish to hang back and pick off the targets at the end of the hall. Alternatively, you can dart quickly into the room on the right, clear it, and then flank the end of the hall via another door exiting the schoolroom.

Once you clear the ground floor, you can ascend the stairs to the second level. Most of the militants firing down at your friendly troops are located here.

When you reach the top of the steps, you face a totally oblivious militant firing out the windows. You can dispatch him easily from behind, but be ready for his buddies. They're located off to the right, down a hall and out of view.

Again, there are two ways to approach the other hostiles. You can go right from the window into the hall, or you can go right through a doorway that leads into another schoolroom, subsequently leading you out behind the militants at the windows.

Taking down the militants at the windows frees up Hunter 2-3, your squad mates who were pinned down. You can now head to the evacuation point, located out the back of the school.

One more hallway filled with militants blocks access to the school's backyard. Stay behind cover and pick them off, or go through another schoolroom to flank them. Then head out the back.

This narrow alley hosts several militants! If you're still packing grenades of any sort, this is a good place to use them, as you don't need to save any for the next mission.

Clear out the few militants in the alley, and then move up until you encounter friendly forces.

## AT THE EXTRACTION POINT

### ⟩ ENGAGEMENT 7

When you reach the rendezvous point, a commanding officer calls upon Private First Class Joseph Allen directly for a special assignment—you find out more about this in an upcoming mission.

For now, your next mission puts you into the boots of a new soldier, in a special task force, working with a very special partner… Put on your cold weather gear and set out for the third mission, Cliffhanger.

ACHIEVEMENT / TROPHY
### DANGER CLOSE

You receive the Danger Close Achievement/Trophy for completing this mission.

## FLANKING POSITIONS

In many encounters, you can find a path leading to the enemies' side or rear rather than facing them head-on.

In some cases, it's much safer to flank your opponents via the alternate route. In other situations, it's not safer, especially on higher difficulty settings—moving up can leave you without the covering fire and distraction that your teammates provide.

Generally speaking, if the alternate route provides ready cover, it's worth using, as you're usually safe from counterattack. But if the alternate route leaves you exposed, think carefully before you attempt to exploit the flank.

We always point out major flanking routes that provide a distinct advantage, but you can always make small adjustments to your position in any engagement. Just keep in mind what you stand to gain from making an aggressive flanking move before you rush headlong into danger!

## ⟩ ENGAGEMENT 6

There's one final skirmish before you reach the extraction point, as the school's back lot leads down into a narrow alley toward the rendezvous.

OPERATIVE: SGT. GARY "ROACH" SANDERSON, TASK FORCE 141

OPFOR: RUSSIAN SOLDIERS

LOCATION: TIAN SHAN RANGE, KAZHAKSTAN

INTEL: 3

OBJECTIVE: INFILTRATE THE RUSSIAN AIRBASE

## INITIAL LOADOUT

**Silenced ACR w/ Heartbeat Sensor**

**USP .45 Silenced**

**4x Flash Grenade**

**4x Frag Grenade**

MISSION 03:

# CLIFFHANGER

## CLIFFSIDE ASCENT

You land in the boots of Sgt. Roach high in the cliffs of Kazhakstan, resting beside one Captain "Soap" MacTavish!

The Captain is enjoying a smoke while you wait on your precarious perch. As a fighter jet screams past from the cliffs above, he prepares to move.

You're now part of a very secret mission for a very secret task force, known as the 141. Your objective here is to infiltrate a Russian airbase and recover a data box from a downed satellite—ideally without making any noise.

You begin the mission high up on the cliffs, just below the airbase located nearby.

## ) ENGAGEMENT 1

To reach it, you have to follow Soap as he makes his climb. You're outfitted with climbing gear to make the perilous ascent. The only part you have to worry about is managing the ice picks in your right and left hands.

Use the ice picks via the Fire button for your right pick, Iron Sights for your left pick. Make sure you don't release a pick when you're reaching with the other one!

Oh, and you *can* fall off the cliff here—don't make a misstep.

Carefully edge after Soap as he sidles along the cliff's edge. Then wait while he begins the ascent up the icy wall.

Once he's in motion, step up to the wall and begin your climb, alternating the left and right ice picks to climb.

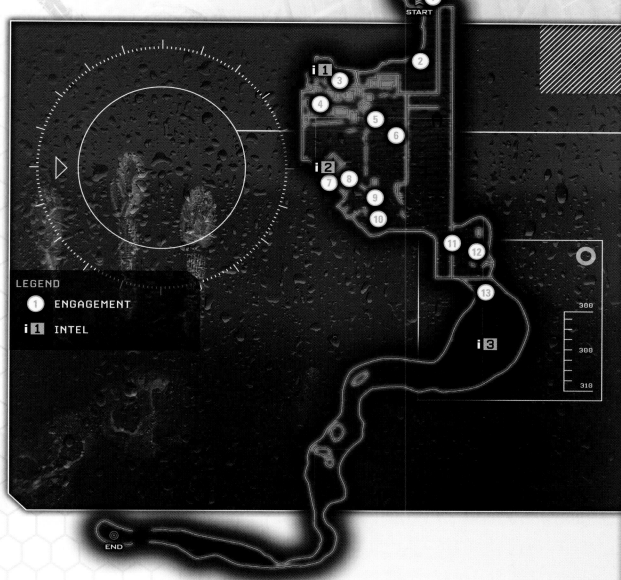

START

**LEGEND**

① ENGAGEMENT

i 1 INTEL

END

300

300

310

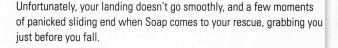

After the initial as-
cent, Soap makes a
running leap across
a gap and hooks
into an ice wall on
the gap's far side.

Follow him—run
and jump over
the gap.

Unfortunately, your landing doesn't go smoothly, and a few moments
of panicked sliding end when Soap comes to your rescue, grabbing you
just before you fall.

Quickly use your ice picks to regain your stability, and then make the
remainder of the climb to the top of the cliffs.

# HEARTBEAT STEALTH

After that panicked moment, you have a bit of
calm as you reach the outskirts of the airbase.
They're oblivious to your presence, and ideally,
you'll keep it that way.

The infiltration of the base begins with Soap giving you a short lesson on your shiny new gear. Activate the Heartbeat Sensor on your ACR and watch the scope. Soap shows up as a small blip, but as you get closer to Russian troops, they will show up as well.

## HEARTBEAT

The Heartbeat Sensor is a powerful tool for a stealth mission like this. It allows you to locate enemies before you can actually see them.

The sensor pulses every few seconds, showing contacts as small blips on the radar screen.

The best way to use this technology is to stop moving every few yards and let a fresh sweep scan the area. Make sure you remain stationary for the sweep, or you can get the enemy troop positions wrong when you're trying to sneak from cover to cover.

## ⟩ ENGAGEMENT 2

Once your sensor is active, follow Soap as you move around the base's perimeter.

You can clearly see the airfield's runway off to your left, but you're going around the right side of a fence to infiltrate from the base's outskirts.

Before you get closer, you must deal with two patrols of two guards. Soap tells you to target the left guard and fire on three.

If you do so, Soap takes out the other guard at the same time. You can fire early and down them both quickly, netting a snarky comment from Soap. Deal with both patrols in the same manner, and then move on.

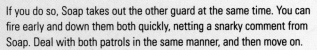

As you get closer to the base, Soap climbs up onto a ridge overlooking the base to provide overwatch for you. Once he's settled in, move up.

The snow begins to fall more heavily as a blizzard brews up, and this is good news for your infiltration. Visibility is cut to almost nothing, but your sensor still works just fine.

## BASE INFILTRATION

With MacTavish on overwatch with his thermal scope, he provides constant radio updates, warning you of nearby guards. In combination with your sensor, you have an edge over the guards, who are blinded by the blizzard and the cold. Plus, they aren't exactly expecting special forces to infiltrate their base.

## ❯ ENGAGEMENT ③

Use the Heartbeat Sensor and your stealthy weapons to make a quiet entry into the base. If you're careful, you can get to your first objective without raising the alarm.

Test out your stealth skills by sneaking in through an opening in the fence just ahead, or by downing the guards at the gate and then sneaking in.

### STEALTH

The most basic and most important aspect of stealth is simply crouching or crawling. While you're crouched, or especially while you're prone, the range at which a hostile can detect you is greatly reduced. You can also conceal yourself in brush, though that doesn't apply here, as you're out in the middle of a snowstorm! Guards can detect you if you use an unsilenced weapon nearby, or if you get too close to their line of sight.

Standing up and sprinting around is a sure way to get spotted quickly if the guards are anywhere nearby. If you do raise the alarm, don't panic. You have to fight off a wave of troops, but the base goes quiet again once they're dispatched.

A patrol can discover bodies that you leave behind, but it takes them awhile to raise the alarm and locate you if this happens. So, don't hesitate to dispatch a troublesome guard impeding your path. Occasionally, you might get spotted at a distance but not fully identified as a threat. If you can get to a hidden position and wait, the alert may be cancelled without a firefight.

## ❯ ENGAGEMENT ④

Once you're inside, you have to make your way over to the airfield, where Soap wants you to plant C4 on the fueling station. It's an insurance policy, in case things go south while you make your way over to the satellite.

You can pass through several of the buildings here, which is useful to avoid foot patrols and a roaming truck that traverses this area.

The truck that drives through holds four guards, so avoid its scrutiny if possible. The truck makes its rounds from the airfield, through the small collection of buildings, and out around the guard tower, near where you entered the base.

If you're safely hidden inside or behind a building, it can't spot you, so just listen for Soap's queues—he lets you know when it's coming.

Carefully make your way through the buildings to the airfield southeast of your position.

## NO REST FOR THE WARY

A few of the buildings have guards inside, but they don't see you coming, and you can spot them with your Heartbeat Sensor before they do. If you move up cautiously, you can eliminate them inside. You can even go for a knife kill if you want to earn the No Rest for the Wary Achievement/Trophy—knifing an enemy while he's unaware of you.

# PLANT C4 ON THE FUELING STATION

## ❯ ENGAGEMENT 5

To reach your first objective, you have to cross this open field with no cover. Use your Heartbeat Sensor and the blizzard's concealment to pass undetected, or at least to quietly eliminate any guards in your path. If you're quick and careful, you shouldn't run into any resistance as you make your way across the airfield.

## ❯ ENGAGEMENT 6

You need to plant a C4 charge at this location. Approach the fueling station and hold the Use button on the target until the C4 is armed.

Once you do this, your backup plan is in place. Now you need to rendezvous with Soap, who is headed toward the hangars at the airfield's west end, where he believes the satellite remains are located.

## GHOST

You receive the Ghost Achievement/Trophy for planting the C4 without getting spotted *and* without killing any guards. It's okay if MacTavish does.

Odds are, you'll get discovered on your first run through this mission. Remember that you can always replay it later and focus on moving cautiously to reach this point undetected, earning the Achievement/Trophy.

# RECOVERING THE SATELLITE

## ❯ ENGAGEMENT 7

Make your way back across the airfield to the snowy ridge just south of the buildings to the north. Use your Heartbeat Sensor and carefully make your way to the airfield's west edge.

Once you're all the way west, you can see the back of the hangars. Proceed due south to link up with Soap.

## OBJECTIVE WAYPOINTS

On many missions, an active waypoint indicator guides you toward your next objective, providing a direction and a distance in meters.

This is very helpful for moving you in the right direction, but be careful about relying on it blindly, especially in a stealthy mission like this one.

Heading straight toward your objective isn't always possible, or in this case, isn't the best idea.

Use the waypoint to get your bearings, but keep an eye on your surroundings as you move. The direct path usually isn't the safest here, as you want to avoid contact with hostiles as you move.

Meet up with MacTavish, and then head inside the hangar.

## TRICKY INTEL, PART I

Most of the Intel in the game is easy to find if you use our maps. However, this mission has two notably tricky pieces.

The first is located *behind* a window into one of the hangars as you make your way to meet Soap. Smash the window with a melee strike or shoot it out to pick up the Intel.

Slip in through the hangar's back door. A lone guard is inside, but MacTavish quickly and brutally takes him down.

Just past the unfortunate guard, the remains of the satellite rest on the hangar's ground floor.

MacTavish begins working on the satellite. He orders you upstairs to find the ACS module.

## ) ENGAGEMENT 8

Head upstairs. The ACS module rests on a table at the back of an office area.

However, once you recover it, the situation goes very bad, very quickly. MacTavish quietly radios to advise you that he's been discovered, and the angry shouts of Russians in the hangar emphasize the point.

Carefully and quietly make your way back out to the hangar. A huge squad of guards has Soap at gunpoint. You have mere seconds to do something—it's time to cash in your insurance!

Your C4 detonator comes up—pull the trigger, and the massive explosion at the fueling station stuns the guards. The entire world slows down, and you have precious seconds to

take down the guards. Take aim and fire, repeatedly tapping the Iron Sights button to switch between targets and down them quickly.

Soap is no less lethal. Between the two of you, the entire squad should be eliminated before your perception of time returns to normal.

Of course, now you have a fully alerted Russian airbase on your scent... It's time to get out!

# ESCAPE THE AIRFIELD!

## 〉ENGAGEMENT 9

Follow MacTavish out into the field, hugging any available cover and providing covering fire for MacTavish as he moves.

When MacTavish calls for you to run, do so. He can provide covering fire as you make your way to another bit of cover.

### FOLLOW DIRECTIONS...OR NOT

Don't feel constrained to follow Soap's directions exactly. You may want to navigate the field via a slightly different path.

The first point Soap directs you to is actually out on the airfield, near a MiG. It's dreadfully exposed, so you may want to sneak along the airfield's edge, behind the concrete barricades and jeeps that line the field's southern reaches.

You have to move east, toward the runway, which you can cross to evade the bulk of the troops on the airfield.

## 〉ENGAGEMENT 10

At this point, snowmobiles with hostile troops begin to arrive. Try to shoot neutralize them, either with a spray of bullets at close range or accurate, aimed fire at a distance.

Several hostiles at a building on the airfield's south side are your last threat before you can escape. Pick them off, or simply sprint for the runway after MacTavish calls that he's covering you.

## 〉ENGAGEMENT 11

Sprint across the runway and then slide down the snowy embankment to the cluster of buildings below.

When you regain your footing, turn 180 degrees and open fire on the line of enemy troops that appear at the top of the rise.

## ) ENGAGEMENT 12

Several more snomobiles show up at this point. Take down any you can get a bead on—they eventually slow down near the buildings, and their riders are vulnerable when they dismount.

Once you dispatch them, quickly hop on an available snowmobile and set off—it's time to make good your escape.

# SNOWMOBILE ESCAPE

## ) ENGAGEMENT 13

The primary extraction point is compromised due to the fireworks at the airbase, so you must flee with MacTavish to a secondary LZ.

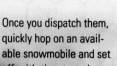

As you drive, your Fire button is the gas, Crouch is reverse, and Scope lets you fire an automatic G18 pistol with unlimited ammo.

### TRICKY INTEL, PART II

Yes, one of the Intel pieces is located on the ground, *during* the crazy snowmobile chase.

To pick it up, you simply have to drive over it, but finding it is the hard part.

The Intel is not far from where you start the chase. It's in a copse of trees off to the right side of the valley you descend.

If you make the jump down into the frozen lake, you've gone too far—restart and check the right side.

You may want to save this Intel for a replay. In that case, on a subsequent play-through, simply drive slowly to track it down, which is usually dangerous.

Follow the waypoint marker and MacTavish's directions as you flee the scene. Fire at any enemy snowmobiles or targets that get in front of you during the wild ride.

The ride leads down through a forested valley, out onto a frozen lake, and finally through a tight gap to a perilously steep slope.

### SNEAKY ROUTE

There's a 'hidden' route through the trees on the valley's left side. It cuts past a good chunk of the route. If you steer to the left and into the trees, you can cut through a narrow path that leads to the lake.

This isn't terribly important during the main campaign, but it is relevant when you play this snowmobile portion of the Spec Ops mission.

See this guide's Spec Ops section for more details—two missions involve racing along these slopes on the snowmobile!

When you reach the end of the line, you have to ride down the slope and make a jump across a chasm to reach the LZ!

Make sure you line up cleanly for the final descent down the mountainside. Do so, and you'll make the jump cleanly. Then you're home free. Drive up to the waiting chopper, and this mission is complete.

🔓 **ACHIEVEMENT / TROPHY**
## COLD SHOULDER

You receive the Cold Shoulder Achievement/Trophy for completing this mission.

## RANGER

OPERATIVE: PFC
JOSEPH ALLEN A.K.A.
ALEXEI BORODIN

OPFOR: RUSSIAN SECURITY

LOCATION: ZAKHAEV
INTERNATIONAL AIRPORT,
MOSCOW, RUSSIA

INTEL: 0

OBJECTIVE: ESCAPE FROM
THE AIRPORT

### INITIAL LOADOUT

**M240**

**M4A1 Grenadier**

**10x Grenade Launcher**

**4x Flash Grenade**

**4x Frag Grenade**

MISSION 04:

# NO RUSSIAN

## SPECIAL NOTE

At the beginning of *Call of Duty: Modern Warfare 2*, you're asked if you have any problems with a mission that contains disturbing content. This is the mission to which that question refers. If you wish, you can skip this mission entirely, and there are no Intel items to be found here, so you don't miss anything by doing so. If you find the content too unpleasant, simply skip it.

For those of you who want to experience it, we avoid spoiling any of the events in the first portion of the mission—the following walkthrough covers only the combat at the end of the mission.

## FOLLOW MAKAROV'S LEAD

Plucked from missions in Afghanistan, Private First Class Joseph Allen has been sent undercover with the arms dealer, Vladimir Makarov.

## ⟩ ENGAGEMENT 1

Follow Makarov through the airport terminal. You can't fail this portion of the mission, short of doing something silly like shooting Makarov.

## FIGHT OFF THE SECURITY GUARDS

After the events in the terminal, a heavily armed assault force is waiting for you.

## ⟩ ENGAGEMENT 2

They come at you armed with Riot Shields and through the cover of a smokescreen.

Use your Grenade Launcher to smash the shield wall and hit them behind their shields. Flash Grenades also work to stun them temporarily, allowing you to shoot them.

You *can* shoot the guards when they attempt to fire at you from behind the shields, but this is difficult compared to using explosives or grenades.

Find some nearby cover—moving behind a baggage cart to your left works fine.

The easiest and fastest way to clear this obstacle is simply to overload them with your Grenade Launcher. If for some reason you don't have enough, or they prove insufficient, simply follow up with Flashbangs until you clear out the riot guards.

## GET CLEAR OF THE AIRPORT

### ❭ ENGAGEMENT 3

You encounter only a few more guard patrols on your way out of the airport. Take cover behind the planes' wheels and any smaller vehicles as you proceed.

More guards arrive, but you should be able to outgun them with your M240 and any remaining grenades. Seek out any available cover, and then open up with your heavy machinegun to neutralize them.

Stay close to Makarov's crew for covering fire and distraction, and move up as they do.

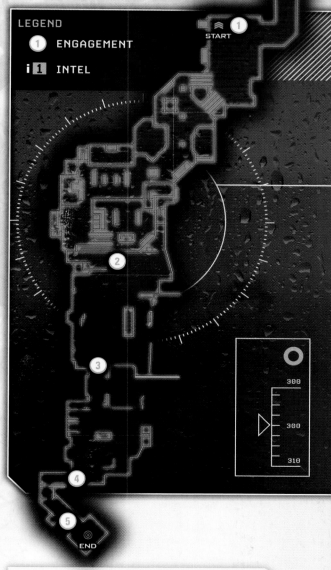

LEGEND

① ENGAGEMENT

i 1 INTEL

START ①

②

③

④

⑤ END

300
300
310

### ❭ ENGAGEMENT 4

You're nearly finished now. Follow Makarov and his men through a service tunnel to reach a small loading bay. A waiting ambulance provides an escape route.

**OPERATIVE: SGT. GARY "ROACH" SANDERSON, TASK FORCE 141**

**OPFOR: FAVELA MILITIA**

**LOCATION: RIO DE JANEIRO, BRAZIL**

**INTEL: 4**

**OBJECTIVE: TRACK DOWN THE ARMS DEALER, ALEJANDRO ROJAS**

**INITIAL LOADOUT**

**M1014**

**ACR Grenadier ACOG Sight**

**10x Grenade Launcher**

MISSION 05:

# TAKEDOWN

## CAPTURE ROJAS' RIGHT-HAND MAN ALIVE

As the mission begins, you're in a truck following a lead on a man who may know the location of Alejandro Rojas. Rojas is an arms dealer who may be able to assist in locating Makarov—willingly or not.

Your truck is following a van filled with local militia believed to be heading to meet this man... But when the van stops, it's clear that Rojas' aide isn't the least bit friendly to them, as he opens fire first on the van and then on your truck!

## ) ENGAGEMENT 1

Duck! Seriously, press the Crouch button. If you don't, you'll get a bullet in the face.

Your driver isn't so quick, and with the driver down, Soap heads out on foot. Get out fast and follow him—you must catch that man!

Captain MacTavish: Get down, get down!

Checkpoint Reached.

Premium

Captain MacTavish: Ghost, our driver's dead! We're on foot! Meet us at the Hotel Rio and cut him off if you can!

Rojas' aide flees into the streets on foot, and you have to follow. Quickly sprint after him. You have to run here, because if he gets away, you immediately fail the mission.

Run through the streets. Explosions and gunfire cause a mass panic. Ignore the civilians and keep moving south—you have to catch up.

# ⟩ ENGAGEMENT 2

When you reach an intersection, turn right, heading west toward the Hotel Rio. Rojas' aide flees into an alley beside the hotel.

Once he reaches the alley, you get one clear shot at him. Do *not* kill him. You need to hit him in the leg to take him down without lethal force. Scope, take steady aim, and fire a short burst.

Once you successfully incapacitate him, MacTavish and another squad member, Ghost, remain behind to interrogate him. You are sent ahead with Meat and Royce to search the favela for Rojas.

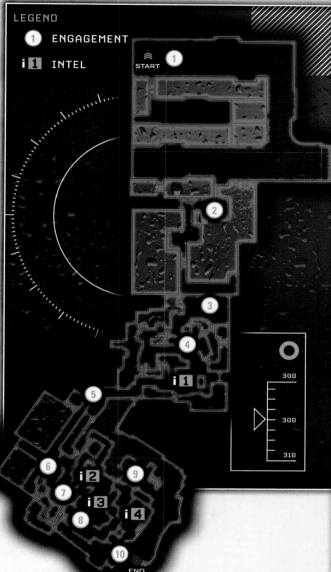

## LEGEND

① ENGAGEMENT

i1 INTEL

START ①

② ③ ④

i1

⑤ ⑥ i2 ⑨ ⑦ i3 ⑧ i4 ⑩

END

300
300
310

## INTO THE DRAGON'S DEN

### GET READY...

The final chapter of Act 1 is significantly more difficult than any of the previous missions.

While you've had some experience with firefights up to this point, the battle through the favela is noticeably more intense than anything that has come before. On Veteran difficulty, the ascent through the favela is downright murderous. To get through in one piece, you need to be patient and make good use of cover. While the hostiles might seem endless, they aren't. If you pick off your opposition systematically and move into cover when you're injured, you can get through the favela intact.

Make your way down the alley with Meat and Royce. The alley exits at the back of the hotel, beside a dilapidated fence that drops down in the rough shantytown below, the favela.

# ) ENGAGEMENT 3

Meat drops down ahead of you to scare off the nearby civilians. The militia here aren't the least bit friendly to your armed squad moving through the area, and you have to avoid any civilian casualties.

Once you drop down, it's go time—favela milita swarm out of the nearby buildings.

## HOT POTATO

You can throw enemy grenades back at hostiles by getting close enough to the tossed weapons and tapping the Grenade button.

However—and this is important—you have only a split-second to decide between a return throw or a dash behind cover.

If you hesitate, odds are the grenade will detonate beside you or in your hand.

When you see the grenade indicator appear, make a quick decision. If you can throw the grenade immediately, it's a simple choice. But if it's merely *nearby*, you must either move quickly to the grenade and throw it back, dash out its range, or get behind hard cover.

This is a difficult firefight, and it doesn't get any easier as you progress to the upper favela, located on the hillside farther south.

# ) ENGAGEMENT 4

Militia troops shoot at you from alleys, from buildings, and from the *tops* of buildings.

Use what little cover is available—mostly walls and the insides of small huts. However, be careful about using the shanties, as enemies can lurk inside. If your back is exposed to the outside, expect to get shot from behind as you sight enemies ahead.

## BURNING BARRELS

The red barrels littered around the favela are explosive. If they take a few shots, they start to burn. A few moments later, they detonate. A hard hit or a nearby explosion sets them off instantly. Keep an eye out for them. While they can be helpful, they can also be dangerous to you or any nearby civilians.

You need to reach the lower favela's southwest corner to get out. Until you do, you can expect militia to harass you continually. The fastest way there is to head west from your starting position, then south.

It's possible to clear out the militia here, but it's safer and easier to cut a path through them. Go directly west and then south until you spot the alley that leads west out of the lower favela.

Clear the way by hugging walls and scanning the low rooftops for enemy presence. Quickly scope and take down any targets at medium range.

For anyone up close, don't waste time sighting. Fire from the hip, or if they're *really* close, knife them.

You may want to use your shotgun here as you fight through. Almost all of the targets you encounter are at relatively close range, and they easy to bag with a quickly aimed shotgun blast.

The militia you dispatch here drop a profusion of weapons. Don't hesitate to swap out your shotgun if you run low on ammo. But don't trade out your ACR until you burn off all of your grenades.

### CHECK YOUR FIRE

Do *not* harm any civilians. If you take down civilians in the favela, you fail the mission instantly. Be sure of your target before you pull that trigger.

Once you break free from the lower favela, you get a momentary reprieve. Make your way through an alley beside a chain-link fence that encloses a soccer field to your right.

## ) ENGAGEMENT 5

An angry dog lunging at the fence is your first warning of further danger, as if the militia isn't bad enough.

Keep moving toward the upper favela, and be ready for the dog... Oh, and avoid killing a dimwitted civvie who thinks its funny to burst out of a window to your left and mime aiming a gun.

## PURSUE ROJAS TO THE TOP OF THE FAVELA

## ) ENGAGEMENT 6

When you get closer to the upper favela, a dog rushes to attack. If you're quick, you can shoot the dog from the hip before it gets on you. If you're unfortunate enough to get tackled, be ready to press your Sprint button to snap the dog's neck. It's unpleasant but necessary, unless you want your throat ripped out!

Past the canine threat, the militia resumes its assault on you. While radio communication from MacTavish indicates that Rojas is indeed in the favela ahead, you have to fight your way right through heavy resistance to get to him.

In terms of enemy presence, the upper favela is every bit as bad as the lower portion. But the terrain makes it even worse, because you're now ascending a hill, and militia forces often occupy building rooftops high above you.

This gives them easy line of sight to you, making grenade and even RPG attacks against you that much worse.

Hug the higher southern wall as you move along the alleys between the buildings. This prevents enemy forces directly above from firing at you.

As you ascend, you can also use Flashbangs to daze hostile forces in the alleys for a few moments. But don't rely on them too heavily—the hanging awnings and ready cover may let one or two hostiles escape the blinding flash. If you try to sprint through, you'll get riddled with bullets.

Proceed methodically—don't let Soap's urgings or the firefight's chaotic nature overwhelm you. Use short, controlled bursts!

The fighting only gets more intense as you approach the top, closing on Rojas as he flees from MacTavish and Ghost's pursuit.

## ) ENGAGEMENT 7

You *can* duck into some of the buildings here. This can take some of the heat off you. Just be careful about your exposure when you emerge to fire from above and ahead at the same time.

Be very careful as you move past the buildings that have doors. Some enemies may open fire, trying to use the door as cover. Remember that you can simply shoot them through their flimsy cover.

If you do move into the buildings, don't let your guard down—several of them have more enemies within.

You need only to reach the final target area to clear the mission. There's no reward for downing the dozens of militia forces that threaten you here. Nevertheless, you'll likely have to clear out quite a few of them to proceed safely.

As before, hug the right, southern wall as you proceed to prevent enemies on rooftops directly above from getting a clear line of sight.

Ghost: Bollocks! Roger that!

Many hostile forces are on higher levels here. Keep an eye on the rooftops and any crosswalks that pass above the shanties.

You'll likely run low on ammo here unless you're exceptionally conservative. Don't hesitate to swap out guns and keep moving.

## ⟩ ENGAGEMENT 8

When you reach the top of the favela, sprint through the final alley. Rojas appears on the second floor of a building ahead of you. Before he can get away, MacTavish slams into him from behind, smashing him into a parked car below.

Rojas is secure, but all is not well. When Ghost radios for helicopter extraction, Command doesn't send it to your position.

Now you have a real problem. Rojas is secure, but your team is trapped in the middle of a favela loaded with an army's worth of hostile militia…

**ACHIEVEMENT / TROPHY**

## TAG 'EM AND BAG 'EM

You receive the Tag 'Em and Bag 'Em Achievement/Trophy for completing this mission.

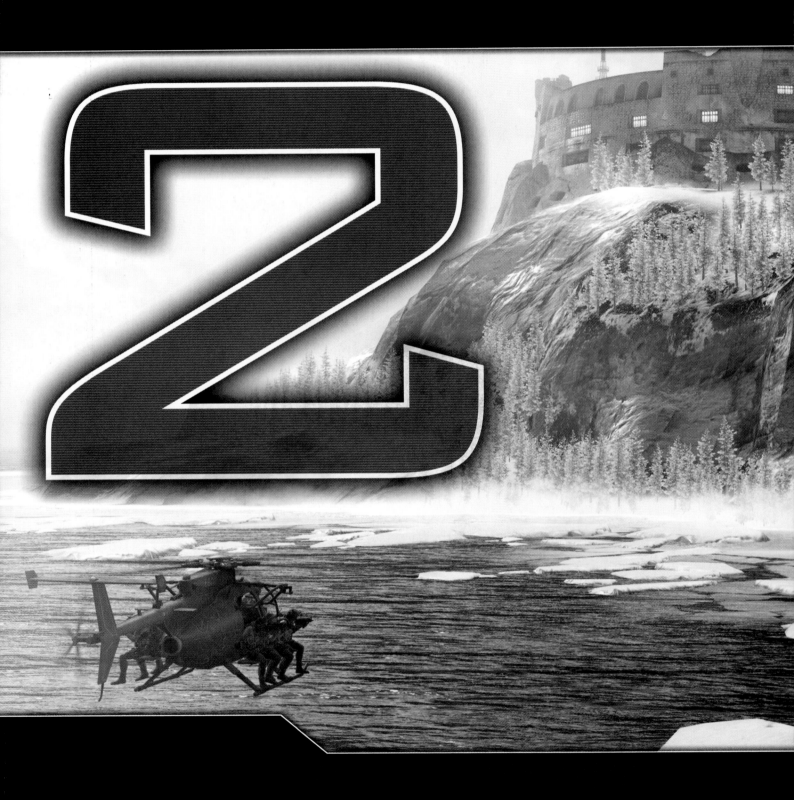

"In war, truth is the first casualty."

—Aeschylus

OPERATIVE: PVT. JAMES RAMIREZ, RANGERS

OPFOR: RUSSIAN MILTARY

LOCATION: NORTHEASTERN VA, USA

INTEL: 4

OBJECTIVE: RECOVER RAPTOR FROM HIS DOWNED HELICOPTER

## INITIAL LOADOUT

**M9**

**SCAR-H Red Dot Sight w/Shotgun**

**4x Smoke Grenade**

**4x Frag Grenade**

MISSION 6

# WOLVERINES!

## RENDEZVOUS WITH RAPTOR'S DOWNED HELICOPTER

Russia has invaded the United States. As a result of events in the first Act, a massive attack has begun. You commence your efforts to repel the assault in the shoes of Private James Ramirez, U.S. Army Rangers.

Your assignment begins in a small U.S. town, as Russian military forces airdrop in and Russian armor rolls through the streets.

## 〉 ENGAGEMENT 1

Sgt. Foley: We got a BTR! Get out, get out!

The mission starts with a bang. As you roll down the street in your transport, a Russian BTR blasts it.

Quickly flee into the cover of a nearby alley, following Sgt. Foley and the rest of your squad.

Foley moves your men behind the houses, avoiding the street and the BTR. Stay with him as he calls for support from Command.

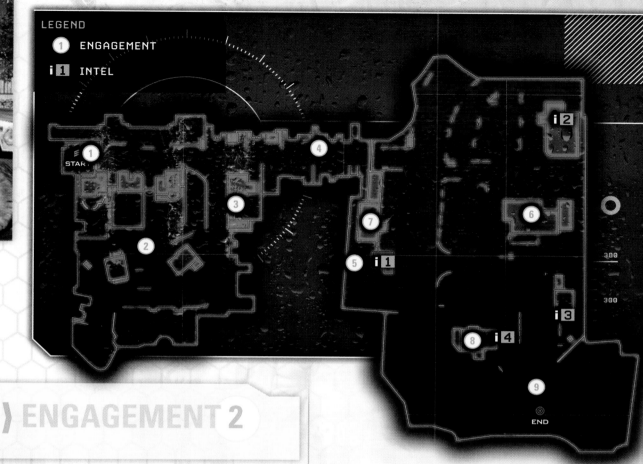

LEGEND

1 ENGAGEMENT

i 1 INTEL

## 〉 ENGAGEMENT 2

Unfortunately, Command is putting out other fires, and you're on your own. You have to reach the target area on foot.

Follow your squad as they move through the backyards and a dry creek bed to the next street ahead. All the while, the eerie scene of Russian troopers parachuting into the town plays out in the distance.

## EVADE THE BTR

## 〉 ENGAGEMENT 3

Be careful when you get to the street. The BTR that ambushed your convoy rolls past the road you were on before. Stay with Sgt. Foley and your squad as he moves up behind a small, green house just across the street.

The BTR moves up the street here, but as long as you don't draw its fire, it won't notice your squad in hiding. Stay out of sight until it moves past, blasting holes in a house off to your right. Then move cautiously out onto the street.

41

As you move up the street, you can see the smoke from Raptor's downed 'copter in the distance. It's beyond a blazing tree in front of a house on the street's left side.

## ⟩ENGAGEMENT 4

Move up the street carefully—the BTR has parked at a barricade in the street up ahead, and you have to sneak past it. To do so, use one or two of your Smoke Grenades—cover the BTR so you can bypass it safely.

 If you miss the BTR badly, you can resupply at an ammo crate on the street's right side.

### AMMO DEPOTS

In certain missions from this point forward, you occasionally run into an ammo drop. Simply approach and hold the Use button to refill your ammo and grenades. Handy!

Be careful about moving up before you clear out any soldiers blocking the alley to the right of the BTR. You don't want to get shot while running!

## FIGHT PAST THE GAS STATION

## ⟩ENGAGEMENT 5

Once you get into the alley, take down an unfortunate Russian soldier who's gotten his chute tangled in some power lines above the gas  station ahead. Then move carefully—more troops are in the alley.

You may want to use the attached shotgun on your SCAR here. You may also wish to swap your M9 sidearm for a more substantial secondary weapon. Keep your eyes peeled for a dropped weapon that you favor.

When you reach the alley's end, you emerge at the side of the gas station, with a concrete wall blocking your right. Be ready—a fully loaded transport truck rolls up and deposits a squad of troops. This is a good time to use your Frag Grenades. However, watch the fuel tanks—you can trigger a massive explosion.

Neutralize the truck's troop complement, and then proceed cautiously. You still aren't fully clear, as more troops are inside the gas station store on the left. Once you eliminate them, you can finally make your way to your destination.

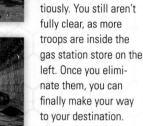

Raptor's copter has crashed just outside Nate's restaurant, one of several local shops still intact. It's in a parking lot east of the gas station, just across the street.

## REPEL THE RUSSIAN ASSAULT

Sprint across the parking lot with your squad. When you arrive, Sgt. Foley speaks with the soldiers defending Raptor, your target VIP for this mission.

Raptor has been secured, unconscious, in the meat locker inside Nate's. He's injured, and Foley sends

Corporal Dunn to check on him. The squad had a supply drop on the restaurant's roof, including an M-5 automatic sentry gun.

## ⟩ ENGAGEMENT 6

Enter Nate's and climb a ladder onto the roof, where you can find another ammo resupply crate, as well as the powerful defensive turret. Take note of the roof's access points—there's the ladder inside Nate's, as well as one on the building's back (east) side.

You can move the automated turret around. Move close to it and hold Reload, then press Fire to drop it. It automatically fires on any hostile forces in its frontal arc of fire.

There's also an M14 EBR Thermal scoped weapon here. It quickly becomes relevant, as hostile Russian forces begin to move on your position from the south, behind the cover of smokescreens.

### SENTRY GUN AND THERMAL SCOPE

The M-5 turret is a powerful tool, but don't rely on it too heavily. Hostile troops can destroy it if it's exposed against a heavy enemy presence for too long. In this case, you can usually make good use of it for both waves that assault Nate's.

The Thermal Scope can be mounted to many different weapons. In this case, it's on an M14, an accurate long-range, semiautomatic rifle. It's ideal for picking off targets concealed in smoke.

Thermal scopes grey-out the world and show heat sources as bright white silhouettes, *including* friendly forces. Friendlies have a slight, pulsing grey glow at center mass, so check your fire if you know or suspect allies may be in your sights.

Use the Thermal Scope to spot hostile forces through the smoke, but be careful about exposing yourself too much on the rooftop's edge.

Once you repel the first wave of troops, more troops soon attack from the north. Move the turret to cover the area, reload your ammo at the ammo crate, and then take an overwatch position.

## CLAYMORES

Claymore anti-personnel mines are also on Nate's roof. You can plant these at the top of the ladders that access the roof, providing a nasty surprise and an early warning against any foes that get too close.

If troops get past the perimeter around Nate's, they climb the ladder at the back (east) of the restaurant, or the one inside, at the roof's center. If you hear Sgt. Foley yell "breach," be sure to turn around and deal with hostiles before they get on the roof and shoot you in the back!

## STINGER

Another important goody is on the rooftop: a case containing a Stinger missile launcher.

While you don't need this weapon immediately, it does come in handy later in the mission. If you're comfortable using only the M14 Thermal, pick it up now as your secondary. Otherwise, just take note of its position in case you need to return and get it later.

Soon after you repulse the ground assaults on Nate's, a new threat arrives. A massive missile slams into the ground nearby. Quickly get off the roof and move away from the building before a missile attack demolishes part of the building.

## RECOVER THE PREDATOR DRONE CONTROL RIG

Corporal Dunn has spotted a Russian trooper controlling a Predator drone. He's located in the diner to the west of the restaurant, back across the street and just north of the gas station where you fought earlier.

## ) ENGAGEMENT 7

Be careful making your way back to the diner. More Russian troops are inside, and more critically, a pair of BTRs rolls down the street from the north. Stay behind cover and wait for them to pass—you don't want to draw their fire.

Once the way is clear, sprint across the street and approach the diner. Sgt. Foley has sent part of the squad with you to assist in the assault, so move in and secure the diner.

Once you clear the structure, watch out for a few more troops coming in the diner's back door (on the west). Don't let them surprise you. With the last soldiers dispatched, you can get your hands on the Drone Control Rig and operate the Predator!

## GRAB THE GOODS

An M240 heavy machine gun is in the diner. Either the M240 or the M14 Thermal makes a good primary weapon for the upcoming battles. The former is attractive for the raw ammo supply, while the latter excels in precision and ease of target-spotting.

Use the Predator to deal hammer blows to the assaulting Russian infantry. Remember that while you control the Predator, you can line up your shot and then pull the trigger to make it fire its booster rockets, propelling it to its target even faster.

Prioritize destroying BTRs and troop transports before you go after clusters of infantry.

## PREDATOR ONLINE

The aerial Predator is armed with tremendously powerful, guided air-to-ground missiles, and you can fire a continuous bombardment of them using the control rig. Simply select the rig, and then press fire to activate it.

Once active, you receive an aerial camera view of the battlefield. Red squares mark mobile hostile targets.

The missile's blast is so powerful that you can take out ten or more infantry with a single shot—in fact, there's an Achievement for doing exactly that! You can easily destroy even heavy armor with a direct hit.

When you fire a missile, you can guide it onto your chosen target. Pulling the trigger while it's in flight activates booster rockets that slam the missile into the ground that much faster.

Abuse the Predator's power enthusiastically. You don't run out of missiles. And, aside from an enemy group located in the Burger Town, all other targets in the open are fair game for bombardment. If they aren't in hard cover, you can take them down.

Soon after you secure the control rig, a flight of enemy fighters bombs Nate's. The building is badly damaged, and you have to escort Sgt. Foley as he carries Raptor to a new location at the Burger Town, just south of Nate's.

## PREPARATION IS KEY

Before you leave the diner, note the Stinger in the room. Either pick up this one, or grab the one from Nate's roof before you proceed to clear out Burger Town.

# DEFEND RAPTOR UNTIL HELP ARRIVES

## ) ENGAGEMENT 8

You have to rid Burger Town of hostile forces before Raptor can be moved. Make your way over to the building and choose an entry point. There isn't a lot of cover as you approach the building, and several Russian troops are inside.

You can use Smoke Grenades to create cover as you move up. If you still have any Frag Grenades, they work well to flush out the hostiles inside.

Once the interior is clear, move in and head up to the roof. You have to provide cover fire while Sgt. Foley moves Raptor. Don't forget to use the Predator!

Once Sgt. Foley moves Raptor safely into the meat locker, continue repulsing the aggressive and relentless Russian assault. Troop transports roll in from semi-random directions. If you're quick with the Predator missiles, you can easily take out both groups before they even get a chance to attack, earning you an Achievement in the process.

Unfortunately, your Predator gets shot down shortly after, leaving you without its protective firepower. Settle in for a firefight.

Mop up any remaining foot soldiers you see approaching your position. They aren't a serious threat, considering your superior elevation and your squad's supporting fire. However, Command radios to warn you about two attack helicopters, and they *are* a threat!

Remember the Stinger we told you to grab earlier? Now is the time to use it. When you see the helicopter move into view, pull out your Stinger, get a clean lock, and fire. One shot is all it takes.

That takes care of one, but another is still on the way. To make matters worse, another large group of Russian troops moves in from the diner to the west.

You have to retrieve another Stinger to deal with the second helicopter. If you picked up the one on Nate's roof, you can still grab another from the same weapons locker. Or, if you prefer, you can go get the one from the diner.

Whichever you choose, make your way there quickly and retrieve the Stinger. You don't want to give the chopper any time to strafe you or your squad.

With the destruction of the second chopper, a friendly convoy finally rolls up to extract Raptor and your squad.

Run to the convoy, just south of Burgertown, and this mission is complete!

ACHIEVEMENT / TROPHY

## ROYALE WITH CHEESE

You receive the Royale with Cheese Achievement/Trophy for completing this mission.

OPERATIVE: SGT. GARY
"ROACH" SANDERSON,
TASK FORCE 141

OPFOR: FAVELA MILITIA

LOCATION: RIO DE
JANEIRO, BRAZIL

INTEL: 4

OBJECTIVE: ESCAPE FROM
THE FAVELA

## INITIAL LOADOUT

**G18**

**UMP45 ACOG Sight**

**4x Flash Grenade**

**4x Frag Grenade**

MISSION 07:

# THE HORNET'S NEST

## ESCAPE FROM THE FAVELA!

When we last left our friends in the 141, they were trapped in the favela with hostile militia closing in from all sides, and no extraction chopper on the way.

The situation hasn't really improved.

## ) ENGAGEMENT 1

MacTavish makes an urgent call to an old friend, one Nikolai, to bring his chopper and meet you at the market, not too far ahead to the south.

That is to say, it's not too far when you aren't facing an army's worth of militia. Get moving!

Follow Soap, Ghost, and the rest of the squad as they move up the slight slope to the south. You emerge in a relatively open square with a large brick building in the center. It houses a large radio tower.

Move up to the building and take cover at the low wall that runs around it. Hostile militia swarm the buildings of the favela that resume to the south. A few are in the small shanty buildings to the east of your position, to your left as you face south from where you entered the square.

Ghost: Technical coming in from the south.

# ) ENGAGEMENT 2

You don't have much time to get settled in before a technical drives in from the south.

If possible, take down the gunner on the mounted machinegun in the back. If you don't, the technical will drive a circle around the radio tower, covering your position with suppressing fire.

Worse, a second technical shows up soon after, in addition to the militia pouring over the buildings around your position. Again, quickly target it and take down the gunner.

Once you deal with the technicals, start moving toward the street to the south where they entered the square.

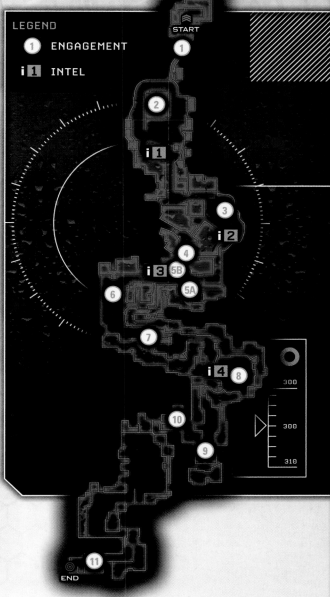

**LEGEND**

1 ENGAGEMENT

i 1 INTEL

START

END

## SNIPING STYLE

A Dragunov sniper rifle rests against the wall on the radio tower building's south side.

This is your first chance to practice long-range sharpshooting. While the Dragunov isn't ideal for all of the combat in this mission, this is a good time to try your hand at sniping.

Remember that you have to press and hold the Run button to steady your breath while you use the scope. Doing so stabilizes the crosshair and lets you make pinpoint shots at a distance, ideal for taking down the militia on the buildings in the distance.

Depending on your weapon preference, you can take the Dragunov with you as you move deeper into the favela. Or you can swap it out for any of the militia's dropped guns when you move up.

## ) ENGAGEMENT 3

Proceed through the gate to the street. You can see several militia fleeing their positions to the east, heading downhill. Try to pick them off as they run, but don't chase too aggressively.

When you reach the turn in the street, you can see an open field below. It's littered with all sorts of cover: burned out vehicles, tires, ruined brick walls, barrels, and other bits of junk.

More critically, hostile militia exploit the abundant cover and try to pick off your squad. This is a good place to use your grenades, Flash or Frag. Toss a few to flush them out, and then mop up the survivors.

Once the field is clear, you can move up, and you have a choice to make. The streets ahead lead to the market, but there are two ways to go: off to the left, or into the streets on the right side.

## REACH NIKOLAI'S LZ IN THE MARKETPLACE

The left route takes you around to the east side of a road that leads uphill toward the market. It passes fairly close to a building that you can enter on the street's left (south) side. The right route takes you near a building that you can enter on your right.

Both buildings give you a good overwatch position on the street, allowing you to take down remaining militia and clear the way for your squad to move up the hill to the west.

## ) ENGAGEMENT 4

There's no reason you can't explore both routes, but you have to pick one and go with it for the initial push. If you don't like the way the fight is going, back off and try the other route from the field into the streets.

To reach either building, you have to deal with some militia that can easily see you coming, both at street level and on the buildings above. Use the buildings' cover and pick them off before you move up.

## ❯ ENGAGEMENT 5A/5B

Position 5A is the southerly building, while 5B is the small shop. Both allow you access to a second floor, where you can fire down on the street.

Likewise, both have hostile militia on the second floor. Be careful as you move in and up—you don't want to get gunned down at pointblank range.

### CAR-BOOM

Multiple cars are parked on the street here. If you see any militia taking cover behind them, either unload on full auto at the vehicle, or throw a Frag Grenade at it.

Cars are *very* explosive, and the resulting blast should take down any nearby hostiles. On the other hand, if you happen to be near a vehicle and you see it catch fire—or worse, a grenade indicator nearby—run!

Once you clear out the street, continue up the road to the west. Ahead, an open field wraps around to the south, where the market waits.

## ❯ ENGAGEMENT 6

However, before you can reach the market, you have to deal with another pack of militia. Some take cover in the field, and more are located in the buildings to the south.

Furthermore, a technical shows up to the party—as always, make this a priority target. Take down the gunner, and then return your attention to any hostiles guarding the market entrance.

### WEAPON SWAP... A CHICKEN'S WORST NIGHTMARE

A lot of enemies are here, and you'll very likely run low on ammunition. Don't hesitate to switch weapons. If possible, pick up a pair of dual Uzis or any heavy machine gun before you reach the market.

You can earn an Achievement for killing seven chickens in the market in less than 10 seconds. It's difficult to do this with the normal clip size in most weapons. Using dual weapons lets you burn all the ammo in one, reload it, and continue firing with the other. A heavy machinegun gives you the ammo load to keep firing, and you can throw grenades to initiate the chicken massacre.

The market battle is intense—the cluttered stalls mixed in with the ramshackle buildings make for a confusing visual profile. The profusion of hostile militia combined with chaos (and a few chickens) doesn't make this any easier.

## ) ENGAGEMENT 7

Grenades work well for clearing out the market. You're nearing the end of the mission, so don't hesitate to use up your remaining stock here.

Hang back and pick off any visible targets before you move into the market itself. Once you do move in, submachine guns or shotguns work quite well in the close confines here.

Dispatch any stragglers hidden at the back of the market, and then follow MacTavish and your team.

**Your team moves through a few buildings to reach the LZ, but it's still too hot; militia with RPGs are in the area.**

## ) ENGAGEMENT 8

Soap waves off Nikolai. You have to neutralize the few remaining militia here before you move on to reach a secondary LZ farther south through the favela.

Follow Soap over to the rooftops, hoist yourself up, and then chase the team.

## ESCAPE TO THE SECONDARY LZ

## ) ENGAGEMENT 9

Sprint across the rooftops with your team. You soon reach Nikolai's chopper hovering over the buildings. The whole team runs and jumps...but you don't quite make it.

You fall, slamming into the ground, dazed and too far for the team to reach.

When you come to, the rest of the team is in the chopper, but you have a major problem. The whole favela is up in arms and after you. You have to get away—now!

The team waits to pick you up at one final LZ, but you don't have much time.

Run as fast as you can. Nikolai's chopper is running out of gas, and you have only 30 seconds to reach it before time runs out!

## ) ENGAGEMENT 11

Follow the path across the rooftops to the chopper. When you reach the end of the line, slide down a sloped roof, hit the ground, and sprint for the chopper. Make a running leap for the hanging ladder!

Land the jump successfully, and Nikolai evacs the area. Your team is finally free of the favela.

## ) ENGAGEMENT 10

Quickly flee through the building in front of you. Don't wait; just sprint as fast as you can as a hail of bullets falls around you.

Through the buildings, you soon find a staircase leading back up to the rooftops. Climb it, and then run across the rooftops.

**RANGER**

OPERATIVE: PVT. JAMES
RAMIREZ, RANGERS

OPFOR: RUSSIAN MILITARY

LOCATION: NORTHEASTERN
VIRGINIA, USA

INTEL: 3

OBJECTIVE: DESTROY THE
AA BATTERIES IN TOWN

INITIAL LOADOUT

**M9**

**SCAR-H Red Dot Sight**

**4x Flash Grenade**

**4x Frag Grenade**

**Laser Designator**

MISSION 08:

# EXODUS

## TARGET ACQUIRED

Back in the boots of Pvt. Ramirez with your squad
under Sgt. Foley, you arrive with an advance force
pushing into town. Your objective is to destroy a set
of Russian anti-aircraft batteries that are preventing
friendly airpower from assisting in the area.

## ) ENGAGEMENT 1

There's one major difference from your last Ranger mission: this time,
you're on the offensive, and you have friendly firepower on your side.
A heavily armed Stryker armored fighting vehicle, codenamed Honey
Badger, accompanies your squad through this mission.

Even better, you get to laser
designate targets for it!

Sgt. Foley orders your squad off the streets. Take his advice and head
toward the buildings to the right side of the street. You can find plenty of
cover there as the Stryker moves up the street.

### CALL THE SHOT

Select the laser targeter and 'fire' at a target or an area to make the Stryker begin
shooting at it.

You can target any hostile infantry, vehicles, or simply an area that you want suppressed.

Use this powerful support ability generously. If you use it well, the Stryker's heavy
firepower greatly eases your advance through the mission.

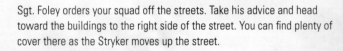

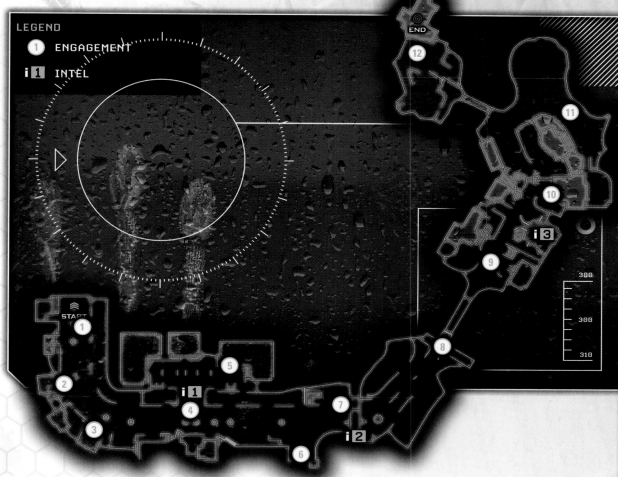

**LEGEND**

1. ENGAGEMENT
i 1. INTEL

## ⟩ ENGAGEMENT 2

Move up into the houses on the street's right side and carefully make your way forward. Continually target the Stryker's machinegun at any visible Russian troops.

If you can't see any targets, simply pick an area up ahead for the Stryker to suppress. If anyone shows up, it'll acquire targets and start shooting at them.

There's plenty of cover available as you move: hedges, trees, cars, between front porch fences, and for a few buildings, household items inside.

Watch for Russian troops inside or behind houses—you don't want to move past them and get flanked.

# ) ENGAGEMENT 3

Partway up the street, you find an ammo crate out on a lawn. You can use it to restock your ammunition and grenades, so you can toss grenades freely against any visible targets during this whole firefight.

Make a point of grabbing a second weapon from a fallen Russian trooper, and refill it at the ammo crate. There's no need to carry your M9 the whole mission, unless you really like to quick-swap to the handgun.

The Stryker slowly moves down the street as you advance. Be sure to continue giving it new target updates as you move.

## CLEAR THE APARTMENT COMPLEX

Keep moving with the Stryker until a set of apartment buildings across the street comes into view.

The first serious battle occurs here, outside the apartment buildings.

# ) ENGAGEMENT 4

Russian choppers fast-rope several squads into the apartment parking lot, and more troops already occupy the ground.

Make sure the Stryker fires at them. Then take position across the street, using any of the ready cover to protect you from incoming fire. Pick off targets at a distance.

## GOING DOWN

If you're quick, you can shortcut much of this fight. When you move up the street across from the apartments, you can see the Russian helicopters before they drop their troop loads.

Immediately target each chopper with your laser targeter. If you do this quickly enough, and the Stryker will blast both 'copters out of the air before they can unload! This reduces the firefight to a very quick battle.

## ) ENGAGEMENT 5

Partway through the battle, RPG fire from the apartments' upper floor starts to wear down the Stryker's anti-missile defenses. Be sure to laser-target the area, and put some of your own rounds onto the targets threatening the Stryker.

Return to clearing out any stragglers on the ground, and then get ready to move on as the Stryker rolls up the street.

## CHECKPOINT BATTLE

The next serious fight occurs as you approach a checkpoint that leads into the Arcadia residential district. The Russians have fortified this position with defensive turrets and a *lot* of infantry.

## ) ENGAGEMENT 6

Have the Stryker fire at the turrets, and try to shoot at them from long range. You don't want to move up while they're still active.

An ammo crate is on the right side of the street leading up to the checkpoint. It's in a grassy field, along with several sandbag barriers that provide decent cover. Use this area to settle in, and start picking off the troops at the checkpoint.

 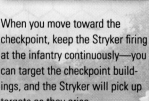

When you move toward the checkpoint, keep the Stryker firing at the infantry continuously—you can target the checkpoint buildings, and the Stryker will pick up targets as they arise.

Stryker Gunner: Badger One to Hunter Two, target area suppressed.

## ⟩ ENGAGEMENT 7

When the volume of fire from the checkpoint thins, start moving up to clear out any remaining guards still inside the checkpoint buildings.

There should be only a few troops left in the checkpoint. Keep the Stryker on overwatch and clear out the buildings.

Once the checkpoint is safely in your hands, you can move up the street into Arcadia, following Honey Badger as it rolls along.

## INTO ARCADIA

As you move into Arcadia, Command radios in a new set of objectives. Your squad is to suppress the AA first, just as your original goal. But after it is removed, you are to move to a specific address along Brookmere Road deeper in the residential area. You aren't given a reason for the detour.

## ⟩ ENGAGEMENT 8

Up ahead, a quaint wooden bridge crosses a stream and leads into the rich houses of Brookmere Road.

Wait for the Stryker to roll across the bridge, as an assault commences as soon as you move into the open. You want its covering fire when you do.

There's one more section of street before you close with the AA batteries in the distance.

As before, move slowly up the street and use the Stryker to provide covering fire. You don't have far to go. You only have to reach a roadblock up

ahead before you must abandon the Stryker. You then move through a mansion beside the roadblock on the street's right side.

## ⟩ ENGAGEMENT 9

However, before you can get there, you have to clear out the Russian troops on the streets.

You can go up the street on either the left or the right side. Both provide plenty of cover, and you can duck into the houses here while the Stryker tears up anyone exposed in the open.

### MORE CARBOMBING

As you might expect, plenty of vehicles are parked vehicles in the streets of Arcadia. If you spot enemy troops near them, toss a grenade for a satisfying explosion. At the same time, be careful about using cars for cover, because the same explosive fate can be yours if you aren't careful.

There's plenty of other cover in the yards, so there's little reason to crouch behind explosive cover!

Be careful moving through the houses. Use standard room-sweeping techniques, and don't rush through them. You don't want to get ambushed by an errant trooper at close range.

Keep moving up the street. When the Stryker stops in front of the large mansion, have it provide covering fire on the house's entrance before you approach.

# DESTROY THE ANTI-AIRCRAFT BATTERIES

The anti-aircraft batteries are just beyond the trees in the distance, near a golf course. To reach them, you have to pass through the large mansion on the side of the street.

## ) ENGAGEMENT 10

Be very careful moving into this house. A lot of Russian soldiers are waiting for you to break in.

You can go in either through the basement level garages, or up the stairs to the second level. Either route allows you to get through to the backyard pool. From there, you can then move on to the AA guns.

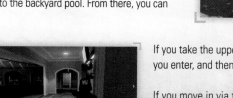

If you take the upper level, toss in a Flashbang or two before you enter, and then clear out any resistance when you enter.

If you move in via the bottom level, throw a few Frags ahead to flush out soldiers hiding with shotguns. You really don't want to let one of them flank you.

Move through the building to the backyard, and the AA guns come into view.

You can now use the laser designator to call in artillery strikes on the anti-aircraft batteries. There are two: one is directly north of your position when you come out of the mansion, the other is a ways west from the first battery.

Set the targets and watch the resulting fireworks as a storm of artillery shells demolish the positions.

## INVESTIGATE 4677 BROOKMERE FOR INTEL

Once the guns are silenced, you can move on to your final task, the mysterious detour to 4677 Brookmere Road.

Follow your squad across another bridge leading to the house in question.

When you emerge on the street across the bridge, you proceed over a short hill and encounter

 a spectacular but distressing sight: a massive C-130 has crashed directly in front of the building.

Your squad is instructed to move in and find a panic room on the second floor. You're told to use the codeword 'Icepick' to identify yourself to the person inside.

Move into the building. On the first floor, you can spot a Russian soldier helping himself at the fridge to the right…

Make your way upstairs. When you get to the panic room, it's clear something isn't right.

The panic room is open, the inhabitant is dead, and there's a dead soldier outside the room with unknown markings and tattoos.

Retrieve the briefcase inside the panic room for intelligence evaluation—this mission is complete.

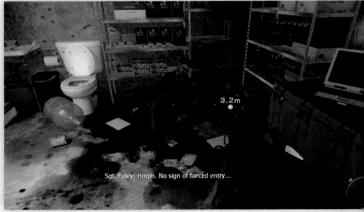

# ACT 2

OPERATIVE: SGT. GARY "ROACH" SANDERSON, TASK FORCE 141

OPFOR: RUSSIAN MILITARY

LOCATION: VIKHOREVKA 36 OIL PLATFORM, RUSSIA

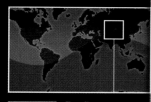

⊘ ⊘

INTEL: 3

OBJECTIVE: DESTROY THE SAM SITES ATOP THE RIG

## INITIAL LOADOUT

**SCAR-H Silenced Thermal Sight**

**M4A1 SOPMOD**

**4x Flash Grenade**

**4x Frag Grenade**

**1x Claymore**

**10x Grenade Launcher**

MISSION 09:

# THE ONLY EASY DAY...WAS YESTERDAY

## INFILTRATE THE OIL RIG

If you've been waiting for a really intense Spec Ops mission, you need wait no longer. How does underwater stealth infiltration of an occupied offshore oil rig strike you?

A prisoner held in a Gulag on Russia's coast has come to the attention of Task Force 141. To get there, your team, along with friendly naval forces on a retaliatory expedition, must clear out SAM sites positioned on top of the rig.

Your squad is dispatched to the rig via underwater insertion vehicles. Enjoy the view of a friendly passing submarine as you make your way beneath the rig.

## ) ENGAGEMENT 1

Once under the rig, your team slowly surfaces. Two bored guards are on the bottom of the rig. Quietly approach in the water. When you're close enough, you can press the Melee button to perform a quick and lethal takedown just as Soap does the same to the second guard.

Climb out of the water and get ready.

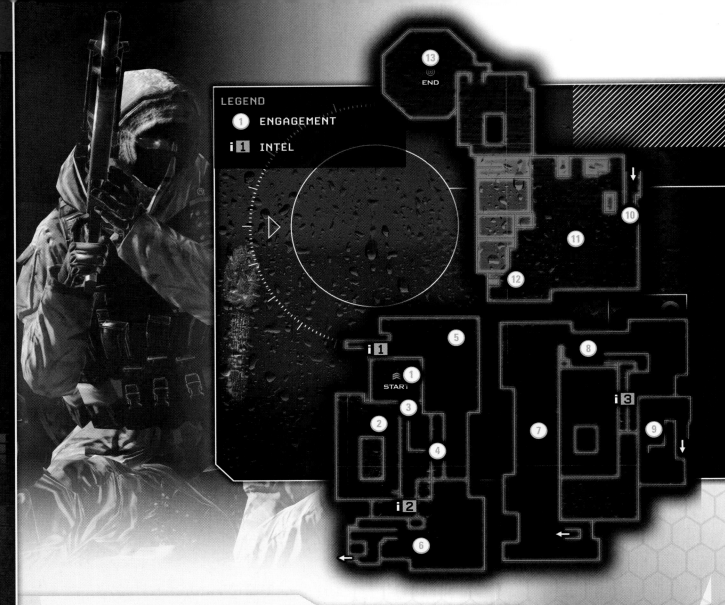

LEGEND

1 — ENGAGEMENT

i 1 — INTEL

13 END

10

11

12

i 1

5

1 START

3

2

4

8

i 3

7

9

i 2

6

## ) ENGAGEMENT 2

Quietly move up the stairs to the second level. Another lone guard waits in the room here, hanging out by a railing, unaware of the lethal team near him.

Take him out quietly with a suppressed weapon.

The Sub Commander radios in—civilian hostages from the rig's crew occupy a room just to your left. You have to breach the room and take out the guards before they can harm any of the hostages.

# BREACH AND CLEAR

You must Breach the hostage room doors and take down the guards inside *without* allowing any hostages to be harmed.

## BREACH!

Breaching is a new mechanic in *Call of Duty: Modern Warfare 2*, and it's a very cool one at that.

When you move up to a doorway marked as a Breach point, you can hold Reload to plant a frame charge on the door. In this case, you can Breach either of the two doors that lead into the hostage room.

Once you do, you automatically move into position to rush the room as soon as the charge detonates.

Your perception of time slows, giving you precious seconds to take down the hostiles inside before they can retaliate or kill a hostage.

In most breaching situations, you have a choice of multiple doors from which to stage your entry.

It doesn't matter which door you use, though it does change your target acquisition slightly. If you fail a Breach at one door, or you simply want to see a different angle the next time, try breaching the alternate door. Your squad mates cover whichever door you don't use.

## ) ENGAGEMENT 3

Make sure you equip your M4, not your thermally scoped weapon, and then plant the frame charge.

When the door blows, you burst into the room in slow motion. Quickly sight and take down any enemies in immediate view. Then hurry to aim for any remaining hostiles.

Enemies aiming to execute a hostage should always be your first priority. You may find some of them holding a hostage, in which case you must make a quick and accurate headshot without harming the civilian.

## ACHIEVEMENT / TROPHY

## KNOCK-KNOCK

You can earn an Achievement/Trophy here, or at any other Breach point, by taking down four targets with four bullets in slow motion. Aim for accurate headshots, and you should claim this Achievement/Trophy easily.

Once the slow motion wears off and the dust settles, you should have a clear room and several safe hostages.

**The Sub Commander contacts your team again, informing you that Team 2 will perform cleanup and rescue operations for the civilians. For now, you must move up to the next floor and rescue the remaining captives as you work your way to the top of the rig.**

## ) ENGAGEMENT 4

Move up to the next level, where you emerge on the walkway around the rig, exposed to the ocean.

Be careful here and seek some cover—an enemy helicopter patrols the rig's perimeter.

A second room of hostages is just around the corner. Again, approach a door of your choice, plant a frame charge, and clear the room.

When the hostages are safe, Ghost picks up enemy radio contacts. You'll have company soon. Soap calls for another 'Plan B' setup.

Plant some C4 on one of the hostile bodies, and then exit the room to the north to prepare the ambush.

## ) ENGAGEMENT 5

Climb the ladder to the scaffolding and go prone alongside MacTavish to wait for the Russian reinforcements to arrive.

Wait patiently for the patrol to arrive and approach. Don't detonate the C4 charge until MacTavish calls for it.

The explosion takes out several guards, and you have to mop up the remainder. You have a good line of sight on the guards in the open. Pick them off first, and then go after any positioned behind cover.

### EXPLOSIVES

Your Grenade Launcher works well during these battles. However, try to save a few for the next level, as well as the top floor.

## ) ENGAGEMENT 6

Fight your way around the corner, past any remaining guards, and then ascend the staircase to the next level.

## BOOM

Numerous fuel storage tanks are scattered around the decks here. Enough concentrated fire makes them rupture and explode. The blast is quite devastating, so during any battle here, keep an eye out for enemies clustered near these tanks. Triggering an explosion can save you time by eliminating multiple hostiles, making the rest of the firefight that much easier.

## BATTLE TO THE TOP

When you move out from the stairs, a long walkway littered with stacks of pipes provides ready cover. This is useful, because another wave of Russian soldiers is about to hit you. They approach from the platform's north end.

## ⟩ ENGAGEMENT 7

Take cover and start picking them off. Use the fuel tanks on the platform's north edge to devastate a pack of guards, and carefully watch a doorway just to your right.

The doorway leads into the center of the oil rig. Enemies occasionally use it to advance on your position. Your most prominent piece of cover is exposed to fire from this doorway.

Partway into the fight, you have a more serious problem: the enemy helicopter shows up. Take it down quickly, before it begins strafing your position with heavy Gatling gun fire.

The hostage rooms up to this point have contained a few launcher weapons. Now you have to retrieve one to take down the chopper. You can find several such explosive toys through the door to your right. Plus, going there gets you out of the chopper's line of fire. Head in, find a Stinger, and then blast the chopper. Using a Stinger is one of the easier ways to take down the 'copter.

## CHOPPER TAKEDOWN

You can also find an AT4 beside the first large piece of cover in this engagement area. If you wish, you can equip it and take down the chopper without even moving through the door to your right.

Wait for the helicopter to arrive. When it sweeps down the platform's side and pauses, hit it!

There's also another way to take down the 'copter. A well-aimed grenade works just as well as an AT4 shot, and you don't even have to swap out a weapon to use it!

## ) ENGAGEMENT 8

Move up and proceed around the corner. You must fight your way to the staircase leading to the platform's top level.

You can tackle this engagement a few different ways. You can go at the guards head-on, or you can detour through the rig's interior and try to get beside them.

To reach the interior, use the stairs attached to the side of the interior to gain some elevation. Eliminate any guards on the stairs up to the third floor. Then duck inside to move down and flank any guards lingering on the ground level.

Whichever route you choose, try to stay behind cover as you move, and pick off any exposed troops as they exchange fire with you.

## ) ENGAGEMENT 9

The staircase up to the rig's top level is located here. Few, if any, guards should remain by the time you reach this area.

Clear out any stragglers, and then climb to the top level—your final battle awaits.

## SMOKESCREEN

Once you finally reach the top of the oil platform, you face a large final battle. The Russians have covered the top of the platform with smoke. The only safe way to fight them through the haze is with a Thermal Scope.

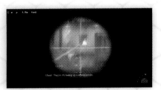

## ) ENGAGEMENT 10

If you kept your initial thermal weapon, you're in good shape, but don't fret if you didn't. A few thermal weapons—an F2000 rifle and a Vector SMG—lean against a shipping crate to the north as you come off the stairs.

Arm yourself, and then turn your attention to the enemies in the smoke.

## ) ENGAGEMENT 11

Multiple hostiles lurk in the smoke on ground level. Enemies also occupy the upper levels of the deck's buildings.

Be sure to visually sweep above eye level in the smoke to spot these elevated hostiles. They aren't always visible, as they tend to duck behind cover. This makes them difficult to spot with thermal vision through the smoke.

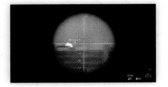

Occasionally pop out of scoped view and look around. It's both easy and dangerous to get overly focused on the enemies in the smoke-screen. You can miss those moving up to flank you.

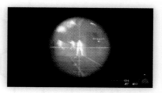

**GRENADO**

Don't hesitate to use the last of your grenades, if you still have any.

This is the last engagement, and there's no point in being conservative.

## ) ENGAGEMENT 12

At this point, a final group of enemies emerges from the smoke and attacks your position. It's better to go after them preemptively.

Ideally, once you clear the center area, you should move off to the left and take cover. Aim into the smoke with a Thermal Scope and pick off the Russian troops as they appear.

Once you eliminate the last of the hostiles, you have to complete one final Breach. Again, you can choose between two doors as entry points. Pick one and get ready. This Breach is the trickiest yet—the reason why becomes apparent when you burst into the room.

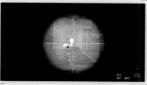

The troops inside have covered the hostages with C4. To make matters worse, they've dragged in several oil drums and covered those with C4 as well!

Check your fire and use precise, single shots or very short bursts to take down the hostiles inside. You really don't want an errant bullet striking one of the massive explosive packages!

## ) ENGAGEMENT 13

Once you secure the last room and save the hostages, Marines arrive to dismantle the SAM sites. You receive a helicopter extraction at this point.

Make your way to the evac chopper and head out—you have a Gulag to visit.

**OPERATIVE: SGT. GARY "ROACH" SANDERSON, TASK FORCE 141**

**OPFOR: RUSSIAN MILITARY**

**LOCATION: GULAG, 40 MILES EAST OF PETROPAVLOVSK, RUSSIA**

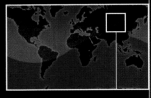

**INTEL: 4**

**OBJECTIVE: RESCUE PRISONER 627**

---

### INITIAL LOADOUT

**M14 EBR Scoped**

**M4A1 Grenadier w/Red Dot Sight**

**4x Flash Grenade**

**4x Frag Grenade**

**10x Grenade Launcher**

**10x Claymore**

**Night Vision Goggles**

MISSION 10:

# THE GULAG

## LAND IN THE GULAG

This mission picks up not long after the previous one. With the SAM sites off the coast disabled, your squad can now move in to the Gulag.

Soap believes a prisoner held in this compound may lead the team to Makarov. Your goal is to get in and extract the target in one piece.

As the mission begins, you hang out the side of a chopper beside Soap as your team flies toward the gulag. Friendly fighter jets streak by, destroying enemy emplacements on the cliffs ahead, clearing the way for your helicopters.

## ⟩ ENGAGEMENT 1

As you get closer to the facility, Soap calls for the chopper to circle the prison, giving you a steady platform for sniping the guards below. Take aim and pick off the Russian troops before they can retaliate with RPGs or activate the remaining SAM batteries on the walls.

## LEGEND

1 ENGAGEMENT

i 1 INTEL

Partway through your battlement clearing,
another set of fighters flies past and blows away
one of the towers completely. The jet wash sends
your helicopter into an unpleasant spin. Soap gets
on the radio with the General in charge of the
operation. The navy is intent on dismantling the
facility, and he tries to buy your team some time
to get in and out before they level the prison.

Once the walls are clear, your chopper moves to
the prison's center and descends, depositing your
squad in the middle of the yard. Disembark and
get moving for cover.

## ) ENGAGEMENT 2

Move over to this
position and take
cover behind one of the
mobile SAMs or behind
the low stone wall
that's nearby.

Hostiles occupy a
rooftop above and to
your right. A friendly
gunship swiftly moves
in and strafes the posi-
tion, clearing it with a
quickness.

You spot more Russian guards through a chain-link fence up ahead, and still more on top of a building to the south.

Use your Grenade Launcher to clear the rooftop, and then turn your attention to the guards at ground level. Eliminate them and move in with your team.

## ) ENGAGEMENT 5

A short hallway leads to the prison's upper control room. A few troops occupy the hall, so don't let your guard down. Eliminate them at a distance, and then move into the control room.

## SWEEP THE GULAG CELLS

## ) ENGAGEMENT 3

A few guards running from the prison below rush past here. Take them out and move up.

The entrance to the belly of the Gulag is just ahead, down a narrow hallway that descends into the prison's heart.

## ) ENGAGEMENT 6

When you reach the control room, Ghost sets up shop to both search for the prisoner and hijack the prison controls to help your team move through the cellblocks. Move out with Soap to start searching the cells the hard way.

### INTO THE PIT

The Gulag's prison area is set up as a large, vertical column. Prison cells are arranged in rings around the column's edges. Centrally located, suspended rooms provide the guards a clear 360-degree view of the cells.

The prison has multiple levels. Your squad begins searching from the top level, just outside the control room.

## ) ENGAGEMENT 4

Enter the tunnel leading below at this engagement point—you have to get inside and find Prisoner 627's location.

## ❯ ENGAGEMENT 7

Proceed down the connecting path that leads to the cells. Then start making your way around the ring. Numerous Russian guards wait for you ahead, so move from cover to cover carefully as you advance. You occasionally find crates, and you can use parts of the prison doors as cover.

Ghost activates a spotlight to shine on enemies ahead of you around the ring. Anywhere you see the light, you can take aim and fire to dispatch more guards. Partway around the ring, you reach a closed security door. Hold tight and keep fighting while Ghost opens it. When the door slides open, keep moving.

Ghost identifies the location of Prisoner 627. He's been transferred from these cells to the Gulag's east wing, which is located far below you.

The fastest way there is through the armory, which is down another connecting pathway. It stretches from your location in the outer ring to another suspended room beneath the control room.

## ❯ ENGAGEMENT 8

Make your way down into the armory to find a plethora of weaponry waiting just for you: pistols, shotguns, submachine guns, and assault rifles. Pick whatever you fancy.

However, you have a problem. The door to the lower level is shut. As Ghost works to open it, a large squad of guards is on its way to your position.

You're dreadfully exposed to weapon fire in the hanging cage that is the armory. You have to find an alternate means of cover—pick up a Riot Shield and get ready.

### THE RIOT SHIELD

The Riot Shield is a powerful new defensive tool. It's practically impenetrable to small arms fire from the front. But it's vulnerable to hits from the sides or rear, in addition to well-aimed explosives.

You've faced enemies armed with Riot Shields earlier in the campaign, but this is your first chance to use one. You can't use a weapon while you have the shield raised, though you can bash someone with it....and earn an Achievement for doing so.

When you take hits with the shield, the bulletproof screen gradually cracks and splinters, becoming increasingly difficult to see through as it absorbs damage. It eventually becomes impractical to use. In this case, you need to use it just long enough for Ghost to open the doors and allow you to escape the armory!

Guards start to pour into the surrounding cell ring and open fire on your position. Keep your back to the weapon rack in the room's center, and use the Riot Shield to soak up enemy fire.

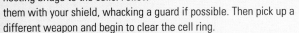

It's unpleasant, but Ghost gets the door open after a short wait. Your squad rushes along the connecting bridge to the cells. Follow them with your shield, whacking a guard if possible. Then pick up a different weapon and begin to clear the cell ring.

MacTavish takes a Riot Shield to sponge up hits, giving you free reign to open fire on the remaining guards.

## SAVE THOSE RIFLE 'NADES

A particularly nasty firefight takes place later in the mission. If possible, conserve your M4 and its large stock of launchable grenades.

## ) ENGAGEMENT 9

Make your way around the ring, and Ghost recommends your squad skip the remaining floors to the basement level by rappelling. Soap acknowledges, and you're headed out the window, so to speak.

Follow Soap to the pair of lines dangling from the cell ring level. Approach and hold Reload to latch on, and then slide down to the bottom of the prison.

# BLACKOUT

The lights are out in the prison's solitary confinement area. Switch on your night vision goggles before you proceed.

## ) ENGAGEMENT 10

A short but intense firefight takes place inside the narrow hall that passes alongside the cells. It's straightforward, as all of your targets are at the end of the hall. However, the bright flashes in your night vision may disorient you a little. A well-placed grenade can work wonders in the narrow confines.

Be very careful about moving down the hall when you eliminate the immediate and obvious threat at the end of the hall. The cells to the sides can hold stragglers—walking past them can be painful at best, fatal at worst.

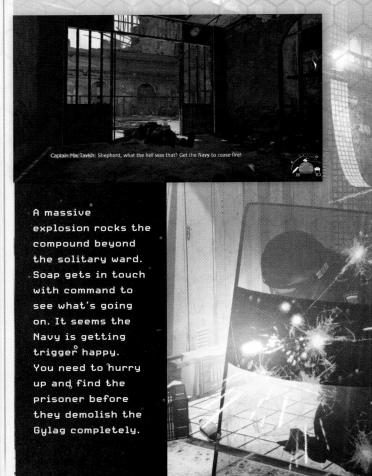

Captain MacTavish: Shepherd, what the hell was that? Get the Navy to cease fire!

A massive explosion rocks the compound beyond the solitary ward. Soap gets in touch with command to see what's going on. It seems the Navy is getting trigger happy. You need to hurry up and find the prisoner before they demolish the Gylag completely.

## ⟩ ENGAGEMENT 11

Keep moving through the tunnels under the Gulag until you reach a room filled with pipes. Watch out—a pair of guards is on the other side of the pipes, using them as cover.

Take them down, and then crawl under the pipes to make your way into the next room.

Be very careful here. A few guards waiting below the walkway can fill you full of holes. Tossing a grenade into the room ahead of you works well. You can then move in while they scramble to avoid the blast.

## A ROCKY RECEPTION

An old shower room is ahead. It can act as a shortcut to the prisoner's current location. To get to it, you must Breach the wall with a frame charge.

## ⟩ ENGAGEMENT 12

Move up to the wall and plant the charge when you're ready—and you'd better *be* ready, because this next firefight is one of the toughest in the game.

When you burst through the wall, take down as many guards as you can see in front of you.

The shower stalls provide ready cover from the abundant guards positioned deeper inside the shower room. The real problem is the two walkways above the shower. They provide perfect line of sight down onto your position…and they're filled with more guards.

There isn't just one "correct" way to fight through this area, but several tips can help:

Use your Grenade Launcher to take out the guards in the upper walkway. This is faster and easier than sighting and shooting at them while they move in elevated cover.

For the enemies on the ground, use your remaining grenades. Duck in and out of cover to pick eliminate them. Use the walls that divide the shower area as protection from foes in the next section.

Don't hesitate to use your Claymores here, but be careful to avoid letting an enemy catch you with a Claymore in your hand.

Finally, near the end of the showers, guards show up with Riot Shields. If you still have any grenades, use them. If not, Flash Grenades work well to stun them, letting you finish them with gunfire.

Frag Grenades can work, but you have to cook them for a few seconds before you throw. Time your tosses so that your grenades detonate just above or behind the guards' shields.

When you manage to fight past the heavy resistance, drop to an even lower tunnel via a hole in the floor at the back of the showers.

## ENGAGEMENT 13

You're nearly there. Follow Ghost's directions as you move through the tunnels beneath the Gulag. The room holding prisoner 627 is just ahead.

When you reach it, you have to do one final Breach to get into the room.

Set the frame charge and lunge in. Take down the guard, and your objective is complete—you've found the prisoner and you can get out!

Of course, that would be easier if the Navy wasn't shelling the building...

## ENGAGEMENT 14

Flee down the hall with your team. As you run down the tunnel to the chopper waiting at the end, another massive explosion triggers a collapse, blocking the hall and your escape route.

Turn around and run the other direction as the tunnels start to give way. You don't get far before a falling piece of the ceiling knocks you down.

At the bottom of a ruined shaft, Soap fires a flare up to his evac chopper. The chopper sends down a SPIE rig onto which your team can hook.

As you are helped to your feet, quickly move to the rig and hook onto it. Your whole team is pulled rapidly up the shaft to freedom as the Gulag goes up in smoke.

Mission complete!

ACHIEVEMENT / TROPHY

## SOAP ON A ROPE

You receive the Soap on a Rope Achievement/Trophy for completing this mission. Clever, eh?

# ACT 2

**OPERATIVE: PVT. JAMES RAMIREZ, RANGERS**

**OPFOR: RUSSIAN MILITARY**

**LOCATION: WASHINGTON, D.C., USA**

INTEL: 2

**OBJECTIVE: AID THE EVACUATION EFFORT**

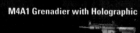

## INITIAL LOADOUT

**M9**

**M4A1 Grenadier with Holographic**

**4x Flash Grenade**

**4x Frag Grenade**

**10x Grenade Launcher**

**10x Claymore**

**Night Vision Goggles**

---

MISSION 11:

# OF THEIR OWN ACCORD

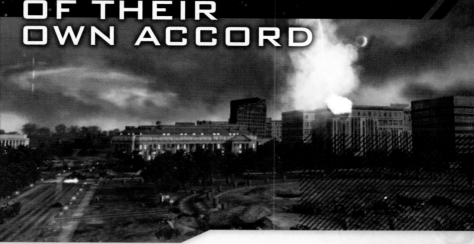

## THE COST OF WAR

Back in the boots of James Ramirez, you find yourself not on the frontlines, but rather in a melancholy makeshift hospital.

Make your way through the rooms. There's no fighting to do here—instead, you witness the cost of the fighting.

## ⟩ ENGAGEMENT 1

When you reach the end of the line, you link up with your squad and Sgt. Foley again. Your squad is being dispatched to assist with an evacuation that is in progress. From where? Step outside and see...

You discover that you're in a trench, just outside a beautiful old building in Washington, D.C.

The entire area is a warzone. Russian troops have invaded the capital, and the fight isn't going well.

---

## ) ENGAGEMENT 2

But you don't have time to worry about that. Right now, you have to get moving. Follow your squad as they move to the front of the trench.

En route to the building ahead, Sgt. Foley makes contact with Command to request an airstrike. Unsurprisingly, air units are already tied up elsewhere.

Foley then requests armored support from a passing armored combat force, which is granted. A light armored vehicle is pulled off to provide suppressing fire to aid your assault on the building.

### ASSAULT THE RUSSIAN-HELD BUILDING POSITION

Once you reach the end of the trenches and razor wire, the fighting begins in earnest. You can head into the building one of two ways: via the stairs up the left side, or those on the right side.

Both lead to the same destination, so just make sure you move up to the same side as your squad—generally they'll follow your lead.

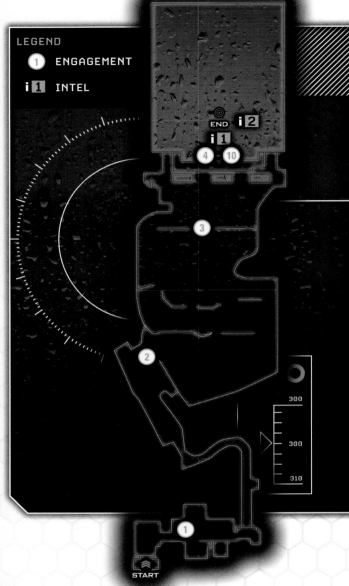

LEGEND

1 ENGAGEMENT

i1 INTEL

## ) ENGAGEMENT 3

The right route is slightly preferable, as an ammo crate is just inside. However, you can reach it from the left, and ammo isn't an issue immediately, so this isn't a problem.

A few Russian troops are on the stairs. Take them down, aided by the LAV's covering fire, and then move inside.

## ) ENGAGEMENT 4

Inside, you face a large, open lobby area with balconies on the second floor overlooking the ground level.

Use your Grenade Launcher to clear out hostiles on the second floor easily. Then pick off any troops on the ground level that threaten you.

An enemy crow's nest is on the building's fifth floor. You have to get up there with your squad to clear it out.

Traverse the central hallway that leads into the building's interior. Elevators are to your left as you go down the hall, but they're out of order—getting up there won't be *that* easy.

A small garden area is in the

middle of the building, and an entrance into the building's inner halls is off to the right.

Once you eliminate the hall guards, move in and make your way south. A few more guards protect a staircase leading up to the next level. Put them down, and then make your way up the stairs.

## CLIMB TO THE CROW'S NEST

On the next level, you soon find the balconies that overlooked the lobby area where you entered. Follow them to the left (east). Then

make your way up a pile of rubble that used to be a hallway, but now serves as makeshift staircase to the next floor.

## ) ENGAGEMENT 5

Be careful moving into that hall. Multiple Russian soldiers guard it, and they have good cover, particularly because you're rather exposed out in the garden area.

Don't hesitate go use some grenades here to flush out the soldiers. You need to penetrate their defenses and make forward progress, and another ammo crate is here.

## ) ENGAGEMENT 6

On the subsequent level, you can immediately spot a SAM site set up in the building's interior, along with a few guards. Pick them off from

the hallway you currently occupy before you step into the inner hallway.

When you decide to move in, watch your left flank. More enemies are to the south, including one that hides behind a door, poking out to take shots—shoot him straight through the door.

You can head over to the SAM and destroy it with C4. While you're out in the center, watch for more hostiles on the building's opposite side.

Clear out any remaining guards protecting the next flight of stairs in the hall. Ascend to the next level. There's plenty of cover here, so you should be able to move swiftly.

## ) ENGAGEMENT 7

You've reached the building's fifth floor. Now you just have to clear out the crow's nest up ahead.

Follow your squad as they carefully edge their way through the rooms. A few Russian troops stand between you and your destination.

Again, there's a lot of cover here. Just make sure you move forward cautiously, checking all sightlines and corners before you proceed— avoid missing a hostile on your flank.

Once you reach the crow's nest, you find that the Russian troops are too distracted firing heavy weaponry at the evacuation site to notice your squad.

Make them pay for their negligence—a cooked grenade followed up by a Grenade Launcher works well. Mop up any survivors and move in to the nest.

## PROVIDE FIRE SUPPORT FROM THE CROW'S NEST

The crow's nest has a clear view of the Mall and the Washington Monument, and it's loaded with heavy weapons.

## ) ENGAGEMENT 8

An M82 .50 cal sniper rifle is hard-mounted to the edge of the wall's blasted-out section. Get on it and take aim.

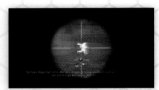

Look to the south of the monument. Hostile targets armed with rocket launchers are firing on friendly forces. Start picking them off!

Partway through your sniping spree, Command advises that incoming troops are headed to your position.

Quickly get off the sniper rifle and set up some Claymores in the hallways just outside the crow's nest. Then back up and get into cover, watching the approaches to the crow's nest.

When you hear the first Claymore detonate, you know you have inbound foes. Open up when they come into view. You have a fairly defensible position, so you should be able to fight off the assault without too much trouble.

**Command warns that an even larger force is on the move to your position, but Sgt. Foley wants more time to take down hostile helicopters and armor advancing on the evac site.**

## ) ENGAGEMENT 9

Pick up a Javelin from the supplies in the nest, and return to the crack in the wall—it's armor-hunting season.

Lock onto and destroy as many ground vehicles and helicopters as you can. You have limited time before the call for you to evacuate sounds.

You have to get to the building's roof now. A friendly SEAL team helicopter waits to extract you there.

## ESCAPE FROM THE RUSSIAN ASSAULT

**You have one minute and 30 seconds to reach the roof. Sprint after your squad mates as they run for the roof. You should get there with time to spare as long as you don't delay.**

**When you reach the rooftop, hop on the Minigun in the chopper. Sgt. Foley contacts Command to check on the evac site's status— fire from the World War II memorial is still pinning them down.**

## ) ENGAGEMENT 10

Your squad sets out in the chopper to do some damage. Your pilot takes you across the Mall to the memorial. Once you're in range, spin up the Minigun and don't let up as your 'copter strafes the memorial.

Unload on all visible infantry, vehicles on the ground, a hostile helicopter attempting takeoff, and anything else that moves.

Your chopper takes a hit during the strafing runs, but it's still functional. You then move to take on a massive SAM battery at the Department of Justice. Again, as you swing past the DoJ, unload with the Minigun on hostile targets visible in the windows.

Unfortunately, when you try to take on the SAM sites, you get blasted out of the sky.

## ) ENGAGEMENT 11

The chopper slams into the ground and everything goes dark. When you come to, your squad is badly shaken and damaged. So are you, and you're critically low on ammo. This is not good, given that hostile Russian forces are converging on your position.

Your ammo situation is grim, and as the Russians start to move in, a massive explosion whites out your vision.

Mission complete?

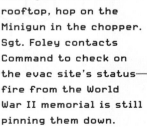

# 3

"Nothing will ever end war unless the people themselves refuse to go to war."

—Albert Einstein

OPERATIVE: SGT. GARY "ROACH" SANDERSON, TASK FORCE 141

OPFOR: RUSSIAN MILITARY

LOCATION: 14 MILES SSE OF PETROPAVLOVSK, RUSSIA

INTEL: 3

OBJECTIVE: REACH THE RUSSIAN NUCLEAR SUBMARINE

## INITIAL LOADOUT

**USP .45 Silenced**

**M14 EBR Scoped Silenced**

**4x Flash Grenade**

**4x Frag Grenade**

MISSION 12:

# CONTINGENCY

## SNEAK THROUGH THE RUSSIAN PATROLS

Back in the boots of Sgt. Roach, you're recovering from a slightly off-target parachute landing, deep in the snowy forests of Russia.

Your goal this time is direct assault on a Russian nuclear submarine, docked at a facility not far from your landing position.

## ❯ ENGAGEMENT 1

The squad is a bit scattered, so you have to work with your squad leader to find your way through the forest and regroup. Follow your leader as you move along the iced-over road.

## ❯ ENGAGEMENT 2

Up ahead, five men and their dog are patrolling the forest. Quickly get into the brush off the side of the road and stay crouched. Or better still, go prone.

As long as you stay quiet and out of sight, they won't bother you.

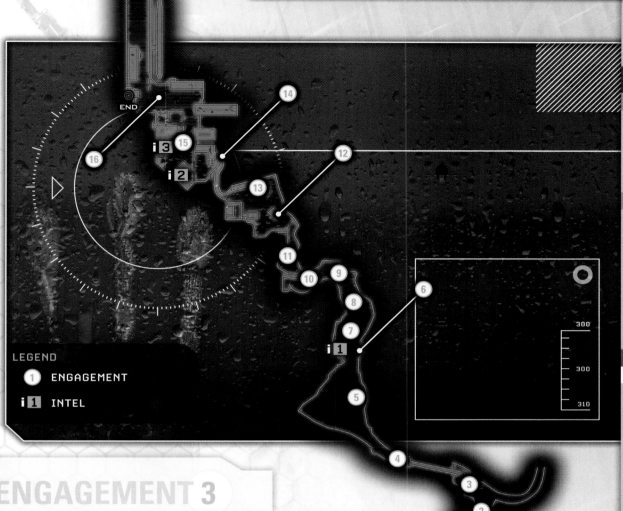

LEGEND

**1** ENGAGEMENT

**i1** INTEL

# ⟩ ENGAGEMENT 3

A convoy soon comes moving down the road. Once the convoy drives past, you have to eliminate the patrol walking along the road.

You can't bypass them and remain in stealth, but you can eliminate them without breaking stealth if you listen to your leader's instructions. Then move up and cross the frozen river via the bridge that spans it.

## OOPS

If you aren't quiet and careful enough, abandon the stealth option and open up on the guards. Use your grenades. You're badly outnumbered, and having attack dogs rush for your throat while troops shoot at you isn't an ideal tactical situation.

If you end up getting into a fight here, don't go swapping out your silenced M14—you need it soon.

## ⟩ ENGAGEMENT 4

Across the bridge, it's a quiet walk for a short distance...all the way until a BTR rolls around the corner and spots you both!

Fighting would be suicidal. Follow your leader as he flees into the forest to the north.

## ⟩ ENGAGEMENT 5

Run! The forest cracks and shudders as the BTR's high-caliber shells rip into the surrounding trees. Don't stop until the fire lets up.

The BTR can't follow you into the dense woods, but that doesn't mean you're completely safe yet. More patrols are ahead. Crouch and follow your leader.

## ⟩ ENGAGEMENT 6

A two-man patrol is here—avoid them if possible.

This entire section is a stealthy operation. If you're careful, you have a chance to avoid every engagement from #6 to #10 in this walkthrough chapter. If you aren't careful, you may have to face all of the guards we note and more when you raise the alarm.

You can quietly take out any of the guards here, and your squad leader helps. But if you're too slow taking down a patrol, if another patrol sees the results of your handiwork, or if they find bodies, you can expect unfriendly company.

If you raise the alarm, you'll have to fight. Fleeing can make a bad situation even worse, as you stumble into more patrols hidden amid the thick brush and trees.

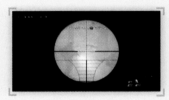

Take down any hostile targets that rush you until the forest quiets. Then keep moving.

## ⟩ ENGAGEMENT 7

Move up and watch for a dog patrol here, soon followed by a three-man patrol. You can skip them or try to take them out. If you go for the lethal takedown, your squad leader opens fire soon after you do.

Just don't take too long firing, or they'll raise the alarm.

## ) ENGAGEMENT 8

Another large patrol: two guards on the right side of the trail, and a guard with a dog on the left.

Use your M14 to pick them off one by one. If you're fast, none of the others will notice as you take them down.

## ) ENGAGEMENT 9

This area reveals several patrols roaming in a circular path as you get close. If you wait patiently in the brush, they move past you and take up positions slightly off the trail, giving you room to sneak past.

Alternatively, you can pick off stragglers at the back of the patrols as they move away from you. If you're careful, the lead patrol doesn't notice the missing tail.

Once you're past the last of the patrols, you can make your way up this hillside to a ridge overlooking a small village just ahead.

Your squad leader gets in touch with Captain MacTavish. An AGM armed Predator Drone is put into the air and you get the control rig.

## ) ENGAGEMENT 10

Activate it to take a look at the village.

Unfortunately, shortly after you do so, a SAM site in the village acquires the Predator and shoots it out of the sky. Oops. Soap will get another one in the air, but that SAM has to go.

## ) ENGAGEMENT 11

Slide down the other side of the ridge to the village below. You find a crate with several weapons on it, including an AUG HBAR with scope, an AA-12 Shotgun, a P90, and an M240 Heartbeat Sensor.

At the very least, grab the M240. The time for stealth has passed, and you're in for some heavy firefighting in a moment.

Around this time, the rest of your squad moves in with a bang—the mobile SAM goes up in smoke, and Ghost and the remainder of your team moves into the village up ahead. Regroup with the squad, and start moving through the village.

Now that the SAM site is gone, you regain control of the Predator. Start abusing your power right away!

The explosion at the SAM site has alerted hostile Russian troops to your attack. They move in on your position immediately.

## ) ENGAGEMENT 12

If you take cover behind one of the village buildings while your squad covers you, you can safely break out the control rig and start dropping enormous missiles on their heads.

Clear out any stragglers with your less exotic weaponry, and then move up through the forest line ahead. You soon arrive at a ridge overlooking the dock facilities. In the distance beneath a crane, you see the submarine you're here to find.

## ENGAGEMENT 13

Open up with the Predator—two hostile BTRs, a helicopter, and numerous foot-mobiles are in the facility.

Take down as many as you can with the Predator. Then start to advance on the facility with your squad. Every time you hear Soap call out that an AGM is online, take cover, bring up the control rig, and unleash another missile on the Russians.

### TEN PLUS FOOT-MOBILES

If you missed your opportunity in the "Wolverines!" mission, this is another chance to get the 10+ kill with a Predator missile Achievement.

You have to fight your way through the first part of the facility to reach the docks. There are two ways through: you can either head left (west), through a building, or follow the right side route.

The left route provides more immediate cover, but the right path provides more cover on the final approach to your destination—it's your choice! The right route also has another AUG HBAR and P90, as well as an RPG-7 resting on a crate.

## ENGAGEMENT 14

Your squad generally follows your lead, depending on which direction you push toward initially. However, if they move away from you, stay with them!

Stay in cover and move with your squad, firing AGM missiles as they come online. Be particularly vigilant for any calls of incoming transports. You should make transport trucks immediate missile targets, as you can take out a truck and all of its passengers with a single shot.

## ENGAGEMENT 15

The final push to your destination comes when you reach this area. One of your squad mates breaks off to head for the submarine. You need to provide cover for him from a nearby guardhouse roof.

## ENGAGEMENT 16

Take down any remaining troops that are too close for the Predator to handle. Then get on top of the guardhouse and grab the Dragunov sniper rifle.

An RPG-7 is also here. It may come in handy if a troop transport arrives and you don't have a Predator missile ready.

Two trucks roll up from the east. Destroy them immediately with an AGM, or use the RPG-7 if the AGM is still reloading.

One more wave of vehicles rolls in from the east. Enemies then come at you from the dock to the north. Use your sniper rifle to dispatch them.

Hold out just a bit longer. To your dismay, you soon see that you're too late, as the submarine's silo doors open and a nuclear missile takes flight… Mission complete, but successful?

**ACHIEVEMENT / TROPHY**
### DESPERATE TIMES

You receive the Desperate Times Achievement/Trophy for completing this mission.

MISSION 13:

# SECOND SUN

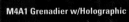

## THE UNTHINKABLE

This is a very brief mission. Consider it a reprieve from the intensity of the last several chapters.

The beginning of this mission plays out identically to the very end of Act 2, Mission 5. You're back in the role of Pvt. Ramirez, fighting off Russian troops as they close on your downed chopper. A massive explosion rips through the sky high above you.

## ⟩ ENGAGEMENT ❶

A massive, *nuclear* explosion. The explosion's EMP shuts down everything electrical for miles, and that's a problem, because there are helicopters over your head.

You need to free yourself from the rubble of the chopper and get off the street, fast!

# ENGAGEMENT 2

Chase after Sgt. Foley and the rest of your squad. Run as fast as you can and get into cover off the street. It's literally raining helicopters.

Once the explosions die down, the surroundings fall eerily quiet. Combat has died down, and everything electrical in the city has gone dead.

Even the optics in your guns no longer work. If you're carrying a weapon with a special scope, the sight is useless. In fact, if you check the Pause screen, even your area mini-map is a mess of static.

Sgt. Foley moves back into the street to investigate. Follow him out. When he moves up the street, stay with him.

Sgt. Foley: Looks like optics are down...comms too. There's not even a street light for blocks.

## FIND YOUR WAY TO WHISKEY HOTEL

A short distance up the street, you encounter a lone Ranger runner. He says that Colonel Marshall is assembling a task force at Whiskey Hotel.

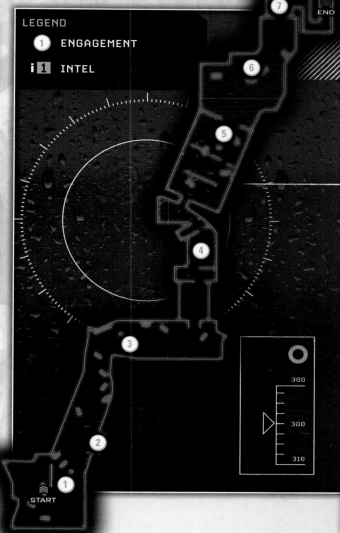

LEGEND

1  ENGAGEMENT

i 1  INTEL

300

300

310

# ENGAGEMENT 3

Your objective now is to reach Whiskey Hotel in one piece. There isn't a whole lot of fighting to do, as the explosion has knocked the fight out of most everyone in the area, but you still have a bit of a hike ahead of you.

Follow your squad into the building up ahead.

## IRONSIGHTS

An M4 with ironsights, rather than a scope, is on the ground near a fallen trooper. Pick it up here, or find another in the building just ahead.

Special scopes are useless after the blast, so traditional ironsights work better for fighting during this mission.

Inside the building, your team moves up a flight of stairs to the second level.

One of your squad members slowly opens a door into the next room. When he calls out a challenge sign, he's swiftly shot down—there are hostiles in the room ahead!

What follows is a particularly challenging firefight. There's precious little light. While the team throws down a few flares, and gunshots briefly light up the room, most of the combat takes place in a darkened office.

## ) ENGAGEMENT 4

Several Russian soldiers hide out in the cubicles and offices ahead. Hang back and watch for any muzzle flashes from the enemy troops. Whenever you see one, spray the area with bullets. You can't rely solely on precisely aimed shots here, though you can occasionally snap to a target by bringing up your sights.

Don't hesitate to use your grenades here, either. This is the mission's only major firefight.

When you clear out the first room, move up. One more office room ahead holds a few more enemies.

The second room has a massive hole in the wall, a bombed-out section that serves as egress from the building. Once you mop up the last of the hostiles, drop down outside with your squad.

## BACK ON THE STREETS

After you drop down, you can make out the Eisenhower building in the distance. Whiskey Hotel isn't far on the other side, so get moving.

## ❭ ENGAGEMENT 5

A short distance through the streets ahead, your team spots three hostiles crawling over a paralyzed Russian AFV. If you wait, your team takes them down without your help, though you can initiate the shooting if you wish.

Your team runs into another squad not too far from the stuck vehicle. They move through the shadows in the street ahead.

You can't tell whether they're friends or foes, but when they respond to a challenge call with bullets, the answer is clear enough.

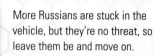

More Russians are stuck in the vehicle, but they're no threat, so leave them be and move on.

## ❭ ENGAGEMENT 6

Take cover behind the short stone wall here, or use any of the stuck vehicles in the street.

This is a good place to use your Grenade Launcher. The open street provides ready lines of fire—if you're quick, you can hit most of the hostile squad in one blast.

## POTUS?

## ❭ ENGAGEMENT 7

You soon reach your destination. Down in the Eisenhower building's basement, your squad finds a door marked with the seal of the President of the United States.

Sgt. Foley orders you inside, and you find a tunnel leading into the distance.

Your mission concludes here, but it picks up immediately in the next, so get ready!

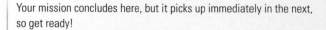

RANGER

OPERATIVE: PVT. JAMES
RAMIREZ, RANGERS

OPFOR: RUSSIAN MILITARY

LOCATION: WASHINGTON,
D.C., USA

INTEL: 2

OBJECTIVE: REGAIN
CONTROL OF WHISKEY
HOTEL

## INITIAL LOADOUT

**M9**

**M4A1 Grenadier**

**4x Flash Grenade**

**4x Frag Grenade**

**10x Rifle Grenade**

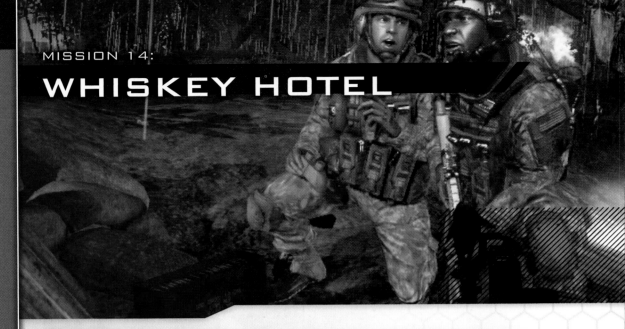

MISSION 14:

# WHISKEY HOTEL

## LOADOUT

The Initial Loadout listed at the beginning assumes you're starting this mission fresh. If you're continuing immediately from Second Sun, you keep whatever gear you had there.

## MEET COLONEL MARSHALL

You pick up where you left off in the Second Sun mission. Your map is still on the fritz and electronics aren't working, but it's pretty easy to know where to go.

## ) ENGAGEMENT 1

Follow Sgt. Foley and your squad down the tunnel. When you start hearing bullets and explosions, you know you've reached your destination.

In the distance, Whiskey Hotel—the White House—is visible. And it's occupied by the Russians.

## BREACH THE WHITEHOUSE

## ) ENGAGEMENT 2

Meet with Colonel Marshall, just up the hill from the tunnel. He's working to retake the White House, as it still has electrical power. If you can help take it, you can get in touch with Central Command.

You have to fight your way up the left flank into the West Wing—get moving!

## LEGEND

**1** ENGAGEMENT

**i1** INTEL

## HEAVY FIREPOWER

There are plenty of dropped weapons here. Try to get your hands on an M240. The extended ammo load comes in handy for clearing out troops rapidly, and you need to move quickly.

To get you started, an M240 ACOG is just to the left of the Colonel in the trench.

A lot of enemies are up in the White House's front façade. The frontline terrain is a maze of hastily constructed razor wire barricades and churned-up mud turf. Off to the left, toward the West Wing, a falling helicopter has dug up a trench of sorts.

The trench is your destination, as it leads directly to the front of the West Wing.

## ) ENGAGEMENT 3

You can proceed one of two ways. The first way is simply to take your chances, stay in cover, and make your way to the West Wing along the trench. You take fire from both the front of the White House and the West Wing, but if you stay in

cover and selectively pick off targets as you approach the West Wing, you can make it safely.

The other way is to hang back and take down targets from long range. This is much slower, as a *lot* of hostiles are up in the White House. It's considerably easier to clear the outer guards at the West Wing. However, it's even easier to accomplish that when you're closer, particularly with optics still down as a result of the nuclear blast.

### MOUNTED MG

A heavy machinegun turret is just to the left of the Colonel where you begin the mission. If you opt for the slower approach, you can use this MG to pick off some targets at the White House front.

## ) ENGAGEMENT 4

Once you're close enough to take down targets outside the West Wing, get in cover and pick off visible hostiles. This is also a good place to use a few launched grenades, but be sure to save some—they come in handy again soon.

Once you eliminate the outer Russian troops, you can move up and enter the Oval Office.

Inside, a radio announcement plays repeatedly—the White House will be bombed to clear its enemy occupiers if green smoke is not popped from the upper floor, and soon!

You have to reach the White House roof and pop that smoke before they ruin your chance to contact Central Command, not to mention destroy the White House!

## ) ENGAGEMENT 5

After listening to the announcement, Corporal Dunn moves up and opens a door into the next room. Move up carefully—Russian troops are waiting for your squad.

Clear out the Russians in the offices ahead, and then make your way forward—the press room awaits!

The press room provides hard cover to its hostile inhabitants, as banks of electronic equipment partially obscure your view of the room's interior. Lobbing a grenade or two ahead of you works well to clear out the troops.

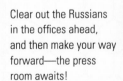

Once the press room is clear, make your way out the back to the walkway behind the White House. Ready a grenade!

# GET TO THE ROOF!

## 〉 ENGAGEMENT 6

Thick stone planters provide ready cover here, but keep an eye up and forward. Multiple Russian troops rappel down the side of the central White House. If you aim up and fire quickly with a Grenade Launcher, you can take down all of them in one shot.

Whether or not you manage the shot, you must deal with a few more hostile troops on the ground ahead. Use the planters as cover, and move up as quickly as you can once you take them down.

Back inside the building, a few more offices behind the press room are your next obstacles. Russian troops use the ready cover to make themselves difficult targets.

## 〉 ENGAGEMENT 7

If you're packing a high-caliber weapon, don't spare the ammo—try to shoot them straight through the thin office cubicle screens.

There are only a few troops here. Once they're down, advance, as Sgt. Foley warns that you have only two minutes to reach the roof!

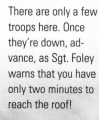

## 〉 ENGAGEMENT 8

Your squad passes through a hole in the kitchen wall, which leads into the White House lobby area.

A few guards are here, but there's no heavy resistance, so take them down quickly. Then ascend the stairs at the back of the lobby to the second floor. You have only seconds remaining—run!

## 〉 ENGAGEMENT 9

Sprint up the stairs to the White House roof. As you get close, a squad mate pops his flares. When you get closer, press the trigger to pop your green flare.

Friendly jets soon streak past overhead— you've made it in time, barely.

You get a moment to soak in the sight of a devastated D.C. stretching out before you, and then this mission is complete.

### ACHIEVEMENT / TROPHY
### WHISKEY HOTEL

You receive the Whiskey Hotel Achievement/Trophy for completing this mission.

# ACT 3

# LOOSE ENDS

---

**OPERATIVE: SGT. GARY "ROACH" SANDERSON, TASK FORCE 141**

**OPFOR: MAKAROV'S FORCES**

**LOCATION: CAUCASUS MOUNTAINS, GEORGIAN-RUSSIAN BORDER**

**INTEL: 3**

**OBJECTIVE: RECOVER INTEL ON MAKAROV**

**INITIAL LOADOUT**

**M9**

**ACR Grenadier Holographic**

**4x Flash Grenade**

**4x Frag Grenade**

**10x Grenade Launcher**

**10x Claymore**

---

## BREACH THE PERIMETER OF MAKAROV'S HIDEOUT

Your squad begins up on a hillside ridge, overlooking Makarov's large cabin in the distance.

You have a large offensive force here with you, including snipers on overwatch, and a large assault force. Your team has come prepared for heavy resistance.

## ⟩ ENGAGEMENT 1

You need to reach that cabin and search for any sign of Makarov or any intel on his location.

Make your way down the ridge to the left, and start moving through the forest toward the cabin.

## ⟩ ENGAGEMENT 2

It doesn't take long to realize that either you've been set up, or Makarov expected company. A Bouncing Betty jumps up from the ground. Go prone immediately! If you don't, you'll get your head blown off.

As it is, the blast shocks and dazes you as hostile forces appear on a ridge to your left, overlooking your squad and opening fire.

LEGEND
1 ENGAGEMENT
i1 INTEL

Shake off the dizziness—you have to return fire quickly and continue moving forward!

The situation rapidly deteriorates, as they have the area sighted for mortar fire. Explosive shells start to fall into the area.

Even pushing ahead isn't safe, as smokescreens go up and hostile fire starts coming in from ahead.

## ) ENGAGEMENT 3

You have to escape this area quickly, before a mortar blasts you or incoming fire that you can't even see through the smoke takes you down. The easiest way to breach this point is to hug the rocky wall to the right and slip through the smoke to the far right side.

If you sprint, you should be able to clear the smoke and come out on the right flank of any hostiles on the other side of the smoke. This gets you clear of the mortar fire, past the smoke, and lets you get a bead on nearby enemies. Move!

Once you're in position, start picking off visible hostiles as the remainder of your squad moves up.

Beyond the smoke-screen ambush, just past a few solar panels powering the cabin, you spot several trucks moving away from the cabin.

Stay back from them! Your friendly overwatch launches a Javelin missile strike on the small convoy. You don't want to be anywhere near the blast when the strike hits.

The trucks are quickly destroyed, but there's no way to tell if Makarov was onboard. You still have to clear the cabin. Move up with your squad toward the cabin's front.

A few hostiles are out in front of the cabin, but they're nothing you can't handle after that intense ambush.

Now you have to decide how to breach the cabin. There are two entrances on the upper floor and one on the lower.

All of them lead into the same cabin, so it doesn't really matter which you choose. Pick a point and get ready to breach!

# SECURE THE DATA

## HOLD THE LINE

Compared to many of the missions you've played up to this point, this one is comparatively simple, but it is an *extremely* intense defensive mission.

Essentially, you fight your way to the target point in just a few minutes. But then you have to hold out as waves and waves of attackers attempt to breach and take down your position.

You have access to a generous arsenal. Don't hesitate to try a different mix of weaponry. Also, a variety of tactics can get you through alive, even on Veteran difficulty.

## ⟩ ENGAGEMENT 4

Once you enter through your chosen breach point, quickly eliminate any hostiles in your sector. Then carefully sweep and clear every room in the cabin.

A *massive* weapon cache is inside the cabin. You find a gigantic spread of weaponry in a downstairs armory, and even more

on the cabin's middle level. Feel free to pick up some new weapons before you finish clearing the cabin.

When you're ready, breach the remaining rooms with frame charges, and eliminate the last of the resistance.

Makarov doesn't seem to be here, but you do find a computer with an absolute jackpot of information about him.

Command reports that they're sending an extraction team to recover you and the intel. But for now, you have to start stripping the computers of data.

You need to sort out your defensive situation—Makarov's men don't intend to let you escape his safe house with this intel in one piece.

Choose your weaponry from the armory's abundant offerings. Then set up as many Claymores as you can just outside and inside the cabin entrances. Expect inbound hostiles very shortly.

Move over to the PC on the main floor and hold Reload to connect the DSM to the machine.

Once it's installed, the DSM begins downloading all data from the hard drives.

The first wave moves in from the southeast. An RPG team then attacks from the west, followed by fast-attack choppers from the northwest.

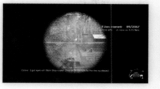

At this point, your sniper overwatch shifts position and you lose coverage for about thirty seconds. Another RPG team moves in from the southwest. Then more enemy 'copters arrive from the northwest and southeast, along with another RPG team from the east.

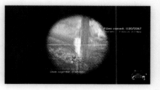

## VETERAN CHECKPOINT

On Veteran difficulty, you get a checkpoint when you pick up the DSM, and you don't get another until you "escape" into the woods just before the end. Save yourself a lot of trouble by thoroughly clearing the house before you pick up the DSM. That way, you don't have to both clear the house and fight to the woods on one checkpoint.

## DEFENSIVE POSITIONS

A high-capacity heavy machinegun and a secondary thermally-scoped weapon is our recommendation here. The former gives you high ammo capacity to maintain a steady stream of fire at incoming hostiles. The latter lets you more easily neutralize baddies moving up through the forest, as you don't have time to waste picking out targets from the brush. You *can* take down the choppers that move in with a sufficiently quick and accurate AT4 or RPG shot. This can give you some much-needed breathing room between attack waves. You may wish to begin your defense of the cabin outside rather than inside, and then gradually retreat inside as their superior numbers push you back.

You can defend from multiple positions inside the cabin, but a good one is just behind the DSM on the cabin's middle floor, which also happens to hold the secondary weapon cache. This gives you ready access to more weapons, and it lets you cover the cabin's upper front and side entrances (the two upper breach points).

Enemies will open fire on the DSM, eventually destroying it. You can't let that happen, so any enemies that breach the cabin perimeter are high-priority targets. The sheer number of foes may be daunting on your first attempt, but hold steady. Listen to your squad mates call out enemy presence, fire in quick, accurate bursts at each target, and immediately take down anyone getting inside the cabin. One last point: When the call to evacuate comes, be sure to clear the area immediately outside the cabin carefully before you flee. You don't want to fight through everything and then die when you step outside. Good luck!

Around this time, the DSM transfer should be complete. You can finally get out of here!

## FLEE TO THE LZ

Ghost calls for evacuation, and it's time to leave the cabin and get to the LZ. The field to the cabin's southeast is your destination. But to get there, you have to get through the forest filled with still more hostiles.

## 〉ENGAGEMENT 5

Make your way outside and get moving, as hostiles may still come up behind you as you flee.

On your way down the slope, try to pick off targets as they become aware of you. When Ghost calls that he's covering you, sprint! He's pretty good at downing targets near your position.

## 〉ENGAGEMENT 6

Once you break free from the forest, the welcome sight of extraction helicopters comes into view. Break free from the tree cover into the field, and this mission is complete!

 ACHIEVEMENT / TROPHY

## THE PAWN

You receive the The Pawn Achievement/Trophy for completing this mission.

# ACT 3.

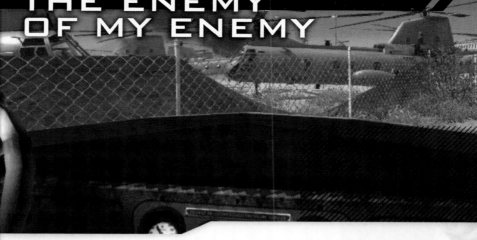

CAMPAIGN
BASICS

CAMPAIGN
WALKTHROUGH

**ACT 1**

M1: S.S.D.D

M2: Team Player

M3: Cliffhanger

M4: No Russian

M5: Takedown

**ACT 2**

M6: Wolverines!

M7: The Hornet's
Nest

M8: Exodus

M9: The Only
Easy Day...
Was Yesterday

M10: The Gulag

M11: Of Their
Own Accord

**ACT 3** ▽

M12: Contingency

M13: Second Sun

M14: Whiskey
Hotel

M15: Loose Ends

M16: The Enemy
of My Enemy

M17: Just Like
Old Times

M18: Endgame

SPECIAL OPS
MISSIONS

MULTIPLAYER
BRIEFING

MULTIPLAYER
WARFARE

TACTICAL

CLANS

INTEL CHARTS

SATELLITE INTEL

ACHIEVEMENTS

OPERATIVE: CAPTAIN
"SOAP" MACTAVISH,
TASK FORCE 141

OPFOR: MAKAROV'S MEN
AND MILITARY FORCES

LOCATION: US VEHICLE
DISPOSAL YARD 437, 160
MILES SW OF KANDAHAR,
AFGHANISTAN

INTEL: 2

OBJECTIVE: SNEAK PAST
THE WARRING FACTIONS

## INITIAL LOADOUT

**MP5K Silenced Red Dot**

**M14 EBR Scoped Silenced**

**4x Flash Grenade**

**4x Frag Grenade**

## MISSION 16:
# THE ENEMY OF MY ENEMY

## SNEAK THROUGH THE FIREFIGHT

At the same time that the assault on Makarov's hideout occurs in
Loose Ends, Soap and his partner investigate another lead, in a vehicle
graveyard in Afghanistan.

On arrival, it's apparent that the tip was good—the area is crawling with
hostiles. Unfortunately, your target is not present, and you need to get
through this mess in one piece.

## 〉 ENGAGEMENT 1

The entire battlefield is covered with hostile military forces, as well as troops loyal to Makarov, each
fighting the other.

If you're careful, quiet, and quick, you can—and should—avoid most conflict here. You'll still engage
in *some* combat, as sneaking through here undetected is extremely difficult.

Nevertheless, make
a point of being as
stealthy as possible. If
you alert an entire area
to your presence and
start shooting indiscrimi-
nately, a huge hostile
force will target you,
making the mission that
much more difficult.

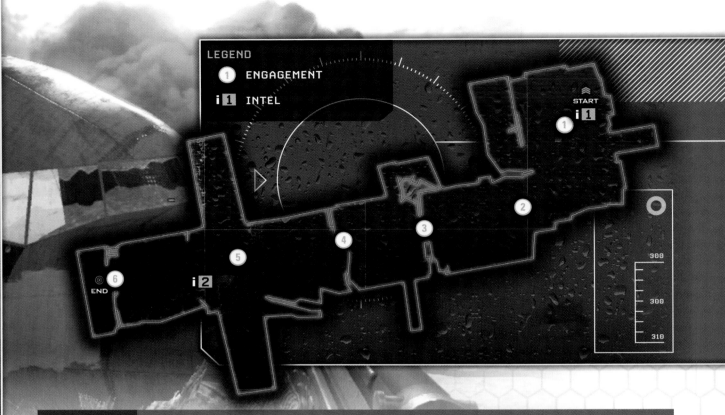

## STEALTHY

This mission isn't *quite* like the sneaking you undertook in the Cliffhanger or Contingency missions. Here, you aren't trying to avoid detection completely, with the threat of hostile patrols coming after you if you fail. Instead, you're simply trying to minimize the number of enemies that you *have* to fight.

Because the forces focus on fighting each other and are unaware of your presence, they engage you only if they spot you directly, or if you fire at them. This is why avoiding firefights as much as possible is a good idea. If enemies *are* alerted to your presence, they come after you, but the entire battlefield doesn't instantly turn on you.

## ⟩ ENGAGEMENT 2

The easiest way to get through the level is to hug the right "wall"— that is to say, the wall of piled-up, scrapped airplanes. Carefully sneak your way along the firefight's outskirts, engaging only those targets directly in your path.

Use the scrap yard's ruined vehicles for cover as you move from position to position. Carefully scan the area for hostiles that might see you,

then move to the next point and see if anyone has noticed. If so, deal with them before you advance in order to avoid attracting a large group.

Carefully make your way from the starting position to this area. You have multiple silenced weapons, so if you see targets directly in your path, take them down and quickly move ahead.

Your target is this ruined plane—you have to crawl through its fuselage. Doing so places you on a perfect spot overlooking a field down the hill below.

As you get close to this narrow gap, Nikolai radios in. He's headed for the runway...and complaining about the ridiculous firefight occurring below. You have to make your way through the remaining forces to reach the runway and get out of this mess!

## ) ENGAGEMENT 4

You may be tempted to open up with your sniper rifle from this position, trying to clear out all the hostiles. Resist the urge. Instead, pick either the left or right side of the field, take out a few targets blocking your descent, quickly leave the airplane, and slide down the slope. Get into cover!

Once you're down the hill and behind solid cover, you can start to pick your way across the field. Proceed up the hill on the other side of the road just ahead.

## ) ENGAGEMENT 3

Keep moving through the airplane rubble. You may find that you have to sprint somewhat in the open from here to Engagement #4. If you move fast, you shouldn't pick up too many hostiles.

# ESCAPE THE AIRPLANE GRAVEYARD!

## ) ENGAGEMENT 5

You have to fight your way through one last chunk of the vehicle graveyard.

Because your destination is just ahead and your squad partner is waiting for you in a vehicle, you can afford to break stealth and blitz to the last target area.

Don't rush ahead rashly, but don't hesitate to open up with your MP5K and grenades to clear the way. You only need to reach the waiting vehicle in one piece!

Aboard the vehicle, you're *almost* out of trouble, but not quite... Hostile troops come after you in their own transportation. While your driver flees the scene, you have to play gunner and try to take down the hostiles on your tail.

## ) ENGAGEMENT 6

At a few points during the crazy chase, a vehicle loaded with troops tries to pull up alongside you. Quickly take out the passengers in the back before they can draw a bead and riddle your ride with bullets.

Once you reach the runway in the distance, Nikolai accelerates down the airstrip with the rear cargo door open. You have to get aboard the plane on the move!

Your driver gets taken out by a stray bullet, and you have to take the wheel at the last second. Carefully aim for the rear of the cargo plane. When you get close enough, one final burst of speed deposits you in the belly of Nikolai's plane.

Nikolai quickly takes off, and this intense mission is finished.

ACHIEVEMENT / TROPHY
### OUT OF THE FRYING PAN

You receive the Out of the Frying Pan Achievement/Trophy for completing this mission.

# ACT 3

**OPERATIVE:** CAPTAIN "SOAP" MACTAVISH, TASK FORCE 141

**OPFOR:** HOSTILE MILITARY FORCE

**LOCATION:** HOTEL BRAVO, AFGHANISTAN

**INTEL:** 4

**OBJECTIVE:** HUNT THE RENEGADE OFFICER

## INITIAL LOADOUT

**Vector Silenced ACOG Sight**

**Intervention Silenced**

**4x Flash Grenade**

**4x Frag Grenade**

**Night Vision Goggles**

MISSION 17:

# JUST LIKE OLD TIMES

## INFILTRATE THE HIDDEN BASE

Discoveries during the previous two missions have brought you here, to a hidden base in Afghanistan. You're tracking down a renegade military officer, and to reach him, you must quietly infiltrate the cliff-side base and locate your target within.

## ENGAGEMENT 1

To get started, head up the dusty slope with your partner.

When you reach the top, stop and take stock of the situation. Down the hillside below you, at the cliff's edge, a road stretches east-west out of sight around the cliff walls to your left.

More critically, the two hostile patrols on the bridge near their vehicles are your first concern.

Don't engage them just yet. Wait for the patrols to separate. As one walks away to the east, you can go after the group on the right. Aim for the two rightmost targets, and open fire with your silenced sniper rifle.

LEGEND

1  ENGAGEMENT

i 1  INTEL

When you eliminate the first group, quickly slide down the slope and aim for the other patrol that's walking away down the road. Eliminate the second patrol in the same way, and then proceed down the road where the patrol was heading.

## ) ENGAGEMENT 2

The entrance to the base is *below* you, through a cave entrance down the cliff. Move up to the road's railing and hold Reload to attach your rappelling rope—then it's over the edge!

Hold Fire to brake, carefully slowing your descent. Below you, two guards watch the cave complex's entrance, and they're completely unaware of your vertical descent.

When you get close enough, attack with a melee strike, and you and your partner take down the guards quickly and silently. Move into the caves.

# LOCATE YOUR TARGET

## ❯ ENGAGEMENT 3

Move in quietly—stay crouched and silent. The guards on the inside have not yet been alerted to your presence, and if you're careful, they won't be.

Follow your partner around the room's left side. A patrol moves through the front part of the cave. If you stay low and quiet, they won't spot you. When they move on, a single guard remains to watch the security cameras. You can take him out quietly and then move on, again on the room's left side.

### ALARM!

It's really in your best interest to avoid conflict in this room, as a very large group of guards is at rest here. If you alert them, you're in for a painful firefight.

If you want to claim the Intel piece that's off to the room's right side, you may wind up alerting them, but you can always come back and get it on a subsequent replay!

You pass a large group of enemies in the center of the cave, then another pair just a short distance ahead. In both cases, stay low and follow your partner. Don't alert them.

Finally, at the rear of the cave, two hostiles with flashlights come down the stairs ahead. You can't let them move past you, so take them down. Fire at the left target when your partner calls the count, and then move up quietly.

One more target is at the top of the stairs, but your partner takes him down. Move into the next room.

When you make it midway into this dimly illuminated cave, radio chatter indicates that your presence has been detected. A breaching team is sent into this room to locate and eliminate you!

## ❯ ENGAGEMENT 4

After a few seconds, an explosion rocks the cavern as the squads move in to attack. You can clearly see their laser pointers in the dark. Given the dim lighting conditions, they are your best indicator for quickly picking out targets.

Don't hesitate to use your grenades. This is a nasty fight, and stunning the breaching squads with a Flashbang or two works wonders to keep the incoming fire at a manageable level.

Once you eliminate the breaching squads, move up through the cavern to an exit at the rear. It leads to the cliff outside, and into open air.

## ) ENGAGEMENT 5

A narrow rock catwalk winds its way along the side of the cliff, leading back into the caverns ahead. You have to traverse this dangerous obstacle in one piece. Pick up a Riot Shield resting against the railing here, and move ahead of your partner, staying crouched.

As long as you move forward slowly crouched, your partner will pick off all hostiles on the catwalk ahead of you. Watch your step! It's hard to see through the Riot Shield's screen, but it's downright lethal to take a misstep here, so move slowly.

When you reach the walkway's opposite side, ditch your shield and pick up a weapon from a fallen guard before you proceed.

## ) ENGAGEMENT 6

This cavern room on the cliff is half exposed to the open air. A bit of camo netting covers its rightmost half.

More hostile guards are in the back of the cavern. Of particular note, several of them carry Riot Shields. If possible, try to pick up a heavy machine gun. Its ammo load comes in handy for taking down this area's hostile presence.

Use your remaining grenades on the troops that carry shields. When you clear out the cavern, search among the fallen troops' guns, along with those littering the room, to find one with an attached grenade launcher—it can come in handy in the next area.

## ) ENGAGEMENT 7

Move into this next cavern, once more inside the cave complex. As you do, a smokescreen pops up to your left, across a deep chasm in the floor. Don't stay across from the smokescreen, though you can toss any remaining grenades into it, or launch a grenade or two into it.

Instead, run straight ahead—a small 'room' ahead loops around the chasm to the smokescreen and, more importantly, a SCAR-H Thermal. Grab it, and you have a perfect flanking position with the perfect weapon to handle the bad guys. An M240 is on the same stand as the Thermal weapon—it makes a good backup.

Take cover in the small, rocky alcove and start picking off enemies through the smoke via your heat-sensing scope. A few targets have Riot Shields. If you take careful aim while scoped, you can hit their exposed limbs, which show up cleanly in the thermal view.

Once you dispatch the last of the enemies in the smokescreen, you can move up.

Shadow Company: Oxide, Butcher Five-Actual. I've got a severed det cord - we're gonna need ten mikes to get the trunk rigged and the EBC primed, over.

## PURSUE THE TARGET

## ) ENGAGEMENT 8

Not too much farther into the cavern, you come to a sealed door leading into the command room. A spread of weapons is on the ground to the left of the door. Pick your favorite, but grab at least one submachine gun, as you need a quick and accurate weapon for the breach.

Move up to the door and plant your Frame Charge. When the door blows and you move in slow motion, check your fire!

The whole command center is laced with C4 charges—you don't want to trip an explosion. Take down as many guards as possible during the breach, and then finish off any stragglers. The door out is sealed, so you have to hit up a console in the room to unlock it.

Get ready to run! You have mere seconds before the detonation of the caves triggers. As soon as the door opens, sprint out of the cave!

# ❭ ENGAGEMENT 9

The massive explosion knocks you off your feet and stuns you for a moment. When you regain consciousness, artillery fire blasts the canyon's open ground ahead, covering the renegade officer's escape.

Wait for the smoke to clear, and then move up. You have to keep chasing him. As you advance, check the cavern's right side for an AT4—it comes in handy in a moment.

Make your way up the right side of the camp just outside the caves. A few guards are here, some staggered by the artillery, so be careful to move around cover.

As you enter the canyon, a hostile helicopter flies in and starts to unload troops. If you're quick with your AT4, you can take it out before it has a chance to unload anyone!

Move up through the camp. Another cave is just ahead on your left, this one leading down to the river you saw at the bottom of the cliff when you began the mission. Your target is fleeing via boat, and you have to pursue!

# ACT 3

**OPERATIVE: CAPTAIN "SOAP" MACTAVISH, TASK FORCE 141**

**OPFOR: NONE**

**LOCATION: RIVER OUTSIDE HOTEL BRAVO, AFGHANISTAN**

**INTEL: 1**

**OBJECTIVE: CHASE DOWN THE ESCAPING OFFICER**

---

**INITIAL LOADOUT**

Mini-Uzi

---

MISSION 18:

# ENDGAME

## PURSUE THE OFFICER

### THE FINAL PUSH

As a good portion of the final mission is cinematic and significant to the story, we intentionally obscure some details in this walkthrough. This is in the interest of not spoiling the final encounters so that you can enjoy the story revelations as they unfold!

Your target has escaped into the river and is fleeing on a Zodiac. Sprint down the stairs to the small dock in the cavern below. Then hop in a boat with your partner.

### FINAL INTEL

The last piece of Intel rests on a crate on the dock. Grab it before you hop in, and then get going!

You have to catch up to the fleeing officer. When you emerge from the cavern onto the wider river ahead, it's clear that you aren't without opposition. Hostile troopers litter the riverbanks, the bridges, in helicopters, and in other boats!

Accelerate via the trigger, and try to steer away from obstacles in your path, as well as helicopters strafing the river. You can fire your Mini-Uzi via the Scope button. It both auto-aims and has infinite ammunition, so don't be shy with the fire.

## HANG ON TIGHT

Partway along the river, you slam through a rough section of rapids. Not long after, your target escapes onto a Pave Low that scoops him up directly from the river!

Hold the boat steady while your partner lines up a shot on the helicopter. A few shots and the helicopter is crippled, plummeting over the waterfall in the distance.

About that waterfall...your boat soon follows!

When you regain your senses, you stagger to your feet, painfully injured. Your weapons are lost, all but your knife. Through the haze of a dust storm, you can just see the crashed remains of the helicopter ahead.

## THE FINAL CONFRONTATION

Stagger your way toward it. As you get close, the officer flees from the wreckage. Stumble after him. When you get close enough to strike, he retaliates too quickly, knocking you to the ground.

What ensues is a desperate struggle for survival. Follow the onscreen prompts to win the battle! When you're finally done, this mission and the campaign are finally complete.

Congratulations—you have finished *Call of Duty: Modern Warfare 2*...but there is still much to do. Check out Special Ops for fun co-op missions. And, of course, hours of enjoyment await you online. Consult the Multiplayer section of this guide for all the details.

If you completed the game on Regular difficulty and you didn't grab all of the Intel, you may want to tackle a replay. Use this guide's Enemy Intelligence section to locate every piece, and go for a higher difficulty level!

 ACHIEVEMENT / TROPHY

### FOR THE RECORD

You receive the For the Record Achievement/Trophy for completing the campaign.

Special Ops is an entirely new mode in *Call of Duty: Modern Warfare 2*, separate from the campaign or multiplayer, though it does include cooperative multiplayer!

Spec Ops missions are divided into Alpha, Bravo, Charlie, Delta, and Echo, with progressively more difficult and unique challenges in each category.

All Spec Ops missions can—and *we* think, should—be played cooperatively. You can play with a friend online, and this is a lot of fun in all of the missions. There are two missions, both in Bravo, that can *only* be played cooperatively. Also, Xbox 360 and PS3 allow you to play these missions cooperatively in Split Screen mode!

In co-op mode, if you fall in battle, your partner can (in most missions) revive you by approaching and holding the Use button. If you are downed, you can yell for help with the Weapon Swap button, or fire with your pistol, as though you're in Last Stand.

Each Spec Ops mission can be played on Regular, Hardened, or Veteran difficulty, corresponding to the one- to three-star rating on each mission. Some missions have specific completion goals to achieve a higher star rating, although most you must simply beat on Veteran to earn three stars.

Earning stars unlocks a few Achievements/Trophies, and unlocks new Spec Ops missions. There are 69 stars to earn in total: three for each of the 23 missions, though you do not need to acquire a full three stars on the early missions to unlock the later ones.

Generally, getting three stars on most missions is easier to do in co-op play, so if you're going for total completion, bring a friend!

Spec Ops missions are usually small chunks of the campaign levels, redone with some type of new objective, be it offense or defense. A few are unique, taking place either on maps that may be familiar to *Call of Duty 4: Modern Warfare* veterans, or entirely new scenarios.

# THE PIT

DESCRIPTION: CLEAR ALL OF THE ENEMY TARGETS AS FAST AS POSSIBLE. SHOOTING CIVILIANS WILL PREVENT YOU FROM GETTING 3 STARS.

ESTIMATED OPPOSITION: NONE

CLASSIFICATION: ASSAULT

ESTIMATED COMPLETION TIME: 1:00.00

IW BEST: 00:22.60

## DIFFICULTY LEVELS

| | | |
|---|---|---|
| ★ | COMPLETE THE COURSE | |
| ★★ | COMPLETION IN LESS THAN 45 SECONDS | |
| ★★★ | COMPLETION IN LESS THAN 35 SECONDS | |

CANNOT HIT ANY CIVILIANS FOR 3-STAR RANKING.

FIVE CIVILIAN CASUALTIES RESULTS IN MISSION FAILURE.

**STARTING GEAR**

M4A1

USP .45

**AVAILABLE GEAR**

M9

Desert Eagle

SCAR-H Foregrip

MP5K Holographic

ACR Holographic

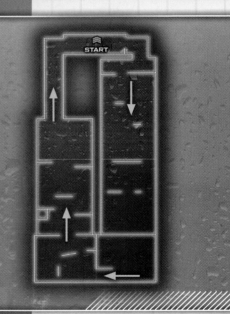

## STAR AWARDS

Upon completion, most Special Ops missions award one star for Regular difficulty, two stars for Hardened, and three stars for Veteran difficulty. However, a few of them have specific requirements to earn stars—check the mission's header for details.

The stars you earn for completing Special Ops missions unlock, among other things, access to each successive mission tier. Note the following table:

| SPECIAL OPS MISSION TIER | STARS NEEDED |
|---|---|
| Bravo | 4 |
| Charlie | 8 |
| Delta | 20 |
| Echo | 40 |

## JUST GETTING WARMED UP

The first Spec Ops mission is very straightforward. It's simply the training run session of S.S.D.D., only this time you can play it co-op.

Most, though not all, Spec Ops missions are small slices of campaign missions, but often with significantly different opposition or goals. Some are target elimination, while some are simple defense.

In this case, you need to clear The Pit quickly and without hitting any civilians. It's good practice for fast movement and weapon swapping!

To start the level, walk through the gate and into The Pit. The first engagement is three enemies and no civilians. You can easily spray down all three of the enemies with an automatic rifle and proceed to the next engagement.

Move forward, and the next crop of enemy targets appears. There is one stationary target to the right, and one moving target, which is occasionally obscured by a civilian target in front. Carefully take out the enemies without hitting the civilian.

The next engagement is immediately behind the previous one. It has enemies on both floors of the destroyed building. The first floor has two moving and one stationary enemy target, while the second floor has one

moving target and one stationary target. Avoid the two civilians on the first floor. Consider switching to your pistol at this point to avoid running out of ammo in the next level.

Move into the building for the next engagement, which consists of one moving and two stationary enemy targets. Take out the two stationary enemy targets to the right before you enter the building. Then carefully take out the moving target behind the civilian. Reload your pistol if necessary, and run up the stairs. Knife the target at the top of the stairs to trigger the next wave.

The next wave consists of four enemies and two civilians. Carefully take out both of the enemies on the left. Next, shoot the two targets to the right while you move toward the rooftop's edge. Drop down for the next wave, reloading as you run.

A precise shot during your fall can take out one hostile in this wave on the left side. Next, move around the right side, carefully taking out the enemy targets and avoiding the civilian in the background. If you're using a Desert Eagle here, the shot will go straight through the two enemies and take out the civilian.

Run straight ahead to the exit as you take out the two enemy targets in your way.

## VETERAN TIPS

While you carry a pistol, you run faster. Consequently, a good way to go for a fast time on this mission is to carry *two* pistols. Take your .45 and grab the M9 at the start.

This gives you the benefit of faster movement *and* faster switching, because you're swapping to a pistol.

Otherwise, simply make sure you're sprinting when you're not shooting!

## MISSION 02

# SNIPER FI

DESCRIPTION: USE A SNIPER RIFLE, CLAYMORES, AND PREDATOR DRONES TO HOLD OFF WAVES OF ENEMIES.

ESTIMATED OPPOSITION: LIGHT

CLASSIFICATION: WAVE DEFENSE

ESTIMATED COMPLETION TIME: 4:00.00

IW BEST: 01:55.50

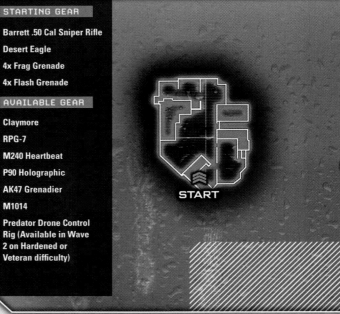

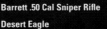

START

### DIFFICULTY LEVELS

| ★ | 3 WAVES OF INFANTRY, 1 JEEP, 1 TRUCK |
| ★★ | 4 WAVES OF INFANTRY, 2 JEEPS, 1 TRUCK |
| ★★★ | 5 WAVES OF INFANTRY, 3 JEEPS, 2 TRUCKS |

This mission takes place in the dock area of Contingency. Instead of fighting your way to a sub, you stay put in one spot, playing defense as waves of hostile troops attack you. To win, you have to survive all of the troop and vehicle waves.

Each wave consists of a set number of infantry and a few vehicles you must kill to progress to the next wave. On the Regular difficulty level, you get the Predator Drone control rig from the beginning; it isn't available until wave two on Hardened or Veteran.

For each wave, try alternately sniping distant enemies, mowing down enemies close to your position, and using the Predator Drone whenever it's available to take out packs of enemies.

At the beginning of the level and between each wave, place Claymore charges near the ladders to protect yourself from enemies that get past your perimeter.

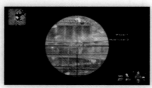

If you change out your Desert Eagle for the M240 with Heartbeat, you can use it to get a quick glimpse of nearby enemies. Use the RPG if necessary to take out any entrenched enemies quickly.

Remember to prioritize troop transport trucks with the Predator, as taking them out can get rid of a huge chunk of a wave, giving you some breathing room.

In co-op, you can have one player stay on the upper platform to snipe, while the other patrols the ground below. The player without the control rig also gets to see the AGM explosions in person, which is always fun…

## VETERAN TIPS

Quickly drop off the upper platform and place a screening perimeter of Claymores. Getting an early warning of an enemy below you can save your life.

Don't expose yourself to enemy fire for long periods. Stay in cover, pop out to pick off a few hostiles, then duck back in cover.

Once you get the Predator, be sure your immediate area is clear of hostiles before you try to use the control rig. Otherwise, you may get killed before you can shoot the AGM.

Remember that once you line up an AGM, you can press Fire again to activate the boosters on the missile, causing it to impact more quickly, and getting you back in control faster.

Use the intel on enemy locations that the Predator provides to pick out enemies behind cover, so you know where to look for them.

Use the M240 Heartbeat heavily to locate flanking enemies if they get close.

Use the M240 along with the Barrett, and the P90 as backup if you run out of M240 ammo.

## MISSION 03

# O CRISTO REDENTOR

DESCRIPTION: HUNT DOWN AND ELIMINATE THE FAVELA GANG. MINIMIZE CIVILIAN CASUALTIES.

ESTIMATED OPPOSITION: LIGHT

CLASSIFICATION: ELIMINATION

ESTIMATED COMPLETION TIME: 2:30.00

IW BEST: 01:16.20

### DIFFICULTY LEVELS

| ★ | 30 ENEMIES, 6 CIVILIAN KILL LIMIT |
| ★★ | 40 ENEMIES, DOGS, AND 4 CIVILIAN KILL LIMIT |
| ★★★ | 50 ENEMIES, DOGS, AND 3 CIVILIAN KILL LIMIT |

In contrast to Sniper Fi, O Cristo has you on the offense, hunting down militia in the favela of the Takedown mission. As in the campaign, civilian casualties are *not* acceptable—you must always avoid killing innocents, or you will fail the mission.

**STARTING GEAR**

TAR-21 Holographic Ranger
4x Flash Grenade
4x Frag Grenade

**AVAILABLE GEAR**

AA-12 Heartbeat
4x Claymore

**LEGEND**

**A** AMMO CACHE

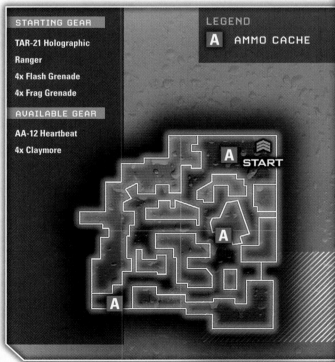

Right from the start, enemies rush at you from all directions. Move from building to building, using them as cover as you methodically take out hostile targets.

Explosive barrels are scattered around the level—blow them up to take out nearby enemies. Additionally, many of the weapons scattered on the ground may give you a tactical advantage in certain situations.

Be careful with the explosive barrels, as they can easily kill nearby civilians (or you!) if they are accidentally detonated.

Your secondary starting weapon is a very, ah, *oldschool* shotgun. We strongly recommend you quickly replace it with the AA-12.

You can duck inside several of the buildings here, but we don't recommend staying in them for too long. Most have multiple openings through which you can take fire, and being stuck inside with a grenade is not an ideal situation.

You have only a few Claymores, so don't hesitate to set them up as booby traps near explosive barrels.

In the Hardened or Veteran levels, a wave of dogs attacks after every 10 enemy kills. Kill the dogs at a distance if possible, or carefully time a melee strike to break a dog's neck.

## VETERAN TIPS

The dogs are the most significant addition, and they can cause you a lot of trouble if you aren't prepared. Remember that they come every 10 kills, and fast, rapid-fire weapons work best for taking them down.

If possible, grab a pair of Mini-Uzis to use on the dogs, as you can fire with one hand, reload it, and continue firing with the other, giving you a constant stream of bullets to take them down before they reach you. You can also duck inside one of the buildings that have only one entrance. That way, the dogs come at you from only one direction.

Try to hang out in one of the corners near the ammo crates, using the crate as cover. The constant ammo resupply can aid you in taking down the waves of militia. If some enemies are hiding, you can use the Heartbeat Sensor to find their location.

# EVASION

DESCRIPTION: USE SILENCED SNIPER RIFLES AND CUNNING TO SLIP PAST THE ENEMY PATROLS.

ESTIMATED OPPOSITION: LIGHT

CLASSIFICATION: STEALTH

ESTIMATED COMPLETION TIME: 3:00.00

IW BEST: 00:43.65

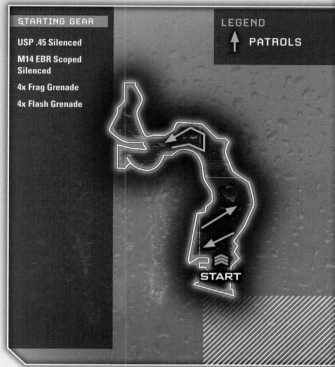

**STARTING GEAR**

USP .45 Silenced

M14 EBR Scoped Silenced

4x Frag Grenade

4x Flash Grenade

**LEGEND**

↑ PATROLS

START

Evasion is the stealth portion of Contingency, ripped out and dropped in as a single, stealthy challenge mission. Completion is simply reaching the target area at the end of the forest in one piece. You are not rewarded, or encouraged, to kill enemies, and there is no time limit, so even on higher difficulties, feel free to take your time being stealthy.

Most of the advice we provide for the Contingency mission applies here. To recap some basic advice: Always stay crouched. When you stand, enemies can detect you from a much greater distance.

If you're trying to avoid detection completely, go prone. Even better, go prone or stay crouched inside heavy brush, which can conceal you from sight.

If you do kill any enemies, pick up an un-silenced assault rifle from a downed guard to replace your USP. It can come in handy if you alert a guard and attract a patrol. If a patrol comes after you, go loud—you don't attract any *more* enemies than you already have. And, trying to fight off a patrol with your sniper rifle or pistol is almost always suicide.

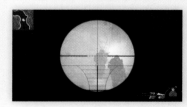

Co-op on this mission is particularly cool, as you can work on tandem sniping, splitting up targets in a patrol, then calling a countdown and eliminating the entire group simultaneously. Give it a try!

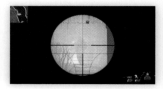

Veteran isn't significantly different in terms of the mission structure, only the enemy behavior. Guards are more alert on Veteran, so stealth becomes paramount. Discovery means almost certain death, so it's best to be as stealthy as possible.

If you do go to take out an enemy, make sure you land upper body or head shots with your M14. You can't afford a wounding shot, or you'll trigger an alarm.

You can avoid the beginning patrol by moving to the far right and going prone. Once they move past, they don't return, so you can continue forward.

You can navigate the river area without a single kill. Wait for the patrol to proceed to the right. One enemy with a dog moves into the riverbed.

Wait for a second enemy to join him, and then carefully move while you're prone to the far right clump of trees (where the large patrol went). Stay prone. When you reach the clearing with two sets of two guards each, look to the right to see a small, elevated ledge.

Quickly jump up out of prone, then immediately return to prone. Proceed to the end of the mission and dispatch the last two guards.

An alternate, more aggressive strategy is to follow the river patrol up, take out the enemy at the back and one enemy with his dog. Follow them up and, as they set up in their new guard positions, sneak past them while they're not looking. Finally, Flashbang the two enemies at the top of the ridge, and then sprint to the finish line.

# MISSION 05:

# SUSPENSION

DESCRIPTION: PUSH THROUGH THE INVADING FORCES ON THE BRIDGE TO REACH THE SAFE ZONE.

ESTIMATED OPPOSITION: MEDIUM

CLASSIFICATION: ASSAULT

ESTIMATED COMPLETION TIME: 3:30.00

IW BEST: 0:53.00

Suspension takes place on a map you won't see anywhere else in the game: a large suspension bridge littered with abandoned vehicles.

Your objective is simply to reach the target extraction point at the end of the bridge. The horde of hostile military forces between you and the target is what makes the mission interesting…

You get a lot of available gear on this mission—pick out your favorites. We recommend using the ACR Grenadier and either a second assault rifle or the M14 sniper rifle.

Don't be stingy with your explosives. While Claymores and C4 are more useful if you play defensively, you can use your grenades and Grenade Launcher to terrific effect offensively.

In particular, you can use Grenade Launcher and Frag Grenades to detonate vehicles, killing enemies using them as cover. Remember that this goes for you as well—be careful about standing behind a car that isn't burned out for too long, or you can be a car bomb victim.

This mission is roughly divided into two chunks. The first half involves an assault by troops rappelling down from the bridge's upper level on the left and right sides.

If you quickly move to the far left or right and line up a shot, you can almost instantly down the entire wave. They conveniently hit the ground almost in a straight line.

Push your way past the first troop wave, and a fighter jet flies by overhead, launching a barrage of missiles at the bridge. The missiles collapse the upper road, providing a makeshift ramp up to the second level.

As soon as you reach the upper level, you find the mid-point weapons cache—grab the Thumper!

You are also given notice of a hostile inbound gunship. You can take down the helicopter with either an RPG shot or a very well aimed Grenade Launcher.

| STARTING GEAR | LEGEND |
|---|---|
| Desert Eagle | **HA** HELICOPTER ATTACK |
| SCAR-H Red Dot Sight | |
| 4x Flash Grenade | **X** TROOP HELICOPTERS |
| 4x Frag Grenade | |
| 5x Claymore | |
| 4x C4 | |

**AVAILABLE GEAR [START]**

P90 Holographic

ACR Grenadier ACOG Sight

TAR-21 Holographic

SCAR-H w/ Shotgun

M14 EBR Scoped

**AVAILABLE GEAR [HALFWAY]**

RPG-7 (Get to da choppa!)

Thumper

In addition to the gunship, hostile troop transport choppers unload the final troop wave in the distance ahead. You can also take these down with well-placed explosive shots, but be very careful of attempting this on Veteran, as you can get taken down quickly by exposing yourself.

Once you're past the last wave of troops, the extraction point isn't far—reach it to complete the mission!

## VETERAN TIPS

Veteran plays very similarly to Regular. The only real distinction is that you need to be much more cautious in your offensive push, as enemies can take you down much more quickly. Be very careful at the ending section. The gunship attack can easily spell the end of your run. Sprint up the slope, grab your weapons, then move back down the slope and take out the chopper.

After that, you can edge up the slope and pick off enemies as they approach you, rather than fighting on the upper level. You can hop up on top of cars and go prone to get a good line of sight on distant enemies. Just be ready to hop back down if they draw a bead on you.

RAPELLING TROOP DROPS

START

# OVERWATCH

**DESCRIPTION: RAIN DEATH FROM ABOVE USING AN AC130 GUNSHIP TO PROTECT YOUR PARTNER.**

**ESTIMATED OPPOSITION: LIGHT**

**CLASSIFICATION: TIMED ESCORT**

**ESTIMATED COMPLETION TIME: 1:30.00**

**IW BEST: 00:35.45**

### DIFFICULTY LEVELS

| REGULAR TARGET | FARMHOUSE BASEMENT |
| --- | --- |
| HARDENED TARGET | WEST OF THE WORKSHOP |
| VETERAN TARGET | BARN NEAR THE GREEN HOUSES |

**STARTING GEAR (ON GROUND)**

| M9 | Night Vision Goggles | 4x Frag Grenade |
| --- | --- | --- |
| SCAR-H Red Dot Sight | Laser Designator | 4x Flash Grenade |

**AVAILABLE GEAR (ON GROUND)**

| SCAR-H Thermal Sight | M1014 Red Dot Sight | M4A1 Grenadier w/ Holographic |
| --- | --- | --- |
| MP5K | M240 | |

**STARTING GEAR (AC130)**

25mm Machine Gun

40mm Cannon

105mm Cannon

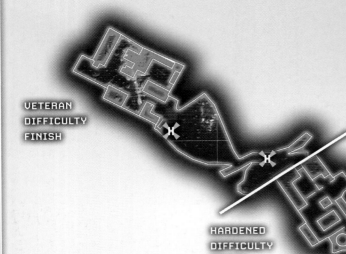

VETERAN DIFFICULTY FINISH

HARDENED DIFFICULTY FINISH

REGULAR DIFFICULTY FINISH

START

LEGEND

✕ TROOP HELICOPTERS

## CO-OP ONLY!

You can play this mission only cooperatively with a partner. You cannot play it alone, for reasons that become apparent immediately.

If you played *Call of Duty 4: Modern Warfare*, you remember the AC130 mission. Everyone remembers that mission. Now, what if you could take control of the AC130…and have a partner on the ground below?

That scenario is exactly what Overwatch lets you reenact. You're back on Hunted, only this time, instead of just providing covering fire for your squad, you provide covering fire from the AC130 for your co-op partner!

This mission's scenario is straightforward: one player takes control of the AC130 gunship, providing overwatch and covering fire. The other player is on the ground, fleeing the constant waves of enemies, attempting to reach the target line in one piece to finish the mission.

## GEAR UP

The ground player has access to Night Vision Goggles, which are helpful for spotting hostiles if you opt not to use a Thermal weapon. You also have access to a laser designator. While this doesn't trigger automatic fire like the laser targeter on the Stryker missions, it provides a clearly visible beam for the player in the AC130. Use it to point out threatening targets!

Either player can control the AC130, while the other runs on the ground below. Expect a bloody pre-mission deathmatch to determine who gets the controls…

For this mission, the objective is the same on each difficulty. Only the target changes—on Hardened and Veteran, the target is located further from the starting point.

The player in the AC130 must provide covering fire for the ground pounder, as the number of enemies here is simply too great for the person on the ground to manage.

Hostile transport helicopter locations are marked on the map for this level. It's very important that the AC130 take these out before the enemies can disembark and threaten the ground player.

Communication is vital while playing this level. The AC130 player must continually inform the player on the ground of enemy positions and their direction of movement. At the same time, the player on the ground must tell the AC130 gunner where and when he's moving, and if he can't handle any immediate threats.

## HEAVY FIREPOWER

The AC130 has three different weapons: a 25mm Gatling gun that's ideal for close support, and two cannons, a smaller 40mm and a huge 105mm.

You can safely use the 40mm relatively close to the ground player to eliminate enemy groups. It has a good rate of fire, so use it often. The 105mm cannon has a long reload and a *massive* explosion, so it's ideal for eliminating large enemy groups that are *not* close to the ground player. Be careful with this—you can easily kill your partner if you aren't cautious. The 25mm also works well for taking out hostile helicopters, though a single well placed 40mm round can also do the trick. As you orbit the ground player, continually switch weapons as necessary.

## MISSION 02:

# BODY COUNT

**DESCRIPTION: RACK UP A LARGE ENOUGH BODY COUNT. QUICK KILLS EARN LARGER BONUSES.**

**ESTIMATED OPPOSITION: MEDIUM**

**CLASSIFICATION: ELIMINATION**

**ESTIMATED COMPLETION TIME: 2:30.00**

**IW BEST: 1:16.20**

**SCORE GOAL: 30000 (ALL DIFFICULTIES)**

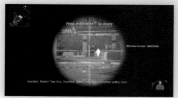

Body Count takes place in the parking lot/shopping area of Wolverines!, and your objective is exactly what the mission name implies. You have to score 30000 points worth of kills to complete the mission.

| STARTING GEAR |
| --- |
| M9 |
| SCAR-H Red Dot Sight |
| 4x Semtex Grenade |
| 4x Frag Grenade |

| AVAILABLE GEAR |
| --- |
| RPG-7 |
| M1014 Holographic |
| AA-12 Red Dot Sight |
| Intervention |
| M14 EBR Thermal |
| AK-47 Grenadier |

**LEGEND**

↑ TROOP TRUCK ROUTE

↑ BTR80 ROUTES

BTR 80          TROOP TRUCK

SUGGESTED ATTACK LOCATIONS

START

You earn 1000 points for a normal killshot, 500 for taking out a downed enemy, and if you string together kills in a combo, each additional kill earns a few hundred bonus points.

To really rack up the points, you can take down a BTR for 4000 points—toss a single Semtex sticky bomb at close range. Don't forget that one of Semtex's unique abilities is to destroy vehicles when it's stuck to them.

There are also hostile troop transports. If you charge the one that arrives just north of your starting position and take it out with an RPG or Grenade Launcher, you can score in excess of 10,000 points immediately!

The fast and aggressive approach works best for completing the mission quickly. But you can also try a more methodical strategy by hanging back inside one of the buildings.

## VETERAN TIPS

Veteran is identical to regular in terms of scoring, only the enemy lethality is increased.

A blitz of the northern troop transport near the bank, followed by destroying the BTRs, is the fastest way to rack up points, leaving only a handful of necessary troop kills to complete the mission.

The mission doesn't begin until you move out of the starting area, so pick your favorite weapons and get moving. Taking the AK-47 Grenadier gives you a good weapon against the transport if you don't want to lug an RPG.

## MISSION 03:

# BOMB SQUAD

DESCRIPTION: RACE THROUGH THE FAVELA MARKETPLACE DEFUSING THE EXPLOSIVES BEFORE IT'S TOO LATE.

ESTIMATED OPPOSITION: MEDIUM

CLASSIFICATION: TIMED ASSAULT

ESTIMATED COMPLETION TIME: 2:30.00

IW BEST: 01:14.20

Bomb Squad is an interesting mission. It takes place near the market area of Hornet's Nest, but with an entirely different objective. Your goal here is to defuse three planted explosive charges within five minutes.

Two bombs are planted on the left (north) side of the mission area, and one is inside the market itself.

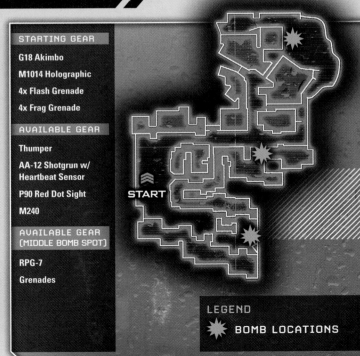

**STARTING GEAR**

G18 Akimbo

M1014 Holographic

4x Flash Grenade

4x Frag Grenade

**AVAILABLE GEAR**

Thumper

AA-12 Shotgun w/ Heartbeat Sensor

P90 Red Dot Sight

M240

**AVAILABLE GEAR (MIDDLE BOMB SPOT)**

RPG-7

Grenades

START

**LEGEND**

✸ BOMB LOCATIONS

The market is marginally easier than the left side to clear out in one shot. The left side is crawling with enemies, so you may want to save it for last. You should need less time to clear it, which can be helpful if you're running low on time.

We recommend using the M240 and the Thumper initially. Burn off the Thumper grenades quickly, then swap to a second weapon for the remainder of the mission.

Don't be shy with your grenades either. You may want to save a few for the push on the final bomb spot, but until that point, use grenades freely to aid your assault.

To defuse a bomb, you have to approach it and hold Reload for a moment, so make sure the nearby area is clear of hostiles before you move in.

## VETERAN TIPS

Veteran is identical to regular difficulty in terms of the time limit, but the more dangerous enemies make it a tougher firefight overall.

This is one mission where having a co-op partner makes completion significantly easier. But if you're flying solo, fully abuse the Thumper and your stock of grenades to keep momentum going.

If you wind up bogged down behind cover, you can easily run down the clock before you can reach the bombs in time.

An additional stock of grenades and an RPG are by the center bomb point. Grab and use them immediately to clear out more hostiles quickly.

## MISSION 04:

# RACE

DESCRIPTION: SPEED YOUR SNOWMOBILE DOWN THE MOUNTAIN, DODGING TREES, ROCKS, AND THOUSAND-FOOT DROPS.

ESTIMATED OPPOSITION: MINIMAL

CLASSIFICATION: DRIVING

ESTIMATED COMPLETION TIME: 1:30.00

IW BEST: 1:05.00

## COMPLETION GOALS

| ★ | COMPLETION IN 2:00 |
|---|---|
| ★★ | COMPLETION IN 1:30 |
| ★★★ | COMPLETION IN 1:10 |

STARTING GEAR

Snowmobile
G18

FOREST

ICE LAKE

SHORTCUT

NARROW CANYON

DOWNHILL

START

## QUICK START!

You can get an early edge by performing a perfect start. Wait to hit the gas just as the timer counts down from one, and you receive a burst of speed off the starting line.

Snowmobiles!

This mission is the snowmobile chase from Cliffhanger, though in this case, you have plenty of time to explore routes down the mountain to try for a three-star time.

The fastest route down is to take the "shortcut" through the trees in the first valley. To reach it, go on the *left* side of the valley and cut through the trees. If you do this correctly, it should quickly deposit you directly out in front of the ice lake.

Finally, in the narrow canyon area, try to avoid skating up the sides of the canyon. Again, going straight and level is the fastest way.

Make your way down the last slope without ramming a tree at high speed, and you're home free for a three-star time.

As you go across the lake, resist the urge to hit the small hills, as doing so actually slows you down.

## MISSION 05:
# BIG BROTHER

DESCRIPTION: EXPLOSIVE AMMUNITION, VULCAN MINIGUN, BLACKHAWK HELICOPTER.
CLEAR THE WAY.

ESTIMATED OPPOSITION: MEDIUM

CLASSIFICATION: TIMED ESCORT

ESTIMATED COMPLETION TIME: 3:00.00

IW BEST: 01:25.90

**STARTING GEAR (ON GROUND)**

Desert Eagle
UMP 45 Holographic
4x Flash
4x Frag
10x Claymore
10x C4

**STARTING GEAR (BLACKHAWK)**

Vulcan Minigun w/ Explosive Rounds

LEGEND
A  AMMO CACHE

## CO-OP ONLY!

This is the second and final Spec Ops mission that can be played *only* cooperatively.

If the AC130 wasn't enough for you, now you can control a mini-gun with explosive rounds in a Blackhawk helicopter! On this mission, you have to escort your ground-based partner as he makes his way  through the small U.S. town of Wolverines!

The target extraction point is on the roof of Nate's restaurant. In this case, whoever is in the helicopter *is* the extraction point! You have six minutes on Regular, seven minutes on Hardened, and ten minutes on Veteran to reach the chopper alive.

Once the ground pounder reaches the roof, the helicopter moves into position for extraction on the rooftop's west side, and you can finish the mission by approaching it.

The Blackhawk continually orbits the player on the ground, with one exception. When the ground player gets close to the barricade at the end of the first street, the Blackhawk leaves its covering role for a moment to strafe the gas station.

The airborne player attacking the gas station has to eliminate all ground targets around the station, including a few truck troop transports that arrive. Once the gas station is clear, the Blackhawk resumes covering the ground player.

At this point, the player on the ground needs to cross the street and the parking lot to reach Nates, and then get up on the roof. There *are* hostile troops inside Nates, so be ready for them—the Blackhawk can't easily shoot them.

When you reach the building's roof, both the chopper and the player on the ground should stay alert, as a swarm of hostiles moves in to assault the rooftop. The ground player can plant a few Claymores to help stem the tide, but otherwise its pure defense for a few moments until you clear the enemies and the chopper moves into position for extraction.

## VETERAN TIPS

Two ammo caches are in the same spots where they were in Wolverines! One is just before the barricade, the other on the roof of Nate's. The ground player can use both to restock his load for whichever weapons he picks up along the way. As with the AC130 mission, communication is critical here, and the ground player is a bit more vulnerable to enemies due to the urban terrain.

The Blackhawk doesn't have the eye in the sky thermal vision that the AC130 did. Plus, it can't hit some targets in and around buildings, so the player on the ground has to be on his game as he moves.

Because the Blackhawk continually orbits the player on the ground, make sure you have line of sight to a new area if the ground player is moving. Again, communicate intent to move, and be sure you have covering fire before you do so.

As you initially move up the street from the starting point, you may want to take the left side of the road, rather than following the right side as you did in the campaign. The left side provides a slightly different angle from which the Blackhawk has a slightly easier time acquiring targets.

# HIDDEN

DESCRIPTION: EVADE ENEMY PATROLS AND GHILLIE SNIPERS NEAR CHERNOBYL.

ESTIMATED OPPOSITION: MEDIUM

CLASSIFICATION: STEALTH

ESTIMATED COMPLETION TIME: 4:30.00

IW BEST: 01:45.60

| STARTING GEAR | AVAILABLE GEAR | LEGEND |
|---|---|---|
| Intervention Silenced | Mini-Uzi Silenced | ⊕ SNIPERS |
| USP .45 Silenced | M1014 Silenced | |
| 4x Frag Grenade | Striker Silenced | 🛡 GUARDS |
| 5x Claymore | MP5KSD | |
| 5x C4 | | |

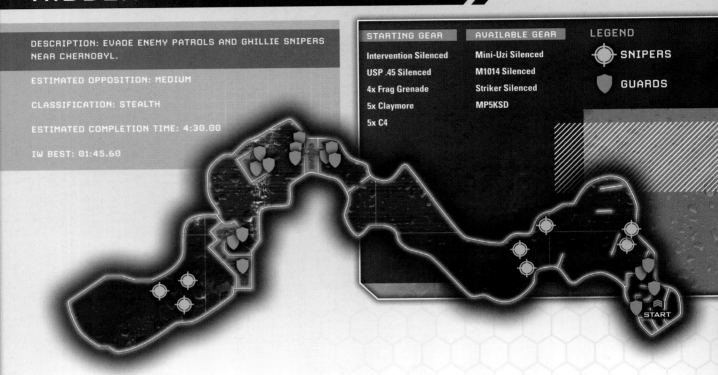

The second major stealth Spec Ops mission, Hidden should be a familiar sight to *Call of Duty 4: Modern Warfare* veterans.

In this mission, you're tasked with reaching the extraction point in the fields near Chernobyl, killing or avoiding enemy patrols along the way, and counter-sniping enemy snipers hiding in the tall brush.

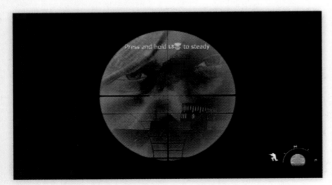

Swap out your USP for either the Mini-Uzi or the MP5—you need a decent secondary weapon if you get spotted by the guards.

There are five major encounters in this mission. The first is the few guards immediately outside the starting area. You can sneak past them or kill the two in your way to the north, and then make your way out into the field.

The next challenge is a pair of snipers in the field ahead. The snipers shift their positions, but you can spot them if you're patient and watch the field carefully.

## WATCH THOSE GLINTS

From time to time, you can catch the sunlight flashing off a concealed sniper's scope. Use these cues to locate and eliminate the threat.

Past the first sniper group, make your way around some ruined tanks and a small lake. Another group of snipers waits in the brush on a small hill ahead. Use the wrecked vehicles for cover and pick them off.

Once the snipers are clear, move up to the next challenge. The old church ahead has guards outside, guards inside, and, on Hardened and Veteran, a sniper up in the bell tower. Be certain to eliminate the sniper from a distance before you move in, or he'll alert the guards to your presence immediately.

Take down the guards on the east side of the church, and then carefully move through. There are more guards in a building to the west, and still more in a checkpoint just ahead.

It's possible to eliminate all of them silently, but if one guard spots another going down, they'll be alerted and come after you. Break out the MP5KSD if this occurs—their rush shouldn't overwhelmed you.

Finally, one last field of snipers bars your path to the extraction point. Be careful here; these snipers move up and flank you if you move forward and stay stationary. Hang back and pick them off from the cover of the barn adjacent to the house, and then make your run for the LZ to finish the mission.

If you're playing co-op, when you tackle the sniper fields, communicate your target areas and sweep halves of the fields for targets to cover more ground.

## VETERAN TIPS

Veteran is more difficult, thanks to the addition of more snipers in the fields, and one in the church bell tower. There's an additional sniper in both of the first encounters, and three more in the final field. Make sure you clear out all of the snipers in each area before you move on! Use Claymores at the doorways of the church and the buildings beyond it as backup in case you break stealth.

## MISSION 02:

# BREACH & CLEAR

DESCRIPTION: SMASH THROUGH ENEMY DEFENSES IN THE GULAG AND ESCAPE.

ESTIMATED OPPOSITION: HEAVY

CLASSIFICATION: ASSAULT

ESTIMATED COMPLETION TIME: 1:30

IW BEST: 0:17.00

The shower battle in The Gulag was an intense firefight, and now you can experience that battle all over again as a Spec Ops mission.

Your objective is simply to reach the hole in the ground at the end of the showers. Note that your goal is *not* to kill every enemy here, so you *can* evade some of the opposition here.

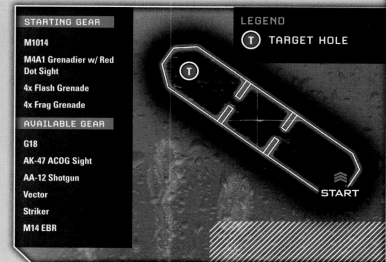

**STARTING GEAR**

**M1014**

**M4A1 Grenadier w/ Red Dot Sight**

**4x Flash Grenade**

**4x Frag Grenade**

**AVAILABLE GEAR**

**G18**

**AK-47 ACOG Sight**

**AA-12 Shotgun**

**Vector**

**Striker**

**M14 EBR**

LEGEND

(T) TARGET HOLE

T

T

START

You may want to grab the G18 as your secondary weapon, changing out your shotgun, as its pistol class lets you swap weapons more quickly. It still gives you enough firepower to take out multiple enemies at close range. When you're ready, plant the breaching charge on the wall and break into the showers.

Numerous enemies are on the ground floor, and multiple hostiles look down from the upper balconies to the left and right. Use your Grenade Launcher to take out enemies on the upper level, and then turn your attention to hostiles on the ground floor.

The showers are separated into three partitions, each section having a pair of walls that extend to the center of the room. Be careful about hiding on the left or right of the gap in the center, as enemy grenades land at your feet.

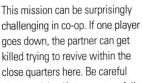

The first two partitions host normal enemies, but the last section has guards with Riot Shields. Use your grenades to take them out, or a Flashbang to stun them, and simply sprint past.

This mission can be surprisingly challenging in co-op. If one player goes down, the partner can get killed trying to revive within the close quarters here. Be careful about reviving if your partner falls in an exposed area!

## VETERAN TIPS

On Veteran, you are limited to three minutes to complete the challenge. The fastest way to get through is to clear the first room quickly as you breach. Then simply use Flash Grenades to stun the enemies in the rooms beyond, and sprint to the exit hole. Get there in one piece, and you can finish the mission in roughly 20 seconds! If you're trying for a blitz finish, remember to use the G18 for the faster running speed.

If you're trying to clear the rooms normally, take down the enemies on the upper ledges as a priority. You can't have Veteran-level enemies alive in an elevated position. Use your Flashbangs to stun large enemy clusters and give you some breathing room, and be sure to save grenades for the Riot Shield enemies in the final section.

## MISSION 03:

# TIME TRIAL

DESCRIPTION: LAUNCH YOUR SNOWMOBILE ACROSS THE CHASM BEFORE THE TIME RUNS OUT. HIT THE FLAG GATES TO GET EXTRA TIME.

ESTIMATED OPPOSITION: LIGHT

CLASSIFICATION: TIMED DRIVING

ESTIMATED COMPLETION TIME: 1:30

IW BEST: 01:07.00

**STARTING GEAR**

Snowmobile

G18

### COMPLETION GOALS

| ★ | 15S STARTING TIME, +4S PER GATE |
|---|---|
| ★★ | 10S STARTING TIME, +4S PER GATE |
| ★★★ | 8S STARTING TIME, +3S PER GATE |

Time Trial puts you on snowmobiles again, but this time you have to complete a slalom course with flag gates placed along the mountain slope.

Each gate gives you a few more seconds of additional time, and you have to hit them continually to reach the finish line in time.

Higher difficulties simply reduce the amount of time you gain per gate; the mission is otherwise identical.

This mission works quite well in co-op. You can have one player go for gates to keep the timer running, while the second player takes the shortcut route, heading for the finish line as fast as possible. Whichever player is behind can pick up gates that the other player misses.

However, if you're going solo, do *not* take the shortcut—there aren't any gates and you'll run out of time!

# MISSION 04:
# HOMELAND SECURITY

**DESCRIPTION: SENTRY GUNS, THERMAL SIGHTS, ROCKET LAUNCHERS AND CLAYMORES. DEFEND YOURSELF FROM FIVE DIFFICULT WAVES OF ATTACKERS.**

**ESTIMATED OPPOSITION: HEAVY**

**CLASSIFICATION: WAVE DEFENSE**

**ESTIMATED COMPLETION TIME: 11:00**

**IW BEST: 07:31.20**

| WAVE 1 | 20 INFANTRY |
|--------|-------------|
| WAVE 2 | 30 INFANTRY, PREDATOR DRONE |
| WAVE 3 | 40 INFANTRY, HELICOPTER, PREDATOR DRONE |
| WAVE 4 | 30 SKILLED INFANTRY, BTR80, PREDATOR DRONE |
| WAVE 5 | 40 SKILLED INFANTRY, BTR80, TWO HELICOPTERS, PREDATOR DRONE |

**STARTING GEAR**

**M9**

**SCAR-H Red Dot Sight**

**4x Frag Grenade**

**4x Semtex**

**AVAILABLE GEAR**

**Claymore Mines**

**Turret**

**Intervention**

**RPG-7**

**M14 EBR Thermal**

**AK47 Grenadier**

LEGEND

**A** AMMO CACHE

**T** THERMAL WEAPON

TURRETS

EXPLOSIVES

START

A heavy-duty wave defense mission, Homeland Security drops you in the parking lot/shopping center area of Wolverines! This time, you're asked to hold the line against five waves of enemy troops.

Be sure to pick up the Claymores at the starting position, and swap out your M9 for a Thermal weapon or the AK-47 Grenadier for its Grenade Launcher.

 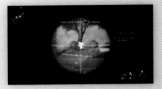

Four M-5 defense turrets are on this map: one at the starting position, one inside the gas station, another in Nate's, and the last one in the bank to the north of the parking lot. Explosive caches are in each location, vital for defeating the helicopters that arrive in the later waves. Using the turrets is vital to success here, particularly on the higher difficulty levels. Proper Sentry turret placement is crucial. Sentry turrets have a 180-degree arc of fire, and should be placed behind crouch-height cover with their backs and flanks protected.

You can tackle this mission in several different ways. One way is to run around quickly and gather the turrets, then place them in one area and hole up. Another way is to move between buildings between each wave, setting up a fresh turret each time.

Make sure you have an AT4 or RPG-7 ready for the helicopters in waves three and five—you want to take them out quickly.

Because the enemy comes at you with a Predator of their own, it's vital to stay in cover. You can use the rooftops for the first wave, but once their Predator comes online, you need to be inside a building!

The fourth wave has a BTR80, along with the infantry. You can take down the BTR with a ranged explosive. Or, if you feel daring, use your Semtex from close range. Don't forget that one of Semtex's unique

abilities is to destroy vehicles when it's stuck to them. However, be careful with that tactic, as the Predator or enemies outside can easily take you down while you're exposed.

Finally, the last wave is infantry, a BTR80, *two* helicopters, and again, a Predator. Eliminate the armor as quickly as possible, and then focus on the remaining infantry.

## VETERAN TIPS

Veteran is significantly more difficult, thanks to the infantry's increased lethality. However, the fundamental tactics don't change. Because you defend from hard cover in buildings, you shouldn't get overwhelmed as long as you're fast and accurate at taking down incoming troops.

Use Claymores to cover your blind spots. A Thermal Scope helps greatly to pick out enemies from the surrounding terrain as they move on your position. Don't expose yourself to infantry fire to take down the vehicles. They're dangerous, but going out in the open to attack them is even more dangerous on Veteran.

One tactic that works quite well is to gather up the turrets and place them together in an overwatch position on the roof of Nate's. Then hole up in whichever building you cover with the turrets. Any enemies that come at you directly take fire from above and behind! This is significantly easier to setup in the first wave if you're playing co-op, but you can generally get one or two in place even by yourself.

# MISSION 05:

## SNATCH & GRAB

DESCRIPTION: BATTLE SHADOW COMPANY AND JUGGERNAUTS IN THE AIRPLANE GRAVEYARD. GRAB THE INTEL TO ESCAPE TO THE EXTRACTION POINT.

ESTIMATED OPPOSITION: MEDIUM

CLASSIFICATION: ASSAULT

ESTIMATED COMPLETION TIME: 3:30

IW BEST: 01:22.40

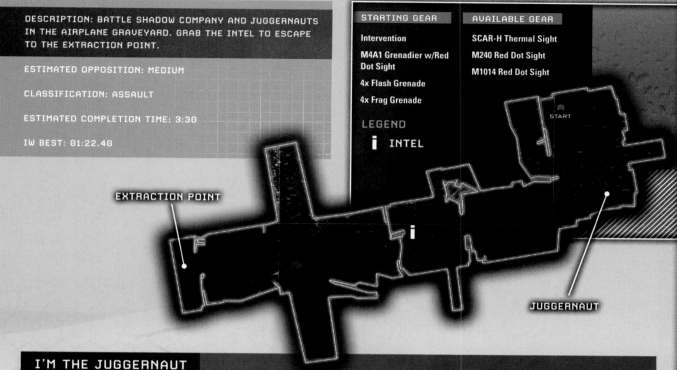

**STARTING GEAR**

Intervention

M4A1 Grenadier w/Red Dot Sight

4x Flash Grenade

4x Frag Grenade

**AVAILABLE GEAR**

SCAR-H Thermal Sight

M240 Red Dot Sight

M1014 Red Dot Sight

**LEGEND**

**i** INTEL

START

EXTRACTION POINT

JUGGERNAUT

## I'M THE JUGGERNAUT

Say hello to an entirely new Spec Ops-exclusive enemy type.

The Juggernaut is a *very* heavily armored assault trooper. He wears a full-body assault suit. Armed with heavy machine guns, these troopers are very, very dangerous.

What's worse is that they act like heat-seeking missiles. The instant they appear in the mission, they make a beeline for your position, not stopping for anything. The only way to slow a Juggernaut is to hit him with a Flashbang or stagger him with a heavy explosive.

You can kill a Juggernaut quickly by landing a headshot with an RPG (very difficult) or a Thumper (still difficult). Otherwise, the best remedy for a Juggernaut is a high-powered sniper rifle. The Intervention works, as does the Barrett. In either case, on-target shots cause the Juggernaut to stagger. If you keep plugging away, he *will* fall.

If a Juggernaut gets into close proximity with you, you're in serious danger. Run away, stun him with a Flashbang, or, if you're daring, hip fire your sniper rifle and keep him stunned until he drops!

Your objective is to sneak through the airplane graveyard, recover an Intel package, and reach the extraction point. Unlike The Enemy of my Enemy, the entire force is hostile to you, and you can't simply sneak through the level.

The presence of the Juggernauts makes this even more challenging. One comes at you immediately as the level starts. Plug him full of holes with your Intervention to take him down, and then begin moving through the level.

The Intel is located midway through the map, just before the airplane fuselage that you have to climb inside.

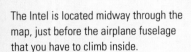

To clear your way to the Intel, sprint from cover to cover. Take down enemies only when they are immediate threats. You want to avoid getting bogged down in an extended firefight if at all possible.

A second Juggernaut spawns in a completely unpredictable location. He may spawn behind you, or he may not spawn until you drop down into the valley.

Once the way is clear, you can pick off any remaining enemies in your path and sprint to the extraction point.

# DELTA MISSIONS

## MISSION 01:
# WARDRIVING

DESCRIPTION: LAZE TARGETS FOR THE STRYKER ARMORED VEHICLE. BATTLE IN THE 'BURBS HOUSE TO HOUSE, ROOM TO ROOM.

ESTIMATED OPPOSITION: HEAVY

CLASSIFICATION: ASSAULT & DEFEND

ESTIMATED COMPLETION TIME: 9:00.00

IW BEST: 3:25.25

### STARTING GEAR

M9
SCAR-H Red Dot Sight
4x Flash Grenade
4x Frag Grenade
Laser Target Painter

### AVAILABLE GEAR

Claymore
Turrets
Thumper

### LEGEND

A — AMMO CACHE

— TURRETS

i — INTEL

START

If you enjoyed painting targets for the Stryker in Exodus, you'll love this mission. You're set up in the small suburban area of Arcadia, along with a friendly Stryker and a laser designator. Your mission is to recover valuable Intel from three laptops in three of the houses here.

Some hostiles are in the streets, but most of the opposition comes when you activate a laptop. You have to download all of the files from each laptop, and if enemies get close to it, their wireless disruptors stop the download—you have to kill them and restart it.

Two houses with Intel on the street's right side have turrets that can aid your defensive efforts.

Because the enemy rush doesn't occur until you start the download, clear the house of any enemies, and set up your Claymores and the M-5 turrets *before* you start the download. Place the turrets outside the house facing it, and set Claymores around the entrances. Proper Sentry turret placement is crucial. Sentry turrets have a 180-degree arc of fire, and should be placed behind crouch-height cover with their backs and flanks protected.

Swap out your starting M9 for a secondary weapon—probably the Thumper initially, but you want something better suited to indoor combat after you're out of grenades.

You can climb to the second floors of some houses and laze targets for the Stryker out in the streets—try to do this whenever you aren't under pressure inside a house.

## MISSION 02:

# WRECKAGE

**DESCRIPTION:** USE C4, GRENADE LAUNCHERS, RPGS, SENTRY GUNS, SEMTEX, AND MORE TO DESTROY EVERY VEHICLE ON THE BRIDGE.

**ESTIMATED OPPOSITION:** MEDIUM

**CLASSIFICATION:** VEHICLE KILLSPREE

**ESTIMATED COMPLETION TIME:** 3:00.00

**IW BEST:** 1:40.40

| STARTING GEAR |
| --- |
| M9 |
| RPG-7 |
| 4x Semtex |
| 4x Frag Grenade |
| 5x Claymore |
| 5x C4 |

| AVAILABLE GEAR |
| --- |
| Turret |
| AK-47 Grenadier |
| M4A1 Grenadier |
| Thumper |
| M16A4 Grenade Launcher |

Looking for a mission where you can simply cut loose with heavy firepower? This is it. Wreckage challenges you to destroy every vehicle on the suspension bridge—36 in all. Additionally, every five vehicles you destroy activates Wreckage mode—unlimited ammunition!

Swap out your M9 for a grenadier weapon or the Thumper, then grab the turret and get moving.

This mission is otherwise identical to Suspension. Troops still rappel down at the beginning, the fighter jet strikes the bridge, and a helicopter and more troops attack you at the end of the bridge.

START

Bring along the RPG to take down the 'copter, unless you're confident with your Grenade Launcher aim. Remember that you only need to take out the vehicles to win. You don't actually have to traverse all the way up the bridge; you can simply lob grenades until you clear the mission!

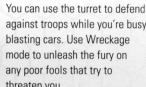

You can use the turret to defend against troops while you're busy blasting cars. Use Wreckage mode to unleash the fury on any poor fools that try to threaten you.

Don't miss the vehicles at the beginning of the level. You'll feel foolish if you get to the end of the bridge and you're missing a few!

## MISSION 03:

# ACCEPTABLE LOSSES

**DESCRIPTION: SABOTAGE THE REMOTE AIRBASE WITH YOUR SILENCED WEAPONS AND HEARTBEAT SENSOR.**

ESTIMATED OPPOSITION: MEDIUM

CLASSIFICATION: STEALTH

ESTIMATED COMPLETION TIME: 7:00.00

IW BEST: 0:48.15

Acceptable Losses challenges you to sneak through the snowy airbase from Cliffhanger, planting three explosive charges and then escaping out the base's north end.

MacTavish provides overwatch on this mission, just as he did on Cliffhanger, and he warns you of threats (or the truck) if they're near your position.

This mission is largely stealthy. You're well advised to use your AA-12 Heartbeat Sensor to detect close-quarters enemies only and simply avoid them. Use the silenced AK or silenced M14 for eliminating patrols, because the short range and wide spread of the AA-12 can easily result in breaking stealth.

Watch out for the truck that patrols the airfield—its patrol path is marked on the map. When you hear it coming, get out of sight until it passes.

**STARTING GEAR**

**USP .45 Silenced**

**AA-12 Shotgun Heartbeat and Silenced**

**4x Flash Grenade**

**4x Frag Grenade**

**AVAILABLE GEAR**

**MP5K Silenced Red Dot**

**AK-47 Silenced**

**M14 EBR Scoped Silenced**

**LEGEND**

✴ **BOMB LOCATIONS**

— **TRUCK PATROL**

START

If you alert an enemy, a hostile enemy patrol attacks you, so be sure to swap out your USP for the MP5K or AK-47 Silenced. If you want to play slightly more aggressively, you can take the M14 and snipe targets as you move from bomb point to bomb point, clearing out guards as you move.

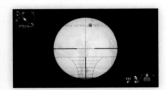

Because you have to escape from the base after you plant all three charges, it's generally best to tackle them in order, from the closest to your start point to the closest to the evac point.

There's no penalty for being spotted, outside of an angry patrol attack, but it's generally easier if you're quiet throughout the mission. Whatever you do, don't go picking up unsilenced weaponry! You can afford to get in a scrape or two, but inviting trouble isn't a good idea.

## VETERAN TIPS

As with the other stealthy missions, on Veteran, the enemies are a bit more alert to your presence. Use cover more carefully, and pay attention to your Heartbeat Sensor to spot them early.

Getting discovered by a patrol on Veteran is seriously bad news. If at all possible, stay out of sight and avoid conflict. If you *do* get spotted, try to retreat to an area with cover. Getting stuck out in the middle of the airfield can be a death sentence.

## MISSION 04:
# TERMINAL

DESCRIPTION: PUMMEL YOUR WAY THROUGH ENEMY RIOT SHIELD AMBUSHES.

ESTIMATED OPPOSITION: HEAVY

CLASSIFICATION: ASSAULT

ESTIMATED COMPLETION TIME: 4:00.00

IW BEST: 0:36.40

This is a tough combat mission. You're challenged to fight through the airport terminal, against a mix of normal troopers and Riot Shielded guards. We recommend grabbing the M240 and an ACR Grenadier, giving you a solid ammo load and the Grenade Launcher you need against the Riot Shields.

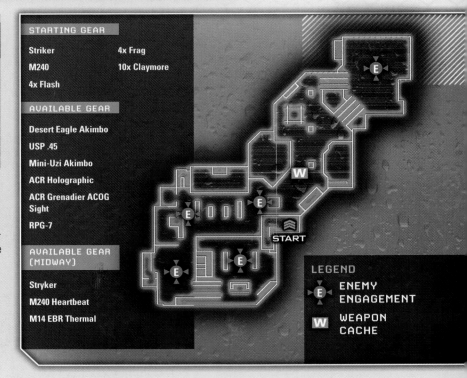

**STARTING GEAR**

| Striker | 4x Frag |
| M240 | 10x Claymore |
| 4x Flash | |

**AVAILABLE GEAR**

Desert Eagle Akimbo

USP .45

Mini-Uzi Akimbo

ACR Holographic

ACR Grenadier ACOG Sight

RPG-7

**AVAILABLE GEAR (MIDWAY)**

Stryker

M240 Heartbeat

M14 EBR Thermal

LEGEND

E ENEMY ENGAGEMENT

W WEAPON CACHE

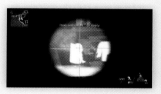

This mission has five major engagements. Two are at the start: one just outside your beginning area, the second up the escalators on the second level. The next two are on the upper level. They lead you to a weapon cache, where you can resupply. The final battle is a wall of Riot Shielded foes down another set of escalators at the terminal's end.

The ammo cache has an M14 Thermal, which can be useful for picking off shielded enemies, as you simply need to snipe their exposed extremities to drop them. Save your grenades and Grenade Launcher for the Riot Shielded foes. You can take out normal enemies with your machine gun or assault rifle.

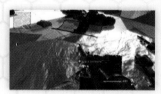

There's *lots* of cover here, so try to play defensively. Move up to trigger each engagement, then back off and let enemies come to you.

There's enough time between each firefight to set up a few Claymores, but don't expose yourself just to plant one last mine!

For the final fight, the Riot Shielded enemies wait for you on the ground level. You can easily take out most of them with a few launched grenades, finishing off any survivors with regular grenades and your weapons. Clear out the enemies that rush you first, and then eliminate the shielded foes at your leisure.

Clear out the last group and head to the evac point to finish the mission!

## VETERAN TIPS

This mission is notably easier with a partner, so bring a friend for co-op if you can.

One fun tactic is to steal a Riot Shield and have one player provide distraction while the other guns down anyone who shoots at the shielded player.

If that's not an option, play each engagement as defensively as possible. Move forward to start a battle, then retreat a good distance to give you room to fight.

Once you get past the first two engagements, the rest of the mission is generally easier, as you have more room to retreat and recover.

# MISSION 05:

# ESTATE TAKEDOWN

**DESCRIPTION: ELIMINATE GHILLIE SNIPERS, ELITE MERCENARIES, AND JUGGERNAUTS GUARDING THE ESTATE.**

**ESTIMATED OPPOSITION: MEDIUM**

**CLASSIFICATION: ELIMINATION**

**ESTIMATED COMPLETION TIME: 9:00.00**

**IW BEST: 2:59.60**

Estate Takedown is an interesting spin on the Loose Ends mission. This time, instead of defending the cabin in the woods, you're tasked with taking down 40 hostiles—including several Juggernauts!

Enemies can appear anywhere on the map, so there isn't any single best location to wait. You have to hunt down enemies to keep the battle moving. The whole map is available to you, so you can roam freely around the cabin, the fields, and the forests surrounding it.

## STARTING GEAR

| | |
|---|---|
| Barrett .50 Cal | 4x Frag Grenade |
| M4A1 Grenadier w/ Holographic | 4x Flash Grenade |

## AVAILABLE GEAR (FIRST HOUSE)

| | | |
|---|---|---|
| AK-47 Holographic | SPAS-12 Holographic | AK-47 w/ Shotgun |
| Striker | Tar-21 Holographic | L86LSW Scoped |
| P90 Silenced | WA2000 Thermal Sight | Dragunov |
| Model 1887 | AUG-HBAR Red Dot Sight | M240 Red Dot Sight |
| MP5KSD | P90 Red Dot Sight | M240 ACOG Sight |
| AUG HBAR Scoped | Vector Red Dot Sight | M240 |
| AK-47 Red Dot Sight | F2000 Thermal Sight | |
| M4 | AA-12 Shotgun | |
| G18 | L86LSW | |
| M9 | | |
| Desert Eagle | | |
| TMP Red Dot Sight | | |
| PP2000 Red Dot Sight | | |
| M4A1 Grenadier w/ Red Dot Sight | | |

### LEGEND

**W** MASSIVE WEAPONS CACHE

**W**

START

We recommend grabbing the L86LSW Scoped or a Thermal weapon to replace your Grenadier after you burn off your Grenade Launcher.

Be patient, stay alert, move from cover to cover, and you'll take down every enemy in the area.

However, you absolutely want to use the Barrett against the Juggernauts. Because Juggernauts always make a beeline for you, you can easily take them down at a distance before they become a threat.

Remember that you can stun Juggernauts with a Flashbang, and if necessary, kill them at pointblank range with hip-fired Barrett shots.

The weapon caches are still inside the cabin, so you may want to make your way inside after you clear the immediate area outside your starting position.

## VETERAN TIPS

This is another difficult mission on Veteran. Bring a friend if possible! Staying in cover and hunting enemies aren't compatible goals, but you can still proceed through the mission methodically.

Clear an area of foes, then move to another position with cover and scan for new threats. Keep particularly alert for hostile snipers at long range. They're hard to spot at a distance, unless you see the glint of sunlight off their scopes, or you're using a Thermal weapon!

You can hole up in the house—just be wary of getting trapped inside by a rushing Juggernaut. One last and very important tip: When a Juggernaut gets close (roughly 200 feet), there's a distinct audio cue. Listen for it, and stay alert!

## MISSION 01:

# WETWORK

DESCRIPTION: BREACH AND CLEAR TWO DEADLY ROOMS FULL
OF ENEMIES AND HOSTAGES TO CAPTURE THE OIL RIG.

ESTIMATED OPPOSITION: MASSIVE

CLASSIFICATION: ASSAULT

ESTIMATED COMPLETION TIME: 5:00.00

IW BEST: 03:10.30

Wetwork is unusual in that it is an almost complete replay of the oil
rig-clearing mission from the campaign. But in this case, you can bring
a friend with you to breach the rooms, which is extremely cool.

Just like in the campaign, you have to clear the oil platform's three
levels of hostiles and rescue the hostages in the breachable rooms. If
you or your partner shoots a hostage, the mission instantly fails.

Be sure you or your partner grabs an AT4 early to deal with the
helicopter that shows up on the second floor. If you're quick, you can
down it before it even makes its first strafing run. There's plenty of
other explosive hardware, even a Stinger (!), on the second level if you
need it, but the helicopter is so close, you can easily take it out with a
Grenade Launcher if necessary.

Use the explosive fuel tanks to take down any enemies hiding near
them, and move from cover to cover as you clear each floor. There's
plenty of hard
cover to hide
behind, so it isn't
difficult to heal if
you get injured.

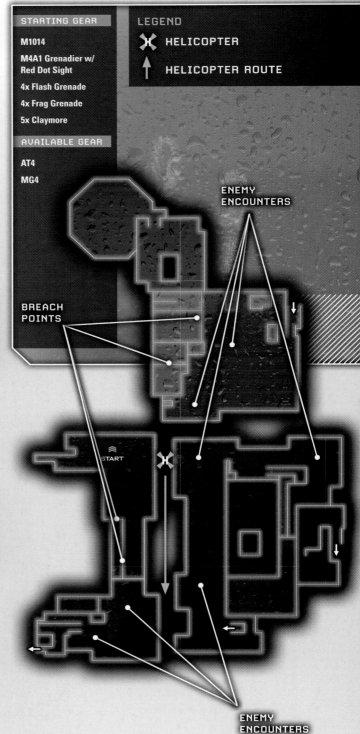

**STARTING GEAR**

M1014

M4A1 Grenadier w/
Red Dot Sight

4x Flash Grenade

4x Frag Grenade

5x Claymore

**AVAILABLE GEAR**

AT4

MG4

**LEGEND**

✖ HELICOPTER

↑ HELICOPTER ROUTE

ENEMY
ENCOUNTERS

BREACH
POINTS

START

ENEMY
ENCOUNTERS

Make sure you grab a Thermal weapon before you engage the top floor, as the smokescreen is still present, and you need a way to see through it.

If you still have grenades, use them up, because once you breach and clear the final room, you're done with the mission. Make sure you have an SMG or assault rifle *without* Thermal sights when you breach the final room. You need clear vision to take down the tangos accurately.

## MISSION 02:

# HIGH EXPLOSIVE

**DESCRIPTION: KILL ALL TEN JUGGERNAUTS USING ONLY EXPLOSIVES AND A KNIFE. YOU'D BE INSANE TO EVEN TRY THIS.**

ESTIMATED OPPOSITION: MASSIVE

CLASSIFICATION: ELIMINATION

ESTIMATED COMPLETION TIME: 6:00.00

IW BEST: 02:47.70

This is a murderously difficult challenge level. You're dropped into the lower part of the favela, the same area as O Cristo Redentor, but this time, your task is to take down *ten* Juggernauts, armed only with an RPG and a Thumper.

As if that isn't bad enough, you eventually have to take on more than one Juggernaut simultaneously. The Juggernauts spawn as 1, 1, then 2, and then 3 for the remainder of the battle. That is to say, each time you kill one of the three, another appears until you take down all ten.

**STARTING GEAR**

RPG-7
Thumper
4x Flash Grenade
4x Frag Grenade
10x C4
10x Claymore

**LEGEND**

**A** AMMO CACHE

Handling one Juggernaut with a sniper rifle isn't too bad, but three *is* bad…and you don't *have* a sniper rifle here.

You can kill Juggernauts with a single headshot from the RPG or Thumper, but landing a headshot with the notoriously inaccurate RPG-7 is a risky proposition.

Your best bet for scoring a quick kill is to stun with a Flashbang, then go for a fairly close-range grenade shot from the Thumper.

## RUN, RUN, RUN

Here's our most important tip for this mission: Counter-intuitively, holing up with the C4 and Claymores available to you is about the worst way to approach this mission. Eventually, you get overwhelmed by multiple Juggernauts, and they take only a few seconds to kill you, *especially* on Veteran.

Instead, the easiest way to take them down is to run! Ammo crates are in the northeast, center, and southwest corners, just like in O Cristo, so you can reload as you run around the level. Follow a large circle around the level's outskirts, stopping periodically to lob Thumper shots back at your pursuers.

Because the Juggernauts are so single-minded, they continue chasing you in a straight line, rather than splitting up and attempting to flank you.

Another very important point: When another Juggernaut spawns, be sure to "round him up" with the others before you continue leading the chase, or you can wind up with two Juggernauts chasing you directly into the third.

If you get pinned, use a Flashbang to stun them, and sprint past. Oh, and destroy the explosive barrels as you run around. Dying from stray Juggernaut fire to a nearby barrel is a frustrating way to go.

This tactic is notable for being slightly *more* difficult in co-op, as you have to worry about keeping your partner's flight synced with yours. Plus, reviving is *extremely* dangerous. Don't go for an immediate revive if your partner falls—lead the Juggernauts away, then circle back and revive!

## MISSION 03:

# ARMOR PIERCING

DESCRIPTION: KILL ALL FIFTEEN JUGGERNAUTS ON THE OIL RIG. THIS PROBABLY ISN'T EVEN POSSIBLE.

ESTIMATED OPPOSITION: MASSIVE

CLASSIFICATION: ELIMINATION

ESTIMATED COMPLETION TIME: 7:00.00

IW BEST: 04:12.25

The final challenge. You're tasked with taking down 15 Juggernauts that spawn randomly throughout the oil rig.

Curiously, this mission is slightly easier than High Explosive, simply because you're given access to both a Barrett and an Intervention right off the bat.

If you're aggressive (and/or suicidal), you can use either of the higher-powered sniper rifles even at pointblank range to stun and then kill a Juggernaut, thus denying him a chance to retaliate.

But other than close-range heroics, most of this mission is simply fleeing from Juggernauts as they spawn and charge you, trying to pick them off at a distance from behind cover.

Because you have room to run around on this level, and there are multiple elevation changes, you can use the layout against the Juggernauts. Dropping from one level to another or moving to a higher level can give you time to recover from a damaging spray of Juggernaut fire. This also gives you a chance to line up a shot when they charge at you in their predictable straight-line fashion.

**STARTING GEAR**

Thumper

M240

4x Frag Grenade

4x Flash Grenade

**AVAILABLE GEAR**

Striker Red Dot Sight

Intervention Thermal Sight

Barrett .50 Cal

AUG HBAR Scoped

AT4

START

Because this mission involves a certain element of randomness, we can't give you a guaranteed perfect hiding spot. Juggernauts can potentially appear anywhere around you, so staying mobile and keeping your eyes peeled for new Juggernauts is vital.

## VETERAN TIPS

This mission is already hard enough. Playing on Veteran doesn't change the tactics or the Juggernauts' threat; you just can't weather their fire as well—which you don't want to do anyway.

We strongly recommend bringing a partner for this mission. Coordinating to take down the Juggernauts is satisfying, and it's a good deal easier than tackling them solo.

While playing co-op, you can have one player stun Juggernauts with a Thumper shot while the other takes them out with a sniper rifle. The ammo crates from the campaign are here, so you can always refill your ammunition, meaning repeated sniper takedowns are absolutely possible.

Practice close-range, hip-fire sniping—it seems crazy, but the combination of stun and damage works well.

We have received your volunteer application for service with the elite forces. We appreciate your dedication. After careful screening, we have decided to accept you as a recruit. Welcome aboard! Your training takes you from the Afghan desert to the radioactive Wasteland. Along the way, you will fight among the best the world has to offer, through the Highrise and the Quarry, the Sub Base and the Underpass. Learn from your mistakes but endeavor to learn from others' as well. We supply you with all of the basics, including weapons training and intel, Perk utilization and implementation, and detailed satellite data for every theater of war. You are cleared to receive advanced intelligence on everything from combat movement and squad management to Killstreak acquisition, weapon Attachment customization, and standard operating procedures for all modes of combat.

You may have done this sort of thing before, but now you can expect deployment in 16 new theaters of war and exposure to a multitude of unfamiliar weapon systems and equipment, so read on. Once you are in country, we will provide you with detailed charts, unlockables, and specs for all Perks, Attachments, equipment, and weapons. You will learn various modes of engagement as you progress. Can you wield dual shotguns effectively? Do you know how to deploy a nuclear warhead? Can you operate the 40mm cannon on an AC-130? We'll show you how. Prepare for deployment...

## BRIEFING

*Call of Duty: Modern Warfare 2* is one of the most beautiful, in-depth, hardcore shooters available today. Players wage war in multiple combat modes and in 16 different theaters of war. Attack with a vast weapon collection, or create many lethal character classes by combining Attachments, equipment, Perks, and Killstreak rewards. Climb the ranks and outfit yourself with a variety of deadly loadout combinations. Engage the most highly skilled soldiers in the world online, challenging up to 18 players in battle. With new modes like Capture the Flag and Demolition, and new weapons like the ACR Assault Rifle and the WA2000 Sniper Rifle, you're in for a completely different experience. Get ready for all of the tactical training you'll need to succeed. Remember, history is written by the victors!

## OPTIONS

Before you engage, you must first establish some preliminary settings, options that enhance the way you operate in battle. Poor choices can hinder your performance, but a savvy setup allows your character to become an extension of yourself.

**Stick Layout:** These four presets determine what each thumbstick does. Carefully decide which setup works best for you.

**Button Layout:** You can select from three choices here. Take your time and figure out which configuration best suits your play style. Pay particular attention to the button you set as your melee combat action.

**Sensitivity:** Three settings are available here, along with a fourth customizable setting. This section allows you to adjust the speed at which your character moves and turns, as well as how sensitive your controls are to input. Too high a setting can spin your crosshairs and make it difficult to target enemies while you're sniping. Too low a setting often results in letting fast-moving targets escape unharmed.

**Look Inversion:** When it's enabled, this option makes your character look down when you press up and look up when you press down.

**Vibration:** If you're using a vibration-enabled controller, this option turns the vibration feature on or off. Leaving vibration on helps you detect silent enemy fire via tactile feedback, in addition to the audible and visual cues.

**Horizontal and Vertical Margins:** These sliders adjust your screen's picture to be either inset from its vertical and horizontal edges or meet them.

**Game Volume and Brightness:** Calibrate these settings so that you can hear everything without distortion and see everything without it being too dark or bright.

# HEAD-UP DISPLAY (HUD)

Your HUD delivers all of the information pertaining to your current objective, from how much time remains in the mission to how much ammo you have left.

Your crosshairs automatically turn red when focused on an enemy. You can use this to your advantage in locations that have a lot of cover. Pass your crosshairs over the cover to see if they turn red. If they do, fire a shot. If you hit someone, your crosshairs turn to an "X," indicating a successful hit.

Your crosshairs also spread apart when you are moving quickly. They tighten again when you stop moving. You can increase your crosshairs' accuracy and size by moving more slowly, crouching, or going prone (to tighten them considerably). When you get hit, your HUD identifies the direction from which the attack originated. This is displayed by a red arc appearing around your crosshair—it points in the direction of attack. This works with bullets as well as grenades or explosions. Use this arc to determine the direction of enemy fire, and evade or engage accordingly.

## Sea Sniper Tip: Where's My HUD?

Hardcore settings remove all elements from your HUD. It's not broken.

SEA SNIPERS

Several indicators inform you of a hit. In addition to controller vibration and the red arc indicator, blood droplets appear onscreen, impairing your vision and movement. This effect subsides over time if you do not suffer any further damage. Seek cover as quickly as possible when you start to bleed.

The HUD displays other important data, including radar with a scrolling map of your location. This map depicts the basic area of engagement as well as your position, your teammates' positions, and enemy positions.

Check the mini-map often, particularly when someone fires a shot. Enemies do not stay visible for long. They appear as a Red Dot on your mini-map, so do your best to call out their locations to your team as soon as you see them. In objective-based game modes, the mini-map also shows your current objectives. Your HUD displays these points in the virtual world with floating icons marking their locations. Look for these when you play modes like Search and Destroy, Sabotage, Domination, or any other objective-based scenario. The bottom-left of your HUD shows the game mode you're currently playing, the score for each side, and how much time remains in the mission. The rank progress bar, a slanted bar along that bottom that spans the screen's width, fills as you rank up. When you reach the next rank, the bar resets, ready to fill again from the beginning. The HUD's bottom right displays your compass, the number of rounds in your current weapon, the special grenades and other explosives you carry, and any Killstreaks you acquire. Use your compass often to call out to your team where you are heading or where you've seen an enemy. Familiarize yourself with the most critical information so you aren't hunting for it when you need it most. Remember that in any Hardcore mode, your HUD disappears. This mode hides all icons and objectives, the mini-map, and even crosshairs! When you play Hardcore modes, choose a weapon you can sight with easily because your crosshairs are inactive.

# GAME MODES

*Call of Duty: Modern Warfare 2* offers several preset modes: Team Deathmatch, Free for All, Domination, Headquarters, Search & Destroy, Demolition, Capture the Flag, and Sabotage. The public playlists change from time to time, so other mode variations may be available to you. Before you head out into the vast online wilderness, let's go over each mode briefly before we delve into more detail later.

**Team Deathmatch:** Team Deathmatch can be played online with up to 18 players at a time in a team-versus-team battle. There are no objectives in this mode, aside acquiring more points than the other team. You can do that. This mode is respawn-based, which means you need to kill as many opponents as you can to get the most points for your team.

**Free for All:** Free for All is just what it sounds like: kill anything that moves. Again, this is a respawn-based mode, and you have a predetermined amount of time to rack up as many kills as possible and land at the top of the list.

**Domination:** Domination mode features three flags that you can capture to rack up points for your team. A captured flag continuously generates points for your team. Multiple captured flags generate more points for your team until the enemy captures them back. Either team can capture a flag, and you can recapture flags at any time. The more teammates you have in the vicinity of a flag, the faster you can capture it. The team with the most points when the round ends wins the match. Domination is a respawn-based type of combat.

**Search & Destroy:** Search & Destroy is *not* respawn-based, so you must be a little more careful when you jump into such matches. This mode is objective-based. One team begins with a bomb and must drop it at either of two plant locations. You can also eliminate the entire enemy contingent to win. Teamwork is crucial for winning in this mode, so cooperate with everyone to clear a path to a drop spot, get the bomb planted, and secure the area before the enemy can defuse it. If you plant the bomb and the enemy defuses it before it explodes, the enemy wins that round.

**Headquarters:** Headquarters is a respawn mode in which your team must capture HQ points before the enemy team can. Once the game randomly selects a headquarters point, you and your team must get to it as quickly as possible and gain control of it. Take control of an HQ by standing in its vicinity until a progress bar appears. A filled bar signifies that you have successfully taken control of the HQ point. Now you must defend it. Once you secure an HQ, your team can no longer respawn. After the enemy destroys the HQ, your team regains the ability to respawn.

**Demolition:** Demolition mode is very similar to Search & Destroy, with the exception that you must plant a bomb at *both* spots to win, instead of just choosing one drop location. This is a respawn-based game mode.

**Capture the Flag:** Capture the Flag is a respawn-based mode that features one flag at each team's base. Each team must grab the other team's flag and bring it back to their base to score points. Someone almost always guards the enemy flag, so avoid rushing in and trying to grab the flag without teammate assistance.

**Sabotage:** Sabotage is kind of a combination of Search & Destroy and Capture the Flag. Each team tries to acquire a centrally located bomb and plant it at the enemy base. The more times you plant the bomb, the more points your team gets. Don't forget that everyone can see a big "kill" arrow over your head when you pick up the bomb. If you defuse a planted bomb, it reappears, giving both teams the chance to plant it again at their enemy's base.

# PLAYING ONLINE

Let's play. When you go to the main Multiplayer screen, choose "Find Match" to join a specific style of game.

From this screen, you can choose from several gameplay modes. Highlight each one to see its description, as well as the number of players currently engaged in it. If you are joining a game by yourself, you get assigned to a random side once the game starts. One of the new online features in *Call of Duty: Modern Warfare 2* is host migration. If you happen to be the host of a game and you lose electrical power, the game pauses, a new host is selected, and the game resumes.

## ) PARTIES

You can invite your friends to play with you online and stay together to fight on the same side by creating a party. Just invite players to your party and join a room. Your party follows you automatically, with all combatants placed on the same side. Occasionally, larger parties may get put into an empty room if there isn't enough space on one side of an existing game. The room eventually fills up as new players join. Before you join a game, remember to check your party's size against the number of players the mode you wish to play supports. If you have seven or more players in your party, modes such as Search & Destroy display as "grayed-out" and unavailable, because those modes are capped at six versus six.

## ) PRIVATE MATCHES

You can also create your own private matches in *Call of Duty: Modern Warfare 2* by selecting "Private Match" from the Multiplayer menu. From this screen, you can choose the map and mode you'd like to play, and even alter the rules to your liking.

Once you choose a map to fight on, select a mode, and then alter the rules as you see fit. You can change everything from the time limit to Kill Cams, Perks, and everything in between.

Private matches are great for holding clan wars or tournaments, or any time you need to create your own customized game mode. Remember that your public character does not gain XP in private matches.

## CREATE A CLASS

Open the Create a Class submenu to outfit your character with all of the weapons and equipment you need in battle. You unlock Custom Classes as you rank up. Once you unlock them, you can rename them as you see fit and include everything, such as your primary weapon, secondary weapon, explosives, equipment, Perks, and Deathstreaks.

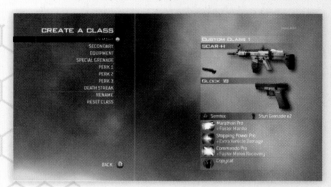

When you create Custom Classes, remember that not every gun is the right tool for a particular job. Try to outfit your classes with a variety of options in case you need to switch classes in the middle of a match. Create classes with close-quarters weaponry, scoped weapons, silenced gear, and even suppressing fire loadouts. The more options you have on the battlefield, the more prepared you are for any situation that might arise. Try to combine the right Perks and Deathstreaks with the right weapons and equipment to get the most out of your Custom Classes. Later in this guide, we provide various Custom Class suggestions, along with explanations of their intended use.

## DEATHSTREAKS

Deathstreaks are a part of the Custom Class setup, but are new to the game. No one likes to die, but it would be nice to get something out of it, right? Enter Deathstreaks. Martyrdom is back, but now you can use it only once and only after you die four times. Copycat lets you steal your killer's class by watching their Kill Cam after your fourth death. Painkiller gives you additional health when you respawn after dying three times without a kill. Choose these based on your individual play style to get the most out of them. You can also refer to a chart that describes all Deathstreaks later in the guide.

# KILLSTREAK REWARDS

Killstreak Rewards are military support bonuses you earn for getting a certain number of kills without dying. For instance, if you kill three people and don't die, you receive a UAV Killstreak. Fifteen different Killstreak Rewards are available throughout your tour, ranging from three-kill streaks to 25-kill streaks!

You can choose three different Killstreak Rewards to earn at different levels. If you select a Killstreak Reward for four consecutive kills, then your next reward must be a five-kill streak or higher, and so on up to a maximum of three. If you know you're not the best player, make the most of your Killstreak Rewards by choosing a three-, four-, and five-kill reward. If you plan to hang back and snipe in silence, maybe you'll do well enough to choose some of the higher rewards. Try using Killstreak Rewards to get more kills and thus advance you to your next Killstreak. Go with a UAV to locate enemies, and then set up a Sentry Gun to push them back. Once you kill six of them, send in a Precision Airstrike to finish off the pack.

## Sea Sniper Tip: AC130

Use the AC130 Killstreak to clear a path for your flag carrier in Capture the Flag mode.

# BARRACKS

The Barracks let you edit how you appear to others online and view your leaderboards, challenges, and highlights. Use this section to stay current on what Challenges to complete in order to rank up and see where you place on the leaderboards. You can also set your Titles, Emblems, and Clan Tags.

## ⟩ TITLES

Titles are graphic bars embellished with a quote that appear when you kill someone. You can unlock and select from a variety of Titles in *Call of Duty: Modern Warfare 2*.

## ⟩ EMBLEMS

Emblems are small icons that appear next to your Title when you kill someone. You can unlock these during your tour of duty, and there are tons to choose from.

## ⟩ CLAN TAGS

Clan tags are prefixes that you can add to your game name. For instance, if your name is "Chief" and your clan is the Sea Snipers, you can make your Clan Tag "SS." The tag then appears in-game with brackets as "[SS]Chief." Once you unlock this feature, use it to designate allegiance to your team.

## LEADERBOARDS

The leaderboards depict your place in the online world rankings. You can view your stats for Score, Wins, Kills, Accuracy, and Skill. Ad-

ditionally, you can sort the leaderboards by friends to see how you stack up against your buddies or clan mates.

## CHALLENGES

Challenges grant you many rewards after you complete them. They range from Weapon Challenges, such as getting a certain number of kills with a particular weapon, to Special Challenges, like Killstreaks and Perk usage. Rewards take the form of experience points or "XP," weapons, Attachments, Perks, Titles and Emblems, and various other goodies. Check

these often to see how close you are to com- pleting different Challenges.

**Sea Sniper Tip: Challenges & XP**

Completing challenges and winning games gives you XP.

## ACCOLADES

Accolades are small, situational rewards for completing things in-game, like singlehandedly killing the entire enemy team, killing the same player the most, or even changing classes the most! Tons of Ac-colades are available in *Call of Duty: Modern Warfare 2*, and you can achieve the same Accolade multiple times. At the end of each match, you can view a list of your top three Accolades, along with a list of the Accolades that everyone else in the room earned. There are pages of Accolades to earn, so try to unlock them all!

**Sea Sniper Tip: XP & Rank**

XP gives you rank, while rank gives you unlocks.

## RANKS

Throughout your tour of duty, you gain experience points, which in turn increase your rank. There are 70 total ranks in *Call of Duty: Modern Warfare 2*. To attain a higher rank, you must accumulate experience points by winning matches, getting kills, completing challenges, and so on. Each rank attained rewards you with different unlocks and XP. Later in the guide, we provide a chart detailing the rewards that accompany each rank. Once you reach rank 70, the game prompts you to "Pres-tige." Prestiging resets your rank back to 1, removing any XP, weapons, and anything you previously earned. What you get in return is a custom icon letting people know your Prestige level. Prestige icons let players know that you've already climbed the ranks and are starting again. Going Prestige gives you the chance to experience the thrill of ranking up all over again, as well as unlock special Prestige Challenges. With ten Prestige levels, you're going to be busy!

## CAMOUFLAGE

Before you jump into a match, you should review your camouflage options. You can select several different options for each type of team. Make sure you choose the best camo for each map's environment. Sometimes it might be better to choose a good camo pattern over a preferred weapon. Remember that the type of weapon you select as your primary determines your camouflage pattern.

You can also camouflage the weapon itself. Once you unlock them, you can choose from a variety of camo styles for your rifles. This helps you hide your entire profile rather than just your body. If you're playing on a snow-covered map, choose an alpine camouflage for your weapon to minimize your visibility to enemies.

**Sea Sniper Tip: Make Your Weapon Blend In**

When loading out your weapon, always consider the environment and choose the appropriate weapon camo.

## WEAPONS

Let's talk weapons. Initially, you don't have too many choices, but once you rank up a bit, many more options become available. Weapon classes include assault rifles, submachine guns, light machine guns, sniper rifles, pistols, machine pistols, grenade launchers, rocket launchers, grenades, and equipment, such as riot shields and tactical knives. Choosing the right weapon for the job is crucial in *Call of Duty: Modern Warfare 2*. Create classes with a variety of weapon systems so you'll be ready for anything. For weapon specs and unlock data, consult the charts later in this chapter.

## ATTACHMENTS

Most weapons can accept optional Attachments to customize your rig and tailor it to your specific play style. Attachments include scopes, such as the ACOG, Red Dot, EOTech Holo-sight, and even Thermal Scopes! Of course, you still have silencers and a grenade launcher Attachment, but you can also select extended magazines, full metal jacket rounds for greater bullet penetration, and the heartbeat sensor, a new Attachment that sweeps the area ahead to locate enemies. Remember that not every weapon or weapon class offers the same Attachments, so check the charts later in this chapter to see what works with what.

## EQUIPMENT

You can also choose from several equipment items. These include Frag Grenades, Semtex sticky grenades, a Throwing Knife, and even a Blast Shield, among others. With all of the weapons, Attachments, equipment, and Perks available throughout the game, you can become unstoppable! One unique addition to the series is Tactical Insertion equipment. Toss this glow stick to "bookmark" a location, and you can respawn right there the next time you die. This is a great piece of equipment for modes like Headquarters. Also new to the series is the Throwing Knife. Yes, you can throw your knife now. Not only can you throw it, you can also pick it back up and throw it again! Use the grenade launcher-type crosshair to gauge your distance to the target, and then chuck it.

## PERKS

Perks are special abilities you unlock throughout the game. They are divided into three sections, labeled as Perk sets 1, 2, and 3. You can choose one Perk from each set for three Perks total. However, the addition of Pro Perks is new to the series. Pro Perks are enhancements to your currently unlocked Perks. By using any of your Perks a certain amount, you can unlock the Pro version of that Perk. For instance, if use the Stopping Power Perk and you kill 100 enemies with it, you can unlock Stopping Power Pro, which increases the damage your bullets inflict on vehicles. Unlocking all Pro versions of your Perks effectively gives you six Perks per class!

You can complement Perks with your weapons and equipment to enhance your online play substantially. Let's say you like to run silent. Grab a silencer for your weapon, a Throwing Knife, and the Bling Perk to add a scope to your primary weapon. Choose Cold Blooded to hide from Thermal Scopes and enemy Killstreaks, and pick the Ninja Perk to make your footfalls nearly silent. You can create a ridiculous amount of combinations with all the available Perks, weapons, and equipment. There really is something here to help everyone excel.

# WARFARE

*Call of Duty: Modern Warfare 2 offers many different types of warfare or gameplay modes. You may remember some and others are brand new, but all of them offer intense combat that just never gets old.*

## FREE FOR ALL

A time-tested standby is the good old Free for All. This is a great mode for blowing off steam. Free for All is the perfect environment to rank up your weapons and increase your kill count with them. Jump into a Free for All room and practice with new weapons or recently acquired Attachments and equipment. Better to try them out here and not in a team-based mode—that way, your teammates don't suffer while you get acquainted with new gear. Other than being a great training ground for your weapons and equipment, Free for All is the best place to practice shooting before matches or tournaments. Everyone is a target, so you're less likely to encounter a lot of campers, especially on the smaller maps.

If you're gunning for the top spot on the leaderboard in your Free for All match, and you already know how your weapons work, here's a great Custom Class to help you dominate:

### MATRIX

| PRIMARY / ATTACHMENT | P90 / Akimbo | | |
|---|---|---|---|
| SECONDARY / ATTACHMENT | PP2000 / Akimbo | | |
| EQUIPMENT | Claymore | | |
| SPECIAL GRENADE | Stun Grenades x2 | | |
| PERK 1 | Marathon | | |
| PERK 2 | Stopping Power | | |
| PERK 3 | Steady Aim | | |
| DEATHSTREAK | Painkiller | | |

The Matrix class delivers a devastating amount of lead in short order. This Custom Class delivers a ton of damage to as many enemies as possible. Your primary weapon is the classic P90, which already contains more rounds than most other weapons in its class. Combine it with the Akimbo Attachment, and you have twice the available lead at your disposal. If you run out of ammo with those, you have the PP2000 with Akimbo, which is no slouch either. Two slots, four guns. Practice firing one and then the other to maintain a constant stream of fire for a much longer duration. You can fire with one weapon using Akimbo. Then, while it's reloading, start shooting with the other. By the time the second gun's out of ammo, your first weapon is fully reloaded.

Choose Claymores for your equipment. These are great for Free for All mode, as you can just plant them and run away. Someone is bound to run into it and die, or at least take major explosive damage. Try planting Claymores around corners in high-traffic areas, inside doorways, in bushes and dense cover, or even at the top of a ladder. Any chokepoint you can find should get a Claymore. Do your best to avoid planting them in highly visible areas. Enemies can toss a grenade or shoot them before the mines can inflict any damage. When you plant a Claymore, check its directional orientation. If you crouch down and plant it at your feet, the direction you face is the direction of the Claymore's blast radius. Make sure you're not too close when one of these babies detonates. Camping near your Claymore isn't the best idea, even if it's directed away from you—it may reflect splash damage if an enemy trips it too close to you.

Stun Grenades x2 should be your choice for your special grenade. Not only do Stun Grenades disorient and slow your enemies, they also prove quite useful for clearing a room. Toss Stun Grenades into a room before you enter. If an enemy is in the room and affected by the grenade, your crosshair turns to an "X," indicating that you stunned someone. You can then take appropriate action. Stun Grenades can also slow your enemy's initial advance. Instead of or in addition to your initial Frag Grenade barrage, toss a few Stun Grenades and rush up to see your enemies running in slow motion. You can use Stun Grenades to beat enemies to sniper locations or other hot spots. Just throw one deep at the start to slow them immediately, and then run to your spot. Now you can take the first shot. Not many players fully exploit the Stun Grenade, but it is a very effective and useful tool when you use it appropriately.

### Sea Sniper Tip: Weapon Attachments & Bonuses

Killing a certain number of enemies with a specific weapon unlocks attachments and bonuses.

Your Perks in this class serve very specific purposes. Marathon gives you unlimited sprint abilities and, if you have earned the Pro version, it enables you to climb obstacles more quickly. This Perk gets you around the map to kill enemies more quickly. It assists you in evading enemies and gets you into hidden positions that opponents may overlook. Remember that when you use Marathon, you cannot fire while sprinting. If you should need to fire, it takes a moment for you to shoulder your weapon. You can counter this by using the Lightweight Pro Perk, which allows you to recover from a sprint to the fire position more quickly.

### Sea Sniper Tip: Smart Crosshair

When you hit someone, your crosshair turns to an "X." Keep firing when you see this, even through walls.

**SEA SNIPERS**

Because you're running dual submachine guns and dual machine pistols that lack power, this class uses Stopping Power for Perk 2. Stopping Power increases the damage your bullets inflict to enemies. In terms of damage, it effectively turns your submachine gun into an assault rifle. By combining Stopping Power with low-damage weapons, you can keep a high rate of fire and deliver much more damage. While Stopping Power Pro increases your damage to vehicles, it does not increase accuracy or bullet penetration through solid surfaces. This Perk is effective only on enemies and vehicles.

Steady Aim is just what its name implies; it stabilizes your aim when you fire from the hip—that's when you don't aim down the barrel of your weapon. This Perk is a perfect companion to your dual Akimbo primary and secondary weapons. Because both of your main weapons use the Akimbo Attachment, you cannot fire them any way other than from the hip. This Perk tightly closes your crosshairs, giving you a much closer grouping of rounds when you fire. If you have the Pro version, which lets you hold your breath longer for scoped weapons, this option doesn't have much benefit. Both of your weapons possess iron sights only, so all you can use is the main crosshair. But overall, this is a great class for Free for All mode. Feel free to swap out Perks or equipment as you see fit to match your play style.

### Sea Sniper Tip: Akimbo Crouch

When using Akimbo, your character crouches slightly lower than normal.

**SEA SNIPERS**

Now that you've set up your class and you know how to use it, let's discuss a few suggestions. When you play Free for All, everyone is your enemy, so shoot anything that moves. Because you're using weapons with limited range, you'll be running quite a bit. Fortunately, your Marathon Perk allows you to run forever. Sprint to where the action is, and then move around the pack, firing into it. Always try to keep your back to a wall so you only need to watch what's in front of you. Circle the general area and keep moving—that is this loadout's *raison d'être*. Use your dual submachine guns in an alternating fashion, firing one weapon for a bit and then the other, so you can reload the empty gun and still fire its companion. Get good at this technique, and you can dominate. Don't forget to plant your Claymores whenever you aren't engaging an enemy. Set them in covered areas. You can also camp in a Free for All game and try to rack up some Killstreak rewards, but this method provides much less action than staying on the move. The Matrix class suggestion isn't particularly suited to camping, so choose a more appropriate class if that's your intention. Nevertheless, earning some Killstreaks before you jump into the fire is a good tactic. Killstreaks can give you massive chunks of kills, and they can start to snowball. Once you get a decent Killstreak and it takes out three or more enemies, you quickly unlock another, more devastating Killstreak. Free for All is all about points. The most points wins, so rack up as many kills as you can before the time runs out—and remember, you're on your own.

## TEAM DEATHMATCH

This is the classic team-versus-team mode. There are no objectives other than to eliminate the enemy team and gain as many points as possible within the time limit. Up to nine players can join each side in Ground War versions of this mode. The standard Team Deathmatch is geared for teams of six players each. Team Deathmatch is a respawn-based game mode, so you have many opportunities to rack up points before time expires. Respawns also help you adapt your play style to the room dynamic. If you realize that everyone on the enemy team is sniping, make the necessary adjustments the next time you respawn. Do your best to befriend the players on your team—you need their help. Your best chance at winning derives from coordinating with your team to cover all of your bases with a sniper, close quarters loadouts, grenadiers, and so on. You must decide which classes are necessary for each map and terrain, as well as the enemy's play style. Here's a class to get you on your way in Team Deathmatch:

### MYSADA

| PRIMARY / ATTACHMENT | ACR / Red Dot & Silencer | |
|---|---|---|
| SECONDARY / ATTACHMENT | Glock 18 / Red Dot & Extended Mags | |
| EQUIPMENT | Frag | |
| SPECIAL GRENADE | Flash Grenades x2 | |
| PERK 1 | Bling | |
| PERK 2 | Lightweight | |
| PERK 3 | Ninja | |
| DEATHSTREAK | Final Stand | |

The Mysada class is a powerful, accurate, and silent loadout designed to keep you hidden while still providing good accuracy. The ACR assault rifle outfitted with a Red Dot Sight and a silencer (via the Bling Perk) is a perfect weapon for Team Deathmatch. You can remain silent and retain precise aiming with the Red Dot. It used to be that you could run with a silencer only by sacrificing an aiming point, such as a Red Dot or any other type of scope. With the addition of the Bling Perk, you can have the best of both worlds. Swap out the Red Dot for an ACOG if you're fighting on a map that requires somewhat greater range. The Red Dot should be fine for basic Team Deathmatches, as we advise you to keep moving. The Red Dot provides a fast and very accurate, minimal zoom point to fire through, so use the Red Dot whenever possible. You may not be able to shoulder your weapon and look through the sight quickly enough every time, but you gain accuracy when you do.

Your secondary weapon is an automatic Glock 18 machine pistol with a Red Dot Sight and Extended Mags. If your ACR runs out of ammunition, or you just want to switch to your secondary weapon instead of reloading, this is a great option. The Glock fires extremely rapidly, burning through ammo before you know it. So, combine it with Extended Mags and add a Red Dot, or even a silencer if you have the Pro version of the Bling Perk. Remember that switching to your secondary weapon is usually faster than reloading your primary weapon.

Your special grenade should be Flash Grenades, which blind and deafen your enemies. You get two of them, and you can use them either to cover a wide spread in quick succession or save them for breaching and clearing rooms. Tossing a Flash Grenade into a confined space affords you time to enter rooms in relative safety. Your crosshairs change to an "X" if you successfully flash someone. This indicates that, more than likely, the enemy in the room is temporarily blind. You won't have much time before the foe regains his sight, so hurry in and eliminate him before he can see you again.

With Bling set to your first Perk, you can run a scope and a silencer on your primary weapon. With the Pro version of Bling, you can also run two Attachments on your secondary weapon system. You can exploit this by creating a silenced, scoped weapon setup, which is far more deadly and accurate than using just one or the other. You can use Bling in many different ways, and it's destined to be a fan favorite in *Call of Duty: Modern Warfare 2*.

Your second Perk is Lightweight, which allows you to move as if your weapons and gear are non-existent. Being able to move faster in Team Deathmatch is a big advantage, letting you sprint from cover to cover or evade enemy ambushes. Lightweight Pro enables you to recover from sprint to aim much faster, too. How many times have you been killed because you were sprinting and couldn't raise your weapon quickly enough against someone who just rounded the corner? Too many times. Thanks, Lightweight Pro!

Your third Perk is Ninja, a Perk that makes you invisible to Heartbeat Sensors. Ninja's Pro version minimizes the amount of noise your character makes when moving, jumping, or falling off high places. Audio is a huge part of *Call of Duty: Modern Warfare 2*. Many players use high-end headphones or surround sound systems that allow them to pinpoint in-game sounds. You can also crouch or go prone to move silently throughout the battlefield, but being able to run, sprint, jump, and fall without having to crouch is a huge advantage.

For your Deathstreak, select Final Stand. This Deathstreak is similar to the Last Stand Perk, but you can actually survive and return to the fight! After four deaths without a kill, your Final Stand kicks in. Once activated, you may use your primary weapon and slowly move around for about ten seconds, at which point you automatically revive. Make sure you finish off all your enemies when you play online, as they may have Last Stand or Final Stand as part of their loadout. Although your enemies might seem dead, continue firing until you see the onscreen text signaling their death.

So that's the Mysada class. Let's take it for a spin in Team Deathmatch. Of course, Team Deathmatch is traditionally a respawn mode, so toss your grenades right off the bat. While they're in the air, use your Lightweight Perk and hustle to where you threw them. Settle down while people either explode or seek cover from which they can attack. As enemies appear out of the explosions and Flash Grenade barrage, pick your shots carefully and take headshots if possible. Although your weapon is silenced, continual fire makes it easier for enemies to pinpoint your location. Try to fire single shots or at least short bursts whenever you can. Coordinate with your teammates to create a perimeter or a backstop to prevent any enemies from flanking behind you. If you can create this formation, you can concentrate your fire on what's ahead of you. Good formations can make everyone's job easier.

Camping is a tradition in Team Deathmatch. It doesn't always work, but it can often get you a Killstreak or two. Camping is a bit of an art. Because you're running silent, you have an even better chance at remaining hidden. Remember that your weapon inflicts a little less damage and has slightly less range with a silencer attached, so set up appropriately. Wait for enemies to pass your position, and then pick them off. You can't stay in your sleeping bag very long, because dead enemies respawn quickly and often proceed directly for your last known location. They can identify your position with the Kill Cam, so you have to relocate quickly.

In Team Deathmatches, it's good to find a buddy. If no one is hanging with you, flip it and shadow someone else on your team. Let them take the lead, and communicate what you see, hear, and think might be happening, or make suggestions regarding what to do next. Let your wingman know where you're looking and what areas you have covered so he or she doesn't duplicate your effort, rendering your team half as effective as it could be. When you move with a buddy, try to split your field of vision to enlarge your combined coverage swath downrange. If your wingman looks 45 degrees northwest, you can look 45 degrees northeast as both of you advance north.

Remember that this mode is based on how many points your team earns in the allotted time. That means you must kill as many enemies as you possibly can. Work on helping everyone on your side by racking up Killstreaks, such as a UAV to reveal enemy locations to your whole team. Get a four-kill streak, and you can call in a Care Package. This sends in a small chopper to airdrop a random Killstreak box. Make sure you tell your teammates where you plan to drop the box—if the package hits someone, it kills him. Airdrop choppers do not care about the map's architecture. They simply drop the Care Packages where you tell them. If you happen to select a rooftop and there is no access to that roof, you just wasted a Killstreak. Find clear locations to drop your Care Packages, and check for unwitting victims below.

Whenever you die and subsequently respawn, you reappear back in the fray, generally near most of your team. If you keep your team together in a particular area, you have a better chance to regroup upon respawn, reinforcing your team as quickly as possible. Vary the class types that your team sends onto the battlefield. If you can't coordinate with your teammates, try to mix it up yourself. If you notice that half your team is sniping, don't go sniping. If no one is sniping and you feel the map requires it, try your hand. Someone has to do it. Sometimes it's better to sacrifice your preferred loadout for one that helps your team win. While you receive points for the kills you get, you earn more XP if your team wins the match. Eventually, you must jump into rooms to complete specific Challenges, such as reaching a Team Deathmatch win quota or finishing a Weapon Challenge. In those cases, determine your goals before you enter the match.

# SEARCH & DESTROY

Search & Destroy is a fantastic competition mode. Here, one team deposits a bomb at one of two plant spots. Remember that Search & Destroy is a non-respawn mode. Work as a team to complete the mission. On offense, you can plant the bomb, while on defense, you can defuse the bomb or prevent it from being planted in the first place. You can also eliminate the other team before the bomb is in play to end the round. One team starts with one bomb and must set it at either of two plant spots located near the enemy spawn. You can bet enemies watch these spots closely, so be careful as you approach to plant. Once a team plants the bomb, the timer counts down to detonation. If you don't pay attention to the bomb you just planted, the enemy team can defuse the bomb for the win. So, set up camp with eyes on the bomb, and shoot anyone that tries to defuse it as quickly as possible. If you can hold off the enemy team for the designated countdown period, the bomb detonates and your team wins. The bomb's detonation also inflicts damage and possibly even kills players near the blast. Smoke is one of the most important elements in winning Search & Destroy, so it's part of the following Custom Class recommendation:

## BOTANIST

| PRIMARY / ATTACHMENT | Vector / Silencer | |
|---|---|---|
| SECONDARY / ATTACHMENT | Thumper x2 | |
| EQUIPMENT | Blast Shield or Claymore | or |
| SPECIAL GRENADE | Smoke | |
| PERK 1 | Scavenger | |
| PERK 2 | Stopping Power | |
| PERK 3 | Last Stand | |
| DEATHSTREAK | N/A in non-respawn rooms | N/A |

The Botanist Custom Class offers many benefits, including silence and protection from explosions. It also provides cover and a last-ditch chance to eliminate the enemy. With the Vector as your primary weapon, you can move quickly with the bomb, and the attached silencer keeps you discreet. Submachine guns have a limited effective range, so you can't take long- or medium-distance shots reliably. Let your teammates take those while you make for the bomb.

Your secondary weapon is the Thumper, a grenade launcher outfitted with two explosives. Break out the Thumper from the start and aim for groups of enemies or even vehicles. Vehicle explosions create a much wider blast radius than grenades alone, so aim for them whenever you can. When you launch grenades at a pack of enemies all headed in the same direction, try to "lead" the pack by aiming where the group is going, not where they currently are. We recommend using the Thumper straight off the bat, and get your grenades off your back as soon as you can. This lets you concentrate on shooting enemies and avoid close quarters combat with a grenade launcher in your hand.

### Sea Sniper Tip: Bigger Bang for the Buck

Using explosives on or near things that explode creates a much larger explosion.

SEA SNIPERS

## Sea Sniper Tip: Death from Above

The Harrier is a great Killstreak for locking down a plant site in Search & Destroy mode.

You can "bonk" enemies with launched grenades if you hit them flush with the projectile itself. If the grenade hits anywhere other than the enemy's body, it explodes. If you hit foes square in the chest or head, they suffer damage from the impact and could possibly die. If you want to get the most out of your Thumper at close range, try aiming it at your enemy's feet. This technique ensures the projectile's detonation and frequently eliminates the threat. The Thumper uses iron sights only and offers hash marks on the crosshairs to help gauge distances. Practice makes perfect with this weapon at range, so try it in a couple of Free for All matches.

This class features a Blast Shield or Claymores for equipment. The choice is yours, and it really comes down to who you have on your team or how you like to play. If you select the Blast Shield as your equipment loadout, you can withstand more explosive damage. This helps you survive initial explosive volleys and stay alive after you plant the bomb to defend it. Often, once enemies discover that the bomb is planted, they toss or launch a few grenades your way. Equipping the Blast Shield minimizes the damage you take from explosions, allowing you to defend the planted bomb.

Should you equip Claymores in place of a Blast Shield, use them to booby-trap the planted bomb. Survey your surroundings and find a good place to set up shop. Identify chokepoints leading to the bomb plant, placing your Claymore at one and keeping your eyes on the others. These devices serve as both a set-and-forget defense and as an audible warning of enemy activity. Listen for it to detonate while you watch the other chokepoints and defend the package.

Without a doubt, choose Smoke Grenades as your special selection for Search & Destroy matches. Use Smokes to make your way to one plant site or another without alerting the enemy to your destination. Also, try to save a Smoke for when you actually go in to plant the bomb. Toss one directly at the plant site, rush in, and set the bomb. Use your Smokes as a distraction as well. If the enemy is accustomed to you popping smoke at your plant site, toss a few at the site you've been planting at, leaving more at the other site. Try using your Smokes as a curtain to mask your movement. If you coordinate a few Smokes to create a line halfway down the map, your entire team can advance to just behind the smoke wall. Enemies can't see you advance, and when the smoke clears, you'll be all up in their grille!

Your first Perk is Scavenger, which allows you to pick up ammo from dead enemies. The Pro version gives you extra mags as well. Because this is a non-respawn mode, you can't just fire away and get a fresh ammo supply when you respawn. Scavenger keeps you loaded so you can continue fending off enemies while you guard the planted bomb. Your submachine gun fires very quickly, which means you burn through ammo rapidly. With extra mags and the ability to nab ammo from the dead, you can keep your Vector loaded.

## Sea Sniper Tip: Demolition vs. Search & Destroy

Demolition mode is the same as Search & Destroy, except for respawn and to the goal to plant at *both* sites to win.

Stopping Power is your second Perk because you pack a submachine gun that delivers minimal damage. The Pro version also gives your bullets more damage against vehicles, so don't be afraid to fire away at abandoned cars. With your silencer and Stopping Power Pro, the autos blow up before enemies can find you.

Choose Last Stand for your third Perk. This drops you to the ground when you get killed, but lets you draw a pistol and fire while crawling. Last Stand's Pro version allows you to use equipment, such as a grenade or throwing knife. Use this Perk for any mode where you may have to defend something. It gives you more time to hold back the enemy while the bomb detonates. The longer you can hold them back, the better.

The Botanist is best suited to Search & Destroy's offensive side. However, you can modify it for defensive use. If you're defending, it may be worthwhile to select Perks like Marathon, which let you run forever and climb obstacles faster, getting you to plant sites before the offense. Try combining that with Lightweight for your second Perk, allowing you to move faster and aim quicker after sprinting. You often encounter enemies while you are sprinting, especially en route to plant sites, so Lightweight helps you shoulder your weapon faster. Think about Dead Silence for your third Perk.

On defense, it's best to split your team into some sort of formation, such as two teams of three. Each squad should watch a separate plant site. Once both squads are set up, they should exchange intel, for example, "they're all coming to A," or, "nothing's happening at B." Depending on the map and the terrain, you may decide to station just one player at each plant site while the rest of your team sets up a perimeter or engages the enemy with sniper rifles from long distance. No matter how you go about defending plant sites, you must do one of three things: kill them all, stop them from planting the bomb at either site, or defuse the bomb after it's planted. If you're the last person alive against multiple enemies, and you have to defend both plant sites, choose a spot between each area. Hopefully, you can get to either site quickly to defuse. Or, if you're lucky, you can find a line of sight to both plant sites. The latter may be trickier than the former.

Occasionally, one plant site is more "popular" than the other is. Send a larger complement that site and just one or two players to the other. Keep on top of the game's dynamic, as the enemy may get wise to your plan and overwhelm the other site when you least expect it.

If you have Claymores in your class, set them as quickly as you can. Place them around corners or directly on the plant site itself. Claymores function almost like another player on your team if you use them correctly. If you're the last surviving teammate and you have a Claymore at one bomb site, defend the other site while your Claymore does its job.

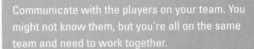

### Sea Sniper Tip: Talk to Me

Communicate with the players on your team. You might not know them, but you're all on the same team and need to work together.

Remember to change position as often as you can. Enemies can learn your location from the Kill Cam and seek you out in the next round. When you're defending on Search & Destroy, you don't have to sit on top of the plant site. You can watch and defend effectively from across the map if necessary. Sometimes this is a great alternative, as enemies often send a few grenades into plant sites to clear the way before they plant a bomb. Try setting up with scoped weaponry and a clear line of sight to the plant spot. If you can see the box, you can see someone planting on it. Avoid sniping from too far away in case you miss or run out of ammo and have to rush down and defuse. Your best bet is to double up and have at least one player sniping site A and one person on the ground at site A. Do the same for site B, and have your last two players act as roving attackers and reinforcements.

If you kill the bomb carrier before he gets to plant it, immediately assess the bomb's location, and reform your team around it. Set up camp and don't take your eyes off the bomb. This is good news for you and your team, as you now have to guard only one location instead two plant sites. Sometimes this occurs in a less than ideal location, but it's still a better scenario than splitting your forces and watching two sites. Again, you don't have to sit on the bomb. Watch it from a window, a building, a rooftop, or anywhere else you can hide and still keep your eyes on it.

Offense is the more difficult side to play on Search & Destroy. You must either kill the entire enemy team or plant the bomb at one of two sites and make sure it doesn't get defused. You do not get to respawn. There are a few ways to engineer a win on Search & Destroy offense. Let's start with a fast plant. This is just what it sounds like: planting the bomb as quickly as you can.

Making a full team rush with grenades and smoke is a great way to force-plant the bomb and seize control of the site. Because many sites are equidistant from each team's spawn point, you frequently encounter the enemy roughly at the same time you reach a site. Throw some smoke at the beginning of the round to mask your initial rush. Then pop more smoke at the plant site. It's a good idea to use smoke as you get into position, then have one Smoke Grenade on the site itself to thwart snipers watching from afar. Be wary, though: many times, defenders who see smoke at the plant site toss in a grenade to kill the planter.

Once you plant the bomb, set up shop and defend it until it explodes. Although it seems like forever, you have to defend it for less than a minute. Set up your teammates in areas where they can watch all chokepoints. It's best if they can see their chokepoint and the plant site simultaneously. Someone on your team should always have eyes on the bomb. It doesn't take long for an enemy to sneak in and defuse it.

Another strategy is to thin the herd. Assume defensive positions after your initial explosives barrage. Set up to snipe or watch highly trafficked areas and chokepoints. Pick off enemies as you see them until you think you have them outnumbered enough to mobilize and attack. Once you whittle them down to at least half, start moving in. Use smoke to mask your direction, then run in and clear one of the plant sites.

You don't need smoke here; just move in and remove the threat, which should be minimal. Plant when your team is set up to defend. Try to allow some time to set up before you plant the bomb so that everyone's in position when the remaining enemies rush the freshly planted bomb. Pick off the last few foes and let the bomb detonate. Remember that you can eliminate as many or as few enemies as you like before planting. Exercise patience here. Sometimes you need most of the round to thin enemy ranks before it's safe to move in. Use your judgment and try to vary your attack style from round to round to keep the enemy guessing.

You can keep the bomb carrier back at your base while you send two teams to "feel out" both plant sites. Each team should enter and clear each site. One or both inevitably encounter resistance, with one team often more threatened than the other. If you can clear one of the sites, call up your bomb carrier and quickly plant there while the second team falls back to regroup with the plant team. You may want to keep another teammate back at your base with the bomb carrier to protect him. This would divide your team into three groups of two. One of your groups may get to a plant site and see that it's impenetrable. They can regroup with the other recon team to assist in clearing the other site. Sometimes one site gets more traffic than the other does. This can work to your advantage if you put in the effort. Compose one team of four and keep your carrier and one protector back. The four-person team should make its way to the "quiet" site and clear it, as it's probably less heavily guarded. Clear it and send in your carrier team to plant, then set up and defend until detonation.

All of the preceding strategies can work if everyone acts together. Communication is the only way to maintain team unity, so keep your comms quick and clear. Search & Destroy is a great mode for clan matches, but it might not be the mode for you if you're not the patient type. With no respawn, you'll be sitting for a few minutes if you die in the round's first few seconds. When your team plays Search & Destroy successfully, it can be one of the most rewarding objective-based modes in *Call of Duty: Modern Warfare 2*.

## DOMINATION

Domination mode is a respawn-based game featuring three flags that either team can capture and recapture at any time. To win, reach 200 points before the enemy does. You receive one point every five seconds for holding one flag, two points every five seconds for holding two flags, and three points every five seconds for holding all three flags. While it may be tempting, you don't always have to capture all three flags to get the most points. It takes teamwork and communication to win. Let's get you loaded out and show you the ropes.

### ICARUS

| PRIMARY / ATTACHMENT | MP5K / Holographic sight | |
|---|---|---|
| SECONDARY / ATTACHMENT | Ranger / Akimbo | |
| EQUIPMENT | Tactical Insertion | |
| SPECIAL GRENADE | Smoke | |
| PERK 1 | Marathon | |
| PERK 2 | Lightweight | |
| PERK 3 | Ninja | |
| DEATHSTREAK | Martyrdom | |

### Sea Sniper Tip: Akimbo Accuracy

Akimbo does not let you sight down the barrel of your weapon. Take the Steady Aim perk to increase your accuracy and tighten up your crosshairs.

SEA SNIPERS

The Icarus class is designed to get you from flag to flag as quickly as possible, providing decent firepower in a lightweight package. The MP5K fires rapidly, so try to fire in bursts through the EOTech holographic sight, or even squeeze off some single shots if you can. You'll be quieter and more accurate. Remember that the MP5K doesn't deliver tons of power, so you may need to fire a few more rounds than you would with an assault rifle. The EOTech sight is very similar to the Red Dot Sight. The reticule is slightly different and the sight's "feel" is also a bit different. But the Attachment ultimately gives you a larger aiming point with about the same amount of zoom and accuracy similar to a Red Dot.

By selecting the Ranger and Akimbo for your Attachment, you can wield dual shotguns, a nice bonus. Shotguns have a wide spread but a short range. Pull these out only when you're in a close quarters battle with an enemy. Otherwise, they don't do you much good. Develop the discipline to switch to them or from them whenever it's appropriate. If you practice, you can learn to fire your dual shotguns in an alternating fashion. This lets you reload one while you continue shooting with the other. This is a great technique for any weapons using the Akimbo Attachment.

Tactical Insertion is your equipment. You can toss this little glow stick onto the battlefield and respawn at its location whenever you die. This can really change the game if you and your team use it correctly. Deploy your Tactical Insertion somewhere the enemy can't easily see it, such as the bushes, on a roof, or anywhere out of sight. If you can get it near a flag you're about to take, all the better. That way, if you die trying to capture it, you can respawn right there and get another chance. If all of your team deploys Tactical Insertions around the central flag, you can dominate that area and control the flag.

Smoke is your special grenade. It can mask your progress toward a particular flag or serve as a distraction. Try to coordinate with your team to create a wall of smoke behind which you can advance and dig in. When the smoke clears, you gain the element of surprise. This Custom Class doesn't carry a silencer, so try to fire only when necessary to avoid helping the opposition find you through the smoke. You can also use smoke as a diversion—fool the enemy into thinking you're headed to one flag when you're actually going for another. It's best to coordinate smoke at multiple points to make the enemy either guess which way to go or divide their forces. Either way, you win.

This configuration's Perks consist of Marathon, Lightweight, and Ninja. Marathon gets you from flag to flag without having to "recharge" your sprint ability. Just sprint all the way and start capturing the flag. Combined with the Lightweight Perk, you move faster overall, and the Pro version lets you fire more quickly exiting a sprint. When you toss in a dash of Ninja, you have an awesome combination of Perks specially tailored to Domination. With Ninja Pro, no one can hear you sprinting from one flag to the next, but remember that flags capture faster with more people taking them at the same time. A lone player grabs flags much slower than two or more. Because you reach the flags very quickly, you can at least start taking them. Once your teammates arrive, the progress bar speeds up until the flag is controlled.

Set your Deathstreak to Martyrdom for this class and mode. After four deaths without earning a kill, Martyrdom lets you drop a live grenade when you perish. You may even consider purposely dying four times just to use it. In Domination, you die most frequently during attempts to take a flag. Most of those times, the enemy is also trying to grab the flag. If your Martyrdom grenade goes boom while they're trying to take the flag, guess who wins that battle?

Note the number of points you receive for each flag you control. Because the team with the most points at the end wins, you want to start earning points as quickly as possible. Have your entire team gather around your base flag to control it as quickly as possible. Once you capture it, have your team grenade the central flag, because the enemy frequently rushes for the most contested flag position. Leave at least one man behind to guard your base flag. The rest should advance to the middle flag. Stick together to capture it more quickly. This strategy

focuses on holding just two flags. So, once you take the second flag, try to divide your team into two equal groups to defend each flag.

After all this, the enemy team starts respawning at their only controlled flag, located at their main base. So, if you reach this critical point, then you know their direction of attack, and you can seal off the chokepoints without having to worry about your flank. Some may try to get behind you to your base flag, but you should keep a few players at that flag to defend it anyway. Now you begin racking up double points for holding two flags, making it difficult for enemies to overtake your score. This containment plan works best if you take adjacent flags.

You can take their base and the central flag, or your base and the central flag, but the strategy isn't as effective if you take your base and their base. Although you can sandwich them as they spawn in the middle, they can more easily fan out from there and go to either flag from the center. If you take two adjacent flags, you can send backup to one flag or another in much closer proximity.

Another option is to run a sniper compliment. Send out two small teams on flag-capturing duty, and assign a sniper to each flag. Once one of your teams grabs its flag, they can move on to help the second team take the other one. The sniper then takes over, covering the first flag you captured. Snipers should run silent in this scenario to avoid detection as much as they can. Once your roving mini-teams capture a flag, that flag's sniper should announce that he is taking over guard duty for that flag from afar. Once all your snipers are in place, your remaining teammates should each camp a flag at close range in case the sniper gets killed or cannot take a shot for some reason. A little backup never hurts. If you can control all three flags at a time, you'll rack up the points very quickly.

You can also rally your whole team to take your flag faster than the enemy when the round starts. If you capture it faster than them, you can run a scenario where you can forego the capturing of any more flags and just camp the central flag from various locations. Using silencers helps this plan excel, so think about running something like an ACOG scope and a silencer on an assault rifle. You can sit back a little further from the central flag and just pick off enemies as they rush in and try to capture it. With multiple riflemen zeroed in on the middle flag, there's not much chance for the enemy to capture it. However, be ready in case they do take it. If they get two flags, their points increase much faster than yours, and they can overtake your score quickly. At that point, make for their base flag and try to capture it. Most of their players are likely defending their newly captured flag.

Domination is very intense and lots of fun to play. You need a team plan before you jump in. Coordinate, and you can steal flags faster and take fewer of them to win. Kills don't matter as much as flags in this mode, so avoid being too bloodthirsty and concentrate on your goal.

## SABOTAGE

This bomb-centric respawn mode can get very competitive and hectic at times. The bomb can be planted and defused many times during a match. In this mode, either team can capture a centrally located bomb. Your objective is to plant it at the enemy's base and defend it until it detonates. If the bomb detonates, the round ends and your team wins. If the enemy can defuse it before it explodes, then the player that defuses the bomb becomes the bomb carrier and can then plant it at your base. The only way to win this mode is to detonate the bomb. If a base is not destroyed within the time limit, the mode goes into overtime. Overtime lasts 30 seconds, and after that, the plant site that the bomb is closest to gets destroyed. Once overtime starts, you don't necessarily have to plant the bomb—just make sure it's closer to the opposing base than it is to yours. Here's a great class to use in Sabotage games:

### CLEANER

| PRIMARY / ATTACHMENT | M4A1 / Heartbeat Sensor | |
|---|---|---|
| SECONDARY / ATTACHMENT | TMP / Red Dot | |
| EQUIPMENT | Semtex | |
| SPECIAL GRENADE | Smoke | |
| PERK 1 | Scavenger | |
| PERK 2 | Hardline | |
| PERK 3 | Scrambler | |
| DEATHSTREAK | Martyrdom | |

This class is designed primarily to locate enemies and deploy Killstreaks. With your friend, the old M4A1, at your side, affixed with a new-fangled Heartbeat Sensor, you can find enemies and put them down with extreme prejudice. The M4A1 is a powerful rifle and can be outfitted in many configurations, but use the Heartbeat Sensor in this mode, as it can help you avoid the enemy pack if you happen to be the bomb carrier. You know you'll have a big "KILL" arrow over your head if you pick it up, right? Don't worry, you can preempt enemy fire by pinpointing their location with your Heartbeat Sensor.

Don't be afraid to shoot through a wall if you detect an enemy behind one—your M4A1 can penetrate most of them. Don't forget that you can't see the Heartbeat Sensor while you're sprinting. With the Heartbeat Sensor attached, you don't have a scope either, so make sure you shoulder your weapon for accuracy.

### Sea Sniper Tip: Watch Your Back

The Heartbeat Sensor picks up enemies only within a 180-degree arc in front of you.

SEA SNIPERS

If you need more accuracy than just iron sights, you can flip to your TMP/Red Dot weapon system. While this weapon setup's range and damage are lower, it allows more precise aim with a little more zoom. The TMP is a submachine gun, so it fires very rapidly but with less power than your M4A1. You may want to use your M4A1 setup to detect enemies, and then quickly switch to your TMP to rush in and eliminate them. This very nimble weapon can get you in and out of close quarters engagements. However, try to keep as your backup weapon, and favor your M4A1's Heartbeat Sensor to spot and dispatch enemies.

Your equipment loadout is Semtex, essentially a timed sticky grenade. It generates about the same blast damage as a Frag Grenade, but sticks to whatever it hits rather than bouncing. You can stick it to enemies' heads, guns, vehicles, walls, just about anything in the game. It's timed to detonate after a few seconds, so you can use it to force your enemy to retreat or run toward the rest of his team. Be careful not to waste these, as you get only one per spawn. It's great for digging enemies out of elevated rooms, as you can toss one through a window and stick it on the ceiling inside. Use Semtex on vehicles, too. It's much easier to destroy a vehicle with Semtex than a Frag Grenade, just because you can place the sticky explosive exactly where you wish.

As your special grenade, smoke helps you and your team plant or defuse the bomb. If you have the bomb, the enemy knows your location, or at least where your bomb carrier is. You need all the help you can get. If you can create your own cover wherever you want it, you might have a chance to plant the bomb. Try to create a perimeter of smoke around and on top of the plant site. This can cloud the enemy's view and might buy enough time to finish the job. If the enemy plants the bomb and you have to defuse it, smoke can still be your friend. Try the same technique, creating a perimeter around the plant site before you run in to defuse. If you succeed, you'll be carrying the bomb, and you can go plant it at the enemy's base.

Take Scavenger as your first Perk. Because you're running the Heartbeat Sensor on your primary weapon, you may need to "wall" some of your enemies. "Walling" someone is the act of killing him or her through a wall. This is costs you some ammunition, but with Scavenger you have extra magazines and can resupply from fallen enemies. This comes in handy as you clean the area.

Hardline, your second Perk, reduces your Killstreak requirements by one kill. This is great for the Cleaner class, because you can rack up the kills knowing where everyone is with the Heartbeat Sensor. Now you can earn your Killstreaks quickly and help your teammates pinpoint enemies by summoning a UAV after only two kills. Based on your opponents' skill, try to gauge whether you can take advantage of the higher Killstreak rewards.

Hardline Pro makes your Deathstreaks require one less death. Try to keep track of how many times you die so you can more effectively use your Deathstreak. If you know your Deathstreak activates the next time you die, you can make the most of it. If Martyrdom is your Deathstreak, run into a pack of enemies so your grenade blasts them all when they kill you.

Martyrdom is a great choice for Sabotage specifically because many teams try to stick together and keep their bomb carrier alive. If you can get close to the bomb carrier when you're one death away from activating your Deathstreak, then rush in and do your worst. You get to use this one death earlier now when you combine it with your second Perk, Hardline Pro. Players instinctively used to run away from dying enemies to avoid a possible Martyrdom grenade. But now that it gets used much less frequently, you might surprise some enemies.

There are many ways to win at Sabotage, from football style to the waiting game. Learn about a few here and then try them, or create your own with bits and pieces from each strategy. Football style is like running the ball in the sport of the same name. Use Smoke Grenades to get your team into position quickly enough to grab the bomb. Once you have it, you have to protect your runner quickly, because his job is to continue sprinting toward the enemy base. If any teammates have Riot Shields, try to get them up ahead of your runner to engage foes before the bomb carrier arrives. The main objective is to keep moving the bomb forward as if you're running a football to the endzone. This mode works very well if a few of your players choose Tactical Insertion for their equipment loadout. Once you get near the enemy base, toss a glow stick to a spot where they won't expect you to come from. You can then respawn there and hit them much faster than they expect. If a handful of your teammates does this, you can hit them hard and push them back far enough to plant the bomb. Once you plant it, you still have to defend it. So, when you place your Tactical Insertions, make sure they're not too far from the plant site. Everyone should take up positions at varying distances to the planted bomb. If you have a scoped weapon, sit back a little farther. If you only have a submachine gun or a shotgun, find a corner and wait for the enemy to arrive. You might get smoked out or flashed or stunned, but if you get smoked, toss a grenade into the smoke and fire away. Better to try to hit something than not try at all. Even better, if you have any Claymores on your team place one right on the bomb. That way, if your opponents smoke the area or you die from a Frag Grenade, your Claymore nails the interloping enemy.

If the enemy defuses the bomb, immediately try to neutralize the carrier before he gets too close to your base. Remember that if the game goes into overtime, the plant site closest to the bomb detonates within 30 seconds. If you can't neutralize the carrier before he gets away, look for an elevated line of sight to your base's plant site. Wait for the carrier to make the drop, and then pick him off from afar. If you eliminate him, you must reacquire the bomb and move it back toward the enemy base before time expires. You can plant and defuse the bomb as many times as the game's duration allows, but if it goes to overtime, you don't have to plant the bomb; you just have to get it closer to their site than yours. Football style is all about pressure. Just keep moving forward and don't stop.

Okay, so you get a big "KILL" arrow over your head when you pick up the bomb, right? Use this to your advantage. Of course, pop some smoke to cover your advance and hoof it to the bomb. Once you grab it, try to keep out of harm's way by sticking to the right or left side of the map. While you do that, the rest of your team should sneak up the opposite side of the map to get behind the enemy and pick them off.

You can use yourself as a distraction, as every opponent focuses directly on you. With their attention fixed, the rest of your team can eliminate them while you make your way to the plant site. This isn't always the best attack plan, but if your bomb carrier equips a Riot Shield, he may be able to withstand the initial assault while the rest of the team engages the enemy and clears a path to the plant site.

One can also play Sabotage from the conservative side. You might be better at letting the enemy come to you. If you take positions quickly enough, you might be able to snipe enemies rushing to pick up the bomb. This is a great strategy against an aggressive team, as you get a steady stream of enemies coming for the bomb, and your team can snipe them from every direction. Keep at this for a while and rack up a few Killstreaks to really pin them down. Remember that you can leave the bomb in the middle for the whole match, but eventually you have to move it closer to the enemy's plant site to win. Even if you move it just a foot closer, you still win. If the bomb goes untouched for the entire round and overtime starts, your snipers have to roll out and hit the ground. It might be prudent to leave at least one sniper watching the bomb while the rest of the team moves in to give it one last push. This is also a good time for Tactical Insertions. Rush up to the bomb and drop one as you try to grab the bomb and move it forward. If you get killed, at least you can respawn right there and keep trying. Chances are, you can push it forward at least a little, and it might be just enough to win. Sabotage is a very mobile mode. There isn't much need for camping, because the objective is to kill the guy with the ball. Even if everyone camps the entire match, it'll boil down to kill the guy with the ball in overtime. Always keep overtime in mind when you choose your loadouts and Custom Classes.

## HEADQUARTERS

Headquarters is a great mode for gaining rank quickly. The game selects a random HQ at the start of each round, and both teams must rush to capture it first. The first team to capture an HQ gains points for the capture, as well as five points every five seconds that they maintain control of the location. This is like getting a kill every five seconds. While you defend an HQ that you control, you and your teammates cannot respawn. Remember this before you rush in to capture the point. The enemy team continues to respawn and tries to destroy the HQ point that you currently control. Once they destroy it, a new HQ is chosen, and it's up for grabs. You receive more points for initially capturing a Headquarters point than for destroying one, and you still get the five points for every five seconds you control it. So, the initial capture of an HQ point is key to victory. Each HQ stays active for one minute. If you control of it for the entire minute, it destroys itself and a new one is selected at random. Remember that the more players you have at the HQ, the faster your team captures it. Keeping all of this in mind, take the following Custom Class into Headquarters games to dominate:

### COLLECTOR

| PRIMARY /<br>ATTACHMENT | Mini-Uzi / Rapid Fire | |
|---|---|---|
| SECONDARY /<br>ATTACHMENT | M93 Raffica / Red Dot | |
| EQUIPMENT | Tactical Insertion | |
| SPECIAL GRENADE | Stun Grenades x2 | |
| PERK 1 | Marathon | |
| PERK 2 | Lightweight | |
| PERK 3 | Last Stand | |
| DEATHSTREAK | Final Stand | |

The Collector class is specially created for Headquarters. A submachine gun lightens your load and makes your character move more quickly, so you get the Mini-Uzi. Because you have to run around to capture HQs, and you'll probably encounter enemies unexpectedly, select Rapid Fire as your primary Attachment. This doubles the Uzi's rate of fire, which comes in handy when you rush into a room and have to hose down a surprise enemy. The Rapid Fire Attachment takes the place of a scope, but you don't need one for this weapon. The Rapid Fire Uzi is what you want for room clearing and spray painting. It has a somewhat fat iron sight, but it's effective and fairly accurate. You don't need to use the iron sights much, as most encounters are surprise attacks that don't allow time to sight down the barrel. Use the crosshairs to get on your target quickly. To increase your hip-fire accuracy, think about swapping out Last Stand for Steady Aim for your third Perk.

For your backup weapon, carry the M93 Raffica machine pistol with a Red Dot Scope. This gun fires a three-round burst and, being a machine pistol, it has minimal range. Equip this when you're on your way to another Headquarters and you spot an enemy either capturing it or on his way to capture it. Stop and shoulder your weapon to look through the Red Dot Sight, and fire a few volleys. Aim for the head to compensate for the Raffica's low power and minimal range. The Red Dot increases accuracy and gives you something for enemies a little further away than the Mini-Uzi can manage with iron sights. Acclimating to three-round burst weapons can be a little difficult, because you pull the trigger and keep aiming but only three rounds come out. Practice pumping the trigger and treat it like a semiautomatic rifle. Once you get used to it, it's a good weapon to have on hand.

## Sea Sniper Tip: Move Slow for Accuracy

The slower you move, the tighter your crosshairs get, improving your aim.

Take Tactical Insertion for your equipment loadout. This allows you to respawn where you place it, which is perfect for Headquarters mode. Remember that it becomes useless after your team takes control of an HQ location (you don't respawn when you defend an HQ). So, don't drop one if your team is about to capture a Headquarters location. However, when you're fighting the enemy team for control over an HQ, deploy one of these bad boys. Drop one as close to the HQ as you can without the enemy seeing you, then rush in to try to take the point. If you die, you can pop right back and finish off the enemy. They won't expect you to rush them again so soon, and they probably won't be ready for you. Hopefully, you already injured them and they haven't had enough time to regenerate much health. Tactical Insertion also works great when you try to destroy an HQ that the enemy has already taken. Again, deploy your glow stick just outside the rave party and move in to clear the HQ. If you die, the party's not over. You'll be back after you hit the bathroom. Now that you've seen the HQ's interior and you know how many enemies are still inside, you can better tailor a plan to dig them out. Try tossing a Stun Grenade at one of them and rush in to finish the job. You have to be quick—again, the enemy gains five points every five seconds they hold the HQ, up to a minute. Don't let them have it. Grab it! Take it!

Your Stun Grenades are great early warning devices. Throw a Stun into any area or room you think enemies occupy. If any enemies are near your blast radius, your crosshairs turn to an "X," indicating you stunned someone. Once you know they're stunned, you can move in, check all of your corners, find the enemy who's probably walking into a wall, and eliminate him. Stuns slow your movement and disorient you. You should experience a Stun Grenade to know what it does to the enemy. Knowledge is power, and you don't have to be the best shot to make the best use of all your tools. Be smarter than your enemies, and you'll be victorious.

The Collector's Perk setup is designed for speed and vengeance. Marathon gives you unlimited sprint ability, and if you've unlocked its Pro version, you can climb obstacles faster. Combine this with your second Perk, Lightweight, and you're the designated driver. With your submachine gun already making you more nimble, the Marathon and Lightweight combo makes you impersonate a trail of light as you bolt from one HQ to the next. Lightweight Pro also lets you aim much more quickly after sprinting. Because you'll be sprinting more often than not, you need to fire fast when someone surprises you. Last Stand is your third Perk. Many times, you're *so* close to taking the HQ and the last little bit of the progress bar, then you get nailed. With Last Stand, you might get enough time to finish taking the HQ and even repay the enemy who tried to kill you. The same applies if you're trying to destroy a Headquarters location.

Final Stand is your Deathstreak. Headquarters mode is so fast-paced, you'll probably die a lot. On your fourth death without a kill, you enable Final Stand. Given the Collector's setup, this puts you in Last Stand, but you can use your primary weapon and continue to move around slowly. After a few seconds, you can regenerate enough to rejoin the fight. Again, this can help you top off the progress bar if you're just about to capture or destroy an HQ. If you're out in the open, crawl to cover so your killer can't find you and finish the job.

One way to win at Headquarters as a team is to mob each point. Don't expect any camping in this mode, as the only way to get points is to capture or destroy Headquarters. Everyone knows your destination because they're going there too. So, make for the first HQ and bring the team. Do everything in your power to get that first HQ before the enemy can. Deploy Stun, Flash, and Frag grenades to hold them back and give your team enough time to get there first. If you take the first HQ, defend it as long as you can to rack up as many points as possible. Dropping a Tactical Insertion is unnecessary once you have control of the point. However, if you're in the process of capturing one, deploying Tactical Insertion might not be a bad idea in case you die before your team captures the point. That way, you can respawn and finish the job. When an HQ that you hold is about to time out (usually about a minute), send most of your team to get a head start on capturing the next Headquarters location. You don't know where it will be, but you should start mobilizing now. Leave a few players to defend the HQ in case you see any more resistance. Once the new HQ appears, everyone should regroup at it and begin to capture it as quickly as possible. Staying together as a group helps you take HQs much faster—the more players you have near the HQ, the quicker the progress bar fills and the faster you can start accumulating points. The group dynamic is also beneficial in terms of having more eyes on the area. If one of your teammates goes down, there's a good chance that another teammate knows where the shot came from and can take appropriate action, either by falling back to a more secure area or by engaging the enemy before he moves in. An entire team can more easily lock down a building, as you can assign one player to each chokepoint. This lets you concentrate on fewer avenues of approach and more effectively focus your fire. You can usually minimize the number of chokepoints by falling back until more become less. Just remember to have someone watching each chokepoint, or you can get flanked and destroy the whole plan.

Alternatively, you can split your team into two squads. One should constitute most of your team. Let's say you're playing six versus six. Organize your squads into four- and two-person units. Your four-person squad should be your powerhouse, focused on taking HQs by force. Your two-person team should sit back from the HQ that your other squad is capturing and oversee its entrances. This technique gives your four-person team some breathing room, making life a little easier for them on the inside, as long as the two-person team thins out the assaulting force. This setup also gives your team a better chance to start capturing the next Headquarters. With one squad inside holding the point, the other squad can mobilize and be en route to the next HQ much faster than the defending squad. Once your two-person guard team begins acquiring the next HQ, your four-person team should converge on it as quickly as possible to aid in the capture. Upon the four-person squad's arrival, your two-person team should bug out and take up watcher positions, repeating the process. The overwatch team should gear up with assault rifles and some sort of scopes and/or silencers. They can't remain in the same spot because of the Kill Cam, so have them vary their locations.

Don't ever wait for an enemy to capture an HQ. If you let them have one, they begin the game with more points than you, and it's difficult to regain momentum on them. Headquarters is fast—you have to think quickly and set up quickly once you find the next HQ's location. You must keep moving from one to the next. Do everything in your power to take it before the enemy team, or you'll never catch up. Use your Tactical Insertion equipment well. Because you die quite a bit, minimize the distance you have to cover to rejoin the fight. Try to drop your Tactical Insertion somewhere close to your desired destination and out of enemy sight. Remember that Headquarters is very fast, lots of fun, and great for ranking up.

# CAPTURE THE FLAG

Capture the Flag is a great new addition to the series. In this mode, you start the match with ten minutes on the clock. You must capture as many flags as possible within that time, or at least more flags than your enemy does. The objective is to steal the enemy flag from their base and bring it back to yours. If the enemy steals your flag while you have control of theirs, then you cannot score a point, even if you bring their flag back to your base. You must first eliminate their flag carrier and secure your flag before you can bring their flag back to your base and score. If time expires and the score is tied, you proceed into overtime. This lasts only 30 seconds, and the winner is the first team to touch an enemy flag. Start thinking about that if you see the time ticking down and the score is tied. The following setup is excellent for Capture the Flag:

## CANNON

| PRIMARY / ATTACHMENT | SCAR-H / Grenade Launcher & Holographic Sight | |
|---|---|---|
| SECONDARY / ATTACHMENT | Thumper x2 | |
| EQUIPMENT | Frag | |
| SPECIAL GRENADE | Flash Grenades x2 | |
| PERK 1 | Bling | |
| PERK 2 | Danger Close | |
| PERK 3 | Scrambler | |
| DEATHSTREAK | Final Stand | |

The Cannon class aims to turn you into just that, a cannon. With five grenades total, you can rain death upon the enemy team and wipe out any enemies near a flag or surrounding a flag carrier. Choose the SCAR-H assault rifle, complete with an undermounted Grenade Launcher and a Holographic Sight. The EOTech gives you a quick, clear, and nicely sized aiming point for fast target acquisition. And the Grenade Launcher…well, we all know what that's for! The launcher comes with two grenades and an iron sight designed to range your target. Gauging the range to your targets takes some practice, but practice makes perfect. Get comfortable with these types of sights in case you need to pick up an enemy rifle with an attached launcher or a separate launcher. The Throwing Knife has the same reticule as the grenade launchers, so get comfortable with that too.

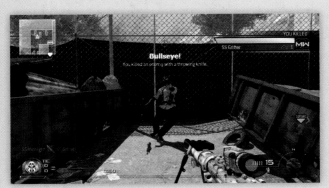

## Sea Sniper Tip: William Tell

Have knife-throwing contests by putting a player up against a wall and having other players take turns trying to get as close to him or her as possible without killing him or her.

The Thumper is your secondary or backup weapon. This standalone grenade launcher comes packed with two projectile grenades. If you wish, switch to this weapon at the spawn and lob both grenades into the enemy base. You can also "bonk" enemies with the Thumper if you absolutely have to. Sometimes a launched grenade might not detonate within a certain distance, and you may actually have to aim directly at the enemy. Set your main crosshair directly on the enemy's center mass, and fire away. You should hit your target square in the chest, inflicting massive damage or even death. Your best option is to save these grenades for more effective uses later in the round. But if it's all you have, you can't switch to your primary, and you're too far away to knife the target, then this is your only choice.

## Sea Sniper Tip: Reclaim the Throwing Knife

You can pick up the throwing knife either from a wall, object, or a dead body.

Your only piece of equipment is the standard-issue Frag Grenade. You can throw this little bad boy quite far, and its causes massive damage, killing everything within its blast radius. You can "cook" Frag Grenades to explode when and where you want them to. To cook a grenade, select your grenade and press the Fire button. Hold the button for a few seconds and release. When you release the Fire button, you throw the grenade. Notice that, within the context of the throw, it detonates much more quickly than if you had just thrown it immediately. It's not that the grenade explodes any faster in absolute terms. Rather, you just hold the live grenade in your hand for part of the time that it otherwise would sit on the ground waiting to explode. Frag Grenades have a timer that makes them detonate several seconds after you pull the pin. If you practice, you can time your throws so that the grenade explodes almost anywhere in its trajectory. Cooking grenades has many uses, such as extracting enemies from rooftops. Just cook a grenade and gauge the building's roof height. Time your throw so that the grenade explodes as soon as it clears the top of the building, and you should frag the enemy. It's much more difficult to land a grenade on the roof than it is to cook one just right and get it to explode as soon as it clears the top. When grenades land, they make noise, and enemies run in the opposite direction. You can cook grenades to thwart their escape. If you cook your frag just right, you can get it to detonate just before or immediately as it hits the ground. If enemies can't hear it, they can't avoid it.

Take Flash Grenades for your special grenade loadout. These let you blind and deafen your enemies, limiting their ability to see or hear incoming grenades or an oncoming assault. Well-timed Flash Grenades can significantly ease your entry into buildings and almost any area, but they are most effective indoors, where the blast can bounce off walls and concentrate its blinding light and concussive sound. Try banking Flash Grenades through doorways to avoid stepping into a hidden enemy's line of fire. When it detonates, quickly but carefully move in and clear the room while everyone inside is temporarily blind. If you get blinded by an enemy Flash Grenade, move backward in the direction from which you came to estimate where you're going. Retrace your steps until the flash wears off, and try to stay out of danger.

Bling is your first Perk. It allows your SCAR-H to have its Grenade Launcher and Holographic Sight. This makes your primary weapon a force to be reckoned with. It's deadly enough without either Attachment, but with both, you can lay waste from a football field away, and accurately dispatch targets from distance or up close with the EOTech sight. Although you can't take advantage of Bling Pro on your secondary weapon because it's a launcher, having the Holographic Sight on your grenade-launching SCAR is worth it. Usually, you should make the most of your Perks, but sometimes you have to sacrifice—this is one of those times.

Danger Close is your second Perk. It increases your explosives damage. Look out. So you have, what, five explosives on you? Nice. Danger Close is made for this. Your explosives already deliver enough damage, but this Perk increases the effect and radius of destruction inflicted on enemies and vehicles. Scout the area for any vehicles near the enemy flag zone and target those first. Vehicles make a much larger explosion than grenades alone, so blow up a car to help your cause. This Perk works with C4, Claymores, grenades, rockets, and launched grenades, so keep that in mind when you customize any of your classes.

Scrambler is your third Perk. It jams enemy radar around you. The Pro version delays enemy Claymore detonations. Because the enemy typically camps their own flag, they may set some booby-traps for you. When you hear a click, start running. You have only a few seconds to get out of the way, but it should be enough for you to escape the blast. Regardless of whether it hits you, the enemy is alerted to your presence, so keep moving. Even though you have Scrambler and they can't see you on radar, they soon sweep the area looking for you. Enemies also get wise to your presence when they notice their radar is jammed. However, you can use this to your advantage. Knowing that they know you're nearby, put your back to something and wait for them to make their rounds. Let them pass, and take a swipe at them with your knife.

Your Deathstreak is Final Stand, and this can keep you alive. You transition to Last Stand on your fourth consecutive death without a kill. You can still fire your primary weapon and crawl, but after ten seconds or so, you revive and rejoin the fight. This is a great choice if you plan on running with multiple friendlies, as they can take the heat off you while you recover. Remember to crawl to cover while you heal, because the enemy tries to finish you off. If you can see the baddie and have a shot, try to kill him before he kills you. You can't move very quickly, so make your shots count.

Let's fight. Leave at least one man behind to guard your team's flag. If you and your teammates have Claymores, set them near your base before you depart. This helps secure your base from flag grabbers and assists your defender if he's alone. Once you place your Claymores, break out the grenades. Fire both Thumper rounds into the enemy base or at vehicles near it. Try to lead your enemies in anticipation of their movement. Switch to your main weapon and fire another few grenades while you continue moving to their base. Switch back to your primary firing mode and toss your final hand grenade. With Danger Close, your grenades inflict much more damage, and hopefully you clear enough enemies to move in and steal their flag. You may even rack up a Killstreak by now. If that's the case, hold on to it. Try to grab their flag as a group and head back to your base. Communicate with your defender to find out if he or she has seen inbound enemies. If not, you have a clear path to your base and can hustle back. The enemy easily sees you on radar if you're the flag carrier, so move fast. Have your teammates create a human shield around you to help protect you from enemy fire. Better they take the damage than the flag carrier. If your defender advises that your flag is still secure, rush back and touch it to get a point. Hopefully by this time, the enemy has been trying to catch you before you make it back home, and is now out of position to defend their own flag.

Try hiding a man back at the enemy base with a silencer and the Cold Blooded and Ninja Perks so he can remain hidden. He they can grab the enemy flag as soon as it reappears back at their base. This is a great tactic if you can manage it. Usually, most of your team should escort the flag carrier and fend off enemies. But, if you keep one player back to defend and leave one at the enemy base to recapture their flag after you score, then that leaves four players to get the flag back to your base. You alter these assignments to suit particular enemies or play styles. There are plenty of squad configuration options, so get a feel for your enemy and decide how to divide your team.

Let's not forget overtime. If you tie at the end of the ten minutes, you go to overtime, which lasts 30 seconds. The first team merely to touch an enemy flag wins the game. You don't have to run it back; you simply have to make contact. This can play out a few ways, and if you saved that Killstreak, now's the time to cash it in. If you can see your enemies are en route to your base, and you think you're closer to theirs, then sprint for their flag and the race is on. If they're camping their own base, then rain fire from above with a Hellfire remote control missile. You can steer this puppy straight down someone's throat. It also creates pretty decent splash damage, so try to land it in the middle of a group when you target multiple enemies.

It's best to keep at least one player back to watch your flag in case enemies get around you, or happen to be invisible to your radar or Heartbeat Sensors. Your defender must keep enemies at bay just until time runs out or your team touches their flag. Be ready to run when overtime hits. Last one to the flag is buying.

## DEMOLITION

Demolition mode is new to the series. This intense mode is very much like Search & Destroy, except that you must plant the bomb at *both* plant sites to win. There are no draws or overtime in this mode. Either you win or you lose. If you don't plant the bomb at both sites before the time runs out, you lose that round. When you defend, you must prevent the enemy from planting a bomb at both sites. If one plant location is destroyed, you no longer have to defend it—move over to help the other part of your team. Assaulting teams can plant at both sites simultaneously. You do not have to wait for one site to be destroyed before destroying the other. In this game mode, everyone on the assaulting team is equipped with a bomb to plant at either site. Once you plant the bomb, you must defend it. The enemy team soon comes to defuse it, so hunker down and keep them away until it detonates. Unlike Search & Destroy, this is a respawn-based mode. Let's gear up!

### GHOST

| PRIMARY / ATTACHMENT | FAMAS / Thermal Scope | |
|---|---|---|
| SECONDARY / ATTACHMENT | N/A | N/A |
| EQUIPMENT | Tactical Insertion | |
| SPECIAL GRENADE | Smoke | |
| PERK 1 | One Man Army | |
| PERK 2 | Cold Blooded | |
| PERK 3 | Ninja | |
| DEATHSTREAK | Martyrdom | |

The Ghost class features the three-round burst FAMAS assault rifle paired with a Thermal Scope as your primary weapon system. The FAMAS is one of the most accurate and powerful weapons in the game. Getting used to its three-round burst firing might take a little practice, but it is a deadly weapon. With the Thermal Scope attached to it, you can spot enemies from quite a distance, but the FAMAS does lack range. Be aware that the scope can sometimes see things that the gun can't reach. This is still a fantastic weapon setup for Demolition. The Thermal Scope can even see through the smoke that many players use.

If you're camping a plant site and someone pops smoke, pull up your Thermal Scope to see who's coming. Because the FAMAS doesn't fire continuously, it reduces your audio footprint to a certain degree. You simulate sniping with this kit. Just practice using the three-round burst, especially because other weapons also use this firing mode.

Using the One Man Army Perk, consider your secondary weapon occupied by an additional Custom Class that you can switch to at any time.

Put Tactical Insertion in your equipment slot. Because this is a respawn mode, and everyone on the assaulting side has a bomb, you want to respawn as close to one of the plant sites as possible. Deploying one between both sites can be even more advantageous, as you may need to reach one and not the other. If your team is busy making a racket over at plant site A, then you can sneak over to plant site B when you respawn at your Tactical Insertion. You can also just join the primary fight if necessary. Make sure you deploy your Tactical Insertion somewhere covert, not just to hide it, but to avoid respawning directly in front of enemies. Try placing it around a corner or on a rooftop, anywhere the enemy can't easily notice and exploit.

Demoliton in particular almost requires you to take Smoke Grenades as your special grenades. You get only one per respawn, so make it count and coordinate with your teammates when and where to throw it. Smoke makes great cover and a wonderful distraction. Get the enemy accustomed to your team planting under smoke, and then try planting at the other site to confuse them. Try popping smoke at both sites simultaneously so the enemy must split its forces in case of attack on either site. Remember that Heartbeat Sensors and Thermal Scopes can see through smoke, so don't get too comfortable in the cloud. Coordinating smoke with your teammates is a valuable skill and doesn't take much effort to accomplish. A little communication yields a nice reward. Use smoke to mask your direction, your numbers, your current location, or to advance your position without the enemy being able to see.

Your first Perk is One Man Army. This Perk takes the place of your secondary weapon slot, but it allows you to swap classes any time during the game. Just press the Switch Weapon button and, instead of switching weapons, you switch your entire class. A screen appears, allowing you to select the class you desire, and then a progress bar appears. Once you choose a class, you can continue playing as normal while the progress bar fills. When it finishes, you're outfitted with your newly selected class.

This Perk's Pro version decreases the time each switch takes from roughly thirty seconds down to only five! This definitely comes in handy, as you have to plant the bomb one minute and defend it the next. Use this Perk to swap between an assault class for planting and a camping class for defending.

Cold Blooded is your second Perk. It makes you undetectable to UAVs, Air Support, Sentry Guns, and Thermal Scopes. This Perk is brilliant combined with the Ninja Perk, which makes you invisible to Heartbeat Sensors. So, you're invisible to electronic detection, a ghost. Enemies can't see you via the preceding methods, and their crosshair doesn't turn red even if it's directly on your head. Your name doesn't appear over your head. This makes the Ghost class great for Demolition and planting bombs. Many times, a defender can just sweep his crosshair slowly through the smoke to see if it turns red as he hunts for enemies. Now your opponents don't see anything until the "bomb planted" message appears. Cold Blooded complements your Tactical Insertion equipment.

Ninja is the cherry on top of this class. With invisibility to Heartbeat Sensors and silent footsteps, you can run without being heard, and you don't have to worry about anyone's radar—ever. Not having to crouch to be quiet is a big advantage in this mode, as you often must rush to a position without detection. Without the Ninja Perk, that's very difficult. Despite your silence, try to avoid running around everywhere. That is, unless you also have the Lightweight Pro Perk, which lets you aim quickly after sprinting. Otherwise, an enemy might nail you because you can't shoulder your weapon quickly enough out of a sprint.

Take Martyrdom with you in case you *just* finish planting a bomb and someone wants to defuse it. Martyrdom doesn't' activate until you die four times without a kill. But man, that fourth time packs a wallop! Try to keep track of how many times you die without getting a kill—not always the easiest thing to do. If you know your Martyrdom is ready to trigger the next time you die, engage in a close quarters battle with a group of enemies. Do whatever damage you can while getting as close to them as possible. Special delivery!

Let's work on some basic tactics before we explore advanced options. Because you have to plant the bomb at both plant sites, take the whole crew to one and then to the other. It sounds simple, and you're thinking you've done this before, but now we add the concept of moving in staggered waves.

Assuming you have a six-person team, break into three teams of two, consisting of a forward team, a support team, and a backup team. Given that you're all headed to the same objective, it doesn't really matter how you get there as long as each team sticks together and the other teams keep them in view. Send your forward team ahead to test the area and clear what they can. They almost certainly encounter resistance. When they begin to engage, they should relay all pertinent information to their support team as quickly as possible, such as, "We see two snipers on the deck, and two gunners directly at the plant." Now your support team can insert and engage, knowing where to look when they reach the kill zone. You can communicate to coordinate attacks, for example, "I've got the sniper on the right," or, "Grenades in at the plant site." Thin out the enemy defense while your backup team closes in. Your backup team should watch for flankers as it continues to move with the pack. The forward team should now try to plant the bomb. The support team should take positions to watch the plant site and defend the bomb once it's planted. When the bomb is planted, the backup team should continue guarding the flanks while it moves into the defense area. The forward team should position themselves in close proximity to the planted bomb. Lock down the area until the bomb detonates, then regroup and move to the next plant site in the same fashion. Use patience. Everyone wants to run to the next plant site, but give your forward team time to go first. The support team can follow at a distance, and the backup team can bring up the rear. It's important to secure the area once you plant the bomb. Otherwise, the enemy can defuse it, negating all your hard work.

Now, get ready to take it to them with both barrels. Split your team into two teams of three, and send one team to each plant site. Organize your formation similar to the previous strategy, this time using individuals rather than small groups. Your front person becomes your forward, your middle person is your support, and your last person serves as your backup. Each three-person team should move to each plant site in this formation: your forward infiltrates and clears, your support follows to pick off snipers, and your backup watches the flank. Once you reach each plant site, it's imperative to communicate and coordinate a smoke and plant action. You can use the game clock to your advantage here, for example, "At 2:30, we smoke and plant." You can also just make sure both teams are in place and communicate that you're popping smoke now. Make sure everyone's in position before you waste your smoke and alert the enemy. With everyone in position and plenty of smoke deployed at the sites, both teams should rush in, engage if necessary, and secure the plant site for defense. You should be in a good position to defend each site, but deploying a Tactical Insertion is a good idea in case you get picked off. Unless both teams plant at exactly the same time, one bomb detonates before the other. Make sure everyone knows which one will blow first, and get clear of it so the free team can help defend the second bomb if there's enough time between detonations, but it can be done. A coordinated, simultaneous assault like this is very difficult to defend. The enemy may think you're creating a distraction at one site and planting at another. You also force them to come out of hiding at both plant sites.

You can also employ a distraction-style assault. In this scenario, you have one player hang back with plenty of ammo and a silencer if possible. The Ghost class often works well for this player. Everyone else should make for one of the plant sites quickly. Once the main team reaches the engagement area, they should slow a bit and remove enemy threats. Remember that enemies respawn quickly, so you have to make this quick. Once you thin out the defense, the enemy will likely concentrate on the plant site that's under attack. This is when your Ghost should move in and plant at the other site. When the enemy hears that you've planted at the other site, they often send their forces over to defuse immediately. Your Ghost should already be set up to defend that site from a distance with a Thermal Scope and FAMAS. When the main team sees everyone from the enemy team leaving to defuse, plant at the second site and split your defenses: leave three at the site you just planted, and send the remaining two to help the Ghost. Your opponents should be disoriented enough for you to push them back and give your explosives time to detonate.

Defending isn't a walk in the park, either, pal. Here are some techniques that can help you fend off the attackers. In this mode, remember that time is on your side. The assaulting force has to traverse the map to get to your plant sites, *and* they have to eliminate your team and plant bombs at both locations before you rejoin the fight. All you really have to do is hold them back and stall for time. Try tossing Smoke, Flash, Stun, and Frag Grenades at any chokepoints when you anticipate their arrival. If you delay them here, there's less time for them to get in and plant. If they surmount your initial barrage, lay down suppressing fire. Fire into the chokepoints, then move, then fire, then move, and so on. Using short bursts and single shots, keep steady fire on the chokepoints, preventing enemies from just waltzing in. However, by this point, the enemy knows your general location and is formulating a way to stop you. Watch for incoming grenades, rockets, and sniper fire. You must defend two separate sets of chokepoints, one for each plant site. Keep your opponents back as long as possible, then you can set up camp to defend.

Usually, you should split your team into two even squads and defend each plant site. One squad may get overpowered, and a bomb might get planted on their site. If that whole squad gets killed, the squad watching the other site should immediately move to clear and defuse the planted site. The respawning squad then heads over to the now unprotected site. The assaulting force is probably en route to that site. So, when you spawn, try to deploy some grenades, along with any other deterrents that might slow them down until you get there. Once you dig in, resume the original strategy, trying to hold back and pick off enemies as best you can.

An interesting approach to this type of warfare is to reassess the entire objective. If you know the assaulting force has to plant at both sites, and planting at one site does *not* win the game, then you can choose to camp your entire team at just *one* plant site. Select the most defensible site, usually the one with the fewest chokepoints or paths into the area. Set up your entire team to defend. Use the techniques described above to hold back the enemy, but try not to reveal that no one is guarding the other site. If you can, set up a sniper at the site you're defending but looking toward the unprotected site. The sniper can try to delay the enemy team at the other site if they try to plant there.

The whole enemy team may come to the site that you're defending, but at least you'll be ready. If they all head to the open site first, your sniper can try to hold them off. For a while, they may think your team is divided to protect each site, which could make them regroup. It's fun to experiment with this strategy, but it takes good communication, willingness, and coordination.

# HARDCORE WARFARE

Hardcore settings remove your HUD, decrease your health, and eliminate your health regeneration abilities. All of the onscreen intel disappears. You have no crosshairs except what you attach to your weapons, such as scopes. If you don't attach a scope, you just have iron sights. You don't get a timer or clock, and you can't see how many points your team has or how much ammo you have left. You don't get any indicators, such as a grenade landing near you, and you don't get any text prompts for things like planting a bomb. On top of all those challenges, Hardcore modes usually require only a bullet or two to kill someone. Killing someone with less powerful weapons, like machine pistols, may take a few more bullets, but it doesn't take many rounds from any gun to put someone down in Hardcore. All of these features make the game feel more realistic. You don't empty entire mags into people in Hardcore, and that encourages somewhat more cautious play.

There's no radar in Hardcore modes. You must rely on UAV support or Heartbeat Sensors, along with your eyes and ears, to locate enemies. You can't see friendlies on radar either. There's nothing onscreen but your environment. Your scopes or iron sights don't turn red if you target someone, as there is no default crosshair. Bug out when you hear the "clink" of a grenade anywhere near you.

Hardcore rooms frequently have you taking shots you normally wouldn't consider worthwhile. Often, you see a leg or a shoulder peeking out from a wall or obstacle. In regular rooms, you might not bother shooting at it with a standard rifle, submachine gun, or even a pistol. However, Hardcore modes drop your health to miniscule levels with each hit, so taking that long shot at someone's toe might be worthwhile. Depending on the weapon's caliber, you just might kill someone with a toe shot. Don't forget that you can shoot through many objects. Don't be afraid to try walling a person you see hiding behind something. Fire directly through the obstacle.

Hardcore settings are great for clan matches and events, or if you just want to test your skills with the big boys. It's nice to have all of that intelligence onscreen, but how good are you without it? Hardcore settings can take some getting used to, but be careful—it's addictive, and you might never want to go back to "regular" rooms again!

# PRIVATE WARFARE

*Call of Duty: Modern Warfare 2* offers private match settings, allowing you to customize your own modes and matches. You don't earn rank or XP in private matches, but you can create exciting and fun modes to play with your clan mates or friends. For some unusual competition, try creating variations on existing modes by turning off Perks or Air Support. You can set the mode, the map, and all of the rules you like.

Try running a Search & Destroy match with Headshots Only enabled and Perks turned off. How about Headquarters with the HQ lifetime set to unlimited? This completely changes Headquarters mode, requiring the enemy to *destroy* the HQ rather than letting it time out for the next one to appear. Try Free for All with no sprint, headshots only, and miniscule health. The possibilities are endless. You can use these features to hold clan matches, special events, and tournaments. You can control which maps to use and how many rounds to play before you switch sides. You can set the time for each round and even how long the bomb takes to detonate in objective-based modes. The smallest tweak can make the biggest difference. Experiment for fun and creative gameplay.

When you play with friends or clan mates, mix things up with a fun stress reliever. For example, try Free for All on a small map, like Rust, set to a five- or ten-minute round. Turn on Hardcore settings, and turn off Perks, headshots, and Air Support. Inform everyone to use knives only. Throwing knives also work. In addition to knives, let players use non-lethal grenades, such as Stuns. If you adjust the settings to Hardcore and miniscule health, you can potentially kill enemies with Stun Grenades. This mode is great fun, sure to have everyone laughing through the match.

Tweak popular game modes, like Team Deathmatch, in private matches and set the number of lives to one. This instantly turns this mode down a notch, forcing players to be much more careful and tactical. Turn the score limit to unlimited and just run a few five-minute rounds instead playing toward a point limit. Turn off sprint to slow down the action significantly. Reduce the game its bare bones by turning off Perks and Air Support and turning on Die Hard mode. This allows teammates to revive you if you are downed. Eliminate campers by setting the radar to always on. Now, everyone can see everyone, and it comes down to who can shoot who first.

Make Domination more tactical by setting the number of lives to three instead of unlimited. This makes players think twice about running out and trying to grab a flag. You have to use communication and teamwork to win this variation. Try turning off sprint too, and watch what happens.

Mess around with friendly fire—set it to reflected to damage the perpetrator instead of the victim. Now, if you're on my team and I shoot you, it's like I'm shooting myself. Set it to shared, and both players take damage. Set up a wave spawn delay to make everyone who dies wait for their wave to respawn. Try third-person mode so you can see your character, as well as around corners. This really changes things. The choice is yours—you can create fun and inventive modes in private matches.

## TACTICAL

Tactical gameplay demands teamwork, communication, good formations, and the ability to employ coordinated actions, such as distractions, sacrifice, close quarters combat, and squad work. The following section discusses each of these topics.

## TEAMWORK

Teamwork requires pre-planning, coordination, skill, and communication. Find a way to communicate with your team prior to a match. You can use party chat, separate applications, such as voice over IP or text chat programs, or even bulletin boards and forums. Formulate solid attack plans for the modes and maps you expect to play. If you access a live voice chat, organize there just before your match. If you pre-plan or brief in something like a bulletin board, make sure you submit your posts well in advance for your teammates to digest the information and make suggestions.

You can use the in-game chat to coordinate assault or defense, for example, "Go on my smoke," or, "Pop smoke in 3, 2, 1, POP!" Coordinated assault or defense can win a round or a match, so assign a chain of command to avoid talking over each other or misunderstanding which orders to follow. Most importantly, assign a leader and make sure everyone knows who it is. Your leader is responsible for coordinating battlefield actions. Fill the chain of command in case your leader falls in combat and cannot communicate. Most modes are respawn-based, so this isn't much of an issue, but non-respawn modes require someone take over if your leader dies. Your leader can coordinate everything from troop numbers to troop actions at any time, so keep the comms clear so he or she can do the job. The leader may decide that the dynamic of the round has changed such that forces need to be reassigned. Be patient when you get your orders, as most times you get an order, you immediately want to carry it out. This should not always be the case. Your leader may call for a timed attack in which separate squads wait for a signal to rush a target at the same time. In cases like these, wait for your go.

Ideally, all of your players should be skilled enough to engage in any type of combat, including sniping, ground pounding, objective completion, and prevention. If this isn't the case, less skilled players should consider practicing. However, the leader should not assign them to positions that they either aren't comfortable with or cannot fulfill. Frequently, you may receive orders to do things you might not want to do but should for the team's welfare. Ultimately, you want the most versatile players you can get, and you need to communicate proficiently.

# COMMUNICATION

Communication is a deciding factor in multiplayer gaming. If, after you get killed, you can speak to surviving teammates, help your them by watching their backs, peeking around corners for them, and so on. If you're camping part of the map and you see three enemies coming toward you, relay that information to the rest of your team as fast as you can. With that intel, the leader can decide if more forces are necessary or if you should hold your ground. If you see enemies but you can't get a shot on them, don't just tell your team that you can't get a shot. Tell them exactly where the enemies are, and use the area names provided on this guide's maps to identify precise locations, for example, "I have one in the warehouse second level—I can't hit him from here." One of your other teammates might be in a position to hit the enemy in question. If the teammate succeeds, he or she should respond back, "Warehouse guy is down." Describe enemy locations quickly, because you may not be able to if you get killed. But don't abuse communication. Avoid hogging the mic singing or talking about what you had for dinner that night. You can make small talk when you're dead. Keep the lines open for tactical comms during matches. Communication often wins matches, even if you have less skilled players on your team.

If you relay information properly, you can drastically improve your situation with communication. If you and a teammate are holding a certain objective and you see movement in an area, let your teammate know. He or she might be able to move into a flanking position and eliminate the threat. Now you've improved the situation by relaying how many enemies are approaching and from where. You can't always prepare for the unknown, so the more information everyone shares, the more likely your team can solve unexpected problems.

Relaying your location allows your leader to verify that all avenues of approach are covered. If you're using this guide's maps, you have a great overview of the battlefield. With this information, you can discern which areas are covered and which aren't. Then you can either reassign players or hold tight. The sooner you let everyone know who's going where, the faster each player can get to a critical location.

Make it your job to know how many enemies are alive, how many of your teammates are alive, and know how much time is left in the round. Relay this as often as necessary to your teammates. You can say something as simple as, "Three of us, five of them, 2:45 left." That takes care of everything in one sentence. Proper communication in *Call of Duty: Modern Warfare 2* helps win you matches.

## Sea Sniper Tip: Just Kill Me Now

Picking up the bomb in Sabotage mode places a big arrow floating over your head that says "KILL," visible to everyone.

SEA SNIPERS

# OFFENSE / DEFENSE

Let's start with offensive strategies. When your team is on the assaulting side, either in Search & Destroy, Demolition, or Sabotage when you have the bomb, know your enemies and think like them. Consider previous rounds you've played against the enemy team. What do they like to do? Snipe? Grenade? Run and gun? Based on that, determine your best course of action as the assaulting force. Look at Search & Destroy as an example. If you're planting the bomb and you know the enemy likes to grenade your spawn, delay your assault. Wait for the initial barrage to end before you assemble and mobilize. There's no need for players to rush past the explosions or try to avoid them. If you know the enemy has skilled snipers, use smoke to conceal your movements. Think about the battle as a whole and consider the details, including how much time is available. Victory lies in forcing enemies out of their game. If they're prepared for one thing, do the other. If they snipe, don't try to snipe back—just go close quarters. If they run and gun, snipe them. If they throw all their grenades at the start, wait for them to finish. Thwarting your enemies' plans not only limits their abilities, it also frustrates them, making them do things they probably shouldn't.

Offense isn't just rushing to the objective. It requires good formations and tactical planning. After you analyze enemy forces and their style of play, you may decide that eliminating a few of them before you move in is the best course of action. From previous rounds, you may know that the enemy doesn't have many players watching a certain area. Consider moving the team to that location and advancing from there. Use your time efficiently and remember that you don't have to rush. Offense isn't rushing; it just means you must complete a given objective.

On assault missions, consider using light weaponry (such as submachine guns with plenty of ammo), Perks like Marathon and Lightweight, and good all-purpose weapons, like an assault rifle with a scope. The submachine gun definitely lightens your load, so if you can get away with that, use it. The faster you move, the better you can attack. Marathon lets you sprint continuously, which makes a great combination. Think about carrying a Thermal Scope in open areas so you can stop and look through it occasionally for enemies waiting to ambush your team. Take some grenades or launchers with you as well. Use them to clear the enemy compounds before you move in on foot. Bring Smoke Grenades to cover your movements and to complete objectives, such as planting bombs.

Defending is a different story. The first thing to keep in mind is that *you are defending!* Too many times, defending teams run into the fray and mix it up with the assaulting force. This is bad. There's no need to do this most of the time. The enemy comes directly to you. If you know they have to come to you, you can more effectively seal off avenues to the objective you defend. If you send players out, there's a good chance for them to get picked off. You'll be down a player. Letting the opposing team come to you allows your team to set up ambushes, chokepoints, and sniping lanes to keep the enemy at bay. Often, the assaulting force has a limited time to complete the objective. All you have to do is keep them off it until time runs out. Defending doesn't always mean killing everyone; it means preventing the enemy from completing the objective. That's all that matters. You won't win or get nearly as much XP if your team can't hold the objective. You can kill the whole enemy team multiple times and die only twice, but if they plant the bomb and it explodes, all your work is meaningless. No one looks to see how many kills the losers got.

Conversely, defending doesn't always mean camping. Defending an area can entail moving up to forward chokepoints quickly, thus reducing the number of entrances to the objective. It can mean sniping enemies at the spawn or on their approach. It can also mean taking a small group to set up forward ambushes or full assaults. Defending is also about keeping the opposition guessing. If you hard camp the objective for a few rounds, send out half your team to ambush the enemy somewhere up the map, where they don't expect it. If you hit them where they least expect it, you might catch them with their guard down and break their squad, forcing them to pull back and regroup. If you want to hit them in a forward ambush, do it quickly and get out of there. Pull back to your objective and regroup. Take up defensive positions and prepare for the next assault. Hopefully, you can cut down their numbers and have a smaller force to deal with.

Defensive equipment includes the Blast Shield, which reduces the damage you take from explosives. This comes in handy, as assaulting forces often attempt to clear areas with grenades. A light machine gun is great for camping, as it comes with so many rounds. You can use it to create an impenetrable wall of suppressing fire, keeping enemies off you and the objective. Shotguns are great for close quarters defense, such as holding a building or a room. Claymores and C4 are some of your best friends on defense. Set up C4 at chokepoints you can see, as you have to detonate it manually. Try to place it inside doorways after enemies enter, so they don't have time to backpedal. Place Claymores at entrances that you can't see. Listen for them to trigger, letting you know someone is coming that way. You can create early warning systems by placing Claymores on or near vehicles that can explode. This trick lets you hear the explosion from much farther away. For hard camping, try the Riot Shield. It replaces your primary weapon, so take that into consideration. You may become a distraction. The Riot Shield can withstand massive damage, and you can use it to focus the enemy on you as you draw them into an ambush.

# DISTRACTION / SACRIFICE

Most players never *want* to serve as a distraction or sacrifice themselves, but volunteering for these roles often proves quite beneficial to your team. Distractions don't always involve players running around screaming, "Hey, look at me!" It can be something as simple as firing a shot, popping smoke, causing an explosion, or even making a sound. If your team needs to plant a bomb in Search & Destroy, and you have two locations to choose from, move with the bomb to the one that's easiest to reach. As you get close to it, pop smoke at the other site and watch to see if enemies relocate there. A distraction can also consist of moving to a location where you know the enemy can hear you. Then just change weapons or reload one. As a last resort, fire blindly. This attracts the enemy. While they're distracted, the remainder of your team can move in the opposite direction to complete the objective. At minimum, these distractions give you a little more time to finish your job, but the enemy doesn't fall for them every time. Use distractions sparingly between your other strategies.

Another great Search & Destroy distraction is to fake-plant or fake-defuse a bomb. This works best when only a few players are alive in the round. To draw out the enemy, all you have to do is move up to the plant site, pull out the bomb, and start to plant it. As soon as it makes noise and your character starts the planting animation, release the Plant button and bug out. Hopefully, the enemy will believe you're really planting and cannot return fire. Little does he know you're waiting for him. This also works for defusing. If you know only one or two players are watching the planted bomb and you have to defuse, make your way there and start to defuse. As soon as your character starts the defuse animation, cease and pull back. Hopefully, this will draw out your enemies, and you can then pick them off.

Splitting up your team into a 4-2 configuration, you can send the two-person squad to wherever you need your distraction. They should carry loud weapons and grenades. Light machine guns let them carry a bunch of ammo. Right from the beginning, this team should proceed to the enemy base with grenades and LMG fire, engaging fast and loud. Once they have the enemy's attention, they should pull back slightly, popping a few shots here and there, or tossing Smoke, Flash, or Stun Grenades—anything to let the enemy know they're still around, even if they can't see them. This lets the enemy believe your team is still trying to attack that site, and there may be more of you than they think. They might even be congratulating themselves for pushing you back. While this goes on, your team of four can easily move up toward the other plant site and complete the objective.

## Sea Sniper Tip: Flank Steak

Flanking enemies creates chaos. Get behind them and rip them apart from their own spawn.

## Sea Sniper Tip: Portable Shelter

When using the riot shield and planting or defusing a bomb, place it on your back to protect you from enemy fire.

Sacrificing a player during a match isn't the best thing to do, and you should use it only as a last ditch effort, or if you know you have the round in the bag due to numbers. Occasionally, your entire team might face just one surviving enemy. In cases like these, you can send out a sacrificial lamb. Have a loud player be the lamb. The rest of the team watches him or her move out from behind cover. Your lamb's footsteps should be loud, and his or her weapon should be unsilenced. Send your victim to comb the battlefield in a grid pattern, covering every area that isn't already secure. He or she can fire a few rounds in succession to alert the lone enemy. The object is to get the enemy to return fire at your lamb so the rest of your team can eliminate the foe. When your opponent finally comes out from hiding to take the lamb, the rest of your team must quickly converge, creating a perimeter from which he or she cannot escape. If you corner the foe, all of you can move in and finish the job. We recommend this strategy only when you have to kill a lone player, and only when you have enough teammates to do the job even if the lamb dies.

Sometimes you must create distraction and make sacrifices for the good of the team and to take the win. It's always better to win than to go for kills and lose.

# SNIPING

Sniping is an art form. *Call of Duty: Modern Warfare 2* offers four different sniper rifles, including the .50 cal Barrett. Choose whichever rifle works best for you or your situation, but try them all before you settle on one. Some rifles have a higher rate of fire, while others pack more punch and can shoot through objects. Choose the rifle that best fits your play style and surroundings. Try to master at least one powerful rifle and one with a high rate of fire. Sometimes you have to fire a few shots in rapid succession, while other times you need to punch a hole through a car.

Snipers are, of course, best utilized in long-distance engagements. The greater the distance at which a sniper is still effective, the better the chance he or she can thin the herd from safety. This minimizes casualties in close quarters combat and makes the enemy backpedal. Practice sniping shorter distances first, then progress to greater distances and increase your accuracy. Try shooting in private rooms on stationary targets or friends. Practice with active targets, too. If you can get some friends to cooperate, try shooting at them as they run across a road in the distance. If you can hit moving targets from distances of 100 yards or more, you should be able to hit anything closer than that. You may have to lead your targets a bit. Gauge their speed and their distance from you to determine how far to aim ahead of their position.

Spot your target, determine which way it's moving, set your crosshairs in that direction, and wait for the target to enter your sights before you fire. Sometimes it's easier to wait for a target to cross into your waiting sights than it is to track the target's movement and fire accurately.

Hold your breath while you snipe. Your aim steadies and your scope sway is much less pronounced. Use the Pro version of Steady Aim to hold your breath even longer. You may want to select Bling for your first Perk if you're sniping, as it allows you to affix a scope and a silencer. Silencing your sniper rifle reduces its effective range slightly, but staying quiet may outweigh that consideration. Cold Blooded should be your second Perk. It makes you invisible to UAVs, Air Support, Sentries, and Thermal Scopes. Your name stays hidden if someone passes their crosshairs over you. Also, enemy crosshairs don't turn red, identifying you as a hostile target. Bling, Cold Blooded, and Steady Aim are great Perks for a sniper, and they help you improve your sniping.

A good sniper is fast, accurate, and rarely in the same place twice. Every sniper knows that a bagged enemy comes looking for his killer in the spot where the sniper fired the fatal shot. Relocate after each successful snipe. You don't have to go far; just move away from the place where you killed your last target. The biggest giveaway to a sniper is movement. Find a good spot to shoot from, like an elevated window or a roof, and get down to minimize your profile. Once you set up, try not to move until you kill a target. If the other team has snipers, your motion is the first thing they'll see. Choose a position where you can see a large area. If the distance isn't too great, stay motionless and not scoped in. When you detect movement, shoulder your rifle and track the target. If you remain scoped in, you give up peripheral vision, and you could get stabbed or flanked. Try not to stay scoped in and instead pan back and forth.

The Heartbeat Sensor is another good Attachment. One of the sniper's biggest weaknesses is getting stabbed or flanked while he's scoped in. Take the Heartbeat Sensor Attachment, and scope in and out to keep checking for enemies. Not all enemies appear on your sensor, especially if they have the Ninja Perk, so trust it only so much. Take a Claymore as backup. Place these set-and-forget trip mines at doorways, or even on top of ladders. Find a spot with minimal entrances. Having just one entrance is best. Set your Claymore there as an early warning device and a backup. If your radar gets jammed, someone with the Scrambler Perk may be nearby. If this person has Scrambler Pro, your Claymore's explosion is delayed when he or she trips it. So, relocate when your radar gets jammed.

Depending on the map, consider a Thermal Scope for sniping. These scopes don't work well on brightly lit battlefields, such as Derail, so choose them only when they're appropriate. The Thermal Scope has good magnification and and makes everything black and white. Enemies and other hot objects appear white. This scope is great on dark maps or maps with a lot of cover. With this scope, even the smallest part of an enemy stands out like a headlight. As always, use the right tool for the job. Try to master all the tools at your disposal, including Attachments, equipment, and Perks. The right combination of this gear can make you virtually unstoppable.

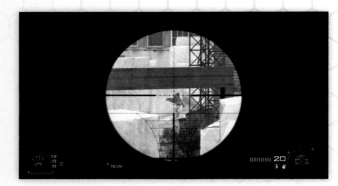

## Sea Sniper Tip: Avoid Camping

If you kill someone and they are using an outside communication application, they generally inform their teammates where you are. Relocate after kills.

SEA SNIPERS

# CLOSE QUARTERS COMBAT

CQB, or Close Quarters Combat, is room-to-room or building-to-building fighting that employs clearing and breaching techniques, rapid-fire weaponry or shotguns, Riot Shields, and fast, accurate coordination on the fly. You encounter lots of close quarters fighting in modes like Headquarters, as many HQ points are located indoors. When your team approaches a building containing an HQ point to secure, you should know the room's exact layout prior to entering. Use this guide's maps to get an overview of the areas you have to clear. Once you have a picture of what you're getting into, your team should stack up. Stacking up is establishing a formation of players, one behind the other, in position to breach a room. Position one player just to the right of the doorway, one behind him, and another on the opposite side of the doorway. You can stack up as many players as you think you need to clear the room. Estimate the number of enemies waiting for you inside before you enter. Formulate a plan beforehand. Assign one of the first players at the door to pop either Flash or Stun Grenades to blind, deafen, disorient, and disable enemies inside. You can also use grenades or C4. Grenade Launchers also work from a little further away. If you plan to use a Grenade Launcher, make sure your stacked players pull away from the door slightly before you launch a grenade into the room. Try to detonate the grenade on the back wall so that the splash damage covers a large area. This works well combined with Flashes or Stuns.

Once you deploy your initial ordnance, designate a primary battering ram player. This person should move into the room quickly and purposefully to the left, while his trailer moves in immediately after, directly to the right. The third and fourth players should follow to clean up any mess that might be made during the breach. As each player enters, he or she should systematically clear the room's perimeter as quickly as possible, including elevated areas such as catwalks, second-story windows, and so on. Once you clear the room, take up defensive positions if the game mode calls for it. In the case of Headquarters, you're moving in to clear and destroy the HQ. Once you do so, you can move out.

Helpful breach gear includes shotguns or submachine guns. Anything that's lethal at close range works perfectly. Try taking the AA-12 shotgun, which is fully automatic. You can enter, firing in spreads that cover the entire room, inflicting heavy damage. Submachine guns are nimble and rapid firing. When you breach with a submachine gun, go in spraying. Spray down all parts of the room, and watch for your crosshair to convert to an "X," indicating that you've made contact. If you see it, retarget that spot and send another clip there. One of the best breaching tools is the light machine gun. This weapon affords massive amounts of high-caliber ammunition. Not only can you clear a room just by mashing the trigger and spinning, but you can clear it from the outside! Because the LMG uses ammunition of a higher caliber than an assault rifle, it's a great choice for walling enemies from the outside. Get familiar with the room's layout, and determine where you would defend it if you were inside. Taking that into consideration, fire a few volleys at the corners you think the enemies may occupy.

Again, watch for your crosshairs to convert to an "X." Spray that position and communicate the enemy location to your team so they can enter the room and take care of business. This is a good way to detect who's inside and where without entering.

Exploit your equipment, Perks, weapons, and Attachments for close quarters combat and breaching whenever you can. The Heartbeat Sensor is one of your best friends for breaching rooms. Just engage it and take a quick look inside. Relay all enemy locations to your team before they enter, and assign players to each enemy. That way, you avoid doubling up two teammates on one enemy while another foe goes untouched and shoots both your buddies in the back. Three Perks are particularly helpful when you expect a lot of breaching and clearing. The first is Scrambler. This slot-three Perk jams enemy radar near your location. This can be good and bad. If enemies see that their radar is jammed, they're alerted to your proximity. However, they can't see exactly where you are or where you're coming from. This Perk's Pro version also delays Claymore explosions, which may allow you to enter unscathed. Ninja, another slot-three Perk, is also worth considering. This Perk makes you invisible to Heartbeat Sensors, and the Pro version makes your footsteps silent. No need to explain why both of these are good. SitRep is the third Perk to consider. SitRep lets you see enemy explosives through walls and obstacles, and it makes enemy footsteps louder. You can bet that when enemies camp or defend a room or building, they also set up explosives nearby. SitRep lets you see them before they turn you into pizza. If you detect an enemy explosive, you can detonate it by either shooting it or tossing a grenade at it. If you detect an explosive indoors and you can't get a direct shot, fire through the wall with a high-caliber weapon to detonate the explosive and possibly eliminate nearby enemies.

Basic close quarters combat requires a tight formation to move as a unit. Employ groups of two to four players, and maintain a staggered line formation. This means having one player in front, the next player behind and to the side, and so on. The last player should watch your six (behind you) in case of enemy flankers. Proceed through areas quickly and quietly, clearing rooms of enemies. The tight formation allows everyone to engage enemies if they fire at your team. If you do get fired upon, your staggered formation should minimize the chances of one bullet taking out multiple players. Don't stand directly behind someone that's getting shot at; the victim's head might explode, sending the bullet straight into you.

## Sea Sniper Tip: Give 'Em Both Barrels

Try using a shotgun with Akimbo for some Wild West fun.

The Riot Shield is a new feature in the series. It's classified as a primary weapon and, if you select it, you cannot carry an assault rifle or any other primary weapon. The Riot Shield is an imposing force. You can stack your teammates behind the player who wields it. For room entry, send in your shield bearer first. That person should stop at the entrance and allow enemies inside to fire at him or her. This move divulges enemy positions and gives the following team a fix on where to shoot. Once you locate the enemies, bring in the rest of your team behind the forward shield carrier, and eliminate the threats. You can also melee with the shield. Shield melee attacks are very handy in clearing situations, because you don't have to shoot—you can just walk up to enemies and smash them with it. Use this technique when you have a shield carrier leading the charge.

# GROUND POUNDING

Also called "running and gunning," this technique is key to reaching forward locations and flanking enemies, but it's reserved for aggressive types. If you like to run and gun, take Perks like Marathon, Lightweight, Cold Blooded, Ninja, or anything to make you fast and undetectable. These characteristics work in your favor, keeping you alive to achieve your goal. Using Tactical Insertion in your equipment slot also helps. If you encounter a large opposing force near your objective and you're close to death, consider deploying Tactical Insertion. This allows you to pop back into the action. Keep your weapons as versatile as possible. You don't know what you'll encounter as you fly into the enemy base. Take something like an AK-47 and an ACOG or Thermal Scope. This helps you with medium- and long-distance engagements. For your secondary weapon, consider something like the TMP machine pistol with Akimbo for close quarters engagements. Because you're on the move most of the time, you may want an assault rifle with a quick-acquisition type of scope, such as the Red Dot or the Holographic Sight. You can't see as far as you can with the ACOG scope, but you get a modicum of zoom and increased accuracy. Silencers are also great for ground pounding. If you expect to flank the enemy, you'll benefit from being as quiet as possible.

Your main objective is to get to the enemy base and clear it from behind. If you employ this tactic correctly, it yields one of the most deadly assaults you can perform. Sometimes, it takes only one player to get behind a team to inflict devastating damage. In certain modes, if most of your team makes it across the "fifty yard line" and kills the enemy

team, they start to respawn behind you, back at your original spawn point. Remember this so you aren't surprised when your opponents suddenly appear behind you. Once you get behind the enemy, skirt the map's perimeter, facing the center and keeping your back to the map's outer borders. Moving in this fashion, you can comb the map and get the drop on enemies respawning at your original base.

If you carry a silenced weapon, try hiding in ambush. When an enemy runs past, you can either knife him if you're close enough, or pick him off silently. Once you eliminate someone, immediately move on, advancing across the map to the enemy spawn. Find another safe zone to ambush the next wave of enemies. Again, pick them off and move along. Continue like this until you reach the end of the map, then make a u-turn and head back. The enemy may be respawning in a different location by now. Consider a light machine gun with a silencer attached. This provides an abundance of high-caliber ammo and keeps you quiet. You can even equip a silenced shotgun! It may not be the best choice for running and gunning, but who doesn't want to roll with a silenced shotty? Stealthy running and gunning can devastate the enemy and force them out of position.

Assembling a full team of runners and gunners can be a great distraction if you first play conservatively for several rounds. Send out the whole team to engage as quickly as possible. Try using Tactical Insertion so you can quickly rejoin the fight if you die. Move fast in a loose group around the battlefield's perimeter. Everyone should keep eyes forward, moving as a pack and eliminating enemies as you progress. Don't stop anywhere; keep the pack together, and keep circling. In ground pounding, objective-based play modes, the entire team should move as a mob to each objective, laying waste to everything in its path.

Ground pounding isn't always rushing—rather, it's just not camping. It's progression through the map, either quickly and semi-recklessly or quickly but tactically. You don't have to run through the middle of the map, throw your grenades, and barrel through the smoke like Rambo. You can rush up to a good vantage point and wait, shoulder your weapon, pick off a few enemies, and then move along. Good ground pounding clears sections of the map that you can secure and control if you have enough willing players. You can move the group around to reform a defense if you need to. It may even be inside the enemy's base. It all depends on what you need to do and when, but it gives some options.

## CAMPING

In the context of a match, camping is the art of the hardcore defensive lockdown. Here's one example of how to camp in Search & Destroy mode. Because there are two plant sites at which the enemy can set bombs, you need to divide your team. Sometimes, one plant sees greater traffic than the other, requiring more defenders or campers. Let's consider a four-two player split. While the team of two moves to the less active site, your four-player squad can set up at the busy site. You have some time to get ready before the enemy can reach your location, but don't waste time. Of course, secure any entrances high and low to your plant site. If there are only a few entrances, try to set up a crossfire. Do this by placing one player back and left of the entrance. Place another player on the right side, opposite the first player. They should both aim at the entrance, creating an imaginary "X" with their lines of fire. The other part of your team should do the same at the other entrance. If possible, you should also have Claymores when you defend. Create a class specifically to defend or camp, so you can switch to it when necessary. Set your Claymores inside the entrance. Place them along the wall, but away from the doorway. Angle them so that one of the lasers is parallel to the entrance wall. This focuses the blast directly on enemies as they cross the threshold. Have your entire team place Claymores on entrances and on the bomb plant site itself. Sometimes enemies rush in to plant the bomb so quickly, they don't take the time to scan the area for explosives. You can also use C4. If you're the only surviving player on your team and you have C4, it can help you guard the other plant site. Determine which site is easier to defend and guard it in person. Set your C4 directly on the plant box at the other. Keep your detonator ready. Watch for enemies coming to your plant site, and be ready to switch to your primary weapon. But, if you hear that the bomb has been planted at the other site, immediately trip your detonator for a good shot at nailing the player that just planted the bomb.

As your team defends your two plant sites, your numbers may dwindle from time to time, forcing you to reorganize your troops. If one site runs short of defenders, send some over to even it up. Reconfigurations like this should happen often, so keep tabs on who's where, how many teammates are alive, and how many enemies remain. If you don't think the enemy will plant at a particular site, you can leave fewer players there, or double up on Claymores and C4 and camp the other site. Enemies may have the SitRep Perk, which allows them to see explosives through walls. If you hear your Claymores or C4 explode and you don't see that anyone dies, you know where the enemy is.

Another way to camp one site is to use a player with a Riot Shield. This player should crouch behind the shield, directly next to the entrance, ready to shoot anyone who comes through the door just as they get hit by Claymores. Another player should be positioned to see the entrance straight on. If enemies make it past the initial Claymore blast and your Riot Shield soldier, this player can shoot them while they're busy trying to shoot the shield carrier in the foot.

Always think about the big picture. When you have to camp a plant site or two, your focus is fully on defense. There's no need to send players out on the map when you need to camp. Risking the loss of a defender isn't worth the one kill he or she may get out there. Let your opponents come to you and face them on your terms. After a few rounds of camping, switch up your techniques. You can't stay in the same spot round after round. Reposition to watch the same area from a different location. Set your Claymores further back than the last time. Go high if you were low. Keep at least two or three options on the table each round, so that the enemy has a hard time adapting. Have a couple of classes set up to help you switch plans.

## SQUADS & FORMATIONS

You can break up a six-player complement several ways, including three teams of two wingmen. A wingman team is a duo used for fast, quiet infiltration, scouting, clearing structures, or even sniper-spotter teams. Sometimes you split split your team in half to create two three-person squads. These require a little more coordination for organizing an assaulting, but they can be more lethal and versatile. Certain maps or modes call for an uneven division, such as a four-two team split. You can also run a five-one split depending on your plan, the map, and the mode.

Let's look at wingman teams first. Comprised of only two players, these buddy teams are great for infiltrating behind enemy lines, clearing buildings and rooms, or forming a sniper-spotter team. Wingman teams can work close together or far from each other, depending on the situation. Most frequently, you work in close proximity. If you're moving toward a particular goal, stick close to each other, using a staggered formation in which the follower is not directly behind the point man. This reduces the chance of one bullet taking down both of you. As you move across the map, note different areas, such as roads you have to cross or buildings you must pass. In areas like these, send the follower out across the street while the point man sits on a corner at the near side, watching for enemy fire. If the follower crosses safely, the point man can proceed and resume the lead. If the follower takes fire, do your best to locate the shots' origin and engage. Watch for tracers and listen for directional cues. Also, use the main radar or your Heartbeat Sensor if you have it. These situations are tailor-made for a UAV if you have that Killstreak.

Sometimes, your wingman team may need to separate a little. You can't support your teammate from close range, so you might have to be creative. Try to get the enemy's attention while your wingman watches for the origin of oncoming fire. It's a little dangerous, but this technique can work very well when you have to dig your teammate out of a jam. Work together with great communication, even when you aren't in the same place. The sniper-spotter team is another great wingman role. Set up the sniper in a good position and have the wingman watch his back. You can usually have a Claymore watch a sniper's back, but its field of view can't match a player's. Your wingman can let you know when an enemy approaches and from which direction. He can then instruct you to remain motionless while he picks off the foe with a silenced weapon. If you're the spotter, choose silenced weapons with medium to short range, and carry tools like the Heartbeat Sensor to help you find incoming threats. Configuring your team into multiple wingman squads can help you cover more ground while keeping a decent force at each point. Maneuver them as you would individuals, and let them configure themselves once they have their orders.

When you need to roll with larger squads, try two groups of three. These three-person teams can provide serious firepower and solid defense. However, movement can be a little trickier. When you have to get your three-person squad across the battlefield quickly, move in a triangular formation. Your point man should lead at the top of the triangle, with each follower at the back points. Move in this formation as the followers keep eyes out to the sides and the point man watches up front. The two players at the back should try to maintain a steady distance from the point man, staying in a tight formation and continuing to move. Think of the point man is the head and the other two players as the body. The body should follow the head at all times, regardless of where it goes. If you need to hold up in a building or secure an area, you can break from the triangle formation and reform into a defensive setup.

If you take your three-person squad on patrol, your movement and formation should be a little different. Move in a staggered line like a lightning bolt, with the rear player watching your backs. As you patrol the battlefield, work the perimeter and keep your eyes forward and inward, while your last player watches your flank in case of ambush. For forward presses, reform into the triangle on the fly and proceed in that fashion. If you're clearing areas, don't use the triangle formation for assault, as you don't need to watch your back as much as you need all eyes forward.

You can use four-two and five-one squad formations for offense and defense. For offense, you can send out your larger squad in a wide chevron formation for clearing purposes. Have your smaller squad bring up the rear from a distance. This is sometimes easier for the protection team, as they don't have to walk backwards. They can just follow the formation from much further back, close enough to help protect, but far enough back to let enemies reveal their positions. You can also use this same tactic and formation in reverse. Send the small squad out front as a scout while the big squad follows at distance more slowly. Wait for your scout to engage, and then your main squad can fall in and dominate the enemy force.

A good time to defend with lopsided squad configurations is when you know you can hold one of your points with fewer players and some explosives. If you just have to defend a single spot, you can hold it down with your main squad and let the smaller squad move out, meet the enemy en route, and hold them off or at least slow them down. Sometimes your objective is just to keep the enemy off your defensive position for a certain amount of time. Your smaller squad can do that by employing Claymores, C4, or even some "high" explosives.

CAMPAIGN
BASICS

CAMPAIGN
WALKTHROUGH

SPECIAL OPS
MISSIONS

ENEMY
INTELLIGENCE

MULTIPLAYER
BRIEFING

MULTIPLAYER
WARFARE

TACTICAL

CLANS

INTEL CHARTS

SATELLITE INTEL

ACHIEVEMENTS

# CLANS

A clan is a group of players who work as a team in structured events, such as clan matches, scrimmages, ladder matches, tournaments, and practices. There are many things to consider when you create a clan. You need a name, Clan Tags, rules, a website or bulletin board, a ranking system or chain of command, somewhere to play, such as a league or a ladder, and obviously clan members. Let's explore what's involved in running your own clan. And, if you already have one, maybe you'll learn something new.

## CLAN NAME / TAGS

Naming your clan is your first job. It might be military-based, or it might just be funny. It all depends on how you plan to run things. Keep in mind that other players might stereotype you based on your name. For instance, if your clan is called the Sea Snipers, many could assume that all the members are good snipers. In our case, that isn't necessarily true. People don't take you seriously if you name your clan something like Paintchip Eaters. That might be your goal, but just take it under advisement. Avoid using vulgar words in your clan name, as many ladder sites or leagues don't allow them. The same goes for racially based clan names or any kind of derogatory names. Once you have your clan name, you need a Clan Tag. A Clan Tag is an abbreviation of your clan's name. It is used in-game to identify members of each clan, and it usually appears before your in-game screen name, like [SS] Chief. You might decide on a Clan Tag before you come up with your clan's name. If you know you want a funny Clan Tag or a military style Clan Tag, you can pick the tag first, like [EOD], which stands for Explosive Ordinance Disposal in the military. You can name your clan after that, or change it up to something like "Elements of Destruction," or whatever you like. Again, refrain from creating Clan Tags that might get you banned from websites. *Call of Duty: Modern Warfare 2* offers a Clan Tag feature, which allows you to add your Clan Tag to your in-game name. This is great for those who don't wish to change their names. Now you can just add the tag to your name through the game. Remember that these tags appear only in *Call of Duty: Modern Warfare 2* and not in other games or anywhere else online. Using the game's Clan Tag naming system is very handy, but sometimes it allows other players to fake being a part of your clan by changing their Clan Tag to match yours. To get around this, you can include your Clan Tag within your screen name, as in SS Chief. Select different characters to create brackets around your tag if your system allows for that. This minimizes the chances that people can fake being part of your clan. So you have your name and you have your tags, now what?

### Sea Sniper Tip: Play Him Off

When you're the last person killed, you get a "Final Kill Cam," which goes into slow motion, allowing everyone to watch you die...slowly.

## RECRUITING

Now to populate your clan. Remember that you'll be playing with these people all the time—practices, matches, on the forums—everywhere, all the time. Look for people that you mesh with on a personal level and on a gameplay level. Avoid recruiting people that always camp if you only rush, and vice versa. Don't recruit loud comedians if you're a quiet, tactical kind of player. You may also want to recruit people within your age range. For example, if you're seventeen, you may not want to play with thirty-five-year-olds...probably as much as they don't want to play with you. So, consider looking for players in your age range with similar gaming goals.

Determine when you plan to play. If you can play only between the hours of 3:00 p.m. and 6:00 p.m., consider that some players may still be at work during those times. Try to set a schedule for things like practices and matches before you recruit players. Recruiting people who can never make a practice or a match is a waste. Skill is another factor to consider. You may be looking specifically for snipers or good ground pounders. Make sure you communicate these things when you recruiting players so they know what you want. You may not care about how good they are as long as they are a good match with you personality-wise. You may already have a good base for your clan, like your friends or even coworkers, but you inevitably have to put the word out to gather new recruits. Bulletin boards or forums are great for this. Compose a post informing readers what kind of players you seek, upcoming tryout information, age ranges, and any other details that recruits might need to know. You can also look for members proactively by playing online and striking up conversations with players that you think would be a good fit. Just hit them up in-game or send a message asking if they're interested.

Once you get some responses, organize tryouts. You can create private matches for your tryouts, and choose a map and mode that best suits what you want to learn from these recruits. You may want to see how well they snipe, so pick an appropriate map and tell them what you're looking for. You can do this for many situations, like defending

or assaulting, running and gunning, or even leading the whole team. Look for everything during tryouts, from skill to communication. See how they handle various situations, including losing and winning. No one wants a sore loser. Run your prospective recruits through a few exercises, let them play as they normally do, and get back to them after you discuss their performance with the rest of your clan mates. They may witness things that you don't see, so have a conversation before you decide whom to let into the clan. Your tryouts might consist of skill challenges, such as "kill 20 guys in 10 minutes." Maybe a recruit gets only 18 kills, but because of his good personality, you might decide to bring him in anyway.

Always give recruits a probationary period. Bring them in, but keep an eye on them. Make sure they don't act in a way that puts your clan in a bad light. Make sure they show up for practices and matches, and that they're generally being good clan members. If, after a certain amount of time, you think they are solid additions to the team, then you can bring them in as members in full standing. You can do as little or as much as you think is necessary to recruit players. Test their dedication by giving them silly things to do, like sing songs. If they're willing to do these things, then you know they really want to be in your clan. While a recruit is in the probationary period, make him or her use recruit tags. For instance, if your recruit's name is JohnSmith, and your Clan Tag is [EOD], then the recruit's tag would be [EODr], where the lowercase "r" designates recruit status. His full name would look like this: [EODr] JohnSmith. When the recruit completes the probationary period, he or she can drop the "r."

### Sea Sniper Tip: Prestige Ranks

Going Prestige resets your rank back to 1 and gives you a new icon that does not change until you Prestige again.

## WEBSITE / FORUMS

Every clan should have a website. If you can't afford one or don't know how to make one, there are plenty of free options and readymade templates you can edit fairly easily, and there are a few free hosting options. You may get some ads on your site, but hey, it's free. Your clan's website should include things like your logo, a list of your crew (it's important to let people know who is actually on your team), your rules, times you play, how to get in touch with you, how to join, and possibly where you compete. You can also install a bulletin board or forums. You can also find these elements for free, and you can customize them to your clan's colors and logo. You can create private forums for your clan to keep in touch with goings on, discuss strategies, and see who can play in the next match. You can make sections like "Match Signups," where you post the next clan event, and players can accept or decline. Create a "Tactics" forum to discuss your plans for the next match. Many forums come with a calendar included, which lets you post event markers on specific days. This is great for at-a-glance schedules for matches and practice. Most forums are very functional and customizable. You can make a public "Recruiting" forum, where prospective recruits can read about your clan and view your requirements. Forums are a terrific meeting place to talk to your team and organize events, and they're a crucial part of reaching the public and new recruits.

Once you get accustomed to running your site and your boards, you can include match records, clan videos, pictures of your clan mates or events in which you've participated, or the history of your clan and how it started. Once you get visitors to your forums, you can get into hosting your own tournament, competitions, or "play with us" nights to involve the community with your clan and possibly even pick up a new recruit or two. Forums are a great tool to make your clan's online presence more interactive and dynamic. If visitors can create their own posts on your forums and speak their minds, they can interact with you and your team. You'll find new clans to play with and set up scrimmages, locate new recruits, and let your team stay in touch from anywhere. You can also use sites like Twitter and Facebook to display your clan information and keep your clan informed. They aren't necessarily the best medium, but they're better than nothing.

### Sea Sniper Tip: Geography Lesson

Use the maps in this guide to find the names of areas on the maps to call out to your teammates in-game.

## RULES

You have to have some semblance of rules. Even if you're just a play-for-fun clan, you need at least a little structure. Post the rules in your forums for your team to see. Rules can be anything from "no cursing in public" to "must attend practice to play in matches." You can be as strict or as laidback as you like, but you should definitely set basic rules and adjust them as your clan evolves. Rules should cover the basics: how to deal with someone cursing at you, things you shouldn't say in public, basic conduct in public settings, how to resolve disputes, and so on. Post your standard operating procedures for matches. This might include things like "never plant the bomb by yourself" and "always call out enemies as soon as you see them." All of these factors depend on how you want to run your clan, how you want to treat others, and how you want the public to perceive your clan. Other clans may avoid playing against you if you always desecrate their dead bodies or use offensive slurs in matches, but maybe you don't care. Just make sure everyone is clear on what the rules are before they join or even try out.

## RANKS

Consider creating a chain of command or ranking system. You can use any form of ranking you like, but many clans use military ranks from the Army, Marines, or the Navy. These organizations use many ranks, probably more than you need. If there are too many for you, just use the major ones, such as Lieutenant, Captain, and so on. You don't need to add intermediate ranks, like First Lieutenant Junior Grade, unless you absolutely need more ranks. Come up with criteria for ranking your fellow teammates. You may decide to give players rank for making practices or doing well in matches. You can promote members based on cumulative deeds, like posting valuable tactics or information on your forums, using good communication, or helping the clan in some other respect. The choice is yours, but make sure your clan mates know how they can rank up.

Once you have your ranking system in place, explain what privileges go along with each rank. Maybe officers get first crack at matches, or Privates have to set up the practice rooms. Your members also need to know the chain of command and who is ranked where. This helps in matches if your clan leader or match leader dies during a round. The next in rank can immediately assume control of the round. You may also have to devise some sort of demotion system. If you plan to promote people, sometimes they have to be demoted. Possible reasons include not showing up for practice or matches, not communicating, or disobeying orders in matches, the forums, or in public. It's up to you to decide. Don't demote someone just because he or she misses a single practice. Try creating a point system in which your players accrue demotion points. When they reach a certain number, they get demoted. You can keep a chart for promotion and demotion points to let your clan monitor their standing.

# SPECIALTIES / CLAN JOBS

Running a clan isn't easy. It takes a lot of time, effort, and planning. You may not be able to do everything yourself. Think about assigning tasks to clan mates who are reliable enough to do them. For example, a "Match Coordinator" would be in charge of setting up and organizing all of your clan's matches. This person would contact the opposing clan to confirm match times, check who is hosting the match, and select the maps and game modes to be played. He or she should handle everything involved with matches. You can also create a "Training Coordinator" to take care of setting up practices, determine skills or tactics to work on, and anything else related to training. Assign these jobs to your higher-ranking members or require a certain rank before one is eligible to take on a job. You can even put someone in charge of recruiting. He or she can post in other forums, set up tryouts, and find people during online play who might wish to join.

Letting members partake in some of the clan's inner workings is beneficial to everyone. It takes pressure off the clan leader and gives members a greater stake in the clan. You want members to be proud to be a part of your clan. It should be fun and structured. Try not to force members into positions, and instead let them volunteer. A member that you least expect might be very good at an essential task. Try to avoid assigning people to tasks that they can't do, either because they lack time or skill.

Sometimes you'll sense a drop in clan morale. For whatever reason, your fault or not, you have to keep the mood up for the sake of the clan. If people are bummed out that you lost your last match, run some fun practices, like knives only in Free for All. If they're fighting amongst each other over silly issues, disrupt it and defuse the situation quickly. Sometimes an intra-clan tournament is a good morale booster. Let them beat the snot out of each other. Try some new graphics for your forums. Any little thing you can do to either give back to your clan mates or provide some fun works wonders for morale. You can even try some different play modes, something you don't usually play in practices or matches. It's a fun change from the norm and a good distraction.

## Sea Sniper Tip: Portable Sentry Gun

When you pick up a sentry gun, you can put it in your inventory and place it later.

SEA SNIPERS

## Sea Sniper Tip: That's All, Folks!

A 25-kill streak gives you a Tactical Nuke that can end the game.

SEA SNIPERS

## Sea Sniper Tip: Slicing Turrets

Knifing turrets destroys them faster than shooting them.

SEA SNIPERS

# AWARDS & COMMENDATIONS

Everyone likes to unlock stuff, right? Come up with a series of medals or awards to give to clan members for various achievements, like killing 20 people in a clan match, or earning a certain amount of explosive kills. Think about it like unlocking Attachments. If you get a certain number of kills with a given weapon, you get a silencer. In this case, the player might earn a medal or some other award. You can give out awards for anything, including good teamwork, communication, or just generally rocking out in a match. You can have specialty medals for specific expertise, like accumulating 100 sniper kills in matches, or 50 pistol kills. There are tons of ways to reward your team. You can create your own clan swag. Hand out trophies for tournaments or have everyone chip in for a prize that someone can win. Awards and commendations can be anything, but they give your members something to work toward. Reward players for time in the clan. If they've been with you for a year, provide a special graphic to add to their signature in the forums, or mark it on their website bio page. It's nice to be recognized for what you've done.

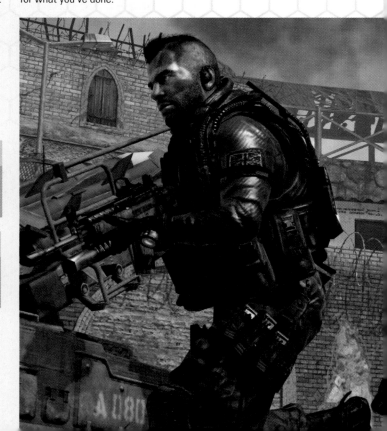

# PRACTICE & TRAINING

Designate at least one day a week for practice and training, even if you think you and your team don't need it. Schedule a practice day and time, and keep it mandatory. This gives your members something to look forward to, maintains the bonds between members, and provides your team with a great environment for practice or just messing around with each other. Make a private match room and invite your friends. Do whatever you can to ensure other random players can't jump into your room. Choose a map and a mode, and divvy up your players. You can also have Auto-Assign randomly place your clan mates on a team to keep them even. If you have an upcoming match, then you can set up scenarios that you think you'll encounter. If you're already comfortable with the match's map and game mode, just play it for the night to get even more familiar with the layout and find some new spots.

You can get as specific as you like in practice. If you know it's hard to plant the bomb at a particular site, tell your OpFor (opposing force) to camp that site and wait for your team to try to plant at it. Scenarios like these really help you develop new ideas. After a few rounds or before you switch sides, end the game and go to the lobby to discuss briefly what worked and what didn't. Don't feel like you're giving away any trade secrets—this is your team, remember? You're all on the same side!

Practice can be a great stress reliever. If your morale is low or you just finished a tournament and you don't really need to work on anything, set up fun scenarios for your members to play. Try things like shotguns only, or pistols and knives in a Team Deathmatch. Maybe try some Free for All, C4 and Semtex only. Take suggestions from your clan mates. Maybe they've played something online that was a lot of fun.

Sometimes you can't field enough clan members to run a practice. In cases like these, try to set up a scrimmage with a friendly clan. Scrimmages are clan matches that don't count toward anything other than bragging rights. If you can't field enough of your own players, and you can't find a clan for scrimmage, create a party and head out into the public. Be warned that when public players see a clan join a room, they may leave. They think that they won't be able to contend with you since you're probably all going to work together. This doesn't happen all the time, but it does occur, so don't be surprised when you join a room and everyone leaves.

### Sea Sniper Tip: Running the Gauntlet

Players look for movement. Try to move from cover to cover when traversing open areas.

# MATCHES

Clan matches are where the magic happens. All of your practicing, all of your training: this is where everything comes together. They're over before you know it, and your blood pressure goes through the roof, but there's nothing like a good clan match. Many different competition sites offer various types of warfare for your clan. Some are ladders set up so you can attack clans higher up the ladder and take their spot, or be challenged by another clan for points and your spot. Various ladders are available for different modes or numbers of players, with different restrictions or none at all. If you enjoy ladder play, find a mode and configuration that best suits your clan, and sign up. Make sure you read all the rules before you sign up. If you fail to abide by the rules, your clan could get banned from the site.

League play is another type of competition. Leagues are different from ladders because you usually play a set number of matches against a set number of clans, ending with an elimination. Some leagues offer playoff series with semi-finals and sets of final matches like hockey. These also feature many configurations, from modes to maps and restrictions, so choose the one that best fits your play style. Furthermore, consider the times that the matches happen. Sometimes league matches involve predetermined times that you have to play. Some ladders let you challenge another clan and work out a date that works for both sides. You have to work with your clan to see when they can get together for matches before you sign up for either a league or a ladder.

Tournaments are another kind of competition. Tournaments usually don't run very long. Sometimes they're done in a day, sometimes a weekend. It may take a little longer, perhaps a week or two, to finish a tournament, depending on the size and number of clans involved, but they are not ongoing events like ladders and leagues. Most tournaments are set up like miniature leagues, and some feature elimination—once you lose a match, you're out. Some tournaments offer cash prizes or swag, like t-shirts or hats. You can also hold your own tournaments, and intra-clan tournaments are lots of fun. It's great to compete against your own members for bragging rights. Try running mini-team tournaments. Break your clan into teams of three or four, and pit them against each other in various types of combat. Try submachine guns on Afghan, or shotguns and knives on Estate. Whoever wins advances to the next tier. There are plenty of ways to configure your own tournaments, from wingman contests to all-against-one survival competitions. Have your clan artist create an award on which you can put the winner's name to display on the clan site for bragging rights. Try running them monthly or annually, however you want. Tournaments are great fun to compete in, and they're good for morale.

The following section provides detailed information to help you make the most of your deployment. You can find weapon stats, Perk descriptions, Deathstreaks, Killstreak Rewards, ranks, unlock data, and much more. Keep these charts handy for quick reference during combat.

# )WEAPONS

## ASSAULT RIFLES/PRIMARY WEAPON

Assault rifles are the Swiss army knives of guns. These rifles have solid power, strong rates of fire, and good penetration. Furthermore, you can outfit them with many Attachments, including silencers and scopes. You can also camouflage this weapon class. Assault rifles have medium to long-range effectiveness and possess adequately sized magazines. They can shoot through a variety of objects, including some walls depending on the rifle's caliber. They're good for close quarters combat and long-range targets.

### AVAILABLE ATTACHMENTS

| ATTACHMENT | | HOW TO UNLOCK |
|---|---|---|
| | Grenade Launcher | Complete Marksman I (10 kills) |
| | Red Dot Sight | Complete Marksman II (25 kills) |
| | Silencer | Complete Marksman III (75 kills) |
| | ACOG Scope | Complete Marksman IV (150 kills) |
| | FMJ | Complete Marksman V (300 kills) |
| | Shotgun Attachment | Get 20 kills with the attached Grenade Launcher |
| | Holographic Sight | Get 60 kills while looking through the Red Dot Sight attached to this weapon |
| | Heartbeat Sensor | Get 15 kills with the Silencer attached to this weapon |
| | Thermal Scope | Get 20 kills while looking through the ACOG Sight attached to this weapon |
| | Extended Mags | Get 40 bullet penetration kills with FMJ attached to this weapon |

### ASSAULT RIFLE QUICK-REFERENCE

| WEAPON | DESCRIPTION | UNLOCKED |
|---|---|---|
| ACR | Fully automatic, all-purpose weapon. | Level 48 |
| M16A4 | Three-round burst. | Level 40 |
| TAR-21 | Fully automatic, all-purpose weapon. | Level 20 |
| F2000 | Fully automatic, all-purpose weapon. | Level 60 |
| M4A1 | Fully automatic, all-purpose weapon. | Level 4 |
| SCAR-H | Fully automatic, all-purpose weapon. | Level 8 |
| AK-47 | Fully automatic, all-purpose weapon. | Level 70 |
| FN FAL | Semi-automatic (single fire). | Level 28 |
| FAMAS | Three-round burst. | Level 4 |

**ACR**

Description: Semi-automatic (single fire).

ACCURACY
DAMAGE
RANGE
FIRE RATE
MOBILITY

UNLOCKED LEVEL 48

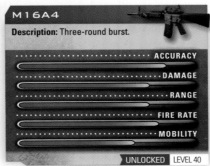

**M16A4**

Description: Three-round burst.

ACCURACY
DAMAGE
RANGE
FIRE RATE
MOBILITY

UNLOCKED LEVEL 40

**TAR-21**

Description: Fully automatic, all-purpose weapon.

ACCURACY
DAMAGE
RANGE
FIRE RATE
MOBILITY

UNLOCKED LEVEL 20

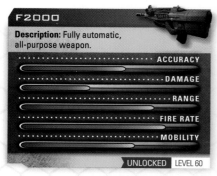

## F2000

**Description:** Fully automatic, all-purpose weapon.

- ACCURACY
- DAMAGE
- RANGE
- FIRE RATE
- MOBILITY

UNLOCKED | LEVEL 60

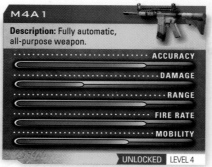

## M4A1

**Description:** Fully automatic, all-purpose weapon.

- ACCURACY
- DAMAGE
- RANGE
- FIRE RATE
- MOBILITY

UNLOCKED | LEVEL 4

## SCAR-H

**Description:** Fully automatic, all-purpose weapon.

- ACCURACY
- DAMAGE
- RANGE
- FIRE RATE
- MOBILITY

UNLOCKED | LEVEL 8

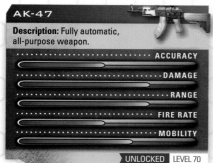

## AK-47

**Description:** Fully automatic, all-purpose weapon.

- ACCURACY
- DAMAGE
- RANGE
- FIRE RATE
- MOBILITY

UNLOCKED | LEVEL 70

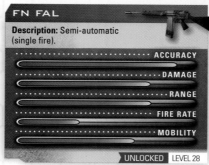

## FN FAL

**Description:** Semi-automatic (single fire).

- ACCURACY
- DAMAGE
- RANGE
- FIRE RATE
- MOBILITY

UNLOCKED | LEVEL 28

## FAMAS

**Description:** Three-round burst.

- ACCURACY
- DAMAGE
- RANGE
- FIRE RATE
- MOBILITY

UNLOCKED | LEVEL 4

# SUBMACHINE GUNS/PRIMARY WEAPON

Submachine guns fire smaller caliber rounds than assault rifles, and they have a much more limited range: short to medium distance. They're great for close quarters combat and a run and gun play style, as they offer a high rate of fire. You can use camouflage and various Attachments on these weapons, making them very flexible for close-range encounters.

## AVAILABLE ATTACHMENTS

| | ATTACHMENT | HOW TO UNLOCK |
|---|---|---|
| | Rapid Fire | Complete Marksman I (10 kills) |
| | Red Dot Sight | Complete Marksman II (25 kills) |
| | Silencer | Complete Marksman III (75 kills) |
| | ACOG Scope | Complete Marksman IV (150 kills) |
| | FMJ | Complete Marksman V (300 kills) |
| | Akimbo | Get 30 kills with Rapid Fire attached to this weapon |
| | Holographic Sight | Get 60 kills while looking through the Red Dot Sight attached to this weapon |
| | Thermal Scope | Get 20 kills while looking through the ACOG Sight attached to this weapon |
| | Extended Mags | Get 40 bullet penetration kills with FMJ attached to this weapon |

## SUBMACHINE GUN QUICK-REFERENCE

| WEAPON | DESCRIPTION | UNLOCKED |
|---|---|---|
| MP5K | Fully automatic, close range. | Level 4 |
| Mini-Uzi | Fully automatic, close range. | Level 44 |
| Vector | Fully automatic, high fire rate. | Level 12 |
| UMP45 | Fully automatic, close range. | Level 4 |
| P90 | Fully automatic, large magazines. | Level 24 |

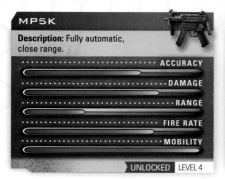

## MP5K

**Description:** Fully automatic, close range.

- ACCURACY
- DAMAGE
- RANGE
- FIRE RATE
- MOBILITY

UNLOCKED | LEVEL 4

## Mini-Uzi

**Description:** Fully automatic, close range.

- ACCURACY
- DAMAGE
- RANGE
- FIRE RATE
- MOBILITY

UNLOCKED | LEVEL 44

## Vector

**Description:** Fully automatic, high fire rate.

- ACCURACY
- DAMAGE
- RANGE
- FIRE RATE
- MOBILITY

UNLOCKED | LEVEL 12

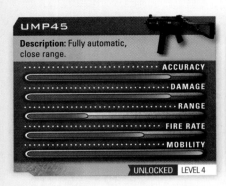

**UMP45**

**Description:** Fully automatic, close range.

- ACCURACY
- DAMAGE
- RANGE
- FIRE RATE
- MOBILITY

UNLOCKED | LEVEL 4

**P90**

**Description:** Fully automatic, large magazines.

- ACCURACY
- DAMAGE
- RANGE
- FIRE RATE
- MOBILITY

UNLOCKED | LEVEL 24

# LIGHT MACHINE GUNS/PRIMARY WEAPON

Light machine guns actually are not very light at all. These slow your mobility but feature huge magazines, fully automatic fire, and high-caliber rounds. You can equip them with various Attachments, including a front grip, and they're best for encounters ranging from short to long distances.

## AVAILABLE ATTACHMENTS

| ATTACHMENT | | HOW TO UNLOCK |
|---|---|---|
| | Grip | Complete Marksman I (10 kills) |
| | Red Dot Sight | Complete Marksman II (25 kills) |
| | Silencer | Complete Marksman III (75 kills) |
| | ACOG | Complete Marksman IV (150 kills) |
| | FMJ | Complete Marksman V (300 kills) |
| | Holographic Sight | Get 60 kills while looking through the Red Dot Sight attached to this weapon |
| | Heartbeat Sensor | Get 15 kills with the Silencer attached to this weapon |
| | Thermal Scope | Get 20 kills while looking through the ACOG Sight attached to this weapon |
| | Extended Mags | Get 40 bullet penetration kills with FMJ attached to this weapon |

### LIGHT MACHINE GUN QUICK-REFERENCE

| WEAPON | DESCRIPTION | UNLOCKED |
|---|---|---|
| M240 | Fully automatic, large magazines. | Level 52 |
| L86 LSW | Fully automatic, large magazines. | Level 4 |
| RPD | Fully automatic, large magazines. | Level 4 |
| AUG HBAR | Fully automatic, high accuracy and damage. | Level 32 |
| MG4 | Fully automatic, large magazines. | Level 16 |

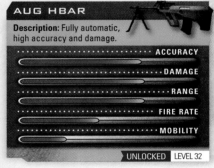

**M240**

**Description:** Fully automatic, large magazines.

- ACCURACY
- DAMAGE
- RANGE
- FIRE RATE
- MOBILITY

UNLOCKED | LEVEL 52

**L86 LSW**

**Description:** Fully automatic, large magazines.

- ACCURACY
- DAMAGE
- RANGE
- FIRE RATE
- MOBILITY

UNLOCKED | LEVEL 4

**RPD**

**Description:** Fully automatic, large magazines.

- ACCURACY
- DAMAGE
- RANGE
- FIRE RATE
- MOBILITY

UNLOCKED | LEVEL 14

**AUG HBAR**

**Description:** Fully automatic, high accuracy and damage.

- ACCURACY
- DAMAGE
- RANGE
- FIRE RATE
- MOBILITY

UNLOCKED | LEVEL 32

**MG4**

**Description:** Fully automatic, large magazines.

- ACCURACY
- DAMAGE
- RANGE
- FIRE RATE
- MOBILITY

UNLOCKED | LEVEL 16

# SNIPER RIFLES/PRIMARY WEAPON

Sniper rifles are long-distance weapons. They are mostly useless without using a scope, but they fire high-caliber rounds, with some even capable of penetrating large objects. Additionally, these guns offer several Attachments and camouflage patterns. Some of these rifles are bolt action and must be reloaded after every shot, but most are semi-automatic.

## SNIPER RIFLES/PRIMARY WEAPON

| WEAPON | DESCRIPTION | UNLOCKED |
|---|---|---|
| Intervention | Bolt action. | Level 4 |
| M21 EBR | Semi-automatic (single fire). | Level 56 |
| Barrett .50 cal | Semi-automatic (single fire). | Level 4 |
| WA2000 | Semi-automatic (single fire). | Level 36 |

## AVAILABLE ATTACHMENTS

| ATTACHMENT | | HOW TO UNLOCK |
|---|---|---|
| | Silencer | Complete Marksman I (10 kills) |
| | ACOG Scope | Complete Marksman II (25 kills) |
| | FMJ | Complete Marksman III (75 kills) |
| | Heartbeat Sensor | Get 15 kills with the Silencer attached to this weapon |
| | Thermal Scope | Get 20 kills while looking through the ACOG Sight attached to this weapon |
| | Extended Mags | Get 40 bullet penetration kills with FMJ attached to this weapon |

### INTERVENTION

**Description:** Bolt action.

- ACCURACY
- DAMAGE
- RANGE
- FIRE RATE
- MOBILITY

UNLOCKED LEVEL 4

### M21 EBR

**Description:** Semi-automatic (single fire).

- ACCURACY
- DAMAGE
- RANGE
- FIRE RATE
- MOBILITY

UNLOCKED LEVEL 56

### BARRETT .50 CAL

**Description:** Semi-automatic (single fire).

- ACCURACY
- DAMAGE
- RANGE
- FIRE RATE
- MOBILITY

UNLOCKED LEVEL 4

### WA2000

**Description:** Semi-automatic (single fire).

- ACCURACY
- DAMAGE
- RANGE
- FIRE RATE
- MOBILITY

UNLOCKED LEVEL 36

# RIOT SHIELD/PRIMARY WEAPON

The Riot Shield is classified as a primary weapon, so selecting it prevents you from carrying any type of rifle. You can melee with the shield, it helps stop rounds of most calibers, and it reduces explosive damage.

### RIOT SHIELD

**Description:** Bullet resistant.

UNLOCKED BY DEFAULT

# MACHINE PISTOLS/SECONDARY WEAPON

## AVAILABLE ATTACHMENTS

| ATTACHMENT | | HOW TO UNLOCK |
|---|---|---|
| | Red Dot Sight | Complete Marksman I (10 kills) |
| | Silencer | Complete Marksman II (25 kills) |
| | FMJ | Complete Marksman III (50 kills) |
| | Akimbo | Complete Marksman IV (75 kills) |
| | Holographic Sight | Complete Marksman V (100 kills) |
| | Extended Mags | Complete Marksman VI (150 kills) |

These rapid-firing pistols are mostly fully automatic and offer many Attachment options, including the Akimbo Attachment, which allows you to wield two of them simultaneously. You cannot add camouflage to this class of weapon.

### MACHINE PISTOL QUICK-REFERENCE

| WEAPON | DESCRIPTION | UNLOCKED |
|---|---|---|
| G18 | Fully automatic, close range. | Level 22 |
| TMP | Fully automatic, close range. | Level 58 |
| M93 Raffica | Three-round burst, close range. | Level 38 |
| PP2000 | Fully automatic, close range. | Level 4 |

**M93 RAFFICAL**

**Description:** Three-round burst, close range.

ACCURACY · DAMAGE · RANGE · FIRE RATE

UNLOCKED — LEVEL 38

**G18**

**Description:** Fully automatic, close range.

ACCURACY · DAMAGE · RANGE · FIRE RATE

UNLOCKED — LEVEL 22

**TMP**

**Description:** Fully automatic, close range.

ACCURACY · DAMAGE · RANGE · FIRE RATE

UNLOCKED — LEVEL 58

**PP2000**

**Description:** Fully automatic, close range.

ACCURACY · DAMAGE · RANGE · FIRE RATE

UNLOCKED — LEVEL 4

# SHOTGUNS/ SECONDARY WEAPON

Shotguns are your man-stoppers. They deal very heavy damage, but only at close range. Most are single shot with various actions, but one type is automatic. Various Attachments are available for shotguns, including a front grip.

## AVAILABLE ATTACHMENTS

| ATTACHMENT | | HOW TO UNLOCK |
|---|---|---|
| | Red Dot Sight | Complete Marksman I (10 kills) |
| | Silencer | Complete Marksman II (25 kills) |
| | Grip | Complete Marksman III (75 kills) |
| | FMJ | Complete Marksman IV (150 kills) |
| | Holographic Sight | Complete Marksman V (250 kills) |
| | Extended Mags | Complete Marksman VI (400 kills) |

### RANGER AND MODEL 1887 SHOTGUNS

| ATTACHMENT | | HOW TO UNLOCK |
|---|---|---|
| | Akimbo | Complete Marksman I (10 kills) |
| | FMJ | Complete Marksman II (50 kills) |

## NOTE

The Ranger and Model 1887 shotguns can only have Akimbo or FMJ as attachments.

### SHOTGUN QUICK-REFERENCE

| WEAPON | DESCRIPTION | UNLOCKED |
|---|---|---|
| Striker | Semi-automatic (single fire). | Level 34 |
| AA-12 | Fully automatic, low ammo. | Level 18 |
| Model 1887 | Lever action. | Level 67 |
| Ranger | Double barrel. | Level 42 |
| M1014 | Semi-automatic (single fire). | Level 54 |
| SPAS-12 | Pump action. | Level 4 |

### STRIKER

**Description:** Semi-automatic (single fire).

- ACCURACY
- DAMAGE
- RANGE
- FIRE RATE

UNLOCKED | LEVEL 34

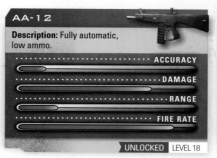

### AA-12

**Description:** Fully automatic, low ammo.

- ACCURACY
- DAMAGE
- RANGE
- FIRE RATE

UNLOCKED | LEVEL 18

### MODEL 1887

**Description:** Lever action.

- ACCURACY
- DAMAGE
- RANGE
- FIRE RATE

UNLOCKED | LEVEL 67

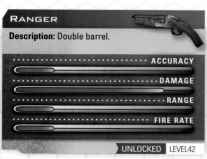

### RANGER

**Description:** Double barrel.

- ACCURACY
- DAMAGE
- RANGE
- FIRE RATE

UNLOCKED | LEVEL42

### M1014

**Description:** Semi-automatic (single fire).

- ACCURACY
- DAMAGE
- RANGE
- FIRE RATE

UNLOCKED | LEVEL 54

### SPAS-12

**Description:** Pump action.

- ACCURACY
- DAMAGE
- RANGE
- FIRE RATE

UNLOCKED | LEVEL 4

# HANDGUNS/SECONDARY WEAPON

Handguns are your backup weapon, featuring semi-automatic action and medium-distance accuracy. Some are very powerful and can inflict massive damage. They are quick to reload but have small magazines. Several Attachments are available for handguns, including the Tactical Knife, which allows you to stab enemies much more quickly than with a regular knife.

## AVAILABLE ATTACHMENTS

### M9 AND USP .45 HANDGUNS

| ATTACHMENT | | HOW TO UNLOCK |
|---|---|---|
| | FMJ | Complete Marksman I (10 kills) |
| | Silencer | Complete Marksman II (25 kills) |
| | Akimbo | Complete Marksman III (50 kills) |
| | Tactical Knife | Complete Marksman IV (100 kills) |
| | Extended Mags | Complete Marksman V (150 kills) |

### DESERT EAGLE AND .44 MAGNUM HANDGUNS

| ATTACHMENT | | HOW TO UNLOCK |
|---|---|---|
| | FMJ | Complete Marksman I (10 kills) |
| | Akimbo | Complete Marksman II (50 kills) |
| | Tactical Knife | Complete Marksman III (100 kills) |

## HANDGUN QUICK-REFERENCE

| WEAPON | DESCRIPTION | UNLOCKED |
|---|---|---|
| USP .45 | Semi-automatic (single fire). | Level 4 |
| .44 Magnum | Revolver. | Level 26 |
| Desert Eagle | Semi-automatic (single fire). | Level 62 |
| M9 | Semi-automatic (single fire). | Level 46 |

### NOTE

The .44 Magnum and Desert Eagle can only have the FMJ, Akimbo, and Tactical Knife as attachments.

### USP .45

**Description:** Semi-automatic (single fire).

- ACCURACY
- DAMAGE
- RANGE
- FIRE RATE

UNLOCKED | LEVEL 4

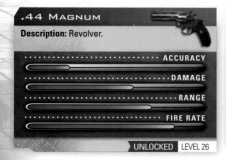

### .44 MAGNUM

**Description:** Revolver.

- ACCURACY
- DAMAGE
- RANGE
- FIRE RATE

UNLOCKED | LEVEL 26

### DESERT EAGLE

**Description:** Semi-automatic (single fire).

- ACCURACY
- DAMAGE
- RANGE
- FIRE RATE

UNLOCKED | LEVEL 62

### M9

**Description:** Semi-automatic (single fire).

- ACCURACY
- DAMAGE
- RANGE
- FIRE RATE

UNLOCKED | LEVEL 46

# LAUNCHERS/SECONDARY WEAPON

Launchers encompass both rockets and grenades, and some feature vehicle lock-on capability. They're great for picking off enemy air support vehicles or large numbers of enemies grouped together. You cannot add camouflage or Attachments to these weapons.

## AVAILABLE ATTACHMENTS

N/A

### LAUNCHER QUICK-REFERENCE

| WEAPON | DESCRIPTION | UNLOCKED |
|--------|-------------|----------|
| AT4-HS | Free fire or vehicle lock-on. | Level 4 |
| RPG-7 x2 | Fires unguided rockets. | Level 65 |
| Javelin | Location and vehicle lock-on. | Level 50 |
| Thumper x2 | Grenade Launcher. | Level 14 |
| Stinger | Vehicle lock-on only. | Level 30 |

**AT4-HS**

**Description:** Free fire or vehicle lock-on.

ACCURACY
DAMAGE
RANGE
FIRE RATE

UNLOCKED LEVEL 4

**RPG-7 x2**

**Description:** Fires unguided rockets.

ACCURACY
DAMAGE
RANGE
FIRE RATE

UNLOCKED LEVEL 65

**JAVELIN**

**Description:** Location and vehicle lock-on.

ACCURACY
DAMAGE
RANGE
FIRE RATE

UNLOCKED LEVEL 50

**THUMPER x2**

**Description:** Grenade launcher.

ACCURACY
DAMAGE
RANGE
FIRE RATE

UNLOCKED LEVEL 14

**STINGER**

**Description:** Vehicle lock-on only.

ACCURACY
DAMAGE
RANGE
FIRE RATE

UNLOCKED LEVEL 30

# WEAPON CAMO
### ASSAULT RIFLES, SNIPER RIFLES, SMGs

| CAMO TYPE | | HOW TO UNLOCK |
|-----------|--|---------------|
| | Desert | Unlocked by Default |
| | Arctic | Unlocked by Default |
| | Woodland | Complete Expert I (5 headshots) |

| CAMO TYPE | | HOW TO UNLOCK |
|-----------|--|---------------|
| | Digital | Complete Expert II (15 headshots) |
| | Urban | Complete Expert III (30 headshots) |
| | Blue Tiger | Complete Expert IV (75 headshots) |

| CAMO TYPE | | HOW TO UNLOCK |
|-----------|--|---------------|
| | Red Tiger | Complete Expert V (150 headshots) |
| | Fall | Complete Expert VI (250 headshots) |

# ATTACHMENTS

| ATTACHMENT | | DESCRIPTION |
|------------|--|-------------|
| Grenade Launcher | | Undermounted grenade launcher. |
| Red Dot Sight | | Precision sight. |
| Silencer | | Invisible on radar when firing. |
| ACOG Scope | | Enhanced zoom ACOG scope. |
| FMJ | | Increased bullet penetration. |
| Shotgun | | Undermounted shotgun attachment. |
| Holographic Sight | | Holographic sight. |

| ATTACHMENT | | DESCRIPTION |
|------------|--|-------------|
| Heartbeat Sensor | | Track enemy locations. |
| Thermal | | Enemies glow white hot. |
| Extended Mags | | Extended Magazines |
| Tactical Knife | | Faster melee attack. |
| Akimbo | | Hip fire two weapons. |
| Grip | | Vertical foregrip for reduced recoil. |
| Rapid Fire | | Increased rate of fire. |

# EQUIPMENT

| EQUIPMENT | | DESCRIPTION | UNLOCKED |
|---|---|---|---|
| Frag | | Cookable frag grenades. | Level 4 |
| Semtex | | Timed sticky explosives. | Level 4 |
| Throwing Knife | | Throw it and pick it back up. | Level 7 |
| Tactical Insertion | | Choose where to respawn. | Level 11 |

| EQUIPMENT | | DESCRIPTION | UNLOCKED |
|---|---|---|---|
| Blast Shield | | Increased explosive resistance. | Level 19 |
| Claymore | | Proximity activated explosive mine. | Level 31 |
| C4 | | Remote detonation explosive. | Level 43 |

# PERKS

## PERK SET 1

| PERK | | DESCRIPTION | PRO | UNLOCK | UNLOCK PRO |
|---|---|---|---|---|---|
| Marathon | | Unlimited Sprint. | Climb obstacles faster. | Level 4 | Run 26 miles using Marathon (Reward XP:5000) |
| Sleight of Hand | | Faster reloading. | Faster Aiming. | Level 4 | Get 120 killls using Sleight of Hand (Reward XP:5000) |
| Scavenger | | Resupply from dead enemies. | Extra mags. | Level 13 | Resupply 100 times while usig Scavenger (Reward XP:5000) |
| Bling | | 2 primary weapon attachments. | 2 secondary weapon attachments. | Level 21 | Get 200 kills using a weapon with 2 attachments (Reward XP:5000) |
| One Man Army | | Swap classes at any time. | Swap classes faster. | Level 45 | Get 120 kills using One Man Army (Reward XP:5000) |

## PERK SET 2

| PERK | | DESCRIPTION | PRO | UNLOCK | UNLOCK PRO |
|---|---|---|---|---|---|
| Stopping Power | | Increased bullet damage | Extra damage vs vehicles | Level 4 | Get 250 kills using Stopping Power (Reward XP:5000) |
| Lightweight | | Move faster | Quick aim after sprinting | Level 4 | Sprint 30 miles using Lightweight (Reward XP:5000) |
| Hardline | | Kill streaks require 1 less kill | Death streaks require 1 less death | Level 9 | Get 40 killstreaks while using Hardline (2 kills in a row) (Reward XP:5000) |
| Cold Blooded | | Undetectable by UAV, air support, sentries and thermal | No red crosshair or name when targeted | Level 25 | Destroy 40 enemy killstreak rewards using Cold Blooded (Reward XP:5000) |
| Danger Close | | Increased explosive weapon damage | Extra air support damage | Level 33 | Get 100 kills with explosives while using Danger Close (Reward XP:5000) |

## PERK SET 3

| PERK | | DESCRIPTION | PRO | UNLOCK | UNLOCK PRO |
|---|---|---|---|---|---|
| Commando | | Increased melee distance | No falling damage | Level 4 | Get 20 melee kills using Commando (Reward XP:5000) |
| Steady Aim | | Increased hip fire accuracy | Hold breath longer when scoped | Level 4 | Get 80 hipfire kills using Steady Aim (Reward XP:5000) |
| Scrambler | | Jam enemy radar near you | Delay enemy claymore explosions | Level 17 | Get 50 close range kills using Scrambler (Reward XP:5000) |
| Ninja | | Invisible to heartbeat sensors | Your footsteps are silent | Level 29 | Get 50 close range kills using Ninja (Reward XP:5000) |
| SitRep | | Detect enemy explosives and tactical insertions | Louder enemy footsteps | Level 37 | Destroy 120 enemy devices using SitRep (Reward XP:5000) |
| Last Stand | | Pull out your pistol before dying | Use equipment in last stand | Level 41 | Get 20 kills while in Last Stand (Reward XP:5000) |

# KILLSTREAK REWARDS

## UNLOCKING KILLSTREAK REWARDS

Killstreak Rewards can be unlocked in any order you choose. The UAV, Care Package, and Predator Killstreak Rewards are default. You earn one point when you reach each milestone rank, as follows: 10, 15, 23, 35, 47, 51, 56, 59, 63, 66, 68, 69.

| KILLSTREAK | | # OF KILLS | DESCRIPTION |
|---|---|---|---|
| UAV | | 3 | Shows enemies on the minimap. Provides an unmanned aerial vehicle sweep. |
| Care Package | | 4 | Airdrop a random killstreak or ammo. This calls in a chopper that drops your care package box. First player to get to it can use it regardless of which team they are on. |
| Counter UAV | | 4 | Temporarily disables enemy GPS. Provides UAV jamming of enemy radar for a short time. |
| Sentry Gun | | 5 | Airdrop a placeable Sentry Gun. A Chopper will drop a box containing the weapon. Walk up to it and pick it up, then you can place it where you like. |
| Predator | | 5 | Remote control missile. Your screen will change to an overhead view allowing you to control the missile. Your body remains on the ground, if you get killed, you can continue your missile attack. |
| Precision Airstrike | | 6 | Call in a directional airstrike. Brings up a map and lets you select the location and direction of the airstrike. |
| Harrier Strike | | 7 | Airstrike with a hovering Harrier. Calls in 2 Harriers, the first drops bombs on the location you select on the map, the second hovers and uses machine guns to defend the selected location. |
| Attack Helicopter | | 7 | Call in a support helicopter. Calls in an armed chopper that patrols the map eliminating enemies. |
| Emergency Airdrop | | 8 | Airdrop 4 random killstreaks or ammo. This calls in a large transport plane that drops 4 care packages of random killstreaks. First to get to them gets to use them regardless of what team you're on. |
| Pave Low | | 9 | Heavily armored assault helicopter. Calls in a heavily armored chopper that patrols the map eliminating enemies. The Pave Low has considerably more armor than the Attack Helicopter. |
| Stealth Bomber | | 9 | Airstrike unknown to the enemy. Calls in a precision airstrike that you can select location and direction, from a stealth bomber which carpet bombs the selected location. |
| Chopper Gunner | | 11 | Be the gunner of an attack helicopter. Calls in a support helicopter which changes your screen to the gunners view. Enemies show up with red boxes around them. Your body is on the ground and can be killed, but you can continue your session. |
| AC130 | | 11 | Be the gunner of an AC130. Calls in an AC130 plane which circles the map while you fire from 3 different types of guns. When it is over, you will return to where you called in this killstreak. You can be killed on the ground but you're able to continue the session. |
| EMP | | 15 | Temporarily disables enemy electronics. A flash of light appears and all enemy electronics do not work including radar minimap, heartbeat sensors, and some scopes. |
| Tactical Nuke | | 25 | End the game with a bang. Calls in a nuclear strike which kills all players on both teams. |

# DEATHSTREAKS

| DEATHSTREAK | | # OF DEATHS | DESCRIPTION | UNLOCKED |
|---|---|---|---|---|
| Copycat | | 4 | Steal your killer's class in a killcam (4 deaths without a kill) | Level 4 |
| Painkiller | | 3 | Big health boost when you spawn. (3 deaths without a kill) | Level 6 |
| Martyrdom | | 4 | Drop a live grenade just after dying. (4 deaths without a kill) | Level 27 |
| Final Stand | | 4 | Get back up after being wounded. (4 deaths without a kill) | Level 39 |

# RANKS

| RANK # | RANK NAME | ICON | XP REQUIRED |
|--------|-----------|------|-------------|
| 1 | Private 1 | | 0 |
| 2 | Private 2 | | 500 |
| 3 | Private 3 | | 1700 |
| 4 | Private First Class 1 | | 3600 |
| 5 | Private First Class 2 | | 6200 |
| 6 | Private First Class 3 | | 9500 |
| 7 | Specialist 1 | | 13500 |
| 8 | Specialist 2 | | 18200 |
| 9 | Specialist 3 | | 23600 |
| 10 | Corporal 1 | | 29700 |
| 11 | Corporal 2 | | 36500 |
| 12 | Corporal 3 | | 44300 |
| 13 | Sergeant 1 | | 53100 |
| 14 | Sergeant 2 | | 62900 |
| 15 | Sergeant 3 | | 73700 |
| 16 | Staff Sergeant 1 | | 85500 |
| 17 | Staff Sergeant 2 | | 98300 |
| 18 | Staff Sergeant 3 | | 112100 |
| 19 | Sergeant First Class 1 | | 126900 |
| 20 | Sergeant First Class 2 | | 142700 |
| 21 | Sergeant First Class 3 | | 159500 |
| 22 | Master Sergeant 1 | | 177300 |
| 23 | Master Sergeant 2 | | 196100 |
| 24 | Master Sergeant 3 | | 215900 |
| 25 | First Sergeant 1 | | 236700 |
| 26 | First Sergeant 2 | | 258500 |
| 27 | First Sergeant 3 | | 281300 |
| 28 | Sergeant Major 1 | | 305100 |
| 29 | Sergeant Major 2 | | 329900 |
| 30 | Sergeant Major 3 | | 355700 |
| 31 | Command Sergeant Major 1 | | 382700 |
| 32 | Command Sergeant Major 2 | | 410900 |
| 33 | Command Sergeant Major 3 | | 440300 |
| 34 | 2nd Lieutenant 1 | | 470900 |
| 35 | 2nd Lieutenant 2 | | 502700 |
| 36 | 2nd Lieutenant 3 | | 535700 |

| RANK # | RANK NAME | ICON | XP REQUIRED |
|--------|-----------|------|-------------|
| 37 | 1st Lieutenant 1 | | 569900 |
| 38 | 1st Lieutenant 2 | | 605300 |
| 39 | 1st Lieutenant 3 | | 641900 |
| 40 | Captain 1 | | 679700 |
| 41 | Captain 2 | | 718700 |
| 42 | Captain 3 | | 758900 |
| 43 | Major 1 | | 800300 |
| 44 | Major 2 | | 842900 |
| 45 | Major 3 | | 886700 |
| 46 | Lieutenant Colonel 1 | | 931700 |
| 47 | Lieutenant Colonel 2 | | 977900 |
| 48 | Lieutenant Colonel 3 | | 1025300 |
| 49 | Lieutenant Colonel 4 | | 1073900 |
| 50 | Colonel 1 | | 1123700 |
| 51 | Colonel 2 | | 1175000 |
| 52 | Colonel 3 | | 1227800 |
| 53 | Colonel 4 | | 1282100 |
| 54 | Brigadier General 1 | | 1337900 |
| 55 | Brigadier General 2 | | 1395200 |
| 56 | Brigadier General 3 | | 1454000 |
| 57 | Brigadier General 4 | | 1514300 |
| 58 | Major General 1 | | 1576100 |
| 59 | Major General 2 | | 1639400 |
| 60 | Major General 3 | | 1704200 |
| 61 | Major General 4 | | 1770500 |
| 62 | Lieutenant General 1 | | 1838300 |
| 63 | Lieutenant General 2 | | 1907600 |
| 64 | Lieutenant General 3 | | 1978400 |
| 65 | Lieutenant General 4 | | 2050700 |
| 66 | General 1 | | 2124500 |
| 67 | General 2 | | 2199800 |
| 68 | General 3 | | 2276600 |
| 69 | General 4 | | 2354900 |
| 70 | Commander | | 2434700 |

# PRESTIGE RANKS

| LEVEL | ICON |
|-------|------|
| 1 | |
| 2 | |
| 3 | |
| 4 | |
| 5 | |

| LEVEL | ICON |
|-------|------|
| 6 | |
| 7 | |
| 8 | |
| 9 | |
| 10 | |

# PRIMARY WEAPON CAMOUFLAGE

| TYPE | PATTERN |
|------|---------|
| Desert | |
| Arctic | |
| Woodland | |
| Digital | |

| TYPE | PATTERN |
|------|---------|
| Urban | |
| Blue Tiger | |
| Red Tiger | |
| Fall | |

# CHALLENGES

## INTERPRETING CHALLENGE DATA

Many of the challenges in the following tables have multiple tiers. For example, the MARKSMAN Weapon Challenges have 8 tiers. In the following tables, the "Target No." columns describe the criteria required to earn XP. Achieving a given Target Number yields the amount of XP listed directly to its right.

Consider the following example for the AK-47 Marksman Challenge:

- Target No. 10 kills with the AK-47 earns 250 XP
- Target No. 25 kills with the AK-47 earns 1000 XP
- Target No. 75 kills with the AK-47 earns 2000 XP
  ...and so on, following the "Target No." columns to the right for each successive tier.

## WEAPON CHALLENGES

| CHALLENGE DESCRIPTION | TITLE | TARGET No. 1 | XP 1 | TARGET No. 2 | XP 2 | TARGET No. 3 | XP 3 | TARGET No. 4 | XP 4 | TARGET No. 5 | XP 5 | TARGET No. 6 | XP 6 | TARGET No. 7 | XP 7 | TARGET No. 8 | XP 8 |
|---|---|---|---|---|---|---|---|---|---|---|---|---|---|---|---|---|---|
| **AK-47 CHALLENGES** | | | | | | | | | | | | | | | | | |
| Get Target No. Kills | Marksman | 10 | 250 | 25 | 1000 | 75 | 2000 | 150 | 5000 | 300 | 10000 | 500 | 10000 | 750 | 10000 | 1000 | 10000 |
| Get Target No. Headshots | Expert | 5 | 500 | 15 | 1000 | 30 | 2500 | 75 | 5000 | 150 | 10000 | 250 | 10000 | 350 | 10000 | 500 | 10000 |
| Get Target No. Kills GL | Attachment: GL | 20 | 750 | N/A | N/A | N/A | N/A | N/A | N/A | N/A | N/A | N/A | N/A | N/A | N/A | N/A | N/A |
| Get Target No. Kills Reflex | Attachment: Reflex | 60 | 1000 | N/A | N/A | N/A | N/A | N/A | N/A | N/A | N/A | N/A | N/A | N/A | N/A | N/A | N/A |
| Get Target No. Kills Silencer | Attachment: Silencer | 15 | 750 | N/A | N/A | N/A | N/A | N/A | N/A | N/A | N/A | N/A | N/A | N/A | N/A | N/A | N/A |
| Get Target No. Kills ACOG | Attachment: ACOG | 20 | 750 | N/A | N/A | N/A | N/A | N/A | N/A | N/A | N/A | N/A | N/A | N/A | N/A | N/A | N/A |
| Get Target No. Kills FMJ | Attachment: FMJ | 40 | 1000 | N/A | N/A | N/A | N/A | N/A | N/A | N/A | N/A | N/A | N/A | N/A | N/A | N/A | N/A |
| Get All Attachments | Mastery | 10 | 10000 | N/A | N/A | N/A | N/A | N/A | N/A | N/A | N/A | N/A | N/A | N/A | N/A | N/A | N/A |
| **FN FAL CHALLENGES** | | | | | | | | | | | | | | | | | |
| Get Target No. Kills | Marksman | 10 | 250 | 25 | 1000 | 75 | 2000 | 150 | 5000 | 300 | 10000 | 500 | 10000 | 750 | 10000 | 1000 | 10000 |
| Get Target No. Headshots | Expert | 5 | 500 | 15 | 1000 | 30 | 2500 | 75 | 5000 | 150 | 10000 | 250 | 10000 | 350 | 10000 | 500 | 10000 |
| Get Target No.Kills GL | Attachment: GL | 20 | 750 | N/A | N/A | N/A | N/A | N/A | N/A | N/A | N/A | N/A | N/A | N/A | N/A | N/A | N/A |
| Get Target No. Kills Reflex | Attachment: Reflex | 60 | 1000 | N/A | N/A | N/A | N/A | N/A | N/A | N/A | N/A | N/A | N/A | N/A | N/A | N/A | N/A |
| Get Target No. Kills Silencer | Attachment: Silencer | 15 | 750 | N/A | N/A | N/A | N/A | N/A | N/A | N/A | N/A | N/A | N/A | N/A | N/A | N/A | N/A |
| Get Target No. Kills ACOG | Attachment: ACOG | 20 | 750 | N/A | N/A | N/A | N/A | N/A | N/A | N/A | N/A | N/A | N/A | N/A | N/A | N/A | N/A |
| Get Target No. Kills FMJ | Attachment: FMJ | 40 | 1000 | N/A | N/A | N/A | N/A | N/A | N/A | N/A | N/A | N/A | N/A | N/A | N/A | N/A | N/A |
| Get All Attachments | Mastery | 10 | 10000 | N/A | N/A | N/A | N/A | N/A | N/A | N/A | N/A | N/A | N/A | N/A | N/A | N/A | N/A |
| **FAMAS CHALLENGES** | | | | | | | | | | | | | | | | | |
| Get Target No. Kills | Marksman | 10 | 250 | 25 | 1000 | 75 | 2000 | 150 | 5000 | 300 | 10000 | 500 | 10000 | 750 | 10000 | 1000 | 10000 |
| Get Target No. Headshots | Expert | 5 | 500 | 15 | 1000 | 30 | 2500 | 75 | 5000 | 150 | 10000 | 250 | 10000 | 350 | 10000 | 500 | 10000 |
| Get Target No. Kills GL | Attachment: GL | 20 | 750 | N/A | N/A | N/A | N/A | N/A | N/A | N/A | N/A | N/A | N/A | N/A | N/A | N/A | N/A |
| Get Target No. Kills Reflex | Attachment: Reflex | 60 | 1000 | N/A | N/A | N/A | N/A | N/A | N/A | N/A | N/A | N/A | N/A | N/A | N/A | N/A | N/A |
| Get Target No. Kills Silencer | Attachment: Silencer | 15 | 750 | N/A | N/A | N/A | N/A | N/A | N/A | N/A | N/A | N/A | N/A | N/A | N/A | N/A | N/A |
| Get Target No. Kills ACOG | Attachment: ACOG | 20 | 750 | N/A | N/A | N/A | N/A | N/A | N/A | N/A | N/A | N/A | N/A | N/A | N/A | N/A | N/A |
| Get Target No. Kills FMJ | Attachment: FMJ | 40 | 1000 | N/A | N/A | N/A | N/A | N/A | N/A | N/A | N/A | N/A | N/A | N/A | N/A | N/A | N/A |
| Get All Attachments | Mastery | 10 | 10000 | N/A | N/A | N/A | N/A | N/A | N/A | N/A | N/A | N/A | N/A | N/A | N/A | N/A | N/A |

## WEAPON CHALLENGES CONT.

| CHALLENGE DESCRIPTION | TITLE | TARGET No. 1 | XP 1 | TARGET No. 2 | XP 2 | TARGET No. 3 | XP 3 | TARGET No. 4 | XP 4 | TARGET No. 5 | XP 5 | TARGET No. 6 | XP 6 | TARGET No. 7 | XP 7 | TARGET No. 8 | XP 8 |
|---|---|---|---|---|---|---|---|---|---|---|---|---|---|---|---|---|---|
| **F2000 CHALLENGES** | | | | | | | | | | | | | | | | | |
| Get Target No. Kills | Marksman | 10 | 250 | 25 | 1000 | 75 | 2000 | 150 | 5000 | 300 | 10000 | 500 | 10000 | 750 | 10000 | 1000 | 10000 |
| Get Target No. Headshots | Expert | 5 | 500 | 15 | 1000 | 30 | 2500 | 75 | 5000 | 150 | 10000 | 250 | 10000 | 350 | 10000 | 500 | 10000 |
| Get Target No. Kills GL | Attachment: GL | 20 | 750 | N/A | N/A | N/A | N/A | N/A | N/A | N/A | N/A | N/A | N/A | N/A | N/A | N/A | N/A |
| Get Target No. Kills Reflex | Attachment: Reflex | 60 | 1000 | N/A | N/A | N/A | N/A | N/A | N/A | N/A | N/A | N/A | N/A | N/A | N/A | N/A | N/A |
| Get Target No. Kills Silencer | Attachment: Silencer | 15 | 750 | N/A | N/A | N/A | N/A | N/A | N/A | N/A | N/A | N/A | N/A | N/A | N/A | N/A | N/A |
| Get Target No. Kills ACOG | Attachment: ACOG | 20 | 750 | N/A | N/A | N/A | N/A | N/A | N/A | N/A | N/A | N/A | N/A | N/A | N/A | N/A | N/A |
| Get Target No. Kills FMJ | Attachment: FMJ | 40 | 1000 | N/A | N/A | N/A | N/A | N/A | N/A | N/A | N/A | N/A | N/A | N/A | N/A | N/A | N/A |
| Get All Attachments | Mastery | 10 | 10000 | N/A | N/A | N/A | N/A | N/A | N/A | N/A | N/A | N/A | N/A | N/A | N/A | N/A | N/A |
| **M4A1 CHALLENGES** | | | | | | | | | | | | | | | | | |
| Get Target No. Kills | Marksman | 10 | 250 | 25 | 1000 | 75 | 2000 | 150 | 5000 | 300 | 10000 | 500 | 10000 | 750 | 10000 | 1000 | 10000 |
| Get Target No. Headshots | Expert | 5 | 500 | 15 | 1000 | 30 | 2500 | 75 | 5000 | 150 | 10000 | 250 | 10000 | 350 | 10000 | 500 | 10000 |
| Get Target No. Kills GL | Attachment: GL | 20 | 750 | N/A | N/A | N/A | N/A | N/A | N/A | N/A | N/A | N/A | N/A | N/A | N/A | N/A | N/A |
| Get Target No. Kills Reflex | Attachment: Reflex | 60 | 1000 | N/A | N/A | N/A | N/A | N/A | N/A | N/A | N/A | N/A | N/A | N/A | N/A | N/A | N/A |
| Get Target No. Kills Silencer | Attachment: Silencer | 15 | 750 | N/A | N/A | N/A | N/A | N/A | N/A | N/A | N/A | N/A | N/A | N/A | N/A | N/A | N/A |
| Get Target No. Kills ACOG | Attachment: ACOG | 20 | 750 | N/A | N/A | N/A | N/A | N/A | N/A | N/A | N/A | N/A | N/A | N/A | N/A | N/A | N/A |
| Get Target No. Kills FMJ | Attachment: FMJ | 40 | 1000 | N/A | N/A | N/A | N/A | N/A | N/A | N/A | N/A | N/A | N/A | N/A | N/A | N/A | N/A |
| Get All Attachments | Mastery | 10 | 10000 | N/A | N/A | N/A | N/A | N/A | N/A | N/A | N/A | N/A | N/A | N/A | N/A | N/A | N/A |
| **M16A4 CHALLENGES** | | | | | | | | | | | | | | | | | |
| Get Target No. Kills | Marksman | 10 | 250 | 25 | 1000 | 75 | 2000 | 150 | 5000 | 300 | 10000 | 500 | 10000 | 750 | 10000 | 1000 | 10000 |
| Get Target No. Headshots | Expert | 5 | 500 | 15 | 1000 | 30 | 2500 | 75 | 5000 | 150 | 10000 | 250 | 10000 | 350 | 10000 | 500 | 10000 |
| Get Target No. Kills GL | Attachment: GL | 20 | 750 | N/A | N/A | N/A | N/A | N/A | N/A | N/A | N/A | N/A | N/A | N/A | N/A | N/A | N/A |
| Get Target No. Kills Reflex | Attachment: Reflex | 60 | 1000 | N/A | N/A | N/A | N/A | N/A | N/A | N/A | N/A | N/A | N/A | N/A | N/A | N/A | N/A |
| Get Target No. Kills Silencer | Attachment: Silencer | 15 | 750 | N/A | N/A | N/A | N/A | N/A | N/A | N/A | N/A | N/A | N/A | N/A | N/A | N/A | N/A |
| Get Target No. Kills ACOG | Attachment: ACOG | 20 | 750 | N/A | N/A | N/A | N/A | N/A | N/A | N/A | N/A | N/A | N/A | N/A | N/A | N/A | N/A |
| Get Target No. Kills FMJ | Attachment: FMJ | 40 | 1000 | N/A | N/A | N/A | N/A | N/A | N/A | N/A | N/A | N/A | N/A | N/A | N/A | N/A | N/A |
| Get All Attachments | Mastery | 10 | 10000 | N/A | N/A | N/A | N/A | N/A | N/A | N/A | N/A | N/A | N/A | N/A | N/A | N/A | N/A |
| **ACR CHALLENGES** | | | | | | | | | | | | | | | | | |
| Get Target No. Kills | Marksman | 10 | 250 | 25 | 1000 | 75 | 2000 | 150 | 5000 | 300 | 10000 | 500 | 10000 | 750 | 10000 | 1000 | 10000 |
| Get Target No. Headshots | Expert | 5 | 500 | 15 | 1000 | 30 | 2500 | 75 | 5000 | 150 | 10000 | 250 | 10000 | 350 | 10000 | 500 | 10000 |
| Get Target No. Kills GL | Attachment: GL | 20 | 750 | N/A | N/A | N/A | N/A | N/A | N/A | N/A | N/A | N/A | N/A | N/A | N/A | N/A | N/A |
| Get Target No. Kills Reflex | Attachment: Reflex | 60 | 1000 | N/A | N/A | N/A | N/A | N/A | N/A | N/A | N/A | N/A | N/A | N/A | N/A | N/A | N/A |
| Get Target No. Kills Silencer | Attachment: Silencer | 15 | 750 | N/A | N/A | N/A | N/A | N/A | N/A | N/A | N/A | N/A | N/A | N/A | N/A | N/A | N/A |
| Get Target No. Kills ACOG | Attachment: ACOG | 20 | 750 | N/A | N/A | N/A | N/A | N/A | N/A | N/A | N/A | N/A | N/A | N/A | N/A | N/A | N/A |
| Get Target No. Kills FMJ | Attachment: FMJ | 40 | 1000 | N/A | N/A | N/A | N/A | N/A | N/A | N/A | N/A | N/A | N/A | N/A | N/A | N/A | N/A |
| Get All Attachments | Mastery | 10 | 10000 | N/A | N/A | N/A | N/A | N/A | N/A | N/A | N/A | N/A | N/A | N/A | N/A | N/A | N/A |

| CHALLENGE DESCRIPTION | TITLE | TARGET No. 1 | XP 1 | TARGET No. 2 | XP 2 | TARGET No. 3 | XP 3 | TARGET No. 4 | XP 4 | TARGET No. 5 | XP 5 | TARGET No. 6 | XP 6 | TARGET No. 7 | XP 7 | TARGET No. 8 | XP 8 |
|---|---|---|---|---|---|---|---|---|---|---|---|---|---|---|---|---|---|
| **SCAR-H CHALLENGES** | | | | | | | | | | | | | | | | | |
| Get Target No. Kills | Marksman | 10 | 250 | 25 | 1000 | 75 | 2000 | 150 | 5000 | 300 | 10000 | 500 | 10000 | 750 | 10000 | 1000 | 10000 |
| Get Target No. Headshots | Expert | 5 | 500 | 15 | 1000 | 30 | 2500 | 75 | 5000 | 150 | 10000 | 250 | 10000 | 350 | 10000 | 500 | 10000 |
| Get Target No. Kills GL | Attachment: GL | 20 | 750 | N/A | N/A | N/A | N/A | N/A | N/A | N/A | N/A | N/A | N/A | N/A | N/A | N/A | N/A |
| Get Target No. Kills Reflex | Attachment: Reflex | 60 | 1000 | N/A | N/A | N/A | N/A | N/A | N/A | N/A | N/A | N/A | N/A | N/A | N/A | N/A | N/A |
| Get Target No. Kills Silencer | Attachment: Silencer | 15 | 750 | N/A | N/A | N/A | N/A | N/A | N/A | N/A | N/A | N/A | N/A | N/A | N/A | N/A | N/A |
| Get Target No. Kills ACOG | Attachment: ACOG | 20 | 750 | N/A | N/A | N/A | N/A | N/A | N/A | N/A | N/A | N/A | N/A | N/A | N/A | N/A | N/A |
| Get Target No. Kills FMJ | Attachment: FMJ | 40 | 1000 | N/A | N/A | N/A | N/A | N/A | N/A | N/A | N/A | N/A | N/A | N/A | N/A | N/A | N/A |
| Get All Attachments | Mastery | 10 | 10000 | N/A | N/A | N/A | N/A | N/A | N/A | N/A | N/A | N/A | N/A | N/A | N/A | N/A | N/A |
| **TAR-21 CHALLENGES** | | | | | | | | | | | | | | | | | |
| Get Target No. Kills | Marksman | 10 | 250 | 25 | 1000 | 75 | 2000 | 150 | 5000 | 300 | 10000 | 500 | 10000 | 750 | 10000 | 1000 | 10000 |
| Get Target No. Headshots | Expert | 5 | 500 | 15 | 1000 | 30 | 2500 | 75 | 5000 | 150 | 10000 | 250 | 10000 | 350 | 10000 | 500 | 10000 |
| Get Target No. Kills GL | Attachment: GL | 20 | 750 | N/A | N/A | N/A | N/A | N/A | N/A | N/A | N/A | N/A | N/A | N/A | N/A | N/A | N/A |
| Get Target No. Kills Reflex | Attachment: Reflex | 60 | 1000 | N/A | N/A | N/A | N/A | N/A | N/A | N/A | N/A | N/A | N/A | N/A | N/A | N/A | N/A |
| Get Target No. Kills Silencer | Attachment: Silencer | 15 | 750 | N/A | N/A | N/A | N/A | N/A | N/A | N/A | N/A | N/A | N/A | N/A | N/A | N/A | N/A |
| Get Target No. Kills ACOG | Attachment: ACOG | 20 | 750 | N/A | N/A | N/A | N/A | N/A | N/A | N/A | N/A | N/A | N/A | N/A | N/A | N/A | N/A |
| Get Target No. Kills FMJ | Attachment: FMJ | 40 | 1000 | N/A | N/A | N/A | N/A | N/A | N/A | N/A | N/A | N/A | N/A | N/A | N/A | N/A | N/A |
| Get All Attachments | Mastery | 10 | 10000 | N/A | N/A | N/A | N/A | N/A | N/A | N/A | N/A | N/A | N/A | N/A | N/A | N/A | N/A |
| **MP5K CHALLENGES** | | | | | | | | | | | | | | | | | |
| Get Target No. Kills | Marksman | 10 | 500 | 25 | 1000 | 75 | 2000 | 150 | 5000 | 300 | 10000 | 500 | 10000 | 750 | 10000 | 1000 | 10000 |
| Get Target No. Headshots | Expert | 5 | 500 | 15 | 1000 | 30 | 2500 | 75 | 5000 | 150 | 10000 | 250 | 10000 | 350 | 10000 | 500 | 10000 |
| Get Target No. Kills Rapidfire | Attachment: Rapidfire | 30 | 1000 | N/A | N/A | N/A | N/A | N/A | N/A | N/A | N/A | N/A | N/A | N/A | N/A | N/A | N/A |
| Get Target No. Kills Reflex | Attachment: Reflex | 60 | 1000 | N/A | N/A | N/A | N/A | N/A | N/A | N/A | N/A | N/A | N/A | N/A | N/A | N/A | N/A |
| Get Target No. Kills ACOG | Attachment: ACOG | 20 | 750 | N/A | N/A | N/A | N/A | N/A | N/A | N/A | N/A | N/A | N/A | N/A | N/A | N/A | N/A |
| Get Target No. Kills FMJ | Attachment: FMJ | 40 | 1000 | N/A | N/A | N/A | N/A | N/A | N/A | N/A | N/A | N/A | N/A | N/A | N/A | N/A | N/A |
| Get All Attachments | Mastery | 9 | 10000 | N/A | N/A | N/A | N/A | N/A | N/A | N/A | N/A | N/A | N/A | N/A | N/A | N/A | N/A |
| **MINI-UZI CHALLENGES** | | | | | | | | | | | | | | | | | |
| Get Target No. Kills | Marksman | 10 | 500 | 25 | 1000 | 75 | 2000 | 150 | 5000 | 300 | 10000 | 500 | 10000 | 750 | 10000 | 1000 | 10000 |
| Get Target No. Headshots | Expert | 5 | 500 | 15 | 1000 | 30 | 2500 | 75 | 5000 | 150 | 10000 | 250 | 10000 | 350 | 10000 | 500 | 10000 |
| Get Target No. Kills Rapidfire | Attachment: Rapidfire | 30 | 1000 | N/A | N/A | N/A | N/A | N/A | N/A | N/A | N/A | N/A | N/A | N/A | N/A | N/A | N/A |
| Get Target No. Kills Reflex | Attachment: Reflex | 60 | 1000 | N/A | N/A | N/A | N/A | N/A | N/A | N/A | N/A | N/A | N/A | N/A | N/A | N/A | N/A |
| Get Target No. Kills ACOG | Attachment: ACOG | 20 | 750 | N/A | N/A | N/A | N/A | N/A | N/A | N/A | N/A | N/A | N/A | N/A | N/A | N/A | N/A |
| Get Target No. Kills FMJ | Attachment: FMJ | 40 | 1000 | N/A | N/A | N/A | N/A | N/A | N/A | N/A | N/A | N/A | N/A | N/A | N/A | N/A | N/A |
| Get All Attachments | Mastery | 9 | 10000 | N/A | N/A | N/A | N/A | N/A | N/A | N/A | N/A | N/A | N/A | N/A | N/A | N/A | N/A |
| **VECTOR CHALLENGES** | | | | | | | | | | | | | | | | | |
| Get Target No. Kills | Marksman | 10 | 500 | 25 | 1000 | 75 | 2000 | 150 | 5000 | 300 | 10000 | 500 | 10000 | 750 | 10000 | 1000 | 10000 |
| Get Target No. Headshots | Expert | 5 | 500 | 15 | 1000 | 30 | 2500 | 75 | 5000 | 150 | 10000 | 250 | 10000 | 350 | 10000 | 500 | 10000 |
| Get Target No. Kills Rapidfire | Attachment: Rapidfire | 30 | 1000 | N/A | N/A | N/A | N/A | N/A | N/A | N/A | N/A | N/A | N/A | N/A | N/A | N/A | N/A |

## WEAPON CHALLENGES CONT.

| CHALLENGE DESCRIPTION | TITLE | TARGET No. 1 | XP 1 | TARGET No. 2 | XP 2 | TARGET No. 3 | XP 3 | TARGET No. 4 | XP 4 | TARGET No. 5 | XP 5 | TARGET No. 6 | XP 6 | TARGET No. 7 | XP 7 | TARGET No. 8 | XP 8 |
|---|---|---|---|---|---|---|---|---|---|---|---|---|---|---|---|---|---|
| Get Target No. Kills Reflex | Attachment: Reflex | 60 | 1000 | N/A | N/A | N/A | N/A | N/A | N/A | N/A | N/A | N/A | N/A | N/A | N/A | N/A | N/A |
| Get Target No. Kills ACOG | Attachment: ACOG | 20 | 750 | N/A | N/A | N/A | N/A | N/A | N/A | N/A | N/A | N/A | N/A | N/A | N/A | N/A | N/A |
| Get Target No. Kills FMJ | Attachment: FMJ | 40 | 1000 | N/A | N/A | N/A | N/A | N/A | N/A | N/A | N/A | N/A | N/A | N/A | N/A | N/A | N/A |
| Get All Attachments | Mastery | 9 | 10000 | N/A | N/A | N/A | N/A | N/A | N/A | N/A | N/A | N/A | N/A | N/A | N/A | N/A | N/A |
| **UMP45 CHALLENGES** | | | | | | | | | | | | | | | | | |
| Get Target No. Kills | Marksman | 10 | 500 | 25 | 1000 | 75 | 2000 | 150 | 5000 | 300 | 10000 | 500 | 10000 | 750 | 10000 | 1000 | 10000 |
| Get Target No. Headshots | Expert | 5 | 500 | 15 | 1000 | 30 | 2500 | 75 | 5000 | 150 | 10000 | 250 | 10000 | 350 | 10000 | 500 | 10000 |
| Get Target No. Kills Rapidfire | Attachment: Rapidfire | 30 | 1000 | N/A | N/A | N/A | N/A | N/A | N/A | N/A | N/A | N/A | N/A | N/A | N/A | N/A | N/A |
| Get Target No. Kills Reflex | Attachment: Reflex | 60 | 1000 | N/A | N/A | N/A | N/A | N/A | N/A | N/A | N/A | N/A | N/A | N/A | N/A | N/A | N/A |
| Get Target No. Kills ACOG | Attachment: ACOG | 20 | 750 | N/A | N/A | N/A | N/A | N/A | N/A | N/A | N/A | N/A | N/A | N/A | N/A | N/A | N/A |
| Get Target No. Kills FMJ | Attachment: FMJ | 40 | 1000 | N/A | N/A | N/A | N/A | N/A | N/A | N/A | N/A | N/A | N/A | N/A | N/A | N/A | N/A |
| Get All Attachments | Mastery | 9 | 10000 | N/A | N/A | N/A | N/A | N/A | N/A | N/A | N/A | N/A | N/A | N/A | N/A | N/A | N/A |
| **P90 CHALLENGES** | | | | | | | | | | | | | | | | | |
| Get Target No. Kills | Marksman | 10 | 500 | 25 | 1000 | 75 | 2000 | 150 | 5000 | 300 | 10000 | 500 | 10000 | 750 | 10000 | 1000 | 10000 |
| Get Target No. Headshots | Expert | 5 | 500 | 15 | 1000 | 30 | 2500 | 75 | 5000 | 150 | 10000 | 250 | 10000 | 350 | 10000 | 500 | 10000 |
| Get Target No. Kills Rapidfire | Attachment: Rapidfire | 30 | 1000 | N/A | N/A | N/A | N/A | N/A | N/A | N/A | N/A | N/A | N/A | N/A | N/A | N/A | N/A |
| Get Target No. Kills Reflex | Attachment: Reflex | 60 | 1000 | N/A | N/A | N/A | N/A | N/A | N/A | N/A | N/A | N/A | N/A | N/A | N/A | N/A | N/A |
| Get Target No. Kills ACOG | Attachment: ACOG | 20 | 750 | N/A | N/A | N/A | N/A | N/A | N/A | N/A | N/A | N/A | N/A | N/A | N/A | N/A | N/A |
| Get Target No. Kills FMJ | Attachment: FMJ | 40 | 1000 | N/A | N/A | N/A | N/A | N/A | N/A | N/A | N/A | N/A | N/A | N/A | N/A | N/A | N/A |
| Get All Attachments | Mastery | 9 | 10000 | N/A | N/A | N/A | N/A | N/A | N/A | N/A | N/A | N/A | N/A | N/A | N/A | N/A | N/A |
| **M240 CHALLENGES** | | | | | | | | | | | | | | | | | |
| Get Target No. Kills | Marksman | 10 | 500 | 25 | 1000 | 75 | 2000 | 150 | 5000 | 300 | 10000 | 500 | 10000 | 750 | 10000 | 1000 | 10000 |
| Get Target No. Headshots | Expert | 5 | 500 | 15 | 1000 | 30 | 2500 | 75 | 5000 | 150 | 10000 | 250 | 10000 | 350 | 10000 | 500 | 10000 |
| Get Target No. Kills Silencer | Attachment: Silencer | 15 | 750 | N/A | N/A | N/A | N/A | N/A | N/A | N/A | N/A | N/A | N/A | N/A | N/A | N/A | N/A |
| Get Target No. Kills Reflex | Attachment: Reflex | 60 | 1000 | N/A | N/A | N/A | N/A | N/A | N/A | N/A | N/A | N/A | N/A | N/A | N/A | N/A | N/A |
| Get Target No. Kills ACOG | Attachment: ACOG | 20 | 750 | N/A | N/A | N/A | N/A | N/A | N/A | N/A | N/A | N/A | N/A | N/A | N/A | N/A | N/A |
| Get Target No. Kills FMJ | Attachment: FMJ | 40 | 1000 | N/A | N/A | N/A | N/A | N/A | N/A | N/A | N/A | N/A | N/A | N/A | N/A | N/A | N/A |
| Get All Attachments | Mastery | 9 | 10000 | N/A | N/A | N/A | N/A | N/A | N/A | N/A | N/A | N/A | N/A | N/A | N/A | N/A | N/A |
| **AUG HBAR CHALLENGES** | | | | | | | | | | | | | | | | | |
| Get Target No. Kills | Marksman | 10 | 500 | 25 | 1000 | 75 | 2000 | 150 | 5000 | 300 | 10000 | 500 | 10000 | 750 | 10000 | 1000 | 10000 |
| Get Target No. Headshots | Expert | 5 | 500 | 15 | 1000 | 30 | 2500 | 75 | 5000 | 150 | 10000 | 250 | 10000 | 350 | 10000 | 500 | 10000 |
| Get Target No. Kills Silencer | Attachment: Silencer | 15 | 750 | N/A | N/A | N/A | N/A | N/A | N/A | N/A | N/A | N/A | N/A | N/A | N/A | N/A | N/A |
| Get Target No. Kills Reflex | Attachment: Reflex | 60 | 1000 | N/A | N/A | N/A | N/A | N/A | N/A | N/A | N/A | N/A | N/A | N/A | N/A | N/A | N/A |
| Get Target No. Kills ACOG | Attachment: ACOG | 20 | 750 | N/A | N/A | N/A | N/A | N/A | N/A | N/A | N/A | N/A | N/A | N/A | N/A | N/A | N/A |
| Get Target No. Kills FMJ | Attachment: FMJ | 40 | 1000 | N/A | N/A | N/A | N/A | N/A | N/A | N/A | N/A | N/A | N/A | N/A | N/A | N/A | N/A |
| Get All Attachments | Mastery | 9 | 10000 | N/A | N/A | N/A | N/A | N/A | N/A | N/A | N/A | N/A | N/A | N/A | N/A | N/A | N/A |

| CHALLENGE DESCRIPTION | TITLE | TARGET No. 1 | XP 1 | TARGET No. 2 | XP 2 | TARGET No. 3 | XP 3 | TARGET No. 4 | XP 4 | TARGET No. 5 | XP 5 | TARGET No. 6 | XP 6 | TARGET No. 7 | XP 7 | TARGET No. 8 | XP 8 |
|---|---|---|---|---|---|---|---|---|---|---|---|---|---|---|---|---|---|
| **L86 LSW CHALLENGES** | | | | | | | | | | | | | | | | | |
| Get Target No. Kills | Marksman | 10 | 500 | 25 | 1000 | 75 | 2000 | 150 | 5000 | 300 | 10000 | 500 | 10000 | 750 | 10000 | 1000 | 10000 |
| Get Target No. Headshots | Expert | 5 | 500 | 15 | 1000 | 30 | 2500 | 75 | 5000 | 150 | 10000 | 250 | 10000 | 350 | 10000 | 500 | 10000 |
| Get Target No. Kills Silencer | Attachment: Silencer | 15 | 750 | N/A | N/A | N/A | N/A | N/A | N/A | N/A | N/A | N/A | N/A | N/A | N/A | N/A | N/A |
| Get Target No. Kills Reflex | Attachment: Reflex | 60 | 1000 | N/A | N/A | N/A | N/A | N/A | N/A | N/A | N/A | N/A | N/A | N/A | N/A | N/A | N/A |
| Get Target No. Kills ACOG | Attachment: ACOG | 20 | 750 | N/A | N/A | N/A | N/A | N/A | N/A | N/A | N/A | N/A | N/A | N/A | N/A | N/A | N/A |
| Get Target No. Kills FMJ | Attachment: FMJ | 40 | 1000 | N/A | N/A | N/A | N/A | N/A | N/A | N/A | N/A | N/A | N/A | N/A | N/A | N/A | N/A |
| Get All Attachments | Mastery | 9 | 10000 | N/A | N/A | N/A | N/A | N/A | N/A | N/A | N/A | N/A | N/A | N/A | N/A | N/A | N/A |
| **RPD CHALLENGES** | | | | | | | | | | | | | | | | | |
| Get Target No. Kills | Marksman | 10 | 500 | 25 | 1000 | 75 | 2000 | 150 | 5000 | 300 | 10000 | 500 | 10000 | 750 | 10000 | 1000 | 10000 |
| Get Target No. Headshots | Expert | 5 | 500 | 15 | 1000 | 30 | 2500 | 75 | 5000 | 150 | 10000 | 250 | 10000 | 350 | 10000 | 500 | 10000 |
| Get Target No. Kills Silencer | Attachment: Silencer | 15 | 750 | N/A | N/A | N/A | N/A | N/A | N/A | N/A | N/A | N/A | N/A | N/A | N/A | N/A | N/A |
| Get Target No. Kills Reflex | Attachment: Reflex | 60 | 1000 | N/A | N/A | N/A | N/A | N/A | N/A | N/A | N/A | N/A | N/A | N/A | N/A | N/A | N/A |
| Get Target No. Kills ACOG | Attachment: ACOG | 20 | 750 | N/A | N/A | N/A | N/A | N/A | N/A | N/A | N/A | N/A | N/A | N/A | N/A | N/A | N/A |
| Get Target No. Kills FMJ | Attachment: FMJ | 40 | 1000 | N/A | N/A | N/A | N/A | N/A | N/A | N/A | N/A | N/A | N/A | N/A | N/A | N/A | N/A |
| Get All Attachments | Mastery | 9 | 10000 | N/A | N/A | N/A | N/A | N/A | N/A | N/A | N/A | N/A | N/A | N/A | N/A | N/A | N/A |
| **MG4 CHALLENGES** | | | | | | | | | | | | | | | | | |
| Get Target No. Kills | Marksman | 10 | 500 | 25 | 1000 | 75 | 2000 | 150 | 5000 | 300 | 10000 | 500 | 10000 | 750 | 10000 | 1000 | 10000 |
| Get Target No. Headshots | Expert | 5 | 500 | 15 | 1000 | 30 | 2500 | 75 | 5000 | 150 | 10000 | 250 | 10000 | 350 | 10000 | 500 | 10000 |
| Get Target No. Kills Silencer | Attachment: Silencer | 15 | 750 | N/A | N/A | N/A | N/A | N/A | N/A | N/A | N/A | N/A | N/A | N/A | N/A | N/A | N/A |
| Get Target No. Kills Reflex | Attachment: Reflex | 60 | 1000 | N/A | N/A | N/A | N/A | N/A | N/A | N/A | N/A | N/A | N/A | N/A | N/A | N/A | N/A |
| Get Target No. Kills ACOG | Attachment: ACOG | 20 | 750 | N/A | N/A | N/A | N/A | N/A | N/A | N/A | N/A | N/A | N/A | N/A | N/A | N/A | N/A |
| Get Target No. Kills FMJ | Attachment: FMJ | 40 | 1000 | N/A | N/A | N/A | N/A | N/A | N/A | N/A | N/A | N/A | N/A | N/A | N/A | N/A | N/A |
| Get All Attachments | Mastery | 9 | 10000 | N/A | N/A | N/A | N/A | N/A | N/A | N/A | N/A | N/A | N/A | N/A | N/A | N/A | N/A |
| **INTERVENTION CHALLENGES** | | | | | | | | | | | | | | | | | |
| Get Target No. Kills | Marksman | 10 | 250 | 25 | 1000 | 75 | 2000 | 150 | 5000 | 300 | 10000 | 500 | 10000 | 750 | 10000 | 1000 | 10000 |
| Get Target No. Headshots | Expert | 5 | 500 | 15 | 1000 | 30 | 2500 | 75 | 5000 | 150 | 10000 | 250 | 10000 | 350 | 10000 | 500 | 10000 |
| Get Target No. Kills Silencer | Attachment: Silencer | 15 | 750 | N/A | N/A | N/A | N/A | N/A | N/A | N/A | N/A | N/A | N/A | N/A | N/A | N/A | N/A |
| Get Target No. Kills ACOG | Attachment: ACOG | 20 | 750 | N/A | N/A | N/A | N/A | N/A | N/A | N/A | N/A | N/A | N/A | N/A | N/A | N/A | N/A |
| Get Target No. Kills FMJ | Attachment: FMJ | 40 | 1000 | N/A | N/A | N/A | N/A | N/A | N/A | N/A | N/A | N/A | N/A | N/A | N/A | N/A | N/A |
| Get All Attachments | Mastery | 6 | 10000 | N/A | N/A | N/A | N/A | N/A | N/A | N/A | N/A | N/A | N/A | N/A | N/A | N/A | N/A |
| **BARRETT .50 CAL CHALLENGES** | | | | | | | | | | | | | | | | | |
| Get Target No. Kills | Marksman | 10 | 250 | 25 | 1000 | 75 | 2000 | 150 | 5000 | 300 | 10000 | 500 | 10000 | 750 | 10000 | 1000 | 10000 |
| Get Target No. Headshots | Expert | 5 | 500 | 15 | 1000 | 30 | 2500 | 75 | 5000 | 150 | 10000 | 250 | 10000 | 350 | 10000 | 500 | 10000 |
| Get Target No. Kills Silencer | Attachment: Silencer | 15 | 750 | N/A | N/A | N/A | N/A | N/A | N/A | N/A | N/A | N/A | N/A | N/A | N/A | N/A | N/A |
| Get Target No. Kills ACOG | Attachment: ACOG | 20 | 750 | N/A | N/A | N/A | N/A | N/A | N/A | N/A | N/A | N/A | N/A | N/A | N/A | N/A | N/A |
| Get Target No. Kills FMJ | Attachment: FMJ | 40 | 1000 | N/A | N/A | N/A | N/A | N/A | N/A | N/A | N/A | N/A | N/A | N/A | N/A | N/A | N/A |
| Get All Attachments | Mastery | 6 | 10000 | N/A | N/A | N/A | N/A | N/A | N/A | N/A | N/A | N/A | N/A | N/A | N/A | N/A | N/A |

## WEAPON CHALLENGES CONT.

| Challenge Description | Title | Target No. 1 | XP 1 | Target No. 2 | XP 2 | Target No. 3 | XP 3 | Target No. 4 | XP 4 | Target No. 5 | XP 5 | Target No. 6 | XP 6 | Target No. 7 | XP 7 | Target No. 8 | XP 8 |
|---|---|---|---|---|---|---|---|---|---|---|---|---|---|---|---|---|---|
| **M21 EBR CHALLENGES** | | | | | | | | | | | | | | | | | |
| Get Target No. Kills | Marksman | 10 | 250 | 25 | 1000 | 75 | 2000 | 150 | 5000 | 300 | 10000 | 500 | 10000 | 750 | 10000 | 1000 | 10000 |
| Get Target No. Headshots | Expert | 5 | 500 | 15 | 1000 | 30 | 2500 | 75 | 5000 | 150 | 10000 | 250 | 10000 | 350 | 10000 | 500 | 10000 |
| Get Target No. Kills Silencer | Attachment: Silencer | 15 | 750 | N/A | N/A | N/A | N/A | N/A | N/A | N/A | N/A | N/A | N/A | N/A | N/A | N/A | N/A |
| Get Target No. Kills ACOG | Attachment: ACOG | 20 | 750 | N/A | N/A | N/A | N/A | N/A | N/A | N/A | N/A | N/A | N/A | N/A | N/A | N/A | N/A |
| Get Target No. Kills FMJ | Attachment: FMJ | 40 | 1000 | N/A | N/A | N/A | N/A | N/A | N/A | N/A | N/A | N/A | N/A | N/A | N/A | N/A | N/A |
| Get All Attachments | Mastery | 6 | 10000 | N/A | N/A | N/A | N/A | N/A | N/A | N/A | N/A | N/A | N/A | N/A | N/A | N/A | N/A |
| **WA2000 CHALLENGES** | | | | | | | | | | | | | | | | | |
| Get Target No. Kills | Marksman | 10 | 250 | 25 | 1000 | 75 | 2000 | 150 | 5000 | 300 | 10000 | 500 | 10000 | 750 | 10000 | 1000 | 10000 |
| Get Target No. Headshots | Expert | 5 | 500 | 15 | 1000 | 30 | 2500 | 75 | 5000 | 150 | 10000 | 250 | 10000 | 350 | 10000 | 500 | 10000 |
| Get Target No. Kills Silencer | Attachment: Silencer | 15 | 750 | N/A | N/A | N/A | N/A | N/A | N/A | N/A | N/A | N/A | N/A | N/A | N/A | N/A | N/A |
| Get Target No. Kills ACOG | Attachment: ACOG | 20 | 750 | N/A | N/A | N/A | N/A | N/A | N/A | N/A | N/A | N/A | N/A | N/A | N/A | N/A | N/A |
| Get Target No. Kills FMJ | Attachment: FMJ | 40 | 1000 | N/A | N/A | N/A | N/A | N/A | N/A | N/A | N/A | N/A | N/A | N/A | N/A | N/A | N/A |
| Get All Attachments | Mastery | 6 | 10000 | N/A | N/A | N/A | N/A | N/A | N/A | N/A | N/A | N/A | N/A | N/A | N/A | N/A | N/A |
| **G18 CHALLENGES** | | | | | | | | | | | | | | | | | |
| Get Target No. Kills | Marksman | 10 | 500 | 25 | 1000 | 50 | 1500 | 75 | 2000 | 100 | 2500 | 150 | 3500 | 300 | 10000 | 1000 | 10000 |
| Get Target No. Headshots | Expert | 5 | 500 | 15 | 1000 | 30 | 2500 | 75 | 5000 | 150 | 10000 | 250 | 10000 | 350 | 10000 | 500 | 10000 |
| **TMP CHALLENGES** | | | | | | | | | | | | | | | | | |
| Get Target No. Kills | Marksman | 10 | 500 | 25 | 1000 | 50 | 1500 | 75 | 2000 | 100 | 2500 | 150 | 3500 | 300 | 10000 | 1000 | 10000 |
| Get Target No. Headshots | Expert | 5 | 500 | 15 | 1000 | 30 | 2500 | 75 | 5000 | 150 | 10000 | 250 | 10000 | 350 | 10000 | 500 | 10000 |
| **M93 RAFFICAL CHALLENGES** | | | | | | | | | | | | | | | | | |
| Get Target No. Kills | Marksman | 10 | 500 | 25 | 1000 | 50 | 1500 | 75 | 2000 | 100 | 2500 | 150 | 3500 | 300 | 10000 | 1000 | 10000 |
| Get Target No. Headshots | Expert | 5 | 500 | 15 | 1000 | 30 | 2500 | 75 | 5000 | 150 | 10000 | 250 | 10000 | 350 | 10000 | 500 | 10000 |
| **PP2000 CHALLENGES** | | | | | | | | | | | | | | | | | |
| Get Target No. Kills | Marksman | 10 | 500 | 25 | 1000 | 50 | 1500 | 75 | 2000 | 100 | 2500 | 150 | 3500 | 300 | 10000 | 1000 | 10000 |
| Get Target No. Headshots | Expert | 5 | 500 | 15 | 1000 | 30 | 2500 | 75 | 5000 | 150 | 10000 | 250 | 10000 | 350 | 10000 | 500 | 10000 |
| **STRIKER CHALLENGES** | | | | | | | | | | | | | | | | | |
| Get Target No. Kills | Marksman | 10 | 500 | 25 | 1000 | 75 | 2500 | 150 | 5000 | 250 | 10000 | 400 | 10000 | 500 | 10000 | 1000 | 10000 |
| Get Target No. Headshots | Expert | 5 | 500 | 10 | 1000 | 20 | 2500 | 40 | 5000 | 100 | 10000 | 200 | 10000 | 350 | 10000 | 500 | 10000 |
| **AA-12 CHALLENGES** | | | | | | | | | | | | | | | | | |
| Get Target No. Kills | Marksman | 10 | 500 | 25 | 1000 | 75 | 2500 | 150 | 5000 | 250 | 10000 | 400 | 10000 | 500 | 10000 | 1000 | 10000 |
| Get Target No. Headshots | Expert | 5 | 500 | 10 | 1000 | 20 | 2500 | 40 | 5000 | 100 | 10000 | 200 | 10000 | 350 | 10000 | 500 | 10000 |
| **M1014 CHALLENGES** | | | | | | | | | | | | | | | | | |
| Get Target No. Kills | Marksman | 10 | 500 | 25 | 1000 | 75 | 2500 | 150 | 5000 | 250 | 10000 | 400 | 10000 | 500 | 10000 | 1000 | 10000 |
| Get Target No. Headshots | Expert | 5 | 500 | 10 | 1000 | 20 | 2500 | 40 | 5000 | 100 | 10000 | 200 | 10000 | 350 | 10000 | 500 | 10000 |
| **SPAS-12 CHALLENGES** | | | | | | | | | | | | | | | | | |
| Get Target No. Kills | Marksman | 10 | 500 | 25 | 1000 | 75 | 2500 | 150 | 5000 | 250 | 10000 | 400 | 10000 | 500 | 10000 | 1000 | 10000 |
| Get Target No. Headshots | Expert | 5 | 500 | 10 | 1000 | 20 | 2500 | 40 | 5000 | 100 | 10000 | 200 | 10000 | 350 | 10000 | 500 | 10000 |
| **RANGER CHALLENGES** | | | | | | | | | | | | | | | | | |
| Get Target No. Kills | Marksman | 10 | 500 | 50 | 1500 | 300 | 10000 | 1000 | 10000 | 2500 | 10000 | N/A | N/A | N/A | N/A | N/A | N/A |
| Get Target No. Headshots | Expert | 5 | 500 | 10 | 1000 | 20 | 2500 | 40 | 5000 | 100 | 10000 | 200 | 10000 | 350 | 10000 | 500 | 10000 |
| **MODEL 1887 CHALLENGES** | | | | | | | | | | | | | | | | | |
| Get Target No. Kills | Marksman | 10 | 500 | 50 | 1500 | 300 | 10000 | 1000 | 10000 | 2500 | 10000 | N/A | N/A | N/A | N/A | N/A | N/A |
| Get Target No. Headshots | Expert | 5 | 500 | 10 | 1000 | 20 | 2500 | 40 | 5000 | 100 | 10000 | 200 | 10000 | 350 | 10000 | 500 | 10000 |

## WEAPON CHALLENGES CONT.

| CHALLENGE DESCRIPTION | TITLE | TARGET No. 1 | XP 1 | TARGET No. 2 | XP 2 | TARGET No. 3 | XP 3 | TARGET No. 4 | XP 4 | TARGET No. 5 | XP 5 | TARGET No. 6 | XP 6 | TARGET No. 7 | XP 7 | TARGET No. 8 | XP 8 |
|---|---|---|---|---|---|---|---|---|---|---|---|---|---|---|---|---|---|
| **USP .45 CHALLENGES** | | | | | | | | | | | | | | | | | |
| Get Target No. Kills | Marksman | 10 | 500 | 25 | 1000 | 50 | 1500 | 100 | 2500 | 150 | 3500 | 300 | 10000 | 1000 | 10000 | 1000 | 10000 |
| Get Target No. Headshots | Expert | 5 | 500 | 15 | 1000 | 30 | 2500 | 75 | 5000 | 150 | 10000 | 250 | 10000 | 350 | 10000 | 500 | 10000 |
| **M9 CHALLENGES** | | | | | | | | | | | | | | | | | |
| Get Target No. Kills | Marksman | 10 | 500 | 25 | 1000 | 50 | 1500 | 100 | 2500 | 150 | 3500 | 300 | 10000 | 1000 | 10000 | 1000 | 10000 |
| Get Target No. Headshots | Expert | 5 | 500 | 15 | 1000 | 30 | 2500 | 75 | 5000 | 150 | 10000 | 250 | 10000 | 350 | 10000 | 500 | 10000 |
| **.44 MAGNUM CHALLENGES** | | | | | | | | | | | | | | | | | |
| Get Target No. Kills | Marksman | 10 | 500 | 50 | 1500 | 100 | 2500 | 300 | 10000 | 1000 | 10000 | 2500 | 10000 | N/A | N/A | N/A | N/A |
| Get Target No. Headshots | Expert | 5 | 500 | 15 | 1000 | 30 | 2500 | 75 | 5000 | 150 | 10000 | 250 | 10000 | 350 | 10000 | 500 | 10000 |
| **DESERT EAGLE CHALLENGES** | | | | | | | | | | | | | | | | | |
| Get Target No. Kills | Marksman | 10 | 500 | 50 | 1500 | 100 | 2500 | 300 | 10000 | 1000 | 10000 | 2500 | 10000 | N/A | N/A | N/A | N/A |
| Get Target No. Headshots | Expert | 5 | 500 | 15 | 1000 | 30 | 2500 | 75 | 5000 | 150 | 10000 | 250 | 10000 | 350 | 10000 | 500 | 10000 |
| **AT4-HS CHALLENGES** | | | | | | | | | | | | | | | | | |
| Get Target No. Kills | Marksman | 10 | 250 | 25 | 1000 | 75 | 2000 | 150 | 5000 | 300 | 10000 | 500 | 10000 | 800 | 10000 | 1200 | 10000 |
| **RPG-7 CHALLENGES** | | | | | | | | | | | | | | | | | |
| Get Target No. Kills | Marksman | 10 | 250 | 25 | 1000 | 75 | 2000 | 150 | 5000 | 300 | 10000 | 500 | 10000 | 800 | 10000 | 1200 | 10000 |
| **JAVELIN CHALLENGES** | | | | | | | | | | | | | | | | | |
| Get Target No. Kills | Marksman | 10 | 250 | 25 | 1000 | 75 | 2000 | 150 | 5000 | 300 | 10000 | 500 | 10000 | 800 | 10000 | 1200 | 10000 |
| **THUMPER CHALLENGES** | | | | | | | | | | | | | | | | | |
| Get Target No. Kills | Marksman | 10 | 250 | 25 | 1000 | 75 | 2000 | 150 | 5000 | 300 | 10000 | 500 | 10000 | 800 | 10000 | 1200 | 10000 |
| **STINGER CHALLENGES** | | | | | | | | | | | | | | | | | |
| Kill Target No. Helicopters | Marksman | 3 | 250 | 8 | 1000 | 15 | 2000 | 25 | 5000 | 40 | 10000 | 60 | 10000 | 100 | 10000 | 250 | 10000 |

## RIOT SHIELD CHALLENGES

| TITLE | CHALLENGE DESCRIPTION | TARGET No. 1 | XP 1 | TARGET No. 2 | XP 2 | TARGET No. 3 | XP 3 |
|---|---|---|---|---|---|---|---|
| Shield Veteran | Kill Target No. Enemies with the Shield Melee Attack | 2 | 500 | 5 | 1000 | 15 | 2500 |
| Smasher | Get a 3-Shield-Kill Streak with the Riot Shield without Dying | 1 | 500 | N/A | N/A | N/A | N/A |
| Back-Smasher | Crush an Enemy from Behind | 1 | 500 | N/A | N/A | N/A | N/A |
| Sponge | Absorb 1000 Damage with your Riot Shield | 1000 | 500 | 10000 | 1000 | 50000 | 2500 |
| Bullet Proof | Deflect 1000 Bullets with your Riot Shield | 1000 | 500 | 10000 | 1000 | 50000 | 2500 |
| Unbreakable | Deflect 10 Explosions with your Riot Shield | 10 | 500 | 50 | 1000 | 100 | 2500 |

## OPERATIONS CHALLENGES

| TITLE | CHALLENGE DESCRIPTION | TARGET No. 1 | XP 1 | TARGET No. 2 | XP 2 | TARGET No. 3 | XP 3 |
|---|---|---|---|---|---|---|---|
| Free For All Victor | Place First, Second or Third in Target No. Free For All Matches | 3 | 500 | 5 | 1000 | 10 | 2500 |
| Team Player | Win Target No. Team Deathmatch Matches | 5 | 500 | 15 | 1000 | 30 | 2500 |
| SD Victor | Win Target No. Search & Destroy Matches | 5 | 500 | 15 | 1000 | 30 | 2500 |
| MVP Team Deathmatch | Play Team Deathmatch Match and Get the Top Score Overall | 1 | 1000 | N/A | N/A | N/A | N/A |
| Hardcore Team Player | Win Target No. Hardcore Team Deathmatch Game(s) | 1 | 500 | 5 | 1000 | 15 | 2500 |
| Sabotage Victor | Win Target No. Sabotage Matches | 5 | 500 | 20 | 1000 | 50 | 2500 |
| MVP Team Hardcore | Win a Team Hardcore Match with the Top Score | 1 | 1000 | N/A | N/A | N/A | N/A |
| Bomb Down | Kill a Bomb Carrier in Sabotage or Search & Destroy | 1 | 1000 | N/A | N/A | N/A | N/A |
| Bomb Defender | Kill Target No. Enemies while They are Defusing a Bomb | 3 | 500 | 10 | 1000 | N/A | N/A |
| Bomb Planter | Kill Target No. Enemies while They are Planting a Bomb | 3 | 500 | 10 | 1000 | N/A | N/A |
| Defuser | Defuse Target No. Bombs in Sabotage | 2 | 500 | 10 | 1000 | N/A | N/A |
| Last Man Standing | Be the Last Man Standing in Search & Destroy | 1 | 1000 | N/A | N/A | N/A | N/A |
| Saboteur | Plant Target No. Bombs | 2 | 500 | 10 | 1000 | N/A | N/A |

## PERK CHALLENGES

| PERK | CHALLENGE DESCRIPTION | TARGET No. 1 | XP 1 | TARGET No. 2 | XP 2 | TARGET No. 3 | XP 3 | TARGET No. 4 | XP 4 | TARGET No. 5 | XP 5 | TARGET No. 6 | XP 6 |
|---|---|---|---|---|---|---|---|---|---|---|---|---|---|
| Marathon Pro | Run Target No. Miles Using Marathon | 5280 | 500 | 26400 | 1000 | 52800 | 2500 | 137280 | 5000 | 274560 | 10000 | 549120 | 10000 |
| Sleight of Hand Pro | Get Target No. Sleight of Hand Kills | 15 | 500 | 30 | 1000 | 60 | 2500 | 120 | 5000 | 300 | 10000 | 750 | 10000 |
| Scavenger Pro | Resupply Target No. Times while Using Scavenger | 10 | 500 | 25 | 1000 | 50 | 2500 | 100 | 5000 | 250 | 10000 | 500 | 10000 |
| Bling Pro | Get Target No. Kills Using a Weapon with 2 Attachments | 25 | 500 | 50 | 1000 | 100 | 2500 | 200 | 5000 | 450 | 10000 | 900 | 10000 |
| One Man Army Pro | Get Target No. Kills Using One Man Army | 15 | 500 | 30 | 1000 | 60 | 2500 | 120 | 5000 | 300 | 10000 | 750 | 10000 |
| Stopping Power Pro | Get Target No. Stopping Power Kills | 30 | 500 | 60 | 1000 | 120 | 2500 | 250 | 5000 | 500 | 10000 | 1000 | 10000 |
| Lightweight Pro | Sprint Target No. Miles Using Lightweight | 10560 | 500 | 42240 | 1000 | 79200 | 2500 | 158400 | 5000 | 528000 | 10000 | 1320000 | 10000 |
| Hardline Pro | Get Target No. Killstreaks while Using Hardline | 3 | 500 | 10 | 1000 | 20 | 2500 | 40 | 5000 | 100 | 10000 | 250 | 10000 |
| Cold-Blooded Pro | Destroy Target No. Enemy Killstreak Rewards Using Cold-Blooded | 3 | 500 | 10 | 1000 | 20 | 2500 | 40 | 5000 | 100 | 10000 | 250 | 10000 |
| Danger Close Pro | Get Target No. Kills with Explosives while Using Danger Close | 10 | 500 | 25 | 1000 | 50 | 2500 | 100 | 5000 | 250 | 10000 | 500 | 10000 |
| Commando Pro | Get Target No. Melee Kills Using Commander | 2 | 500 | 5 | 1000 | 10 | 2500 | 20 | 5000 | 50 | 10000 | 100 | 10000 |
| Steady Aim Pro | Get Target No. Hipfire Kills Using Steady Aim | 10 | 500 | 20 | 1000 | 40 | 2500 | 80 | 5000 | 200 | 10000 | 500 | 10000 |
| Scrambler Pro | Get Target No. Close-Range Kills Using Scrambler | 5 | 500 | 10 | 1000 | 25 | 2500 | 50 | 5000 | 125 | 10000 | 250 | 10000 |
| Ninja Pro | Get Target No. Close-Range Kills Using Ninja | 5 | 500 | 10 | 1000 | 25 | 2500 | 50 | 5000 | 125 | 10000 | 250 | 10000 |
| SitRep Pro | Destroy Target No. Enemy Devices while Using SitRep | 15 | 500 | 30 | 1000 | 60 | 2500 | 120 | 5000 | 300 | 10000 | 750 | 10000 |
| Last Stand Pro | Get Target No. Last Stand Kills | 2 | 500 | 5 | 1000 | 10 | 2500 | 20 | 5000 | 50 | 10000 | 100 | 10000 |

## BASIC TRAINING CHALLENGES

| TITLE | CHALLENGE DESCRIPTION | TARGET No. 1 | XP 1 | TARGET No. 2 | XP 2 | TARGET No. 3 | XP 3 |
|---|---|---|---|---|---|---|---|
| Ghillie in the Mist | Get Target No. One-Shot Kills with Sniper Rifles | 50 | 1000 | 100 | 2500 | 200 | 5000 |
| Goodbye | Fall 30 Feet or More to Your Death | 1 | 500 | N/A | N/A | N/A | N/A |
| Base Jump | Fall 15 Feet or More and Survive | 1 | 750 | N/A | N/A | N/A | N/A |
| Flyswatter | Shoot Down an Enemy Helicopter | 1 | 1000 | N/A | N/A | N/A | N/A |
| Vandalism | Kill 1 Enemy by Destroying a Car | 1 | 750 | N/A | N/A | N/A | N/A |
| Crouch Shot | Kill Target No. Enemies while Crouching | 5 | 500 | 15 | 1000 | 30 | 2500 |
| Prone Shot | Kill Target No. Enemies while Prone | 5 | 500 | 15 | 1000 | 30 | 2500 |
| Point Guard | Get Target No. Assists | 5 | 500 | 15 | 1000 | 30 | 2500 |
| X-Ray Vision | Kill Target No. Enemy through a Surface using Bullet Penetration | 2 | 500 | 5 | 1000 | 15 | 2500 |
| Backdraft | Destroy Target No. Enemy Explosives | 2 | 500 | 5 | 1000 | 15 | 2500 |

## KILLSTREAK CHALLENGES

| TITLE | CHALLENGE DESCRIPTION | TARGET No. 1 | XP 1 | TARGET No. 2 | XP 2 | TARGET No. 3 | XP 3 |
|---|---|---|---|---|---|---|---|
| Exposed | Call in Target No. UAVs | 5 | 1000 | 25 | 2500 | 50 | 5000 |
| Air Mail | Call in Target No. Care Packages | 5 | 1000 | 25 | 2500 | 50 | 5000 |
| Interference | Call in Target No. Counter-UAVs | 5 | 1000 | 25 | 2500 | 50 | 5000 |
| Sentry Veteran | Call in Target No. Sentry Guns | 5 | 1000 | 25 | 2500 | 50 | 5000 |
| Air to Ground | Call in Target No. Predator Missiles | 5 | 1000 | 25 | 2500 | 50 | 5000 |
| Airstrike Veteran | Call in Target No. Precision Airstrikes | 5 | 1500 | 25 | 3000 | 50 | 6000 |
| Vertical Takeoff | Call in Target No. Harrier Strikes | 5 | 1500 | 25 | 3000 | 50 | 6000 |
| Attack Helicopter Veteran | Call in Target No. Attack Helicopters | 5 | 1500 | 25 | 3000 | 50 | 6000 |
| Special Delivery | Call in Target No. Emergency Airdrops | 3 | 1500 | 10 | 3000 | 25 | 6000 |
| 21 Ton Giants | Call in Target No. Pave Lows | 3 | 1500 | 10 | 3000 | 25 | 6000 |
| Stealth Bomber Veteran | Call in Target No. Stealth Bombers | 3 | 1500 | 10 | 3000 | 25 | 6000 |
| Chopper Gunner Veteran | Call in Target No. Chopper Gunners | 3 | 2500 | 10 | 5000 | 25 | 10000 |
| AC130 Veteran | Call in Target No. AC130s | 3 | 2500 | 10 | 5000 | 25 | 10000 |
| Blackout | Call in Target No. EMPs | 2 | 2500 | 5 | 5000 | 10 | 10000 |
| End Game | Call in Target No. Nukes | 2 | 5000 | 5 | 10000 | 10 | 10000 |
| Radar Inbound | Call in Target No. UAVs or Counter-UAVs | 50 | 2500 | 100 | 5000 | 1000 | 10000 |
| Airstrike Inbound | Call in Target No. Precision, Stealth or Harrier Airstrikes | 50 | 2500 | 100 | 5000 | 1000 | 10000 |
| Helicopter Inbound | Call in Target No. Armed Helicopters | 50 | 2500 | 100 | 5000 | 1000 | 10000 |
| Airdrop Inbound | Call in Target No. Total Airdrop Crates Using Care Package, Sentry Gun, and Emergency Airdrop | 50 | 2500 | 100 | 5000 | 1000 | 10000 |

## INTIMIDATION CHALLENGES

| TITLE | CHALLENGE DESCRIPTION | TARGET No. 1 | XP 1 |
|---|---|---|---|
| Omnicide! | Kill the Entire Enemy Team within 10 Seconds | 1 | 5000 |
| Wargasm | Get All 3 of Your Killstreak Rewards within 20 Seconds | 1 | 3500 |
| The Bigger They Are… | Kill the Top Player 3 Times in a Row | 1 | 2500 |
| …The Harder They Fall | Kill the Top Player 5 Times in a Row | 1 | 5000 |
| Crab Meat | Kill 10 Enemies with a Single Killstreak | 1 | 7500 |
| Ultimate Sacrifice | Nuke the Enemy while Your Team is Losing | 1 | 10000 |
| The Denier | Kill an Enemy Before They Earn a 10 or Higher Killstreak Reward | 1 | 5000 |
| Carpet Bomb | Kill 5 Enemies with a Single Airstrike | 1 | 5000 |
| Red Carpet | Kill 6 Enemies with a Single Stealth Bomber | 1 | 5000 |
| Grim Reaper | Kill 5 Enemies with a Single Predator Missile | 1 | 5000 |
| No Secrets | Call in a UAV 3 Times in a Single Match | 1 | 2500 |
| Sunblock | Counter the Enemy's UAV 3 Times in a Single Match | 1 | 2500 |
| Afterburner | Call in an Airstrike 2 Times in a Single Match | 1 | 2500 |
| Air Superiority | Call in a Helicopter 2 Times in a Single Match | 1 | 2500 |
| MG Master | Get a 5-Kill Streak while on a Mounted Machine Gun | 1 | 2500 |
| Slasher | Get a 3-Melee Kill Streak without Dying | 1 | 3500 |

## PRECISION CHALLENGES

| TITLE | CHALLENGE DESCRIPTION | TARGET No. 1 | XP1 | TARGET No. 2 | XP2 | TARGET No. 3 | XP3 |
|---|---|---|---|---|---|---|---|
| Assault Expert | Kill Target No. Enemies with a Headshot while Using an Assault Rifle | 5 | 2000 | 25 | 5000 | 50 | 10000 |
| SMG Expert | Kill Target No. Enemies with a Headshot while Using an SMG | 5 | 2000 | 25 | 5000 | 50 | 10000 |
| LMG Expert | Kill Target No. Enemies with a Headshot while Using an LMG | 5 | 2000 | 25 | 5000 | 50 | 10000 |
| The Surgical | Fire an Entire Assault Rifle Magazine into Your Enemies without Missing | 1 | 2000 | N/A | N/A | N/A | N/A |
| Mach 5 | Fire an Entire SMG Magazine into an Enemy without Missing | 1 | 2000 | N/A | N/A | N/A | N/A |
| Dictator | Fire an Entire LMG Magazine into an Enemy without Missing | 1 | 2000 | N/A | N/A | N/A | N/A |
| Perfectionist | Fire an Entire Sniper Magazine into an Enemy without Missing | 1 | 2000 | N/A | N/A | N/A | N/A |
| Multi-RPG | Kill 2 or More Enemies with a Single AT4-HS or RPG Shot, Target No. Times | 5 | 2000 | 25 | 5000 | 50 | 10000 |
| Clay More | Kill 2 or More Enemies with a Single Claymore, Target No. Times | 5 | 2000 | 25 | 5000 | 50 | 10000 |
| Multi-Frag | Kill 2 or More Enemies with a Single Frag Grenade, Target No. Times | 5 | 2000 | 25 | 5000 | 50 | 10000 |
| ch_multic4 | Kill 2 or More Enemies with a Single C4 Pack, Target No. Times | 5 | 2000 | 25 | 5000 | 50 | 10000 |
| Collateral Damage | Kill 2 or More Enemies with a Single Sniper Rifle Bullet | 1 | 2000 | N/A | N/A | N/A | N/A |
| Flawless | Play an Entire Full-Length Match without Dying | 1 | 2000 | N/A | N/A | N/A | N/A |
| Fearless | Kill 10 Enemies in a Single Match without Dying | 1 | 2000 | N/A | N/A | N/A | N/A |
| Group Hug | Kill Multiple Enemies with a Semtex Stuck to One of Them | 1 | 2000 | N/A | N/A | N/A | N/A |
| NBK | Get 3 Longshots in One Life | 1 | 2000 | N/A | N/A | N/A | N/A |
| All Pro | Headshot 2+ Enemies with 1 Bullet | 1 | 2000 | N/A | N/A | N/A | N/A |
| Airborne | Get a 2-Kill Streak with Bullets while in Midair | 1 | 2000 | N/A | N/A | N/A | N/A |

## HUMILIATION CHALLENGES

| TITLE | CHALLENGE DESCRIPTION | TARGET No. 1 | XP 1 | TARGET No. 2 | XP 2 |
|---|---|---|---|---|---|
| Hot Potato | Kill Target No. Enemies with Thrown-Back Grenades | 5 | 3000 | 10 | 5000 |
| Car Bomb | Kill Target No. Enemies by Destroying Cars | 5 | 3000 | 10 | 5000 |
| Backstabber | Stab an Enemy in the Back with Your Knife | 1 | 3000 | N/A | N/A |
| Slow But Sure | Kill 1 Enemy while Being Stunned by a Stun Grenade | 1 | 3000 | N/A | N/A |
| Misery Loves Company | Kill Yourself and 1 Enemy by Cooking a Grenade without Throwing it | 1 | 3000 | N/A | N/A |
| Ouch | Kill an Enemy with a Rifle-Mounted Grenade Launcher without Detonation (Direct Impact) | 1 | 3000 | N/A | N/A |
| Rival | Kill the Same Enemy 5 Times in a Single Match | 1 | 3000 | N/A | N/A |
| Cruelty | Kill an Enemy, Pick Up His Weapon, then Kill Him Again with His Own Weapon | 1 | 3000 | N/A | N/A |
| Think Fast | Finish an Enemy off by Hitting Them with a Frag Grenade (Direct Impact) | 1 | 3000 | N/A | N/A |
| Think Fast Stun | Finish an Enemy off by Hitting Them with a Stun Grenade (Direct Impact) | 1 | 3000 | N/A | N/A |
| Think Fast Flash | Finish an Enemy off by Hitting Them with a Flashbang (Direct Impact) | 1 | 3000 | N/A | N/A |
| Return to Sender | Kill 1 Enemy by Shooting Their Own Explosive | 1 | 3000 | N/A | N/A |
| Blindfire | Kill an Enemy while You Are Still Dazed by a Flashbang | 1 | 3000 | N/A | N/A |
| Hard Landing | Kill an Enemy that is in Mid-Air | 1 | 3000 | N/A | N/A |
| Extreme Cruelty | Kill Every Member of the Enemy Team (at Least 4 Enemies) without Dying | 1 | 3000 | N/A | N/A |
| Tango Down | Kill Every Member of the Enemy Team (4 Enemy Minimum) | 1 | 3000 | N/A | N/A |
| Counter-MVP | Kill the #1 Player on the Enemy Team 10 Times in a Single Match | 1 | 3000 | N/A | N/A |

## FINISHING MOVE CHALLENGES

| TITLE | CHALLENGE DESCRIPTION | TARGET No. 1 | XP 1 |
|---|---|---|---|
| Droppin' Crates | Get a Game Winning Killcam by Dropping a Crate on the Enemy | 1 | 2500 |
| Absentee Killer | Get a Game Winning Killcam with a Sentry Gun | 1 | 2500 |
| Drone Killer | Get a Predator Missile Kill in the Game Winning Killcam | 1 | 2500 |
| Finishing Touch | Get a Game Winning Killcam with a Precision Airstrike | 1 | 2500 |
| True Liar | Get a Game Winning Killcam with a Harrier | 1 | 2500 |
| OG | Get a Game Winning Killcam with an Attack Helicopter | 1 | 2500 |
| Transformer | Get a Game Winning Killcam with a Pave Low | 1 | 2500 |
| Techno Killer | Get a Game Winning Killcam with a Stealth Bomber | 1 | 2500 |
| Hi Def | Get a Game Winning Killcam with a Chopper Gunner | 1 | 2500 |
| Death From Above | Get a Game Winning Killcam with an AC130 | 1 | 2500 |
| Unbelievable | Get a Throwing Knife Kill in a Game Winning Killcam | 1 | 2500 |
| Owned | Get a Riot Shield Melee Kill in a Game Winning Killcam | 1 | 2500 |
| Stickman | Stick a Semtex to the Enemy in a Game Winning Killcam | 1 | 2500 |
| Last Resort | Get a Last Stand or Final Stand Kill in a Game Winning Killcam | 1 | 2500 |

## PAYBACK CHALLENGES

| TITLE | CHALLENGE DESCRIPTION | TARGET No. 1 | XP 1 | TARGET No. 2 | XP 2 |
|---|---|---|---|---|---|
| Money Shot! | Get a Payback in the Game Winning Killcam | 1 | 3500 | N/A | N/A |
| Robin Hood | Get Payback Target No. Times while in Last Stand | 5 | 3500 | 25 | 10000 |
| Bang for Your Buck | Get a Payback Target No. Times with Frag Grenades | 5 | 3500 | 25 | 10000 |
| Overdraft | Get a Payback that Sticks to the Victim | 1 | 3500 | N/A | N/A |
| Identity Thief | Get a Payback with the Killer's Copycat Class | 1 | 3500 | N/A | N/A |
| ATM | Get a Payback with a Throwing Knife | 1 | 3500 | N/A | N/A |
| Time is Money | Get Payback Target No. Times with Semtex | 5 | 3500 | 25 | 10000 |
| I'm Rich! | Get Payback Target No. Times with C4 | 5 | 3500 | 25 | 10000 |
| Break the Bank | Get a Payback with a Claymore | 1 | 3500 | N/A | N/A |
| Color Of Money | Get Payback Target No. Times with Headshots | 5 | 3500 | 25 | 10000 |

## ELITE CHALLENGES

| TITLE | CHALLENGE DESCRIPTION | TARGET No. 1 | XP 1 | TARGET No. 2 | XP 2 | TARGET No. 3 | XP 3 |
|---|---|---|---|---|---|---|---|
| The Brink | Get a 3 or More Kill Streak while Near Death (Screen Flashing Red) | 1 | 4500 | N/A | N/A | N/A | N/A |
| Fast Swap | Hurt an Enemy with a Primary Weapon, then Finish Them off with a Pistol | 1 | 4500 | N/A | N/A | N/A | N/A |
| Star Player | Play an Entire Match of any Game Type with a 5:1 Kill/Death Ratio | 1 | 4500 | N/A | N/A | N/A | N/A |
| How the ? | Kill an Enemy by Using Bullet Penetration to Shoot an Explosive Device through a Wall | 1 | 4500 | N/A | N/A | N/A | N/A |
| Dominos | Kill an Enemy by Setting Off Chain Reactions of Explosives | 1 | 4500 | N/A | N/A | N/A | N/A |
| Master Chef | Kill Target No. Enemies with Cooked Grenades | 5 | 2500 | 10 | 5000 | 20 | 10000 |
| Invincible | Get 5 Health Regenerations from Enemy Damage in a Row, without Dying | 1 | 4500 | N/A | N/A | N/A | N/A |
| Survivalist | Survive for 5 Consecutive Minutes | 1 | 4500 | N/A | N/A | N/A | N/A |
| Counter-Claymore | Kill Target No. Enemies by Shooting a Claymore | 3 | 2500 | 10 | 5000 | 20 | 10000 |
| Counter-C4 | Kill Target No. Enemies by Shooting C4 | 3 | 2500 | 10 | 5000 | 20 | 10000 |
| Enemy of the State | Kill 3 Enemies while You are the Only Surviving Member of Your Team | 1 | 4500 | N/A | N/A | N/A | N/A |
| The Resourceful | Kill an Enemy by Sticking Semtex to a Teammate | 1 | 4500 | N/A | N/A | N/A | N/A |
| The Survivor | Get a Knife Kill when All of Your Ammo is Empty | 1 | 4500 | N/A | N/A | N/A | N/A |
| Both Barrels | Kill an Enemy with the Ranger by Firing Both Barrels at the Same Time | 1 | 4500 | N/A | N/A | N/A | N/A |

## EQUIPMENT CHALLENGES

| TITLE | CHALLENGE DESCRIPTION | TARGET No. 1 | XP 1 | TARGET No. 2 | XP 2 | TARGET No. 3 | XP 3 |
|---|---|---|---|---|---|---|---|
| Grenade Kill | Kill Target No. Enemies with Grenades | 10 | 500 | 25 | 2500 | 50 | 5000 |
| Claymore Shot | Kill 5 Enemies with Claymores | 5 | 500 | 15 | 2500 | 30 | 5000 |
| Jack-in-the-Box | Kill an Enemy within 5 Seconds of Tactically Inserting, Target No. Times | 10 | 500 | 25 | 2500 | 50 | 5000 |
| Carnie | Kill Target No. Players with a Throwing Knife | 5 | 500 | 15 | 2500 | 30 | 5000 |
| Solid Steel | Survive Target No. Explosions while Using Blast Shield | 10 | 500 | 25 | 2500 | 50 | 5000 |
| Plastered | Stick Target No. Players with a Semtex Grenade | 5 | 500 | 15 | 2500 | 30 | 5000 |
| C4 Shot | Kill Target No. Enemies by Using C4 | 5 | 500 | 15 | 2500 | 30 | 5000 |
| Did You See That? | Kill Someone with a Throwing Knife when Flashed or Stunned | 1 | 1000 | N/A | N/A | N/A | N/A |
| Darkbringer | Prevent Target No. Tactical Insertions | 25 | 1000 | N/A | N/A | N/A | N/A |
| Tactical Deletion | Kill Target No. Players that Spawn Using Tactical Insertion | 25 | 1000 | N/A | N/A | N/A | N/A |
| It's Personal! | Hurt an Enemy, then Finish Them with a Throwing Knife | 1 | 1000 | N/A | N/A | N/A | N/A |

# SATELLITE INTEL

The following section provides satellite data for all the theaters of war you encounter in multiplayer deployment. This intelligence suggests class loadouts, location-based tips, routes, and map callout markers specific to several game modes. Familiarize yourself with all of the info contained in this file. This is your bread and butter. Study your maps, know them inside and out, and you'll come back alive.

## › AFGHAN

### MODE: CAPTURE THE FLAG

TERRAIN: ROCKY, MOUNTAINOUS, DESERT • FACTIONS: OP FOR/TF 141 • WEATHER/T.O.D.: BLOWING SAND, DUST / MID-DAY

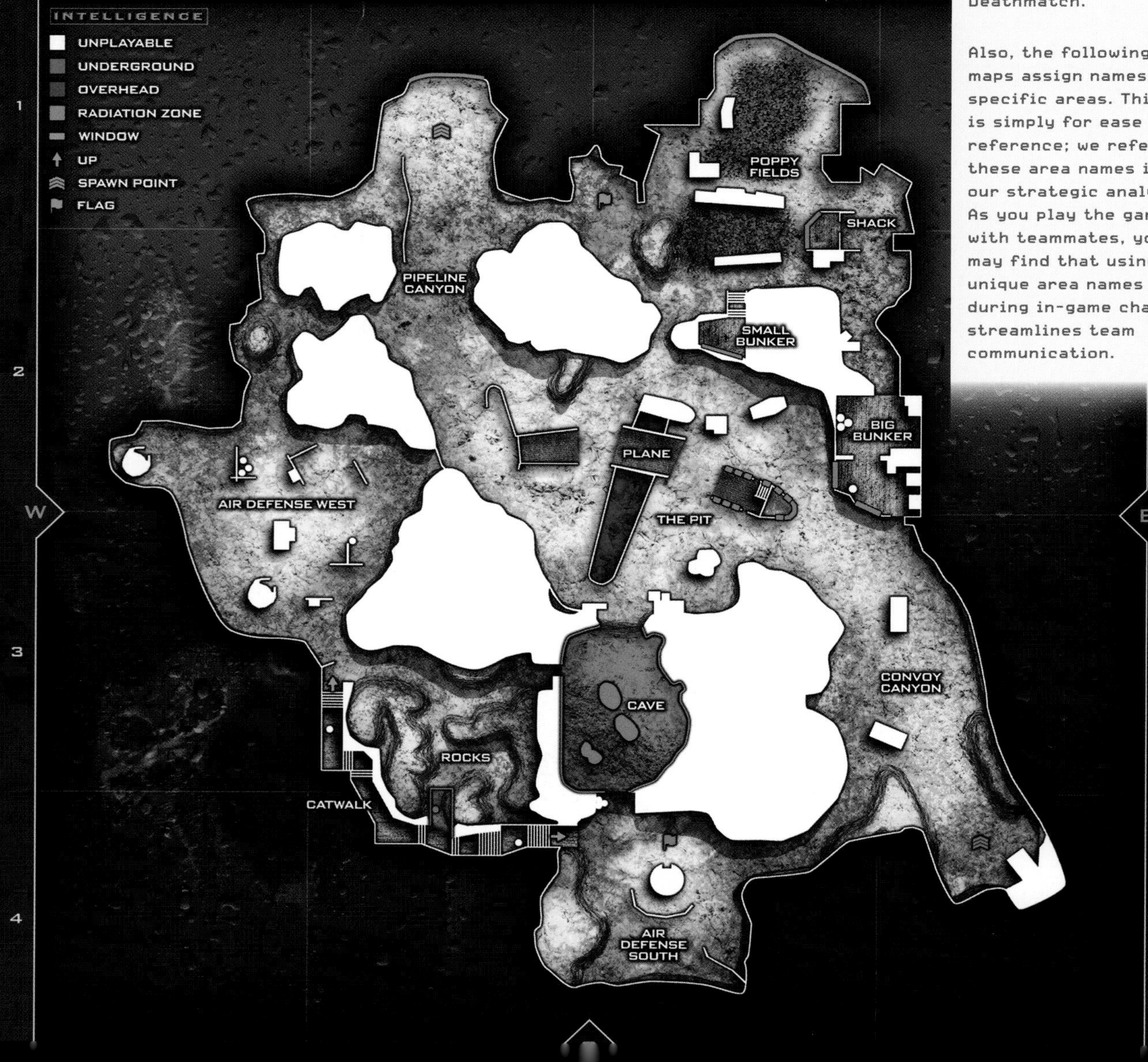

**INTELLIGENCE**

- ☐ UNPLAYABLE
- ▨ UNDERGROUND
- ▨ OVERHEAD
- ▨ RADIATION ZONE
- ▬ WINDOW
- ↑ UP
- ⟫ SPAWN POINT
- ⚑ FLAG

Map callout markers:
- POPPY FIELDS
- SHACK
- PIPELINE CANYON
- SMALL BUNKER
- BIG BUNKER
- PLANE
- AIR DEFENSE WEST
- THE PIT
- CONVOY CANYON
- CAVE
- ROCKS
- CATWALK
- AIR DEFENSE SOUTH

## MAP VARIATIONS/ LOCATION NAMES

Our analyses of the MP levels include six variations of each map. Each map variation displays callout markers for a specific MP game mode: Capture the Flag, Domination, Headquarters, Sabotage, Search & Destroy / Demolition, and Team Deathmatch.

Also, the following maps assign names to specific areas. This is simply for ease of reference; we refer to these area names in our strategic analyses. As you play the game with teammates, you may find that using unique area names during in-game chatter streamlines team communication.

ghan's mountainous desert region features a centrally located
wned plane, a cave system, cliff-side catwalks, bunker complex-
poppy fields, and plenty of cover. Your insertion occurs during
middle of the day, sending you off into some blowing sand. You
uld be aware of a few radiation zones in this part of the country.
id them, as passing into them inflicts damage—you must back-
ck as quickly as possible before you die of radiation poisoning.
e's a suggested character class for the Afghan map:

### SANDBLASTER

| PRIMARY/ATTACHMENT | Barrett .50 cal / Silencer |
| --- | --- |
| SECONDARY/ATTACHMENT | Model 1887 / Akimbo |
| EQUIPMENT | Claymore |
| SPECIAL GRENADE | Smoke |
| PERK 1 | Sleight of Hand |
| PERK 2 | Stopping Power |
| PERK 3 | Steady Aim |
| DEATHSTREAK | Final Stand |

## MODE: DOMINATION

TERRAIN: ROCKY, MOUNTAINOUS, DESERT • FACTIONS: OP FOR/TF 141 • WEATHER/T.O.D.: BLOWING SAND, DUST / MID-DAY

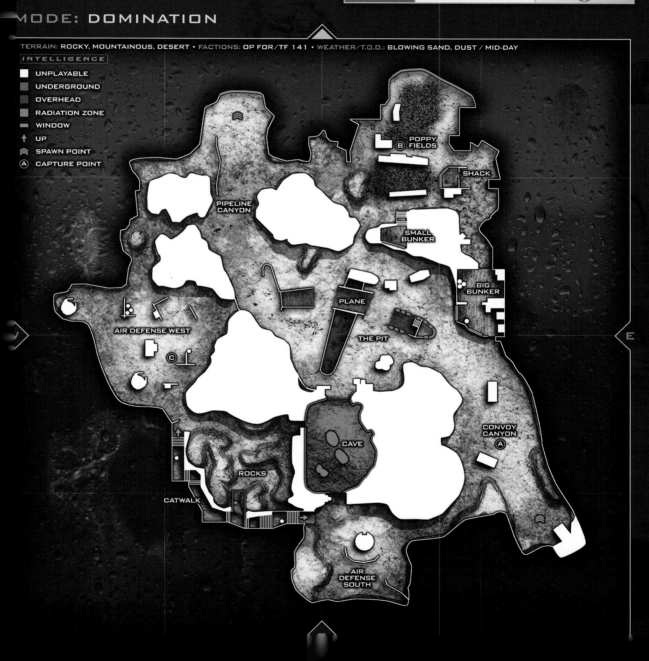

### INTELLIGENCE

- ▨ UNPLAYABLE
- ▨ UNDERGROUND
- ▨ OVERHEAD
- ▨ RADIATION ZONE
- — WINDOW
- ↑ UP
- ⩙ SPAWN POINT
- Ⓐ CAPTURE POINT

Map labels: POPPY FIELDS, SHACK, PIPELINE CANYON, SMALL BUNKER, BIG BUNKER, PLANE, THE PIT, AIR DEFENSE WEST, CONVOY CANYON, CAVE, ROCKS, CATWALK, AIR DEFENSE SOUTH

This loadout is specifically designed for Afghan's environment. Choose desert camo for your primary weapon. Your best bet for survival is picking enemies off from distance using your silenced sniper rifle, the big ol' Barrett .50 cal. Be patient and wait for enemies to pop up their heads, then blow them clean off. The Barrett makes one of the biggest booms in the game, but not with the silencer affixed to it. While you should try to relocate once you picked someone off anyway, the silencer prevents nearby enemies from echo-locating you.

Your secondary or backup weapon is actually two weapons: dual-wielded Model 1887 shotguns. Break these out when you have to move from one location to the next and might encounter close quarters resistance. With Stopping Power as your second Perk, these bad boys can slam the door in your enemies' faces. Sleight of Hand lets you aim and reload much faster than normal, while Steady Aim tightens up your spread for more accurate shots even with the shotguns. This is a big help, because you're running the Akimbo Attachment and cannot look down the sights of your shotguns.

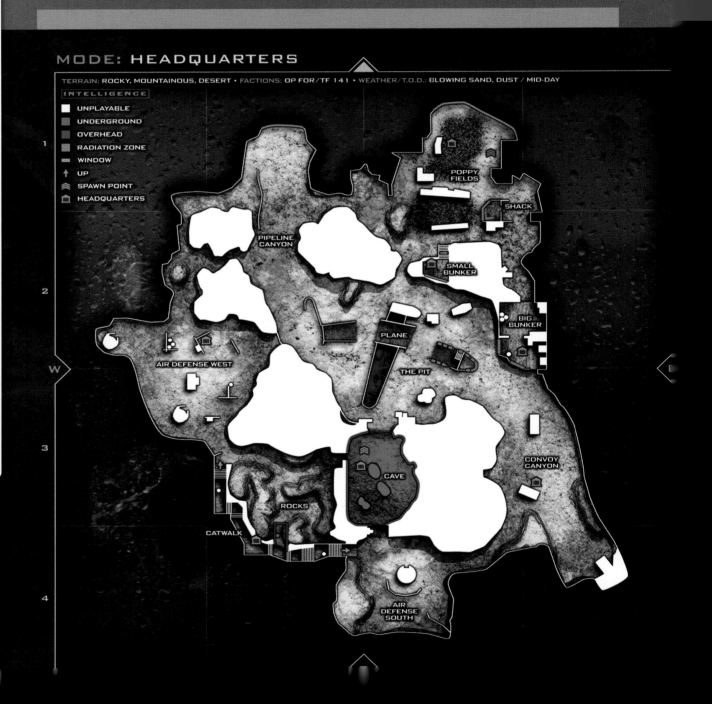

MODE: HEADQUARTERS

TERRAIN: ROCKY, MOUNTAINOUS, DESERT • FACTIONS: OP FOR/TF 141 • WEATHER/T.O.D.: BLOWING SAND, DUST / MID-DAY

INTELLIGENCE
UNPLAYABLE
UNDERGROUND
OVERHEAD
RADIATION ZONE
WINDOW
UP
SPAWN POINT
HEADQUARTERS

POPPY FIELDS

SHACK

SMALL BUNKER

BIG BUNKER

PIPELINE CANYON

PLANE

THE PIT

AIR DEFENSE WEST

CONVOY CANYON

CAVE

ROCKS

CATWALK

AIR DEFENSE SOUTH

# MODE: SABOTAGE

TERRAIN: ROCKY, MOUNTAINOUS, DESERT • FACTIONS: OP FOR/TF 141 • WEATHER/T.O.D.: BLOWING SAND, DUST / MID-DAY

### INTELLIGENCE

- ⬜ UNPLAYABLE
- ⬛ UNDERGROUND
- ⬛ OVERHEAD
- ⬛ RADIATION ZONE
- ▬ WINDOW
- ↑ UP
- ⬙ SPAWN POINT
- ⬙ BOMB
- ☀ BOMB PLANT

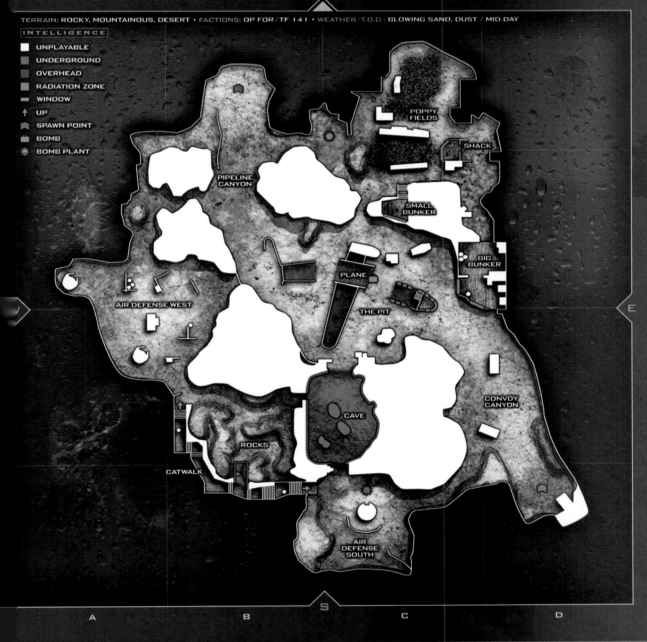

Take a Claymore mine to protect your back while you snipe, but don't rely on it completely. Enemies may have Scrambler on, which delays your Claymore's explosion, giving them time pass it without damage and possibly eliminate you.

These mines usually do the trick, but avoid setting one so close to your position that its blast injures you. Furthermore, setting it a little further back gives time to react to incoming threats if an enemy has the Scrambler Perk. Because more than just one sniper appears on this map, select Final Stand as your Death-streak. This gives you a chance to crawl to cover from an enemy sniper, possibly allowing you to recover and rejoin the fight.

Try to use your Smoke Grenades when you relocate. Use the smoke as a curtain to set up under cover and resume business where the enemy isn't looking for you.

There are lots of great sniping spots, regardless of the side on witch you start. From the Pipeline Canyon area, you can keep overwatch on the Plane, the Pit, and the Bunker Complex. If you need to watch the Catwalk, you can cover its entirety from the southwest corner of Air Defense South. Because there are many ways around, it's difficult to put your back against anything on this map, so work with a buddy to make sure you don't get flanked.

# MODE: SEARCH & DESTROY / DEMOLITION

**TERRAIN:** ROCKY, MOUNTAINOUS, DESERT • **FACTIONS:** OP FOR/TF 141 • **WEATHER/T.O.D.:** BLOWING SAND, DUST / MID-DAY

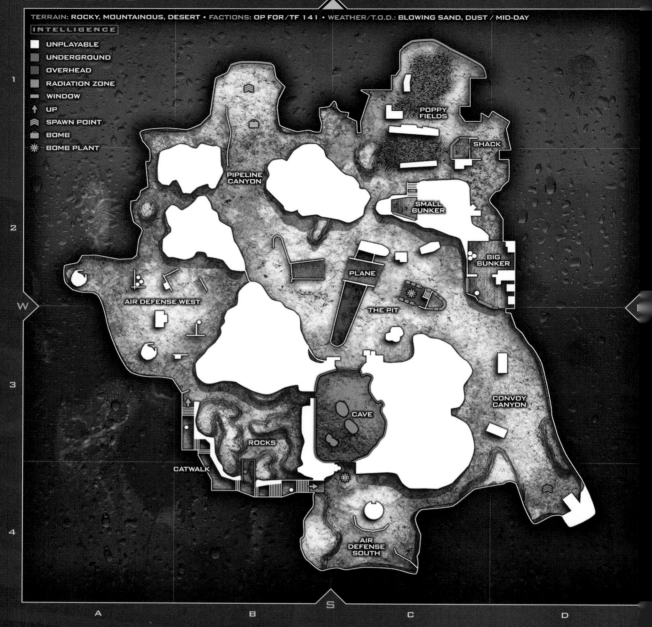

**INTELLIGENCE**

- ☐ UNPLAYABLE
- ☐ UNDERGROUND
- ☐ OVERHEAD
- ☐ RADIATION ZONE
- ▬ WINDOW
- ↑ UP
- ⟰ SPAWN POINT
- ◼ BOMB
- ☀ BOMB PLANT

*Map labels: PIPELINE CANYON, POPPY FIELDS, SHACK, SMALL BUNKER, BIG BUNKER, PLANE, THE PIT, AIR DEFENSE WEST, CAVE, CONVOY CANYON, ROCKS, CATWALK, AIR DEFENSE SOUTH*

If you check the sat map, you can work out defensible areas by locating chokepoints. The Bunker Complex is a great place from which to control the middle of the map.

With a medium- to long-range scoped rifle, one or two players can cover almost every avenue of approach to the center of the map. Use the Air Defense West area and the Catwalk to get around central firefights, or to flank enemies. If you carry light weapons and are nimble enough, you can make the jump from the plane's wing to a small ledge just outside the Cave's north entrance. This makes a great roost from which to snipe if you

have a silenced weapon. The Cave is a great place for patient players to set up an ambush. Place Claymores and choose a silenced weapon, stay close to the walls and corners, and wait for unsuspecting enemies to file in, trying to flank your team. If you plan to use the Catwalk, be wary of the explosive barrels that line it. There isn't anywhere to hide if an enemy tosses a grenade while you traverse the area. Medium- to long-range weaponry is key on this map. Continue moving from cover to cover as much as possible, and use smoke whenever you can. Check the additional mode variations of our sat maps to determine which areas work best for overwatching mode-based objectives.

# MODE: TEAM DEATHMATCH

TERRAIN: ROCKY, MOUNTAINOUS, DESERT • FACTIONS: OP FOR/TF 141 • WEATHER/T.O.D.: BLOWING SAND, DUST / MID-DAY

**INTELLIGENCE**

- ⬜ UNPLAYABLE
- ⬛ UNDERGROUND
- ⬛ OVERHEAD
- ⬛ RADIATION ZONE
- ▬ WINDOW
- ↑ UP
- ⌃ SPAWN POINT

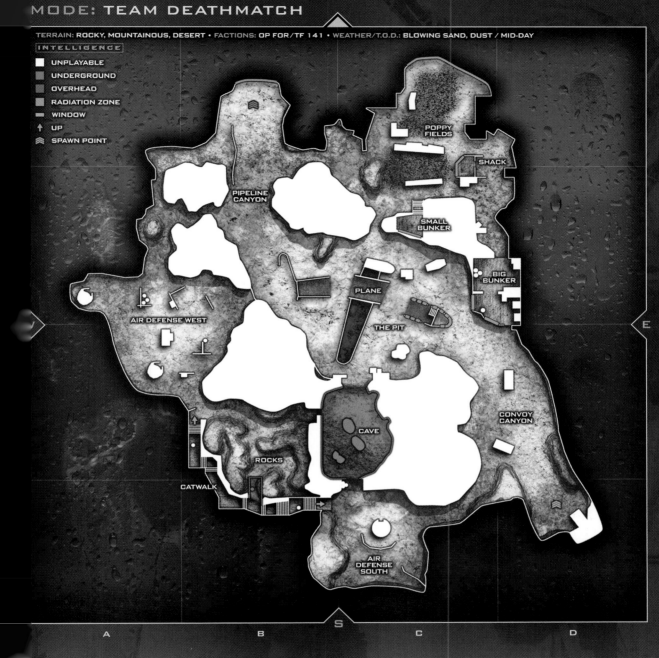

POPPY FIELDS
SHACK
SMALL BUNKER
BIG BUNKER
PLANE
THE PIT
PIPELINE CANYON
AIR DEFENSE WEST
CONVOY CANYON
CAVE
ROCKS
CATWALK
AIR DEFENSE SOUTH

# ❯DERAIL

This locale is a small shipping town in the snowy backcountry. A derailed train splits the map in half, west to east. A small town with a garage and gas station covers the map's east side, while warehouses, offices, power stations, and other industrial elements dominate the west side. A frozen creek that can be used for cover cuts through the center of the map from north to south. Exploit this map's wooded cover as much as you can. This is a very sniper-heavy map, so feel free to carry what you like, but keep the following option in mind.

## WHITE NINJA

| | | |
|---|---|---|
| PRIMARY/ ATTACHMENT | ACR / ACOG & Silencer | |
| SECONDARY/ ATTACHMENT | TMP / Akimbo & Silencer | |
| EQUIPMENT | Tactical Insertion | |
| SPECIAL GRENADE | Smoke | |
| PERK 1 | Bling | |
| PERK 2 | Cold Blooded | |
| PERK 3 | Ninja | |
| DEATHSTREAK | Martyrdom | |

## MODE: CAPTURE THE FLAG

TERRAIN: HILLS, SEMI-WOODED, SHIPPING COMPLEX • FACTIONS: OP FOR/TF 141 • WEATHER/T.O.D.: LIGHT BLOWING SNOW/LATE AFTERNOON

INTELLIGENCE

- ◻ UNPLAYABLE
- ◻ UNDERGROUND
- ◻ OVERHEAD
- ▬ WINDOW
- ▯ LADDER
- ↑ UP
- ⚐ SPAWN POINT
- ⚑ FLAG

WAREHOUSE 2ND LEVEL

WAREHOUSE 3RD LEVEL

LOADING DOCK 2ND LEVEL

OFFICES 2ND LEVEL

GAS STATION ROOF

GARAGE ROOF

NORTH TOWERS

WAREHOUSE

CREEK

NORTH WOODS

GAS TANKS

LOADING DOCK

BRIDGE

TRAIN STATION

CONTAINERS

OFFICES

CRASH

GAS STATION

STRIP MALL

POWER STATION

WATER TOWER

GARAGE

SOUTH WOODS

BARRACKS

SOUTH TOWERS

Skin your ACR with the Arctic camo. Given that most outdoor areas are snow-covered, this helps you blend in. The ACR has a good range and solid power, and with the ACOG scope and a silencer attached, you can engage enemies at both medium distance and long range. The silencer reduces your effective range a little, but you should still be able to hit someone from quite a distance without alerting nearby enemies. The ACR has a good rate of fire and feels comfortable to shoot. You can use it to snipe or run and gun, but the weapon works best in close quarters firefights with a Red Dot Scope or a Holographic Sight.

Your backup weapon is the TMP with Akimbo and silencers attached. If you get into hot water, wave these at anything that slithers. While they're a little difficult to control at first, dual TMPs can be deadly and accurate if you learn to burst-fire them. Try the burst firing technique paired with the pump technique (i.e. alternating fire between the two weapons). This method lets you continue shooting one weapon while you reload the other. If you aren't comfortable firing both weapons or incorporating both techniques, you can still fire one weapon until it's empty and then empty the other one. By that time, the first one's reloaded, and you can repeat.

## MODE: DOMINATION

TERRAIN: HILLS, SEMI-WOODED, SHIPPING COMPLEX • FACTIONS: OP FOR/TF 141 • WEATHER/T.O.D.: LIGHT BLOWING SNOW/LATE AFTERNOON

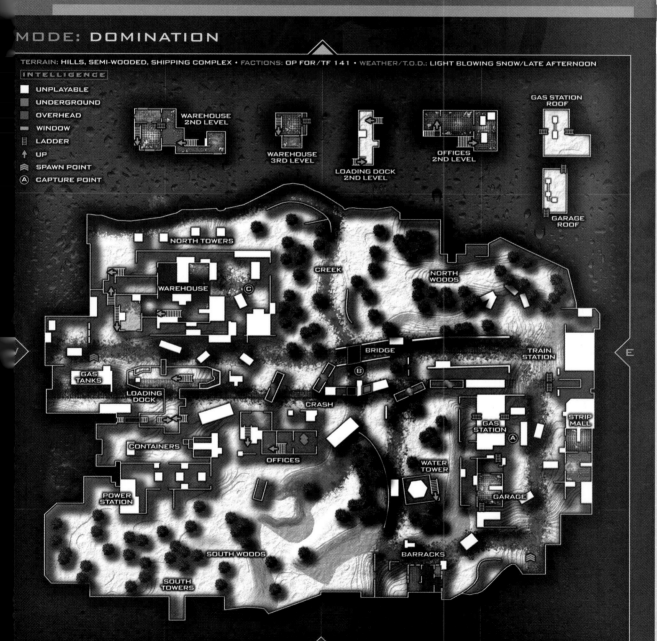

INTELLIGENCE
- UNPLAYABLE
- UNDERGROUND
- OVERHEAD
- WINDOW
- LADDER
- UP
- SPAWN POINT
- Ⓐ CAPTURE POINT

WAREHOUSE 2ND LEVEL

WAREHOUSE 3RD LEVEL

LOADING DOCK 2ND LEVEL

OFFICES 2ND LEVEL

GAS STATION ROOF

GARAGE ROOF

NORTH TOWERS

WAREHOUSE Ⓒ

CREEK

NORTH WOODS

BRIDGE Ⓑ

TRAIN STATION

GAS TANKS

LOADING DOCK

CRASH

GAS STATION Ⓐ

STRIP MALL

CONTAINERS

OFFICES

WATER TOWER

GARAGE

POWER STATION

SOUTH WOODS

BARRACKS

SOUTH TOWERS

E

The alternating technique is a valuable trick for any weapons sporting the Akimbo Attachment.

Choose Tactical Insertion for your equipment slot. If you see a group of enemies coming your way, you can throw smoke at your feet ninja-style and then toss your Tactical Insertion in the same spot. Come out fighting, and eliminating as many foes as you can, staying silent with your suppressors. If you die, you can respawn and immediately resume the assault. Keep your Tactical Insertion ready for deployment if you approach a hot zone, or if you traverse a large area and don't want to repeat the lengthy jog. Always use smoke to cover this action.

Plenty of snipers scan the horizon for movement, but they can't shoot you if they can't see you.

So, Bling is your first Perk, allowing you to run a scope and silencer on your primary weapon, and Akimbo and silencers on your secondary. Cold Blooded keeps you off the radar, Thermals, UAVs, and Sentries. The Pro version also removes your name and red crosshairs from enemy view. And you have Ninja for Perk three, making you invisible to Heartbeat Sensors (Pro adds silent footsteps). With two silenced weapons and all of your Perks keeping you off of the grid, you're nearly invisible.

## MODE: HEADQUARTERS

TERRAIN: HILLS, SEMI-WOODED, SHIPPING COMPLEX • FACTIONS: OP FOR/TF 141 • WEATHER/T.O.D.: LIGHT BLOWING SNOW/LATE AFTERNOON

### INTELLIGENCE

- □ UNPLAYABLE
- ■ UNDERGROUND
- ▣ OVERHEAD
- ▬ WINDOW
- ▯ LADDER
- ↑ UP
- ⬗ SPAWN POINT
- ⛪ HEADQUARTERS

WAREHOUSE 2ND LEVEL

WAREHOUSE 3RD LEVEL

LOADING DOCK 2ND LEVEL

OFFICES 2ND LEVEL

GAS STATION ROOF

GARAGE ROOF

NORTH TOWERS

CREEK

NORTH WOODS

WAREHOUSE

BRIDGE

TRAIN STATION

GAS TANKS

LOADING DOCK

CRASH

GAS STATION

STRIP MALL

CONTAINERS

OFFICES

WATER TOWER

GARAGE

POWER STATION

SOUTH WOODS

BARRACKS

SOUTH TOWERS

# MODE: SABOTAGE

TERRAIN: HILLS, SEMI-WOODED, SHIPPING COMPLEX • FACTIONS: OP FOR/TF 141 • WEATHER/T.O.D.: LIGHT BLOWING SNOW/LATE AFTERNOON

**INTELLIGENCE**

- ☐ UNPLAYABLE
- ☐ UNDERGROUND
- ☐ OVERHEAD
- ▬ WINDOW
- ▯ LADDER
- ↑ UP
- ◈ SPAWN POINT
- ▤ BOMB
- ☀ BOMB PLANT

Look for several crashed train cars you can enter in the middle of this map. Watch out for enemies hiding inside, and use them whenever you wish, for example to watch an objective or to snipe. This map contains many sniping lanes, especially down the center near the trains, so you may have to duck into the train cars from time to time. Be careful not to make too much noise when you're inside them. The North Woods and the wooded area just north of the Water Tower are great sniping spots, as is the Warehouse's third-floor balcony. The roofs of the Gas Station and the Garage are also high vantage points. Just be careful getting to them, as many snipers focus their attention on them.

A good way to get from east to west covertly is to move through the north side of the train tracks in the North Woods, up to the frozen creek. Take that north and west to the back of the Warehouse. This lets you infiltrate the enemy spawn, while the route hides you from view. The Loading Dock just south of the Warehouse has a second level that gives scoped shooters an elevated platform from which to shoot. The Containers, Power Station areas, and the Offices offer good ambush locations. Consider bringing Claymores into these areas.

## MODE: SEARCH & DESTROY / DEMOLITION

TERRAIN: HILLS, SEMI-WOODED, SHIPPING COMPLEX • FACTIONS: OP FOR/TF 141 • WEATHER/T.O.D.: LIGHT BLOWING SNOW/LATE AFTERNOON

**INTELLIGENCE**

- ☐ UNPLAYABLE
- ◼ UNDERGROUND
- ◼ OVERHEAD
- ▬ WINDOW
- ▯ LADDER
- ↑ UP
- ⧯ SPAWN POINT
- ▬ BOMB
- ✳ BOMB PLANT

WAREHOUSE 2ND LEVEL

WAREHOUSE 3RD LEVEL

LOADING DOCK 2ND LEVEL

OFFICES 2ND LEVEL

GAS STATION ROOF

GARAGE ROOF

NORTH TOWERS

CREEK

NORTH WOODS

WAREHOUSE

BRIDGE

TRAIN STATION

GAS TANKS

LOADING DOCK

CRASH

GAS STATION

STRIP MALL

CONTAINERS

OFFICES

WATER TOWER

POWER STATION

GARAGE

SOUTH WOODS

BARRACKS

SOUTH TOWERS

Most of the fighting takes place up and down the train tracks and around the Warehouse. Keep this in mind when you look for snipers or plan your team's route toward an objective. Think about where you would watch if you were on that side, and keep your eyes open for traps like C4 and Claymores. As with many maps, sticking near the perimeter to maneuver from one side to the other is a good bet. This map offers many trees and some hills to shield you from enemy view. If necessary, use smoke to cover areas where you have to maneuver in the open. Remember, you only get one Smoke Grenade, so coordinate with your team to stagger them, and never use more than you need.

# MODE: TEAM DEATHMATCH

**TERRAIN:** HILLS, SEMI-WOODED, SHIPPING COMPLEX • **FACTIONS:** OP FOR/TF 141 • **WEATHER/T.O.D.:** LIGHT BLOWING SNOW/LATE AFTERNOON

**INTELLIGENCE**

- ☐ UNPLAYABLE
- ☐ UNDERGROUND
- ☐ OVERHEAD
- ▬ WINDOW
- ▯ LADDER
- ↑ UP
- ⇗ SPAWN POINT

WAREHOUSE 2ND LEVEL
WAREHOUSE 3RD LEVEL
LOADING DOCK 2ND LEVEL
OFFICES 2ND LEVEL
GAS STATION ROOF
GARAGE ROOF

NORTH TOWERS
WAREHOUSE
CREEK
NORTH WOODS
BRIDGE
TRAIN STATION
GAS TANKS
LOADING DOCK
CRASH
STRIP MALL
CONTAINERS
OFFICES
GAS STATION
POWER STATION
WATER TOWER
GARAGE
SOUTH WOODS
BARRACKS
SOUTH TOWERS

E

S

A    B    C    D

# ESTATE

This mountainside complex has many elevation changes and several multi-level buildings, including a main Lodge with three levels. This area is heavily wooded, so take appropriate camouflage. Many buildings offer second-story windows where you can get a good look at the map from different vantage points. The Boathouse sits atop the Overlook, and it can be a good defense point. The Workshop in the map's northwest corner can be quite defensible as well, depending on your objectives. You can play this map many ways, and it usually offers a good mix of sniping and ground pounding, so here's a suggested loadout:

## RENAISSANCE MAN

| | | |
|---|---|---|
| PRIMARY/ ATTACHMENT | FAMAS / Thermal Scope | |
| SECONDARY/ ATTACHMENT | .44 Magnum / Tactical Knife | |
| EQUIPMENT | Blast Shield | |
| SPECIAL GRENADE | Stun x2 | |
| PERK 1 | Sleight of Hand | |
| PERK 2 | Hardline | |
| PERK 3 | Commando | |
| DEATHSTREAK | Final Stand | |

## MODE: CAPTURE THE FLAG

TERRAIN: MOUNTAINOUS, WOODED, MULTIPLE MULTI-LEVEL STRUCTURES • FACTIONS: OP FOR/TF 141 • WEATHER/T.O.D.: CLEAR/MORNING

**INTELLIGENCE**

- ☐ UNPLAYABLE
- ▢ OVERHEAD
- ▬ WINDOW
- ▤ LADDER
- ↑ UP
- ⋙ SPAWN POINT
- ⚑ FLAG

POWER PLANT ROOF

POWER PLANT

SNOWMOBILE GARAGE 2ND LEVEL

MOON

WORKSHOP

SNOWMOBILE GARAGE

OVERLOOK

MAIN ROAD

WORKSHOP 2ND LEVEL

SPORT'S STAIRS

BOATHOUSE

LODGE

GREENHOUSE

LODGE 2ND LEVEL

GREENHOUSE LOWER LEVEL

LODGE BASEMENT

BACK WOODS

Designed as a multi-purpose tool, this class allows you to pick off enemies you wouldn't normally see, and it provides decent skills and protection to hold down areas. Equip your FAMAS with a Thermal Scope. This is perfect for spotting enemies through the trees and those perched in second-story windows. Such foes glow bright white even in the daytime. Your FAMAS is set to a three-round burst, which is very accurate and should be enough to down a man at range with a hit in the torso. Be careful when you take this weapon running and gunning, as getting used to the pumping action you need for a three-round burst weapon is difficult.

Your secondary weapon is the .44 Magnum with the Tactical Knife. The knife allows you to stab enemies much faster than with a regular knife. Combining it with the Commando Perk further increases your melee versatility. This combo weapon serves as a great backup for unexpected close quarters situations. Although it's a semiautomatic, it might be easier to handle than the FAMAS in close quarters. Try to dial in your melee stabbing radius. It's always better to stab someone than to shoot them and alert nearby enemies.

## MODE: DOMINATION

TERRAIN: MOUNTAINOUS, WOODED, MULTIPLE MULTI-LEVEL STRUCTURES • FACTIONS: OP FOR/TF 141 • WEATHER/T.O.D.: CLEAR/MORNING

**INTELLIGENCE**
- UNPLAYABLE
- OVERHEAD
- WINDOW
- LADDER
- UP
- SPAWN POINT
- (A) CAPTURE POINT

POWER PLANT ROOF

POWER PLANT

SNOWMOBILE GARAGE 2ND LEVEL

MOON

WORKSHOP

SNOWMOBILE GARAGE

OVERLOOK

WORKSHOP 2ND LEVEL

MAIN ROAD

BOATHOUSE

SPORT'S STAIRS

LODGE

GREENHOUSE

GREENHOUSE LOWER LEVEL

LODGE 2ND LEVEL

BACK WOODS

LODGE BASEMENT

Take the Blast Shield for your equipment. This item reduces the damage you take from explosives, such as Claymores, C4, grenades, Semtex, and even rockets. It's great for defending a confined space, like the Lodge or the Greenhouse. Explosive concussions bounce off walls still harm you, but the Blast Shield significantly lessens the effect. If you're entering a defensive mode, choose Sleight of Hand for your first slot and Hardline for your second. You never want to get caught in a reload, so Sleight of Hand lets you reload much faster than normal, and the Pro version lets you aim faster. You often rack up kills when you defend or camp, so Hardline is a great choice for your second Perk slot. It reduces your Killstreak Reward quotas by one kill. Once you pick off a few foes trying to come through your door, activate a Killstreak and push them back until your reinforcements arrive. Select Final Stand for your Deathstreak. You can live through getting downed if you can crawl away and survive long enough to recover. Because this map is heavily wooded and mountainous, you may be able to crawl out of the way long enough to rejoin the fight.

## MODE: HEADQUARTERS

TERRAIN: MOUNTAINOUS, WOODED, MULTIPLE MULTI-LEVEL STRUCTURES • FACTIONS: OP FOR/TF 141 • WEATHER/T.O.D.: CLEAR/MORNING

INTELLIGENCE

- UNPLAYABLE
- OVERHEAD
- WINDOW
- LADDER
- UP
- SPAWN POINT
- HEADQUARTERS

POWER PLANT ROOF

POWER PLANT

SNOWMOBILE GARAGE 2ND LEVEL

MOON

WORKSHOP

SNOWMOBILE GARAGE

OVERLOOK

MAIN ROAD

WORKSHOP 2ND LEVEL

SPORT'S STAIRS

BOATHOUSE

LODGE

GREENHOUSE

GREENHOUSE LOWER LEVEL

LODGE 2ND LEVEL

BACK WOODS

LODGE BASEMENT

# MODE: SABOTAGE

TERRAIN: MOUNTAINOUS, WOODED, MULTIPLE MULTI-LEVEL STRUCTURES • FACTIONS: OP FOR/TF 141 • WEATHER/T.O.D.: CLEAR/MORNING

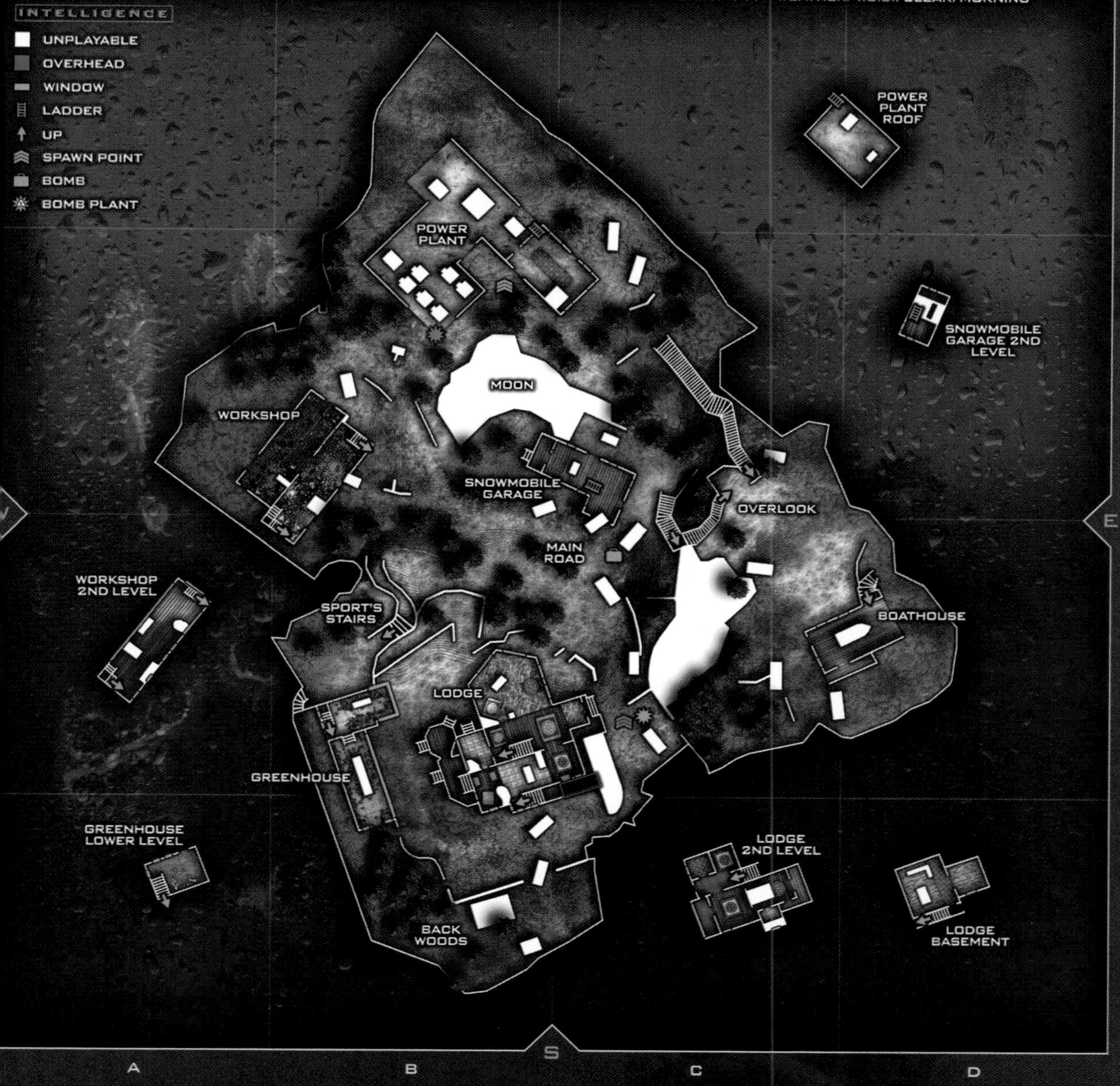

## INTELLIGENCE

- ☐ UNPLAYABLE
- ☐ OVERHEAD
- ▬ WINDOW
- ▯ LADDER
- ↑ UP
- ◈ SPAWN POINT
- ▪ BOMB
- ✳ BOMB PLANT

POWER PLANT ROOF

POWER PLANT

SNOWMOBILE GARAGE 2ND LEVEL

MOON

WORKSHOP

SNOWMOBILE GARAGE

OVERLOOK

MAIN ROAD

WORKSHOP 2ND LEVEL

SPORT'S STAIRS

BOATHOUSE

LODGE

GREENHOUSE

GREENHOUSE LOWER LEVEL

LODGE 2ND LEVEL

BACK WOODS

LODGE BASEMENT

A    B    C    D

The Lodge is where most of the action normally takes place. It's one of the map's most contested areas, depending on the mode and objective locations. It features a basement, a main floor with several rooms, and a second level with various windows from which you can scope enemies. This structure is very accessible, so watch your back when you move through it. The Boathouse located in the map's eastern portion sits on top of the Overlook, a large mountain crest looking down over the map. There are only two main ways to the Boathouse, so you can defend this area if necessary. You can even see the entrance to the Lodge from here. The Workshop in the northwest corner is also a good place to camp. Featuring a second level with well-hidden sniper slots, you can use your Thermal Scope to lay waste to anyone trying to creep toward you through the woods. You can use the trees just north of the Workshop to maneuver between the Workshop and the Power Plant. However, the Power Plant doesn't offer much cover or advantage other than its main building's roof. This small rooftop gives you a decent elevated sniping spot, despite its location at the map's lowest elevation. The Snowmobile Garage is very open and not the best place to hide, but you can set up good crossfire through it toward the Main Road. It also has a second level with windows for sniping.

# MODE: SEARCH & DESTROY / DEMOLITION

TERRAIN: MOUNTAINOUS, WOODED, MULTIPLE MULTI-LEVEL STRUCTURES • FACTIONS: OP FOR/TF 141 • WEATHER/T.O.D.: CLEAR/MORNING

**INTELLIGENCE**

- ☐ UNPLAYABLE
- ☐ OVERHEAD
- ▬ WINDOW
- ▦ LADDER
- ↑ UP
- ⬙ SPAWN POINT
- ▬ BOMB
- ✳ BOMB PLANT

POWER PLANT ROOF

POWER PLANT

SNOWMOBILE GARAGE 2ND LEVEL

MOON

WORKSHOP

SNOWMOBILE GARAGE

OVERLOOK

MAIN ROAD

WORKSHOP 2ND LEVEL

BOATHOUSE

SPORT'S STAIRS

LODGE

GREENHOUSE

LODGE 2ND LEVEL

GREENHOUSE LOWER LEVEL

BACK WOODS

LODGE BASEMENT

Use the terrain to your advantage on this map. Sometimes higher ground isn't always the best, especially if you have a Thermal Scope. Enemies stand out really well in the woods and peeking out of windows. If they come down the mountain toward you, they stand out sharply against the mountainside. Watch Sport's Stairs, the Main Road, and the Overlook stairways for approaching enemies. The same goes for the map's densely wooded areas. When you work your way up the hill to the Lodge, try to get to an elevated area and thin out the enemy before you push further. Clear a side or a path for yourself, and then move forward. If you can push past the Greenhouse into the Back Woods, you can flank the enemy in the Lodge. Just watch for enemies in the Boathouse looking west toward you.

# MODE: TEAM DEATHMATCH

TERRAIN: MOUNTAINOUS, WOODED, MULTIPLE MULTI-LEVEL STRUCTURES • FACTIONS: OP FOR/TF 141 • WEATHER/T.O.D.: CLEAR/MORNING

**INTELLIGENCE**

- ☐ UNPLAYABLE
- ☐ OVERHEAD
- ▬ WINDOW
- ▤ LADDER
- ↑ UP
- ⏬ SPAWN POINT

POWER PLANT ROOF

POWER PLANT

SNOWMOBILE GARAGE 2ND LEVEL

MOON

WORKSHOP

SNOWMOBILE GARAGE

OVERLOOK

MAIN ROAD

BOATHOUSE

WORKSHOP 2ND LEVEL

SPORT'S STAIRS

LODGE

GREENHOUSE

GREENHOUSE LOWER LEVEL

LODGE 2ND LEVEL

LODGE BASEMENT

BACK WOODS

# FAVELA

Favela is littered with multi-level buildings and structures, making combat a little more precarious, as you must think vertically. You must keep your eyes on many rooftops. The map offers great alternate routes if you get cornered. From the Main Street, you can cut through the Barber Shop, out to the Cemetery, and continue up behind the Laundromat. From the southwest corner, you can sneak through the Grassy Knoll, into the Junkyard, and back through the Playground. A good plan is to work the borders and make your way into the center. You often encounter close quarters gunplay, so try the following class:

## Eraser

| | | |
|---|---|---|
| PRIMARY/ ATTACHMENT | M240 / Grip & Red Dot | |
| SECONDARY/ ATTACHMENT | Model 1887 / FMJ | |
| EQUIPMENT | Claymore | |
| SPECIAL GRENADE | Stun x2 | |
| PERK 1 | Bling | |
| PERK 2 | Stopping Power | |
| PERK 3 | Steady Aim | |
| DEATHSTREAK | Painkiller | |

## MODE: CAPTURE THE FLAG

TERRAIN: FLAT, INNER CITY, MULTIPLE MULTI-LEVEL STRUCTURES • FACTIONS: MILITIA/TF 141 • WEATHER/T.O.D.: CLEAR/MID-MORNING

### INTELLIGENCE

- ■ UNPLAYABLE
- ▬ WINDOW
- ▯ LADDER
- ↑ UP
- ◤ SPAWN POINT
- ⚑ FLAG

BAR 3RD LEVEL

SHACKS

PLAYGROUND

FRUIT STAND

ROOF GARDEN

JUNKYARD

YELLOW BUILDING

SOCCER FIELD

LAUNDROMAT

BAR 2ND LEVEL

CRACKHOUSE

GRASSY KNOLL

SIDE STREET

ICE CREAM SHOP

GRIFTER'S GREEN HOUSE

BARBER SHOP

CEMETARY

MAIN STREET

BRICKHOUSE

LAUNDROMAT 2ND LEVEL

GREEN HOUSE 2ND LEVEL

GRIFTER'S GREEN HOUSE 3RD LEVEL

BARBER SHOP 2ND LEVEL

ICE CREAM SHOP 2ND LEVEL

LAUNDROMAT 3RD LEVEL

The Eraser loadout provides lots of massive firepower. Because there are so many buildings in this map, you need something to help open doors. The M240 lets you shoot straight through them. Fire through walls where you think enemies are hiding, and watch for the "X" telling you you've found a target. With its large magazine, the M240 can get you in and out of tough situations without reloading. The Grip and Red Dot Scope decrease your recoil and increase your accuracy. With Steady Aim as your third Perk, you don't even have to look through the sight to keep a tight spread.

Your backup weapon is the Model 1887 lever action shotgun with FMJ. Stopping power and FMJ combined on this weapon make it a man-stopper. Putting someone in the grave shouldn't take more than a blast or two. Swap to this weapon whenever you move quickly from one place to another, in case an unexpected engagement arises. The shotgun pushes enemies back a bit and slows their reaction, which should give you enough time to finish them off. If you maneuver into the middle of the map, bring your Claymore. Drop one inside a doorway to a heavily trafficked area, and then move on. Do this every chance you get, as you can often learn whether someone is following you when that person triggers your Claymore.

# MODE: DOMINATION

TERRAIN: FLAT, INNER CITY, MULTIPLE MULTI-LEVEL STRUCTURES • FACTIONS: MILITIA/TF 141 • WEATHER/T.O.D.: CLEAR/MID-MORNING

**INTELLIGENCE**

- ▪ UNPLAYABLE
- ▬ WINDOW
- ▯ LADDER
- ⬆ UP
- ⩙ SPAWN POINT
- Ⓐ CAPTURE POINT

BAR 3RD LEVEL

SHACKS

PLAYGROUND

FRUIT STAND

ROOF GARDEN

YELLOW BUILDING

SOCCER FIELD

JUNKYARD

BAR 2ND LEVEL

LAUNDROMAT

CRACKHOUSE

GRASSY KNOLL

SIDE STREET

ICE CREAM SHOP

GRIFTER'S GREEN HOUSE

BARBER SHOP

CEMETARY

MAIN STREET

BRICKHOUSE

LAUNDROMAT 2ND LEVEL

GREEN HOUSE 2ND LEVEL

GRIFTER'S GREEN HOUSE 3RD LEVEL

BARBER SHOP 2ND LEVEL

ICE CREAM SHOP 2ND LEVEL

LAUNDROMAT 3RD LEVEL

Bring Stun Grenades to help clear rooms. Toss in a Stun and see if you get an "X." If you do, break out the M240 and start walling. If you see the "X" again, either keep going or toss in another Stun and break out the shotgun. Move in, eliminate the squatter, and secure the area with a Claymore. With Steady Aim tightening your groupings, close quarters battles won't be very close at all. Remember that this is a very tight map. It's large enough to get around without being seen, but most battles occur in medium to short distances. You respawn into fire many times, so the Painkiller Deathstreak works well.

This map offers tons of places in which to hide, defend, and lock down. With so much close quarters combat, think about taking a submachine gun with lots of rounds, such as the P90 over your LMG. It's not crucial, but it's a decent option. The Main Street typically sees a lot of action, so be ready to check both ends before you head out there. Also check the Brickhouse windows and the roof of Grifter's Green House. You can easily get picked off from either of these areas if you don't look up. This map lets you maneuver around enemies via several rooftops and ledges, so try to use them whenever you can.

## MODE: HEADQUARTERS

TERRAIN: FLAT, INNER CITY, MULTIPLE MULTI-LEVEL STRUCTURES • FACTIONS: MILITIA/TF 141 • WEATHER/T.O.D.: CLEAR/MID-MORNING

**INTELLIGENCE**
- ☐ UNPLAYABLE
- ▬ WINDOW
- ☷ LADDER
- ↑ UP
- ⬙ SPAWN POINT
- ⛫ HEADQUARTERS

BAR 3RD LEVEL

SHACKS

PLAYGROUND

FRUIT STAND

ROOF GARDEN

YELLOW BUILDING

JUNKYARD

SOCCER FIELD

LAUNDROMAT

BAR 2ND LEVEL

CRACKHOUSE

GRASSY KNOLL

SIDE STREET

ICE CREAM SHOP

GRIFTER'S GREEN HOUSE

BARBER SHOP

CEMETARY

MAIN STREET

BRICKHOUSE

LAUNDROMAT 2ND LEVEL

GREEN HOUSE 2ND LEVEL

GRIFTER'S GREEN HOUSE 3RD LEVEL

BARBER SHOP 2ND LEVEL

ICE CREAM SHOP 2ND LEVEL

LAUNDROMAT 3RD LEVEL

# MODE: SABOTAGE

TERRAIN: FLAT, INNER CITY, MULTIPLE MULTI-LEVEL STRUCTURES • FACTIONS: MILITIA/TF 141 • WEATHER/T.O.D.: CLEAR/MID-MORNING

**INTELLIGENCE**
- ☐ UNPLAYABLE
- ▭ WINDOW
- ▤ LADDER
- ↑ UP
- ⬙ SPAWN POINT
- ▣ BOMB
- ✸ BOMB PLANT

The Barber Shop second story offers windows for watching part of Main Street and the Brickhouse. The Laundromat complex has a third-story rooftop to watch over the Soccer Field and the northern strip of Shacks. Be careful to avoid getting picked off here from the Roof Garden or the Green House roof. Check there first before you venture out on the rooftops. The Junkyard and the Grassy Knoll are defensible positions, but watch the Crackhouse's second story for enemies trying to pop a shot at your team. You must watch four chokepoints in this area, but they're large enough that one or two players can cover more than one of them.

For long-range fighting, select an ACOG scope and set up on either side of the Main Street, or in the street's southeast corner, looking north toward the Soccer Field. Enemies frequent these areas, so be patient and let them cross before you take them down. If you're running by yourself, consider a silencer to remain hidden from nearby enemies. Remember that enemies you kill can view your Kill Cam and identify the location from where you shot them. Chances are, they'll try to engage you when they respawn, assuming the game mode allows respawns.

TERRAIN: FLAT, INNER CITY, MULTIPLE MULTI-LEVEL STRUCTURES • FACTIONS: **MILITIA/TF 141** • WEATHER/T.O.D.: CLEAR/MID-MORNING

## INTELLIGENCE

■ UNPLAYABLE
▬ WINDOW
▤ LADDER
↑ UP
☰ SPAWN POINT
▮ BOMB
✳ BOMB PLANT

BAR
3RD LEVEL

PLAYGROUND

SHACKS

FRUIT
STAND

ROOF
GARDEN

JUNKYARD

YELLOW
BUILDING

SOCCER
FIELD

LAUNDROMAT

BAR
2ND LEVEL

CRACKHOUSE

GRASSY
KNOLL

SIDE
STREET

ICE
CREAM
SHOP

GRIFTER'S
GREEN
HOUSE

BARBER
SHOP

CEMETARY

MAIN STREET

BRICKHOUSE

LAUNDROMAT
2ND LEVEL

GREEN HOUSE
2ND LEVEL

GRIFTER'S GREEN
HOUSE 3RD LEVEL

BARBER
SHOP 2ND LEVEL

ICE CREAM
SHOP 2ND LEVEL

LAUNDROMAT
3RD LEVEL

W

S

1

2

3

4

A

B

C

D

# MODE: TEAM DEATHMATCH

TERRAIN: FLAT, INNER CITY, MULTIPLE MULTI-LEVEL STRUCTURES • FACTIONS: MILITIA/TF 141 • WEATHER/T.O.D.: CLEAR/MID-MORNING

**INTELLIGENCE**

- ⬜ UNPLAYABLE
- ▭ WINDOW
- ▯ LADDER
- ↑ UP
- ⧩ SPAWN POINT

BAR
3RD LEVEL

SHACKS

PLAYGROUND

FRUIT
STAND

ROOF
GARDEN

YELLOW
BUILDING

JUNKYARD

SOCCER
FIELD

BAR
2ND LEVEL

LAUNDROMAT

CRACKHOUSE

GRASSY
KNOLL

SIDE
STREET

ICE
CREAM
SHOP

GRIFTER'S
GREEN
HOUSE

BARBER
SHOP

CEMETARY

MAIN STREET

BRICKHOUSE

LAUNDROMAT
2ND LEVEL

GREEN HOUSE
2ND LEVEL

GRIFTER'S GREEN
HOUSE 3RD LEVEL

BARBER
SHOP 2ND LEVEL

ICE CREAM
SHOP 2ND LEVEL

LAUNDROMAT
3RD LEVEL

A     B     C     D

# HIGHRISE

Be ready for anything, especially snipers and getting flanked. There's a large pit in this map's center and two office building complexes on either end. You can use the tunnel system to get from one side to the other without contending with the snipers up top. However, be wary of close quarters engagements down below. Watch the Helipad and the office complex windows for elevated enemies. There isn't a lot of elevation change, but you should keep your eyes on several upper and lower locations. Sniper rifles work well here, so that's what we suggest in the following character class:

## OVER-UNDER

| PRIMARY/ATTACHMENT | WA2000 / Silencer | |
|---|---|---|
| SECONDARY/ATTACHMENT | M93 Raffica / Holographic Sight | |
| EQUIPMENT | Throwing Knife | |
| SPECIAL GRENADE | Smoke | |
| PERK 1 | One Man Army | |
| PERK 2 | Hardline | |
| PERK 3 | Ninja | |
| DEATHSTREAK | Final Stand | |

## MODE: CAPTURE THE FLAG

TERRAIN: FLAT, SKYSCRAPER ROOF & OFFICES • FACTIONS: OP FOR/RANGERS • WEATHER/T.O.D.: LIGHT WIND, BLOWING DEBRIS/EVENING

**INTELLIGENCE**

- ◻ UNPLAYABLE
- ▬ WINDOW
- ▯ LADDER
- ▶ MOUNTED GUN
- ↑ UP
- ⬆ SPAWN POINT
- ⚑ FLAG

STORE ROOM

MAIL ROOM

NORTH OFFICES

CAFE

HELIPAD TOP LEVEL

TO NORTH OFFICES

ELEVATOR ROOF

NORTH TUNNEL

FENCE SHACK ROOF

PROPANE SHACK

PROPANE SHACK ROOF

RED PIT

POWER CENTER

ELEVATORS

PROPANE TANK

HELIPAD

RED PIT

RED PIT

TO HELIPAD

FENCE SHACK

SOUTH TUNNEL

SOUTH OFFICES

EXECUTIVE OFFICES

TO SOUTH OFFICES

For this encounter, be ready for anything either topside or underground. Take a sniper rifle and machine pistol just in case. Your primary weapon has great penetration and range. Try setting up with your back to something and snipe across the center of the map. With the attached silencer, you remain elusive, which is beneficial because enemies can flank you on this map. The Ninja Perk keeps you off enemy Heartbeat Sensors, and the Pro version keeps you quiet if you have to bug out. You may have to use a smoke screen to divert the enemy's attention, or to create cover for relocation. If snipers can't see you, they may fire blindly into the smoke, so be careful.

Your backup weapon is the M93 Raffica, which is a three-round burst, close-range weapon. Switch to this when you have to get from one point to another. With the Holographic Sight attached, you'll have a better chance to headshot enemies. Always aim for the head with three-round burst rifles, especially with underpowered weapons like machine pistols. If you run low on ammo, prepare to switch to the Throwing Knife occupying your equipment slot. If you miss with this, you can always go back and retrieve it.

## MODE: DOMINATION

This loadout offers a nice selection of Perks, including One Man Army, which lets you switch classes at any time. Have a secondary class rigged for medium to close quarters combat. If the dynamic of the game changes, you'll be ready for anything. We recommend Hardline, your second Perk, hoping you can rack up Killstreaks by quietly sniping enemies across the map. With one fewer kill to achieve a Killstreak Reward, try to wait until you hit four, and then send in a Predator or a Sentry Gun. With Ninja as your last Perk, you stay off enemy Heartbeat Sensors. Because this map provides lots of cover, from cubicles to rooftop structures, choose Final Stand for your Deathstreak. The abundant cover helps you crawl to safety and recover.

Both the North and South Offices offer great sniping locations. Find a slot that offers cover from the sides and, if possible, from the back. Try to pick off enemies milling around in the opposite office complexes, or those trying to cross the middle without going underground. These make easy pickings—just lead them sufficiently. Getting from one side to the other requires you to go underground. The tunnels are tight, then they open up in the center, where you are potentially vulnerable to shooters from above.

## MODE: HEADQUARTERS

TERRAIN: FLAT, SKYSCRAPER ROOF & OFFICES • FACTIONS: OP FOR/RANGERS • WEATHER/T.O.D.: LIGHT WIND, BLOWING DEBRIS/EVENING

### INTELLIGENCE

- UNPLAYABLE
- WINDOW
- LADDER
- MOUNTED GUN
- UP
- SPAWN POINT
- HEADQUARTERS

# MODE: SABOTAGE

TERRAIN: FLAT, SKYSCRAPER ROOF & OFFICES • FACTIONS: OP FOR/RANGERS • WEATHER/T.O.D.: LIGHT WIND, BLOWING DEBRIS/EVENING

**INTELLIGENCE**

- ◻ UNPLAYABLE
- ▬ WINDOW
- ▯ LADDER
- ▶ MOUNTED GUN
- ↑ UP
- ⌇ SPAWN POINT
- ▮ BOMB
- ✳ BOMB PLANT

You can shoot from a few elevated areas aside from the office building windows, such as the top of the Elevators, Propane Tank, and the Fence Shack. Use these areas sparingly, as you stand out to snipers. They may give you a decent vantage point on certain enemies, but the exposure may not be worth it. Make sure it's clear before you pop your head up there.

The Helipad offers an elevated platform from which to scan east to west toward the Elevators. It has a little more cover than the other rooftop areas. You can see across, through the Power Center and to the Elevators, and you can use this as a good cross-sniping platform. If you need to lock down the Red Pit and tunnel system, take at least five players to do so. Although there are five points to watch, it could be a great place to set up shop. Watch every entrance to the Red Pit, including those from the Offices. Have the last player watch the Helipad entrance. Enemies can drop in over the sides and down the stairs, so have your Red Pit players watch for them. The Offices are the best defensible areas. While players can gain access through many windows, two teammates can set up a crossfire to prevent enemies from coming through them.

## MODE: SEARCH & DESTROY / DEMOLITION

TERRAIN: FLAT, SKYSCRAPER ROOF & OFFICES • FACTIONS: OP FOR/RANGERS • WEATHER/T.O.D.: LIGHT WIND, BLOWING DEBRIS/EVENING

**INTELLIGENCE**

- ☐ UNPLAYABLE
- ▬ WINDOW
- ▦ LADDER
- ▶ MOUNTED GUN
- ↑ UP
- ≫ SPAWN POINT
- 📦 BOMB
- ✹ BOMB PLANT

Labels on map:
STORE ROOM, MAIL ROOM, NORTH OFFICES, CAFE, HELIPAD TOP LEVEL, ELEVATOR ROOF, TO NORTH OFFICES, NORTH TUNNEL, FENCE SHACK ROOF, PROPANE SHACK, PROPANE SHACK ROOF, RED PIT, POWER CENTER, ELEVATORS, HELIPAD, PROPANE TANK, RED PIT, TO HELIPAD, FENCE SHACK, SOUTH TUNNEL, SOUTH OFFICES, EXECUTIVE OFFICES, TO SOUTH OFFICES

W — E
S

Column labels: A  B  C  D
Row labels: 1  2  3  4

Just assign another player to cover the stairs that lead up from the Red Pit to avoid getting flanked. This setup can let you use two or three snipers to lay waste to the enemy contingent heading toward you. This map is very linear, and it's like a cattle chute, so be careful crossing, and focus on enemies trying to do the same.

# MODE: TEAM DEATHMATCH

TERRAIN: FLAT, SKYSCRAPER ROOF & OFFICES • FACTIONS: OP FOR/RANGERS • WEATHER/T.O.D.: LIGHT WIND, BLOWING DEBRIS/EVENING

**INTELLIGENCE**

- ☐ UNPLAYABLE
- ▬ WINDOW
- 🪜 LADDER
- ▶ MOUNTED GUN
- ↑ UP
- ⟩⟩ SPAWN POINT

# ❱ INVASION

This war-torn part of the city features a large, two-story base in the northwest corner. Make sure what you see is actually an enemy and not a newspaper before you fire. One team starts on the Convoy road near the base, but the map is covered with multiple buildings, offering several upper levels from which to gain decent vantage points. Watch for snipers camped in the eastern part of this map, in the Sniper Apartment and the Loft. Players usually frequent these two areas. Much fighting occurs in the map's center, in and around the Café, but the conflict moves around the map quite a bit. Gear up with a good all-purpose kit.

## INVADER

| PRIMARY/ATTACHMENT | SCAR-H / Heartbeat Sensor | |
|---|---|---|
| SECONDARY/ATTACHMENT | AA-12 / Extended Mags | |
| EQUIPMENT | Frag | |
| SPECIAL GRENADE | Stun x2 | |
| PERK 1 | Scavenger | |
| PERK 2 | Danger Close | |
| PERK 3 | Scrambler | |
| DEATHSTREAK | Martyrdom | |

## MODE: CAPTURE THE FLAG

TERRAIN: FLAT, CITY, MULTIPLE MULTI-LEVEL BUILDINGS • FACTIONS: OP FOR/RANGERS • WEATHER/T.O.D.: HAZY, BLOWING DEBRIS/AFTERNOON

INTELLIGENCE
- ■ UNPLAYABLE
- ▬ WINDOW
- ▐ LADDER
- ↑ UP
- ⫸ SPAWN POINT
- ⚑ FLAG

COFFEE SHOP 2ND LEVEL

LOFT 2ND LEVEL

SODA SHOP ROOF

U.S. BASE

GENERAL STORE

SNIPER APARTMENT 2ND LEVEL

FIELD

CONVOY

COURTYARD

SNIPER APARTMENT

ALCOVE

CAFE

VIDEO STORE

LOFT

U.S. BASE 2ND LEVEL

BATHROOMS

BOUTIQUE

COFFEE SHOP

SODA SHOP

GAS STATION

PARKING LOT

Attaching the Heartbeat Sensor to your SCAR-H provides a two-in-one system with great firepower and accuracy, as well as enemy detection abilities. This weapon proves accurate at most distances you engage on this map. You can dart into and out of many places, so try not to sprint in order to see your Heartbeat Sensor. Frequently check it for enemies holed up in nearby buildings. Your secondary weapon is the fully automatic AA-12 shotgun. It has a limited amount of ammunition, so take Extended Mags as your Attachment.

Try using your Stun and Frag Grenades in combination. Pop a Stun into rooms or buildings that may contain enemies, and watch for the "X." If you get the "X," follow your Stun with a quick, cooked Frag to clean out the target. If you don't kill the foe, toss in your last Stun Grenade and move in with your auto shotgun to finish the job. Whenever you can kill someone with a grenade instead of engaging in a firefight, do so. You may not get out alive if more than one enemy is inside, so select Martyrdom for your Deathstreak. If they kill you before you kill them, hopefully you can take them with you.

## MODE: DOMINATION

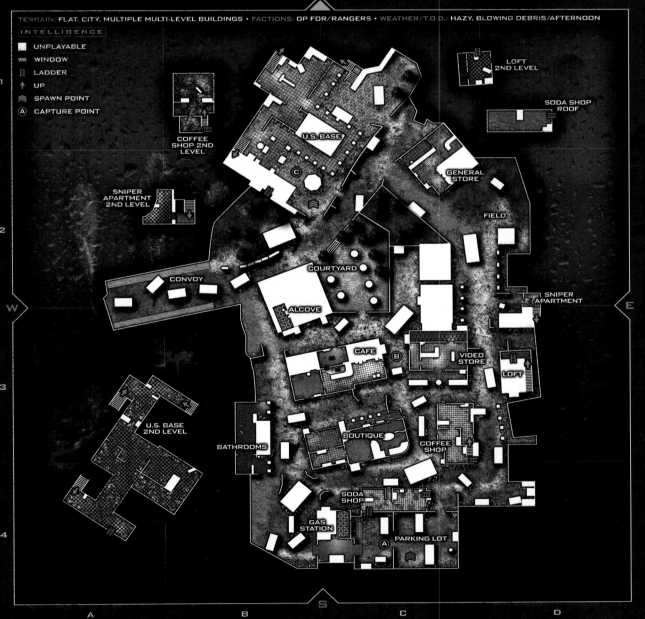

TERRAIN: FLAT, CITY, MULTIPLE MULTI-LEVEL BUILDINGS • FACTIONS: OP FOR/RANGERS • WEATHER/T.O.D.: HAZY, BLOWING DEBRIS/AFTERNOON

INTELLIGENCE

- UNPLAYABLE
- WINDOW
- LADDER
- UP
- SPAWN POINT
- Ⓐ CAPTURE POINT

We intend this loadout's Perks to minimize your visibility and keep you stocked with ammo. The Scavenger Perk lets you resupply from dead enemies, while the Scrambler Perk jams enemy radar near your location. Again, be careful using this Perk, as enemies can tell you're in close proximity. They may find you by using your own Perk against you. Danger Close is your second Perk, giving your explosives more damage and (in the Pro version) increasing air support damage. This group of Perks is well suited to this environment, keeping you firing on the line longer, forcing enemies have to hunt for you without using radar.

The Parking Lot complex to the south is a decent defensible area. There are only two chokepoints to defend here, and you don't have to worry about the Soda Shop roof, as you can see the only accessible points from the Parking Lot. You can also defend the Bathrooms on the map's western side with a small group, albeit not as easily. Set up crossfire between the Café and the Boutique, as many players cross back and forth here and at the Coffee Shop and Video Store. The Coffee Shop's demolished second story offers great vistas of the map; just watch for sniper fire from the Sniper Apartment and the Loft in the east.

## MODE: HEADQUARTERS

TERRAIN: FLAT, CITY, MULTIPLE MULTI-LEVEL BUILDINGS • FACTIONS: OP FOR/RANGERS • WEATHER/T.O.D.: HAZY, BLOWING DEBRIS/AFTERNOON

INTELLIGENCE
- UNPLAYABLE
- WINDOW
- LADDER
- UP
- SPAWN POINT
- HEADQUARTERS

COFFEE SHOP 2ND LEVEL
LOFT 2ND LEVEL
U.S. BASE
SODA SHOP ROOF
SNIPER APARTMENT 2ND LEVEL
GENERAL STORE
FIELD
CONVOY
COURTYARD
SNIPER APARTMENT
ALCOVE
CAFE
VIDEO STORE
LOFT
U.S. BASE 2ND LEVEL
BATHROOMS
BOUTIQUE
COFFEE SHOP
SODA SHOP
GAS STATION
PARKING LOT

1
2
3
4
W
E
A
B
C
D
S
N

# MODE: SABOTAGE

TERRAIN: FLAT, CITY, MULTIPLE MULTI-LEVEL BUILDINGS • FACTIONS: OP FOR/RANGERS • WEATHER/T.O.D.: HAZY, BLOWING DEBRIS/AFTERNOON

## INTELLIGENCE

- ☐ UNPLAYABLE
- ▬ WINDOW
- 𝄃 LADDER
- ↑ UP
- ☰ SPAWN POINT
- ▣ BOMB
- ✳ BOMB PLANT

COFFEE SHOP 2ND LEVEL

SNIPER APARTMENT 2ND LEVEL

LOFT 2ND LEVEL

SODA SHOP ROOF

U.S. BASE

GENERAL STORE

FIELD

CONVOY

COURTYARD

SNIPER APARTMENT

ALCOVE

CAFE

VIDEO STORE

LOFT

U.S. BASE 2ND LEVEL

BATHROOMS

BOUTIQUE

COFFEE SHOP

SODA SHOP

GAS STATION

PARKING LOT

While the U.S. Base may seem like a great place to camp and hold off enemies, it may not be the best choice. Three stairways lead up to the second level, along with a ladder accessible from the base wall's south side. You can hold this second level with three players if one takes the window facing south to watch the south stairs and ladder, one player watches the northwestern stairs, and another watches the northeast stairs.

Be careful venturing through this map's top-middle section, near the Courtyard and Alcove areas. There are many places to hide here, including the trees, and you're exposed when you move through this area. Think about taking a longer way around to reach your destination. Head south toward the Bathrooms, then back up through the middle, between the Coffee Shop and Boutique. This map favors a run and gun play style, so our suggested loadout is geared for that. Don't feel like you have to move constantly. Moving up, stopping to wait for enemies to pass by, and stabbing them in the back isn't a bad strategy. The Invasion map offers many opportunities for this kind of up close, personal play.

TERRAIN: FLAT, CITY, MULTIPLE MULTI-LEVEL BUILDINGS • FACTIONS: OP FOR/RANGERS • WEATHER/T.O.D.: HAZY, BLOWING DEBRIS/AFTERNOON

**INTELLIGENCE**

- ■ UNPLAYABLE
- ▬ WINDOW
- ▤ LADDER
- ↑ UP
- ⧫ SPAWN POINT
- ✦ BOMB
- ✳ BOMB PLANT

1

2

W

3

4

COFFEE SHOP 2ND LEVEL

LOFT 2ND LEVEL

SODA SHOP ROOF

U.S. BASE

GENERAL STORE

FIELD

SNIPER APARTMENT 2ND LEVEL

CONVOY

COURTYARD

ALCOVE

SNIPER APARTMENT

CAFE

VIDEO STORE

LOFT

U.S. BASE 2ND LEVEL

BOUTIQUE

COFFEE SHOP

BATHROOMS

SODA SHOP

GAS STATION

PARKING LOT

A          B          S          C          D

# MODE: TEAM DEATHMATCH

TERRAIN: FLAT, CITY, MULTIPLE MULTI-LEVEL BUILDINGS • FACTIONS: OP FOR/RANGERS • WEATHER/T.O.D.: HAZY, BLOWING DEBRIS/AFTERNOON

**INTELLIGENCE**

- ☐ UNPLAYABLE
- ▦ WINDOW
- ▤ LADDER
- ↑ UP
- ◣ SPAWN POINT

LOFT 2ND LEVEL

COFFEE SHOP 2ND LEVEL

SODA SHOP ROOF

U.S. BASE

GENERAL STORE

SNIPER APARTMENT 2ND LEVEL

FIELD

CONVOY

COURTYARD

ALCOVE

SNIPER APARTMENT

CAFE

VIDEO STORE

LOFT

U.S. BASE 2ND LEVEL

BATHROOMS

BOUTIQUE

COFFEE SHOP

SODA SHOP

GAS STATION

PARKING LOT

A    B    S    C    D    E

ROSE

# ❭ KARACHI

This mission takes place in a burned-out desert town at dusk, with clear conditions and decent visibility. Ground Zero dots the center of this map, so watch your step, as Claymores can lurk in the rubble. This map's southern section has an outdoor market with a couple of multi-story buildings. The northern section features a good-sized Hotel, Bus Station, and Café. With a large Parking Lot to the east and a Warehouse and Waterfront to the west, there are plenty of places to get into trouble. There aren't many lines of fire for sniping, but you may have to make a long shot or two. Here's a good class for this map:

## GRUNT

| | | |
|---|---|---|
| PRIMARY/ATTACHMENT | M4A1 / Holographic Sight & Extended Mags | |
| SECONDARY/ATTACHMENT | M9 / FMJ & Extended Mags | |
| EQUIPMENT | Frag | |
| SPECIAL GRENADE | Stun x2 | |
| PERK 1 | Bling | |
| PERK 2 | Stopping Power | |
| PERK 3 | Last Stand | |
| DEATHSTREAK | Final Stand | |

## MODE: CAPTURE THE FLAG

TERRAIN: FLAT, DESERT TOWN, MULTI-LEVEL STRUCTURES • FACTIONS: OP FOR/SEALS • WEATHER/T.O.D.: CLEAR, LIGHT WIND / DUSK

### INTELLIGENCE

- ☐ UNPLAYABLE
- ☐ UNDERGROUND
- ☐ OVERHEAD
- ▬ WINDOW
- ▯ LADDER
- ▶ MOUNTED GUN
- ↑ UP
- ⩘ SPAWN POINT
- ⚑ FLAG

SHAKAR MART 2ND LEVEL

STOREROOM 2ND LEVEL

APARTMENTS 2ND LEVEL

HOTEL 2ND LEVEL

CAFE

BUS STATION

SHACKS

HOTEL

PARKING LOT

WATERFRONT

APARTMENTS

MINI MART

GROUND ZERO

WALLY'S WAREHOUSE

MOSQUE

STORE ROOM

PARKING LOT

MAIN ST.

SHAKAR MART

CHICKEN MARKET

CLOCK TOWER

You are a deadly, almost unkillable Grunt with our suggested loadout. Your standard-issue M4A1 assault rifle complete with Extended Mags is fitted with the highly accurate Holographic Sight. Great for all distances, the M4A1 is a stable, reliable, and powerful weapon. Don't hesitate to fire a few shots at distant enemies, especially with Stopping Power as your second Perk. This, along with the FMJ Attachment makes your pistol much deadlier than ever. You carry Extended Mags for both your primary and secondary weapons, so you shouldn't have to scavenge for ammo.

Use your Frag Grenades with your Stun Grenades to root out enemies and then turn them into paste. Last Stand is your third Perk. They thought they could kill you. They were wrong. With your extra-potent pistol, you can squeeze a few rounds at your killer before you die. If you run Last Stand's Pro version, you can even use a Frag Grenade. If you die four times without killing anyone, your Final Stand Deathstreak activates. Now, when you go into Last Stand, you can use your primary weapon and survive being downed if you don't endure further damage. This is a very simple class, but it excels at that. You can put a different scope on your rifle if you're more comfortable that way, but the Holographic Sight is good for almost any engagement.

## MODE: DOMINATION

TERRAIN: FLAT, DESERT TOWN, MULTI-LEVEL STRUCTURES • FACTIONS: OP FOR / SEALS • WEATHER/T.O.D.: CLEAR, LIGHT WIND / DUSK

INTELLIGENCE

- UNPLAYABLE
- UNDERGROUND
- OVERHEAD
- WINDOW
- LADDER
- MOUNTED GUN
- UP
- SPAWN POINT
- Ⓐ CAPTURE POINT

There are many ways to move around this map without being noticed. To get from east to west, try going through the Parking Lot to the Store Room, and move upstairs. Up there, you can move to the Apartments and easily get to the Waterfront. Use this map's upper levels to circumvent enemies and appear where they least expect you. The Shacks are a great place to spring an ambush. Set up in the Shacks' northeast corner to reduce nearby chokepoints to two. Place Claymores just inside the entrances to the Shacks. The Hotel's second level and the Apartments are also defensible areas, as they have limited chokepoints.

There's usually a lot of movement on this map, so consider sending a few volleys of grenades (either thrown or launched) over the buildings and into Ground Zero. Many players inevitably end up here when they try to rush their enemies. A well-placed grenade can get them out of the way before you even arrive. Early grenades are a big part of the game and can really decimate a team if you know where to place them. From the east side, try sending initial grenades out onto Main Street, into Ground Zero, into the Shacks, and over the Hotel. From the west, toss some into Ground Zero, the Shacks, the Mini Mart, and the Chicken Market. If you coordinate these grenades with your team so that each player places one at each spot, you'll avoid sending several

# MODE: SABOTAGE

TERRAIN: FLAT, DESERT TOWN, MULTI-LEVEL STRUCTURES • FACTIONS: OP FOR/SEALS • WEATHER/T.O.D.: CLEAR, LIGHT WIND / DUSK

## INTELLIGENCE

- ⬜ UNPLAYABLE
- ▦ UNDERGROUND
- ▨ OVERHEAD
- ▬ WINDOW
- ▯ LADDER
- ▶ MOUNTED GUN
- ↑ UP
- ⩘ SPAWN POINT
- ▭ BOMB
- ☀ BOMB PLANT

SHAKAR MART
2ND LEVEL

STOREROOM
2ND LEVEL

APARTMENTS
2ND LEVEL

HOTEL
2ND LEVEL

CAFE

BUS STATION

SHACKS

HOTEL

PARKING LOT

WATERFRONT

APARTMENTS

MINI
MART

MOSQUE

GROUND ZERO

PARKING LOT

WALLY'S
WAREHOUSE

STORE
ROOM

MAIN ST.

SHAKAR
MART

CHICKEN
MARKET

CLOCK
TOWER

E

A          B          S          C          D

grenades to one spot and none to the others. If you have a grenade launcher, send some into the enemy's spawn point right from the start. Just find their spawn on the maps in this guide and lob one in there. Coordinating with your teammates, try to create a spread of grenades to cover a larger area.

The Hotel can be a good spot for putting eyes on the map's northern section. You can get a good overview of the Shacks, the Café, and Bus Station from the second floor. Just watch your back for enemies sneaking up behind you. If possible, set Claymores at the top of the stairs, as that is the only way up.

If you get into the Shakar Mart's second level, you can cross a plank to access scaffolding, which affords a good look down Main Street. Just move slowly getting up there, as enemies may already be scoping that part of the map for snipers. The Chicken Market adjacent to the Shakar Mart is somewhat noisy, which is good for masking sounds. If you don't have the Ninja Perk and need to reload or move around, the Chicken Market is a good place to do it.

TERRAIN: FLAT, DESERT TOWN, MULTI-LEVEL STRUCTURES • FACTIONS: OP FOR/SEALS • WEATHER/T.O.D.: CLEAR, LIGHT WIND / DUSK

**INTELLIGENCE**

- ☐ UNPLAYABLE
- ▦ UNDERGROUND
- ▦ OVERHEAD
- ▬ WINDOW
- ▥ LADDER
- ▶ MOUNTED GUN
- ↑ UP
- ⌄ SPAWN POINT
- ▭ BOMB
- ✵ BOMB PLANT

SHAKAR MART
2ND LEVEL

STOREROOM
2ND LEVEL

APARTMENTS
2ND LEVEL

HOTEL
2ND LEVEL

CAFE

BUS STATION

SHACKS

HOTEL

PARKING LOT

W

WATERFRONT

APARTMENTS

MINI
MART

GROUND ZERO

WALLY'S
WAREHOUSE

MOSQUE

STORE
ROOM

PARKING LOT

MAIN ST.

SHAKAR
MART

CHICKEN
MARKET

CLOCK
TOWER

S

A        B        C        D

1

2

3

4

# MODE: TEAM DEATHMATCH

TERRAIN: FLAT, DESERT TOWN, MULTI-LEVEL STRUCTURES • FACTIONS: OP FOR/SEALS • WEATHER/T.O.D.: CLEAR, LIGHT WIND / DUSK

**INTELLIGENCE**

- ☐ UNPLAYABLE
- ▪ UNDERGROUND
- ▪ OVERHEAD
- ▬ WINDOW
- ▤ LADDER
- ▶ MOUNTED GUN
- ↑ UP
- ⌄ SPAWN POINT

SHAKAR MART 2ND LEVEL

STOREROOM 2ND LEVEL

APARTMENTS 2ND LEVEL

HOTEL 2ND LEVEL

CAFE

BUS STATION

SHACKS

WATERFRONT

HOTEL

PARKING LOT

APARTMENTS

MINI MART

WALLY'S WAREHOUSE

MOSQUE

GROUND ZERO

MAIN ST.

STORE ROOM

PARKING LOT

SHAKAR MART

CLOCK TOWER

CHICKEN MARKET

A B S C D

E

# QUARRY

This working stone quarry features massive elevation changes. It's a clear afternoon, but enemies can lurk both high and low. So, despite the daylight, enemies can evade your detection. It's a large map with multiple roads and paths throughout. There are many buildings, such as offices, warehouses, and garages. Two huge tanks with a platform around them for elevated engagements stand in the map's northeast section. A heavy-duty crane with three player-accessible levels sits in the map's center. You can climb many of the chiseled-out marble blocks. While it may take time to scale them, finding a nice corner up top can be worth the effort.

## ICU

| | | |
|---|---|---|
| PRIMARY/ ATTACHMENT | AUG HBAR / Thermal Scope & Grip | |
| SECONDARY/ ATTACHMENT | Javelin | |
| EQUIPMENT | Tactical Insertion | |
| SPECIAL GRENADE | Smoke | |
| PERK 1 | Bling | |
| PERK 2 | Danger Close | |
| PERK 3 | SitRep | |
| DEATHSTREAK | Martyrdom | |

## MODE: CAPTURE THE FLAG

TERRAIN: MULTI-LEVEL STONE QUARRY, MULTI-LEVEL BUILDINGS • FACTIONS: MILITIA/TF 141 • WEATHER/T.O.D.: CLEAR/EARLY AFTERNOON

**INTELLIGENCE**
- ☐ UNPLAYABLE
- ☐ OVERHEAD
- ▭ WINDOW
- ☰ LADDER
- ↑ UP
- ⟫ SPAWN POINT
- ⚑ FLAG

STORAGE FACILITY 2ND LEVEL
CRANE 3RD LEVEL
OFFICES 2ND LEVEL
WAREHOUSE 14 2ND LEVEL
LOADING BAY 2ND LEVEL
STORAGE FACILITY
TANK GARAGE 3RD LEVEL
TANK GARAGE 2ND LEVEL
INDUSTRIAL ROAD
CRANE 2ND LEVEL
THE DUMP
TO TANK GARAGE
EQUIPMENT GARAGE
BIG TANK
FLAG TANK
TANK GARAGE
CRANE
WAREHOUSE 14 3RD LEVEL
GARAGE
LOADING BAY
WAREHOUSE 14
OFFICES
RED TANKS
BACK ROAD

The ICU class provides a high-caliber, stable weapon in the AUG, and increases its capabilities by adding the Thermal Scope. This scope attached to this weapon might just have the opposing team taking nonstop bathroom breaks. You can see enemies who think they're hiding. On vertical maps like this, the Thermal Scope is a great tool for locating enemies. The AUG features high damage and great accuracy, especially combined with the Thermal Scope. The front grip reduces the weapon's recoil, keeping you on target longer with much less barrel rise. Although it's classified as a light machine gun, this heavy weapon can weigh you down a bit, but you won't need to run too much if you're smart.

Due to this environment's elevation, consider the Javelin. The difference between this rocket launcher and something like the RPG is that the RPG fires straight at enemies and can also lock onto vehicles. However, the Javelin lets you lock onto a location as well as vehicles, and it launches straight up into the air rather than directly at your target. This makes the Javelin an ideal tool for this map, because you often have to eliminate enemies hiding way up on top of something that you just can't hit with a direct shot. Enter the Javelin, which can shoot straight up into the air and come straight down on your target.

## MODE: DOMINATION

Because of the map's generous size, bring the Tactical Insertion to avoid having to cover so much ground each time you die. Take a Smoke Grenade to mask your team's advances or to escape a pinned-down situation if a sniper finds you. Choose Danger Close and SitRep for your last two Perks. Danger Close increases your explosive damage so your Javelins inflict more pain, and SitRep lets you detect enemy explosives and Tactical Insertions.

The Quarry features a perimeter path obstructed only in two places: the Loading Bay in the southeast corner, and the Storage Facility in the northwest corner. If your plan is to move around the map's outer edge, duck into these buildings when you get to them, then exit and continue. The large building complex in the southern region is a big engagement spot. It features multiple access points, over- and underpasses, and a second level that connects all three buildings with catwalks. This is not a good place to defend, but it is a good place to eye the map[md]for example, the Loading Bay's second-level windows. You can see any enemies setting up on the tanks or coming down from the Industrial Road.

## MODE: HEADQUARTERS

TERRAIN: MULTI-LEVEL STONE QUARRY, MULTI-LEVEL BUILDINGS • FACTIONS: MILITIA/TF 141 • WEATHER/T.O.D.: CLEAR/EARLY AFTERNOON

**INTELLIGENCE**

- UNPLAYABLE
- OVERHEAD
- WINDOW
- LADDER
- UP
- SPAWN POINT
- HEADQUARTERS

STORAGE FACILITY 2ND LEVEL

CRANE 3RD LEVEL

WAREHOUSE 14 2ND LEVEL

LOADING BAY 2ND LEVEL

OFFICES 2ND LEVEL

TANK GARAGE 2ND LEVEL

STORAGE FACILITY

TANK GARAGE 3RD LEVEL

INDUSTRIAL ROAD

THE DUMP

CRANE 2ND LEVEL

TO TANK GARAGE

BIG TANK

EQUIPMENT GARAGE

FLAG TANK

WAREHOUSE 14 3RD LEVEL

TANK GARAGE

CRANE

GARAGE

LOADING BAY

WAREHOUSE 14

RED TANKS

OFFICES

BACK ROAD

# MODE: SABOTAGE

TERRAIN: MULTI-LEVEL STONE QUARRY, MULTI-LEVEL BUILDINGS • FACTIONS: MILITIA/TF 141 • WEATHER/T.O.D.: CLEAR/EARLY AFTERNOON

## INTELLIGENCE

- ☐ UNPLAYABLE
- ▨ OVERHEAD
- ▬ WINDOW
- ▤ LADDER
- ↑ UP
- ⚑ SPAWN POINT
- ▣ BOMB
- ✳ BOMB PLANT

Map labels: STORAGE FACILITY 2ND LEVEL, CRANE 3RD LEVEL, OFFICES 2ND LEVEL, WAREHOUSE 14 2ND LEVEL, LOADING BAY 2ND LEVEL, STORAGE FACILITY, INDUSTRIAL ROAD, THE DUMP, EQUIPMENT GARAGE, TANK GARAGE 3RD LEVEL, TANK GARAGE 2ND LEVEL, CRANE 2ND LEVEL, TO TANK GARAGE, BIG TANK, FLAG TANK, CRANE, TANK GARAGE, GARAGE, WAREHOUSE 14 3RD LEVEL, WAREHOUSE 14, LOADING BAY, OFFICES, RED TANKS, BACK ROAD

Another hot zone is near the Tank Garage, Crane, and Equipment Garage. These three structures are semi-connected and feature multiple levels and great overviews of the map. The adjacent marble blocks on the Equipment Garage's south side let you look all the way south and east across the map. Enemy snipers frequently look here as well, so keep a low profile. The Storage Facility is a little north of the Equipment Garage. This building also boasts two levels and a few great sniping windows. Use this place to avoid major incursions and pick off people from a adistance, and always watch for counter-snipers.

A long chute from the Back Road's east end to the Red Tanks features some explosive barrels; you can snipe these barrels to kill hidden enemies. Try firing your Javelin into this location to create a huge explosion. A large, explosive truck is just outside the Warehouse 14 building to the south. Blow it up to create a large smoke screen you can use for cover. Keep your eyes moving up and down, check your Thermal Scope, and you'll fare well on this map.

# DEMOLITION

TERRAIN: MULTI-LEVEL STONE QUARRY, MULTI-LEVEL BUILDINGS • FACTIONS: MILITIA/TF 141 • WEATHER/T.O.D.: CLEAR/EARLY AFTERNOON

## INTELLIGENCE

- ■ UNPLAYABLE
- ■ OVERHEAD
- ▬ WINDOW
- ▯ LADDER
- ↑ UP
- ⬆ SPAWN POINT
- ▥ BOMB
- ✳ BOMB PLANT

STORAGE FACILITY 2ND LEVEL

CRANE 3RD LEVEL

WAREHOUSE 14 2ND LEVEL

LOADING BAY 2ND LEVEL

OFFICES 2ND LEVEL

STORAGE FACILITY

TANK GARAGE 2ND LEVEL

TANK GARAGE 3RD LEVEL

INDUSTRIAL ROAD

CRANE 2ND LEVEL

THE DUMP

EQUIPMENT GARAGE

BIG TANK

TO TANK GARAGE

FLAG TANK

TANK GARAGE

CRANE

WAREHOUSE 14 3RD LEVEL

GARAGE

LOADING BAY

WAREHOUSE 14

OFFICES

RED TANKS

BACK ROAD

252

# MODE: TEAM DEATHMATCH

TERRAIN: MULTI-LEVEL STONE QUARRY, MULTI-LEVEL BUILDINGS • FACTIONS: MILITIA/TF 141 • WEATHER/T.O.D.: CLEAR/EARLY AFTERNOON

### INTELLIGENCE

- ▢ UNPLAYABLE
- ▨ OVERHEAD
- ▬ WINDOW
- ▥ LADDER
- ↑ UP
- ⟩⟩ SPAWN POINT

STORAGE FACILITY 2ND LEVEL

CRANE 3RD LEVEL

OFFICES 2ND LEVEL

WAREHOUSE 14 2ND LEVEL

LOADING BAY 2ND LEVEL

STORAGE FACILITY

INDUSTRIAL ROAD

TANK GARAGE 3RD LEVEL

TANK GARAGE 2ND LEVEL

CRANE 2ND LEVEL

TO TANK GARAGE

THE DUMP

EQUIPMENT GARAGE

BIG TANK

TANK GARAGE

CRANE

FLAG TANK

WAREHOUSE 14 3RD LEVEL

GARAGE

LOADING BAY

WAREHOUSE 14

OFFICES

RED TANKS

BACK ROAD

A    B    C    D

# ⟩RUNDOWN

This suburban town's main feature is a crescent-shaped river splitting it from north to south. Three bridges facilitate pedestrian and vehicle traffic, and you can engage in combat in the river itself. A large, two-story Villa in the map's northeast corner overlooks a cluster of homes in the Neighborhood across the street. This map has a little of everything, from a Fish Market and Church to a Cantina and a Gas Station. Move from building to building or cover to cover, and watch for second-story shooters. Try the following class with Woodland camouflage on your primary weapon:

## PREDATOR

| | | |
|---|---|---|
| PRIMARY/ ATTACHMENT | F2000 / ACOG & Grenade Launcher | |
| SECONDARY/ ATTACHMENT | Ranger / Silencer & FMJ | |
| EQUIPMENT | Claymore | |
| SPECIAL GRENADE | Smoke | |
| PERK 1 | Bling | |
| PERK 2 | Lightweight | |
| PERK 3 | Ninja | |
| DEATHSTREAK | Painkiller | |

## MODE: CAPTURE THE FLAG

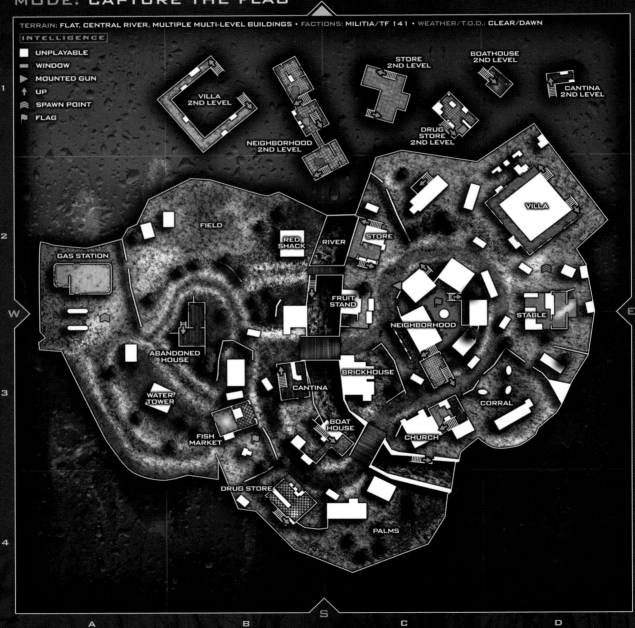

TERRAIN: FLAT, CENTRAL RIVER, MULTIPLE MULTI-LEVEL BUILDINGS • FACTIONS: MILITIA/TF 141 • WEATHER/T.O.D.: CLEAR/DAWN

**INTELLIGENCE**

- ▪ UNPLAYABLE
- ▬ WINDOW
- ▶ MOUNTED GUN
- ↑ UP
- ⟱ SPAWN POINT
- ⚑ FLAG

The F2000 is a very capable rifle with great range and a high fire rate. Its accuracy leaves something to be desired, so take along the ACOG scope. You may use a few extra rounds to finish someone off, but this weapon's increased range makes your enemies spin around looking for their shooter. This may allow you to get another few shots. Launch grenades into enemy courtyards or just over buildings to create splash damage off adjacent buildings. Try not to use the launcher at close range, as its projectiles don't explode until they reach a decent distance. If you don't have a choice, hit the enemy square in the chest or head. If you do, your opponent takes massive damage and might even die.

Your backup weapon is the double barrel Ranger shotgun. Switch to this brutal weapon if you're moving from room to room inside buildings, or any place you consider close quarters. This proves a much better close-range choice over the scoped F2000. The Ranger has a silencer to keep her quiet, along with an FMJ Attachment to compensate for the silencer's damage penalty. Bring along a Claymore, as you can place it in many heavily trafficked areas. Just set it and forget it[md]someone will trip it. Take along a Smoke Grenade in case you get pinned down or need a distraction.

## MODE: DOMINATION

TERRAIN: FLAT, CENTRAL RIVER, MULTIPLE MULTI-LEVEL BUILDINGS • FACTIONS: MILITIA/TF 141 • WEATHER/T.O.D.: CLEAR/DAWN

Your second and third Perks are Lightweight and Ninja. Of course, the Ninja Perk makes you invisible to Heartbeat Sensors and quiets your movements (Pro version), but the Lightweight Perk allows you to move faster and aim quickly after sprinting (again, Pro version). Running very quietly on this map is advantageous if you're assaulting or escaping. All of these tools combine to make a formidable package.

This map can very easily create a standoff. Because you have to cross the river for many objectives, you must use one of the three bridges or the stairs in the river by the Church. This small number of chokepoints could encourage both teams to just sit tight and watch them, waiting for the enemy to cross. Use the secret stairs by the Church if you want to remain hidden while you cross. Just make sure you have a long-range gunner watch the Church area to make sure no one's waiting for you when you climb up.

## MODE: HEADQUARTERS

TERRAIN: FLAT, CENTRAL RIVER, MULTIPLE MULTI-LEVEL BUILDINGS • FACTIONS: MILITIA/TF 141 • WEATHER/T.O.D.: CLEAR/DAWN

INTELLIGENCE
- ☐ UNPLAYABLE
- ▬ WINDOW
- ▶ MOUNTED GUN
- ↑ UP
- ⌄⌄ SPAWN POINT
- 🏛 HEADQUARTERS

# MODE: SABOTAGE

TERRAIN: FLAT, CENTRAL RIVER, MULTIPLE MULTI-LEVEL BUILDINGS • FACTIONS: MILITIA/TF 141 • WEATHER/T.O.D.: CLEAR/DAWN

**INTELLIGENCE**

- ☐ UNPLAYABLE
- ▭ WINDOW
- ▶ MOUNTED GUN
- ↑ UP
- ⫸ SPAWN POINT
- BOMB
- ☀ BOMB PLANT

The Boathouse offers a great view of the Neighborhood area, and the Cantina has a small window to watch east. The Drug Store can provide snipers with a great line of sight across the river to the Neighborhood. One of this map's hot zones is the Neighborhood and its second levels. Bridges and catwalks or overpasses connect the three forward buildings in the Neighborhood. The northernmost room has windows useful for sniping across the river. In Search & Destroy, you can use the middle building's north side, second-floor window to watch over one of the plant sites. Use the Villa's second-level balcony to watch over the other. There are many places to hide and seek on this map, so watch your back.

This map offers decent cover for making your way around its perimeter. Use small chunks of cover, like cows or hay bales, if you need to hide quickly and wait for enemies to pass. Jump into the River to escape enemies if you have to, but moving too quickly in it makes quite a bit of noise. Try to move from high point to high point, as staying on the ground limits your field of view even with your scope. Don't stick around in windows too long, as this is where most snipers first look for counter-snipers. Try setting up further back from windows, in the shadows, to be less visible to snipers.

# MODE: SEARCH & DESTROY / DEMOLITION

TERRAIN: FLAT, CENTRAL RIVER, MULTIPLE MULTI-LEVEL BUILDINGS • FACTIONS: MILITIA/TF 141 • WEATHER/T.O.D.: CLEAR/DAWN

### INTELLIGENCE

- ▫ UNPLAYABLE
- ▬ WINDOW
- ▶ MOUNTED GUN
- ↑ UP
- ⏶ SPAWN POINT
- 🜄 BOMB
- ☀ BOMB PLANT

VILLA 2ND LEVEL

STORE 2ND LEVEL

BOATHOUSE 2ND LEVEL

CANTINA 2ND LEVEL

NEIGHBORHOOD 2ND LEVEL

DRUG STORE 2ND LEVEL

FIELD

RED SHACK

RIVER

STORE

VILLA

GAS STATION

FRUIT STAND

NEIGHBORHOOD

STABLE

W

E

ABANDONED HOUSE

CANTINA

BRICKHOUSE

CORRAL

WATER TOWER

BOAT HOUSE

CHURCH

FISH MARKET

DRUG STORE

PALMS

1

2

3

4

A

B

S

C

D

# MODE: TEAM DEATHMATCH

TERRAIN: FLAT, CENTRAL RIVER, MULTIPLE MULTI-LEVEL BUILDINGS • FACTIONS: MILITIA/TF 141 • WEATHER/T.O.D.: CLEAR/DAWN

**INTELLIGENCE**

- ☐ UNPLAYABLE
- ▬ WINDOW
- ▶ MOUNTED GUN
- ↑ UP
- ⚞ SPAWN POINT

VILLA 2ND LEVEL
STORE 2ND LEVEL
BOATHOUSE 2ND LEVEL
CANTINA 2ND LEVEL
NEIGHBORHOOD 2ND LEVEL
DRUG STORE 2ND LEVEL
FIELD
GAS STATION
RED SHACK
RIVER
STORE
VILLA
FRUIT STAND
ABANDONED HOUSE
NEIGHBORHOOD
STABLE
WATER TOWER
BRICKHOUSE
CANTINA
FISH MARKET
BOAT HOUSE
CORRAL
CHURCH
DRUG STORE
PALMS

# ⟩RUST

Rust is a very small oil refinery complex in the desert. Lots of blowing sand at sunset makes discerning friend and foe difficult. The main refinery has three levels, though not full ones. It features many little places to climb to and look down, although most players who get up there don't last very long. Use the available cover, as it's hard to stay alive here. The pace is very fast, and grenades fly everywhere. Try out this class if you want to survive:

## CYCLONE

| | | |
|---|---|---|
| PRIMARY/ ATTACHMENT | P90 / Rapid Fire & Extended Mags | |
| SECONDARY/ ATTACHMENT | PP2000 / Akimbo & Extended Mags | |
| EQUIPMENT | Blast Shield | |
| SPECIAL GRENADE | Stun x2 | |
| PERK 1 | Bling | |
| PERK 2 | Stopping Power | |
| PERK 3 | Steady Aim | |
| DEATHSTREAK | Martyrdom | |

## MODE: CAPTURE THE FLAG

TERRAIN: FLAT, SAND, BROKEN REFINERY COMPLEX • FACTIONS: OP FOR/TF 141 • WEATHER/T.O.D.: DUST STORM/SUNSET

**INTELLIGENCE**

- ☐ UNPLAYABLE
- ☐ OVERHEAD
- ▤ LADDER
- ≪ SPAWN POINT
- ⚑ FLAG

REFINERY 2ND LEVEL

PROPANE TANK

OIL TANKS

SHACK

REFINERY

TRAILER

OIL RIG

OIL TRUCK

PICKUP

The Cyclone class turns you into a Tasmanian devil with guns. The P90 submachine gun starts with a high rate of fire. Adding the Rapid Fire Attachment lets it shred everything in sight. Pack Extended Mags to keep it full of fuel. This gun doesn't have a great range, but you don't have to make very long shots on this map. With Extended Mags, you can put enough bullets downrange to make it look like horizontal rain.

For your backup weapon, take the PP2000 machine pistol with Akimbo and Extended Mags. This combo is nearly as deadly as your P90. Stopping Power is your first Perk, which increases the damage your bullets inflict. With Akimbo on your PP2000, you can wield two at the same time. Use one until it's out of ammo, then use the second while thie first reloads. By the time second gun is out of ammo, the other gun has reloaded[md]you can maintain a nearly continuous stream of horizontal rain. With the Extended Mags Attachment on both of these weapons, you should be able to sustain fire for quite awhile, especially if you use the alternating Akimbo weapon technique.

## MODE: DOMINATION

TERRAIN: FLAT, SAND, BROKEN REFINERY COMPLEX • FACTIONS: OP FOR/TF 141 • WEATHER/T.O.D.: DUST STORM/SUNSET

INTELLIGENCE

- ■ UNPLAYABLE
- ▨ OVERHEAD
- ▤ LADDER
- ≋ SPAWN POINT
- Ⓐ CAPTURE POINT

REFINERY 2ND LEVEL

PROPANE TANK

OIL TANKS

SHACK

Ⓑ

Ⓐ

REFINERY

TRAILER

OIL RIG

Ⓒ

OIL TRUCK

PICKUP

Because this map is so small, enemies launch grenades and fire Javelins right off the bat. The Blast Shield is a good choice to minimize explosive damage. Follow your enemy's example and send some explosive ordinance and Stun Grenades their way. There aren't many places to hide on this map, so use your Stuns to slow enemies, and pick them off while they slowly try to react.

Take Steady Aim for your third Perk, as both your weapons have only iron sights. It comes in handy, especially when you switch to the PP2000s. You can't aim down the barrel of your secondary weapon or any weapon with Akimbo attached to it. You only get a crosshair, so consider taking Steady Aim whenever you run Akimbo on a weapon.

You can jump climb several areas on the main refinery to reach higher ground. Definitely crouch if you reach one of the Refinery's highest points. It's a just a matter of time before an enemy spots and kills you, so seize the moment and kill as many of 'em as you can.

## MODE: HEADQUARTERS

TERRAIN: FLAT, SAND, BROKEN REFINERY COMPLEX • FACTIONS: OP FOR/TF 141 • WEATHER/T.O.D.: DUST STORM/SUNSET

INTELLIGENCE

- UNPLAYABLE
- OVERHEAD
- LADDER
- SPAWN POINT
- HEADQUARTERS

REFINERY 2ND LEVEL

PROPANE TANK

OIL TANKS

SHACK

REFINERY

TRAILER

OIL RIG

OIL TRUCK

PICKUP

# MODE: SABOTAGE

TERRAIN: FLAT, SAND, BROKEN REFINERY COMPLEX • FACTIONS: OP FOR/TF 141 • WEATHER/T.O.D.: DUST STORM/SUNSET

**INTELLIGENCE**

- ◻ UNPLAYABLE
- ◼ OVERHEAD
- ▯ LADDER
- ⬢ SPAWN POINT
- ◼ BOMB
- ✳ BOMB PLANT

REFINERY 2ND LEVEL

PROPANE TANK

OIL TANKS

SHACK

REFINERY

TRAILER

OIL RIG

OIL TRUCK

PICKUP

A          B          S          C          D

E

If you hang on long enough to acquire a Killstreak Reward, they can be deadly on this map. One Killstreak can take out the entire team. On this map, Killstreak acquisition ends up being the key to many victories.

You can use the refinery's lower areas to proceed from one side to the other, but be ready for enemies doing the same. You can use the map's perimeter to circle around enemies, especially with blowing sand and dust masking your movements. Your best bets are to either find a good hiding place down on the ground and rack up Killstreaks, or ground pound to circle the enemy into the center.

# MODE: SEARCH & DESTROY / DEMOLITION

TERRAIN: **FLAT, SAND, BROKEN REFINERY COMPLEX** • FACTIONS: **OP FOR/TF 141** • WEATHER/T.O.D.: **DUST STORM/SUNSET**

### INTELLIGENCE

- ⬜ UNPLAYABLE
- ◻ OVERHEAD
- ▤ LADDER
- ⧁ SPAWN POINT
- ▬ BOMB
- ☀ BOMB PLANT

REFINERY
2ND LEVEL

PROPANE TANK

OIL TANKS

SHACK

OIL TANKS

TRAILER

REFINERY

OIL RIG

OIL TRUCK

PICKUP

264

# MODE: TEAM DEATHMATCH

TERRAIN: FLAT, SAND, BROKEN REFINERY COMPLEX • FACTIONS: OP FOR/TF 141 • WEATHER/T.O.D.: DUST STORM/SUNSET

**INTELLIGENCE**

- □ UNPLAYABLE
- ■ OVERHEAD
- ▯ LADDER
- ≋ SPAWN POINT

265

# SCRAPYARD

This location is a vehicle junkyard bordered by warehouses, offices, loading docks, and other structures necessary to run the yard. Several scrapped planes encircled by a road line the center of this map. Warehouse 3 features three levels from which to engage enemies, whereas the Offices have a second level. Both of these structures offer windows from which you can snipe or call out enemy locations. You can find plenty of ground fighting here, but also lots of sniper work. Watch for Office-to-Warehouse sniping at all times, and dish out some of your own sniping here.

## Bipod

| | | |
|---|---|---|
| PRIMARY/ ATTACHMENT | Intervention / Thermal | |
| SECONDARY/ ATTACHMENT | TMP / Red Dot Sight | |
| EQUIPMENT | Frag | |
| SPECIAL GRENADE | Smoke | |
| PERK 1 | Sleight of Hand | |
| PERK 2 | Stopping Power | |
| PERK 3 | Last Stand | |
| DEATHSTREAK | Painkiller | |

## MODE: CAPTURE THE FLAG

TERRAIN: FLAT, VEHICLE JUNKYARD, MULTI-LEVEL BUILDINGS • FACTIONS: OP FOR/TF 141 • WEATHER/T.O.D.: CLEAR, BLOWING DEBRIS/DUSK

**INTELLIGENCE**
- ☐ UNPLAYABLE
- ▬ WINDOW
- ▤ LADDER
- ↑ UP
- ❯ SPAWN POINT
- ⚑ FLAG

OFFICES

CRANE

POWER STATION

TAIL SECTIONS

WAREHOUSE 4

OFFICES 2ND LEVEL

LOADING BAY

WAREHOUSE 3 2ND LEVEL

BLUE PLANE

818

BURNING TRUCK

PROPANE TANKS

WAREHOUSE 3 3RD LEVEL

RED TANKS

PARKING LOT

WAREHOUSE 3

W

E

S

A       B       C       D

1

2

3

4

This class gives you the option of sniping or ground pounding. The Intervention sniper rifle inflicts about as much damage as the Barrett .50 cal, but possesses slightly better accuracy. Stopping Power for your second Perk increases its power. With Sleight of Hand as your first Perk, you reload much faster, which is necessary because your rifle is bolt-action. This rifle has the Thermal Scope attached, a perfect tool for sneaking peeks at slices of enemies who might be trying to counter-snipe you. Look for slivers of white in the windows across the map, and fire directly through the wall if necessary. The Intervention is powerful enough to penetrate.

The TMP you carry certainly isn't as powerful as the Intervention, but it's fully automatic. Use it whenever you aren't sniping. In fact, it should be your main weapon here. Switch to your sniper rifle only when it's necessary. The TMP with Stopping Power and Sleight of Hand lets you deal much more damage, even with the weapon's low caliber. The Sleight of Hand Perk quickly slams in another mag. The Red Dot Scope helps you acquire targets quickly. It offers a small amount of zoom, so, if you want to shoot someone too close for the sniper rifle but far enough to warrant a little zoom, this is the best choice.

## MODE: DOMINATION

TERRAIN: FLAT, VEHICLE JUNKYARD, MULTI-LEVEL BUILDINGS • FACTIONS: OP FOR/TF 141 • WEATHER/T.O.D.: CLEAR, BLOWING DEBRIS/DUSK

Launch a Frag Grenade over the center of the map and each corner of the far building. Try to nail someone right at the spawn. Grenades soon come in your direction as well, so be prepared to take cover quickly. If a sniper pins you down, which is very possible on this map, and you can't escape without getting shot, pop smoke and wait for it to spread before you jump up and boogie out. If you get flanked while you're sniping, at least you have Last Stand for your third Perk. Fire a few rounds at your assailant's head. Make him pay for trying to kill you. This Perk's Pro version lets you use equipment in Last Stand to throw a grenade if your nemesis is too far away to kill with your pistol. By the way, take a Painkiller if you die three times without a kill. Jumping back into battle only for a sniper to blow off your head is supremely frustrating. Painkiller gives you a nice health boost when you respawn, but the effect lasts for a short time.

You can navigate the Scrapyard a few ways depending on your mission. If you're playing Search & Destroy, and you need to plant the bomb, try going straight up the east side through Warehouse 4. This route keeps you under cover as you advance. Proceed through the Warehouse, between the Propane Tanks and the Burning Truck. Then continue around the back of the Red

## MODE: HEADQUARTERS

TERRAIN: FLAT, VEHICLE JUNKYARD, MULTI-LEVEL BUILDINGS • FACTIONS: OP FOR/TF 141 • WEATHER/T.O.D.: CLEAR, BLOWING DEBRIS/DUSK

INTELLIGENCE
- ☐ UNPLAYABLE
- ▬ WINDOW
- ▯ LADDER
- ⬆ UP
- ⩘ SPAWN POINT
- ⛫ HEADQUARTERS

# MODE: SABOTAGE

TERRAIN: FLAT, VEHICLE JUNKYARD, MULTI-LEVEL BUILDINGS • FACTIONS: OP FOR/TF 141 • WEATHER/T.O.D.: CLEAR, BLOWING DEBRIS/DUSK

### INTELLIGENCE

- ◻ UNPLAYABLE
- ▭ WINDOW
- ▯ LADDER
- ↑ UP
- ≫ SPAWN POINT
- ▦ BOMB
- ☀ BOMB PLANT

Tanks to the "B" bomb plant site. If you want to plant the bomb at "A," head through the plane's Tail Sections, southwesterly toward the Loading Bay. Expect some grenades and a few enemies waiting to meet you there, but toss in some grenades early to clear your way. The Loading Bay has decent cover, but don't peek your head out through the garage doors. Otherwise, Warehouse 3 snipers can get a look at you.

The scrapped planes in the middle offer good cover when you're just moving through, but they aren't good campsites. You can even stop and fire a few shots if you see someone through the windows, but don't try to hold this position very long. This map's elevated areas are generally the most contested, so keep looking north and south at the Offices and Warehouse 3, specifically the upper levels. Watch for snipers in the windows. If you can lock down one of these buildings with a teammate or two, you can do some real damage and rack up Killstreaks. If you don't have enough teammates to cover your back, Claymores can help. Even if they don't kill the intruder, they serve as an early warning device for you to get up and watch your back.

## MODE: SEARCH & DESTROY / DEMOLITION

TERRAIN: FLAT, VEHICLE JUNKYARD, MULTI-LEVEL BUILDINGS • FACTIONS: OP FOR/TF 141 • WEATHER/T.O.D.: CLEAR, BLOWING DEBRIS/DUSK

**INTELLIGENCE**

- ☐ UNPLAYABLE
- ▬ WINDOW
- ▤ LADDER
- ↑ UP
- ⧨ SPAWN POINT
- ▣ BOMB
- ☀ BOMB PLANT

This map has great corners for ambushing enemies as they run back and forth. The Blue Plane's northwest inside corner is a nice spot. The northeast corner just outside Warehouse 4 is another good location. If you want to ambush, remember to run silent and keep adjusting your position. Some good sniping lanes are just outside the west entrance to Warehouse 3, in the Parking Lot corner. You can see between the Loading Bay and the Blue Plane. Enemies are much easier to spot with your Thermal Scope engaged. Try positioning yourself on the Crane's southwest corner. This can give you a great line of sight through to the map's center, where many players run back and forth. If you set up by Warehouse 4, you can get a decent line on the center of the map and look into the Loading Bay. A mobile sniper is a living sniper. With the Kill Cam on, you can't camp very long at any one place.

# MODE: TEAM DEATHMATCH

TERRAIN: FLAT, VEHICLE JUNKYARD, MULTI-LEVEL BUILDINGS • FACTIONS: OP FOR/TF 141 • WEATHER/T.O.D.: CLEAR, BLOWING DEBRIS/DUSK

**INTELLIGENCE**

- ☐ UNPLAYABLE
- ▬ WINDOW
- 🪜 LADDER
- ⬆ UP
- ⏬ SPAWN POINT

Labels on map:
OFFICES
CRANE
POWER STATION
TAIL SECTIONS
WAREHOUSE 4
OFFICES 2ND LEVEL
LOADING BAY
WAREHOUSE 3 2ND LEVEL
BLUE PLANE
B18
BURNING TRUCK
PROPANE TANKS
WAREHOUSE 3 3RD LEVEL
RED TANKS
PARKING LOT
WAREHOUSE 3

# ⟩ SKIDROW

This part of the inner city centers on a large apartment building with two levels and multiple interiors to navigate. A Parking Lot in the map's northern tip serves as a makeshift triage center, while a Playground and Laundromat occupy the southern end. The centrally located complex features a movie store on the lower level, various apartments on the second level, and even a rooftop from which you can oversee the West Lot. There are many corners, and while sniping is possible, you only need something like an assault rifle with a scope.

## CURFEW

| | | |
|---|---|---|
| PRIMARY/ ATTACHMENT | M16A4 / FMJ & ACOG | |
| SECONDARY/ ATTACHMENT | AA-12 / FMJ & Extended Mags | |
| EQUIPMENT | Tactical Insertion | |
| SPECIAL GRENADE | Stun x2 | |
| PERK 1 | Bling | |
| PERK 2 | Stopping Power | |
| PERK 3 | SitRep | |
| DEATHSTREAK | Copycat | |

## MODE: CAPTURE THE FLAG

TERRAIN: FLAT, INNER-CITY, MULTI-LEVEL BUILDINGS • FACTIONS: OP FOR/RANGERS • WEATHER/T.O.D.: CLEAR, BLOWING DEBRIS/MORNING

INTELLIGENCE
- ⬜ UNPLAYABLE
- ▬ WINDOW
- ▶ MOUNTED GUN
- ↑ UP
- ⋙ SPAWN POINT
- ⚑ FLAG

There are many places to hide in this piece of the city. You want something that can penetrate walls if necessary. The M16 is a good choice. With FMJ increasing your power and an ACOG scope to zero in on enemy targets, you're accurate, and you can eliminate enemies who think they're safe from damage. The M16 is a very stable weapon. Its accuracy is great, and its power is already high. With the FMJ Attachment, it's even deadlier. The ACOG Scope allows you to zero in on enemies almost anywhere on this map. There aren't that many long-distance shots to be had here.

Your secondary weapon is the AA-12 automatic shotgun. This likewise gets FMJ. It also has Extended Mags since it has low ammo to begin with. Break this out when you're running from one place to another. You don't want to get caught with a three-round burst rifle in your hands when an enemy rounds the corner of the Movie Store. Just mash the trigger on the AA-12, and it's clear sailing. This weapon has very little range but great power, and the fact that it's fully automatic turns it into a street sweeper.

## MODE: DOMINATION

TERRAIN: FLAT, INNER-CITY, MULTI-LEVEL BUILDINGS • FACTIONS: OP FOR/RANGERS • WEATHER/T.O.D.: CLEAR, BLOWING DEBRIS/MORNING

**INTELLIGENCE**

■ UNPLAYABLE
▨ WINDOW
▶ MOUNTED GUN
↑ UP
⏫ SPAWN POINT
Ⓐ CAPTURE POINT

PARKING LOT
OFFICES
LOADING DOCK
GARAGE
WEST LOT
BLUE ROOM
WEST ALLEY
MOVIE STORE
TUNNEL
TO 2ND LEVELS
TO 2ND LEVELS
TO 2ND LEVELS
HOUSE
BACK ALLEY
LAUNDROMAT
PLAYGROUND
APARTMENT
OFFICES 2ND LEVEL
STUDY
ROOF
GREEN ROOM
MAIN HALL
FROM 1ST LEVEL
FROM 1ST LEVEL
FROM 1ST LEVEL
KITCHEN
CAMERA ROOM

Using Tactical Insertion on this map is key to staying in the fight. You don't want to traverse areas filled with enemy crossfire, especially if you've already crossed them before. Drop a Tactical Insertion somewhere out of the way as soon as you can. Try placing it somewhere in the middle of the map so that, when you respawn, you don't have to run from one end to the other just to fire a few rounds and die again. Take Stun Grenades to help clear rooms. These are great for digging enemies out of holes in upper-level rooms, like the Green Room or the Kitchen. Toss a Stun in there to see who's home. Follow it up with a Frag, or show them your automatic shotgun.

Your Perks are Bling for dual Attachments on both weapons (the Pro version covers secondary weapons) and Stopping Power for additional damage from both weapons. SitRep for your third Perk. It lets you see enemy explosives through walls so you can either wall them to make them detonate or avoid them altogether. This Perk also allows you to see enemy Tactical Insertions, which you can camp, waiting for enemies to respawn.

## MODE: HEADQUARTERS

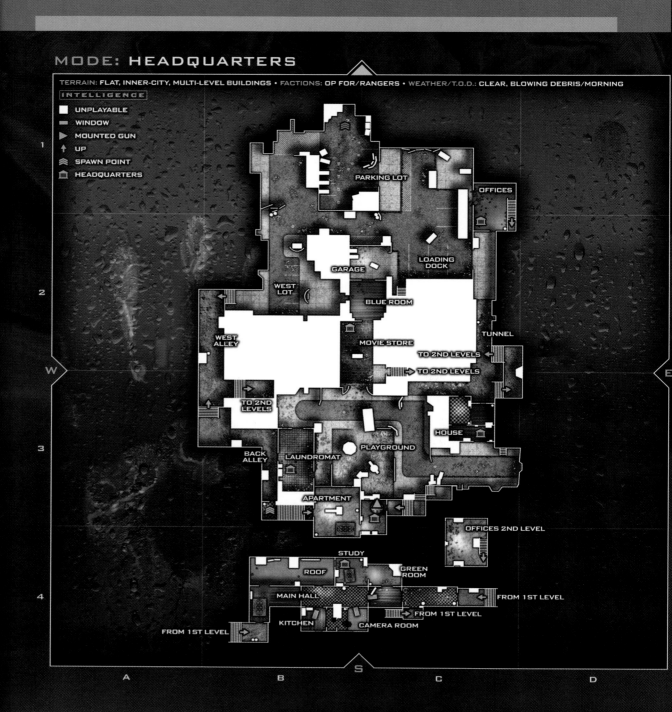

TERRAIN: FLAT, INNER-CITY, MULTI-LEVEL BUILDINGS • FACTIONS: OP FOR/RANGERS • WEATHER/T.O.D.: CLEAR, BLOWING DEBRIS/MORNING

INTELLIGENCE

- ☐ UNPLAYABLE
- ▬ WINDOW
- ▶ MOUNTED GUN
- ↑ UP
- ⚞ SPAWN POINT
- 🏛 HEADQUARTERS

# MODE: SABOTAGE

**TERRAIN:** FLAT, INNER-CITY, MULTI-LEVEL BUILDINGS • **FACTIONS:** OP FOR/RANGERS • **WEATHER/T.O.D.:** CLEAR, BLOWING DEBRIS/MORNING

### INTELLIGENCE

- ▢ UNPLAYABLE
- ▬ WINDOW
- ▶ MOUNTED GUN
- ↑ UP
- ⩘ SPAWN POINT
- ▣ BOMB
- ✳ BOMB PLANT

PARKING LOT

OFFICES

GARAGE

LOADING DOCK

WEST LOT

BLUE ROOM

WEST ALLEY

MOVIE STORE

TUNNEL

TO 2ND LEVELS

TO 2ND LEVELS

TO 2ND LEVELS

HOUSE

BACK ALLEY

LAUNDROMAT

PLAYGROUND

APARTMENT

OFFICES 2ND LEVEL

STUDY

ROOF

GREEN ROOM

MAIN HALL

FROM 1ST LEVEL

FROM 1ST LEVEL

KITCHEN

CAMERA ROOM

FROM 1ST LEVEL

A    B    C    D

This Perk's Pro version makes all enemy footsteps louder than normal. If you have a decent surround sound setup or some nice headphones for your audio, you can hear the footsteps from a mile away and echolocate their position, too.

The main apartment complex's second story is one of this level's hottest zones. The roof is open and overlooks the West Lot, and the second story's south side overlooks the Playground and the Apartment. Always watch for snipers in the Kitchen and the Camera Room. They often perch in the Apartment, looking back at you and possibly even using the mounted gun there. This high-caliber mounted machine gun can tear

through enemies and shoot through walls, so if you're across the Playground upstairs, relocate or kill the operator quick.

A decent length sniper sight line leads from the north Offices through the Tunnel looking at the House. You can counter-snipe from a window in the House that faces that way. Even here, for one of the longest shots on the map, you don't need more than your ACOG Scope to hit your target. On the House's north side, a set of stairs leads up into the main apartment complex's second story. Another entrance stairway is in the middle, in the Movie Store, and from the West Alley.

# MODE: SEARCH & DESTROY / DEMOLITION

TERRAIN: **FLAT, INNER-CITY, MULTI-LEVEL BUILDINGS** • FACTIONS: **OP FOR/RANGERS** • WEATHER/T.O.D.: **CLEAR, BLOWING DEBRIS/MORNING**

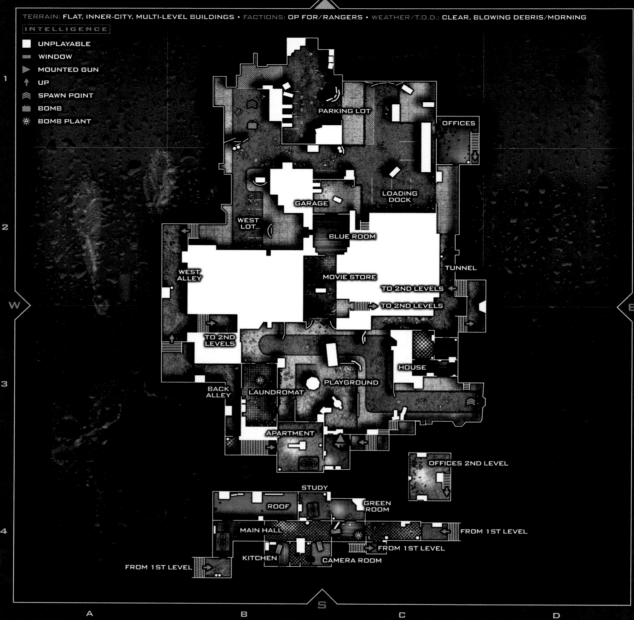

**INTELLIGENCE**

- ☐ UNPLAYABLE
- ▭ WINDOW
- ▶ MOUNTED GUN
- ↑ UP
- ⩘ SPAWN POINT
- ▧ BOMB
- ✳ BOMB PLANT

1

PARKING LOT

OFFICES

LOADING DOCK

GARAGE

WEST LOT

BLUE ROOM

2

TUNNEL

WEST ALLEY

MOVIE STORE

TO 2ND LEVELS

TO 2ND LEVELS

W
E

TO 2ND LEVELS

HOUSE

BACK ALLEY

LAUNDROMAT

PLAYGROUND

3

APARTMENT

OFFICES 2ND LEVEL

STUDY

ROOF

GREEN ROOM

FROM 1ST LEVEL

4

MAIN HALL

FROM 1ST LEVEL

KITCHEN

CAMERA ROOM

FROM 1ST LEVEL

FROM 1ST LEVEL

S

A          B          C          D

Chances are, you can't cover all three locations to keep enemies out, but the main complex's entire second story is a great place to defend. Just be sure to clear the upstairs before you hunker down.

Move through the map with your shotgun, and level anything that moves. When you approach areas that enemies frequent, and you need more accuracy and range, switch to the M16 and let 'em have it. Don't be afraid to shoot through walls. Choose the right weapon for the task. Moving west toward the Movie Store and Laundromat from just southeast of the House might require your M16. Conversely, when you move up through the Movie Store into the second-story rooms, keep your AA-12 on hand.

# MODE: TEAM DEATHMATCH

TERRAIN: FLAT, INNER-CITY, MULTI-LEVEL BUILDINGS • FACTIONS: OP FOR/RANGERS • WEATHER/T.O.D.: CLEAR, BLOWING DEBRIS/MORNING

**INTELLIGENCE**

- ■ UNPLAYABLE
- ▬ WINDOW
- ▶ MOUNTED GUN
- ↑ UP
- ⪡ SPAWN POINT

PARKING LOT
OFFICES
LOADING DOCK
GARAGE
WEST LOT
BLUE ROOM
WEST ALLEY
MOVIE STORE
TUNNEL
TO 2ND LEVELS
TO 2ND LEVELS
TO 2ND LEVELS
HOUSE
BACK ALLEY
LAUNDROMAT
PLAYGROUND
APARTMENT
OFFICES 2ND LEVEL
STUDY
ROOF
GREEN ROOM
MAIN HALL
FROM 1ST LEVEL
FROM 1ST LEVEL
KITCHEN
CAMERA ROOM
FROM 1ST LEVEL
FROM 1ST LEVEL

# SUB BASE

With light snow blowing in the morning, visibility isn't very high. This naval yard complex builds and maintains the few subs in port. The Loading Bay restocks them, and the Garage Bay services maintenance vehicles. A sub is in dry dock now, so don't fall over the edge. It's in the map's far west side, by the Maintenance Yard. You encounter the most resistance at the Base Entrance and the Loading Bay, as they are the most centrally located areas. Try using the Warehouse to flank enemies from either side. This is a large map, and it features plenty of sniping spots. Camouflage your weapon with an arctic pattern before you head out.

## SEA SNIPER

| | | |
|---|---|---|
| PRIMARY/ ATTACHMENT | Barrett .50 cal / Silencer & Heartbeat Sensor | |
| SECONDARY/ ATTACHMENT | G18 / Silencer & Akimbo | |
| EQUIPMENT | Throwing Knife | |
| SPECIAL GRENADE | Smoke | |
| PERK 1 | Bling | |
| PERK 2 | Cold Blooded | |
| PERK 3 | Ninja | |
| DEATHSTREAK | Final Stand | |

## MODE: CAPTURE THE FLAG

TERRAIN: FLAT, CONCRETE, MULTIPLE MULTI-LEVEL BUILDINGS • FACTIONS: OP FOR/SEALS • WEATHER/T.O.D.: LIGHT SNOW/MORNING

**INTELLIGENCE**
- ☐ UNPLAYABLE
- ▬ WINDOW
- ▯ LADDER
- ↑ UP
- ⟩⟩ SPAWN POINT
- ⚑ FLAG

Remaining silent is your top priority. The preceding class is designed specifically for that purpose and more. There are many places from which to snipe, and there's potential for close quarters fighting, so choose the silenced Barrett .50 cal sniper rifle. It can shoot through walls, so don't be shy. It's also loud even with the silencer Attachment, but at least you don't show up on radar. The Heartbeat Sensor Attachment lets you pinpoint enemy locations from a sniper roost.

The G18 machine pistol is very nimble but it lacks power. Use it with the silencer to stay off radar, and employ Akimbo when you relocate after sniping. Just before you bug out, check your Heartbeat Sensor and switch to your G18s. Combine all of your stealth with the Throwing Knife, and you'll have enemies scrambling to find you while the rest of your team proceeds with the objective. Use the Throwing Knife only if you need to conserve ammo, and if you have a clear shot. The knife requires some practice.

## MODE: DOMINATION

TERRAIN: FLAT, CONCRETE, MULTIPLE MULTI-LEVEL BUILDINGS • FACTIONS: OP FOR/SEALS • WEATHER/T.O.D.: LIGHT SNOW/MORNING

**INTELLIGENCE**

- UNPLAYABLE
- WINDOW
- LADDER
- UP
- SPAWN POINT
- Ⓐ CAPTURE POINT

You have smoke in case you need to escape your position. When you're high on a rooftop or catwalk, put smoke directly at the enemy's feet. Don't smoke you're area, smoke the enemy instead. Bling allows you to carry two silenced G18s and a silenced sniper rifle with a Heartbeat Sensor. With Cold Blooded as your second Perk, UAVs don't see you, air support can't hit you, Sentry Guns don't fire at you, and Thermal Scopes don't work on you. Add the Pro version to that, and enemy crosshairs don't turn red when they're on you. Your last Perk is Ninja, making you completely invisible to Heartbeat Sensors. This is a huge advantage.

The Loading Bay area cuts this map vertically down the center, and it's one of this map's major hot zones. When you attack from the west, get up on the Catwalks by way of the Garage Bay, and eventually onto the Catwalk's roof. From these locations, you can overwatch the Loading Bay and prevent enemies from moving across from the Warehouse or the Tunnel. Keep an eye on the enormous second-story level over the Warehouse and the Power Station. There are many places to hide and snipe, so don't stay in one place too long. Help your team by clearing a path for them on the map's north side, and get them into the Base Entrance.

## MODE: HEADQUARTERS

TERRAIN: FLAT, CONCRETE, MULTIPLE MULTI-LEVEL BUILDINGS • FACTIONS: OP FOR/SEALS • WEATHER/T.O.D.: LIGHT SNOW/MORNING

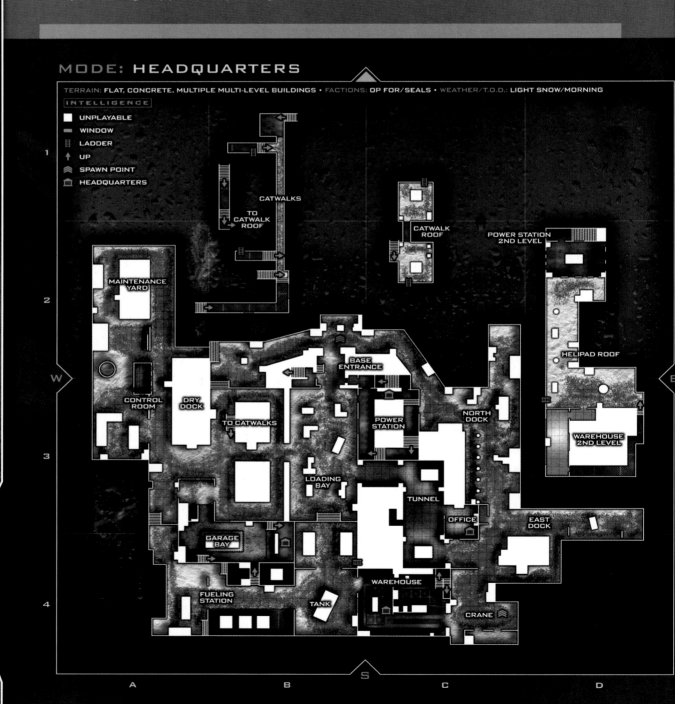

# MODE: SABOTAGE

TERRAIN: FLAT, CONCRETE, MULTIPLE MULTI-LEVEL BUILDINGS • FACTIONS: OP FOR/SEALS • WEATHER/T.O.D.: LIGHT SNOW/MORNING

**INTELLIGENCE**

- ■ UNPLAYABLE
- ▬ WINDOW
- ▯ LADDER
- ↑ UP
- ⌇ SPAWN POINT
- ▣ BOMB
- ✳ BOMB PLANT

You can do this from the Dry Dock's northeast corner. Sight down the northern strip and make sure it's clear of enemies before you let your team advance. If you have to make it past the Tank, have a sniper up on the Catwalks look that way to make sure it's safe before you proceed.

When you advance from the east, try to get to the top of the Warehouse, which gives you a great vantage point over most of the Loading Bay. Keep a buddy with you to look for enemies approaching from the Helipad Roof. When you have to relocate, try moving across the roof by bouncing from cover to cover. Make your way out through the Power Station to the North Dock. Head out on the tip of the dock and look west toward the Base Entrance. You're almost certain to scope someone trying to get in that way. If you can lock that down from your location, your teammates can worry about getting flanked from one less direction.

## MODE: SEARCH & DESTROY / DEMOLITION

TERRAIN: FLAT, CONCRETE, MULTIPLE MULTI-LEVEL BUILDINGS • FACTIONS: OP FOR/SEALS • WEATHER/T.O.D.: LIGHT SNOW/MORNING

**INTELLIGENCE**
- ⬜ UNPLAYABLE
- ▬ WINDOW
- 🪜 LADDER
- ↑ UP
- 🏳 SPAWN POINT
- 🧰 BOMB
- ☀ BOMB PLANT

CATWALKS
TO CATWALK ROOF
CATWALK ROOF
POWER STATION 2ND LEVEL
MAINTENANCE YARD
HELIPAD ROOF
BASE ENTRANCE
CONTROL ROOM
DRY DOCK
TO CATWALKS
NORTH DOCK
POWER STATION
WAREHOUSE 2ND LEVEL
LOADING BAY
TUNNEL
OFFICE
EAST DOCK
GARAGE BAY
FUELING STATION
TANK
WAREHOUSE
CRANE

All-out, head-on assaults can use the most central route. Be wary of incoming grenades, and move through the Loading Bay either from the Dry Dock or the Tunnels. Proceed as far as you can while you try to get to the end of the map. From there, make perimeter sweeps of the level. Keep your back to the map's outer edge in modes like Team Deathmatch. It's a good way to stay alive and pick off stragglers that might try to bug out of the hot zones to flank your team. Make the absolute most of your gear on this map. The Sea Sniper class is one of the most deadly classes we've provided. You can also use it on several other maps and missions with minor tweaks.

# MODE: TEAM DEATHMATCH

TERRAIN: FLAT, CONCRETE, MULTIPLE MULTI-LEVEL BUILDINGS • FACTIONS: OP FOR/SEALS • WEATHER/T.O.D.: LIGHT SNOW/MORNING

**INTELLIGENCE**

- ▢ UNPLAYABLE
- ▬ WINDOW
- ▤ LADDER
- ↑ UP
- ≋ SPAWN POINT

CATWALKS
TO CATWALK ROOF

CATWALK ROOF

POWER STATION 2ND LEVEL

MAINTENANCE YARD

HELIPAD ROOF

BASE ENTRANCE

CONTROL ROOM

DRY DOCK

TO CATWALKS

POWER STATION

NORTH DOCK

WAREHOUSE 2ND LEVEL

LOADING BAY

TUNNEL

OFFICE

EAST DOCK

GARAGE BAY

FUELING STATION

TANK

WAREHOUSE

CRANE

A    B    S    C    D

E

# )TERMINAL

The Terminal doesn't look so bad in the middle of the day under clear conditions, but inside it's a slaughterhouse. The Lobby and Waiting areas are two hot zones, as are Midnight's Bookstore and the Hallway. Be careful maneuvering through these locations. There is a lot of cover to use, and Killstreaks can crash through the skylights at any time to crush you. You have to bounce from cover to cover quickly on the Tarmac to avoid getting pinned down. This map also has a few long-distance firing lanes, but the best tools to take with you are an assault rifle and a backup.

## SKYCAP

| | | |
|---|---|---|
| PRIMARY/ ATTACHMENT | ACR / ACOG & Heartbeat Sensor | |
| SECONDARY/ ATTACHMENT | Desert Eagle / FMJ & Akimbo | |
| EQUIPMENT | Claymore | |
| SPECIAL GRENADE | Smoke | |
| PERK 1 | Bling | |
| PERK 2 | Hardline | |
| PERK 3 | Steady Aim | |
| DEATHSTREAK | Final Stand | |

## MODE: CAPTURE THE FLAG

TERRAIN: FLAT, AIRPORT, MULTIPLE MULTI-LEVEL STRUCTURES • FACTIONS: OP FOR/RANGERS • WEATHER/T.O.D.: CLEAR/MID-DAY

**INTELLIGENCE**

- ☐ UNPLAYABLE
- ☐ UNDERGROUND
- ☐ OVERHEAD
- ▬ WINDOW
- ▯ LADDER
- ↑ UP
- ⌄ SPAWN POINT
- ⚑ FLAG

Use the Heartbeat Sensor with your ACOG Scope to hunt down and eliminate enemies. This deadly combination is perfect for most distances you encounter on this map. There aren't any overlapping areas, such as upper and lower levels, so you have an easier time locating enemies with the Heartbeat Sensor. The ACR can also wall people, so don't be afraid to shoot through barriers to eliminate targets hiding behind cover. Your backup weapon is the Desert Eagle, or two of them to be more specific. Packed with additional power via the FMJ Attachment, these two bad boys are no joke. Steady Aim allows tight targeting when you Akimbo the two Desert Eagles. This is a great set of backup weapons when desperate times call for desperate measures.

This map features tons of corners and shortcuts, so plant your Claymore in places the enemy tends to run past without looking. Try places like the Bookstore and the top of the escalators in the Lobby. Just around corners are great places for booby traps, too. Set them in new locations all the time, so the enemy doesn't try to detonate them from afar. You have Smoke Grenades, so if someone chases you, toss one at your feet while you're running to smoke out your pursuer. As soon as it billows up enough to cover you, stop and turn back to engage as your opponent runs through the smoke. He or she won't expect you to be right there, and you can knife the enemy quickly.

## MODE: DOMINATION

TERRAIN: **FLAT, AIRPORT, MULTIPLE MULTI-LEVEL STRUCTURES** • FACTIONS: **OP FOR/RANGERS** • WEATHER/T.O.D.: **CLEAR/MID-DAY**

INTELLIGENCE
- UNPLAYABLE
- UNDERGROUND
- OVERHEAD
- WINDOW
- LADDER
- UP
- SPAWN POINT
- Ⓐ CAPTURE POINT

Bling gives you the ability to run a scope and radar on your primary weapon, and to wield two Desert Eagles with additional power (Bling Pro covers secondary weapons). Take the Hardline Perk, because you should probably get at least two kills before you die, and then you can call in a UAV. Save up and summon a sentry gun. The Hallway is a great place for one of these—just don't get shot trying to place one. Be careful of any Killstreak air drops you call in on this map. Make sure you place them in an accessible area. If they land on an inaccessible roof, it's too bad. However, air-dropped Killstreaks can be dropped through glass ceilings, crushing anyone who happens to be underneath them. Bring Steady Aim as a fallback Perk in case you need to go double Desert Eagle on someone. This Perk makes it easier to aim and tightens your crosshairs.

When your team spawns in the western Security area, send two players to each of three areas: left, down through the Food Court; straight through Midnight's Bookstore; and right to the Luggage Store. These locations create the three major chokepoints on this map. Seal off these areas to prevent the enemy from getting around you. For the team watching the Luggage Store area, keep eyes on the Plane's jetway in particular. Enemies can come from the Tarmac, up through the Plane, and into the hallway.

## MODE: HEADQUARTERS

TERRAIN: FLAT, AIRPORT, MULTIPLE MULTI-LEVEL STRUCTURES • FACTIONS: OP FOR/RANGERS • WEATHER/T.O.D.: CLEAR/MID-DAY

INTELLIGENCE

- UNPLAYABLE
- UNDERGROUND
- OVERHEAD
- WINDOW
- LADDER
- UP
- SPAWN POINT
- HEADQUARTERS

BURGER TOWN
WAITING AREA
LOBBY
BAGGAGE AREA
FOOD COURT
ROOF
CONTROL ROOM
MIDNIGHTS BOOKSTORE
SECURITY
SECURITY LOBBY
TARMAC
HALLWAY
TO PLANE
RESERVATION DESK
SECURITY OFFICE
TO PLANE
TO PLANE
CHECK IN
PLANE
LUGGAGE STORE

# MODE: SABOTAGE

TERRAIN: FLAT, AIRPORT, MULTIPLE MULTI-LEVEL STRUCTURES • FACTIONS: OP FOR/RANGERS • WEATHER/T.O.D.: CLEAR/MID-DAY

**INTELLIGENCE**

- ▢ UNPLAYABLE
- ▢ UNDERGROUND
- ▭ OVERHEAD
- ▬ WINDOW
- ▯ LADDER
- ↑ UP
- ⚑ SPAWN POINT
- ▬ BOMB
- ✷ BOMB PLANT

Map labels: BURGER TOWN, WAITING AREA, LOBBY, BAGGAGE AREA, FOOD COURT, MIDNIGHTS BOOKSTORE, ROOF, CONTROL ROOM, TARMAC, SECURITY, SECURITY LOBBY, HALLWAY, TO PLANE, RESERVATION DESK, SECURITY OFFICE, TO PLANE, TO PLANE, CHECK IN, PLANE, LUGGAGE STORE

Pick them off before they make it out of the Plane. For the team heading through the Food Court, try getting grenades out to the Waiting area and to the top of the escalators. The idea is to push back enemies trying to advance that way. You might end up pushing them down the Hallway and into the waiting trap at the Bookstore.

When you advance from the Tarmac, maneuver your team through the Lobby and up into the Waiting Area. Be careful of incoming grenades. Split your team to have one group continue through the Waiting Area and into the Food Court. Meanwhile, the second group heads down the Hallway. If your Hallway group makes it all the way down to the Luggage Store, they have a better chance at getting around enemies by moving through the Luggage Store itself and taking cover in the Security Office or heading around the Reservation Desk. Once you make it through this way, check the bookstore, and flank the enemy team if any of them are camping inside. Detonate any explosives they may have set as well. You'll be happy you brought your Heartbeat Sensor for just such occasions. This map has plenty of places to hide, but not from radar.

# MODE: SEARCH & DESTROY / DEMOLITION

TERRAIN: FLAT, AIRPORT, MULTIPLE MULTI-LEVEL STRUCTURES • FACTIONS: OP FOR/RANGERS • WEATHER/T.O.D.: CLEAR/MID-DAY

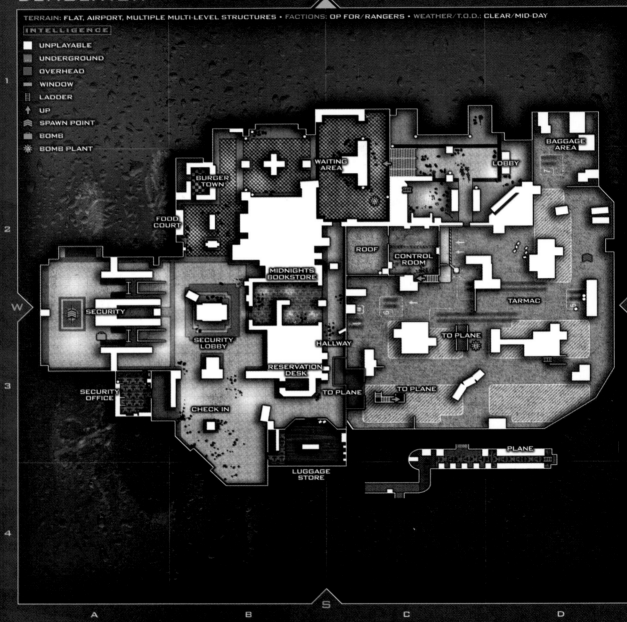

**INTELLIGENCE**

- □ UNPLAYABLE
- ▨ UNDERGROUND
- ▩ OVERHEAD
- ▬ WINDOW
- ▤ LADDER
- ↑ UP
- ⧩ SPAWN POINT
- ▭ BOMB
- ☀ BOMB PLANT

*Map labels: BAGGAGE AREA, LOBBY, WAITING AREA, BURGER TOWN, FOOD COURT, MIDNIGHTS BOOKSTORE, ROOF, CONTROL ROOM, TARMAC, SECURITY, SECURITY LOBBY, HALLWAY, TO PLANE, RESERVATION DESK, SECURITY OFFICE, CHECK IN, TO PLANE, TO PLANE, LUGGAGE STORE, PLANE*

*Grid: W, E, N, S, A, B, C, D, 1, 2, 3, 4*

Try maneuvering back and forth through the center instead of doing a perimeter sweep. From the east and Tarmac, head into the Plane and upstairs into the Hallway. Then proceed through Midnight's Bookstore and out into the Security Lobby. Once you clear all of these areas, turn around and head back the way you came. This route is a good for encountering the most resistance. You probably need to fire from the hip when you run this route, which is another good reason to take Steady Aim. Your ACOG comes in handy once you hit the Hallway or the Security Lobby, but for all other close encounters, you can either fire it from the hip with increased accuracy or break out the Desert Eagles.

# MODE: TEAM DEATHMATCH

TERRAIN: FLAT, AIRPORT, MULTIPLE MULTI-LEVEL STRUCTURES • FACTIONS: OP FOR/RANGERS • WEATHER/T.O.D.: CLEAR/MID-DAY

## INTELLIGENCE

- ☐ UNPLAYABLE
- ▨ UNDERGROUND
- ▨ OVERHEAD
- ▬ WINDOW
- ▤ LADDER
- ▲ UP
- ⟰ SPAWN POINT

BURGER TOWN

WAITING AREA

LOBBY

BAGGAGE AREA

FOOD COURT

ROOF

CONTROL ROOM

MIDNIGHTS BOOKSTORE

SECURITY

TARMAC

SECURITY LOBBY

HALLWAY

TO PLANE

SECURITY OFFICE

RESERVATION DESK

TO PLANE

TO PLANE

CHECK IN

PLANE

LUGGAGE STORE

A    B    S    C    D

E

FLUGRUGER

# ❯UNDERPASS

Bring your raincoat. This map is set in a heavy afternoon downpour under a broken highway. With a hastily made Shanty Town to the south and a Drainage Ditch running through the west from north to south, this map also features a small village, an industrial area, and some warehouses. Use the conditions to mask your movements and always keep an eye on upper-level overlooks, as you can get shot from many rooftops and second-floor windows. Use the buildings and cover to navigate the map's edges, and be careful of ambushes in open spaces. You need different kinds of gear on this mission, so consider the following:

## CHAMELEON

| PRIMARY/ATTACHMENT | FAMAS / Shotgun & Thermal Scope |
|---|---|
| SECONDARY/ATTACHMENT | PP2000 / Red Dot Sight & Silencer |
| EQUIPMENT | Claymore |
| SPECIAL GRENADE | Smoke |
| PERK 1 | Bling |
| PERK 2 | Lightweight |
| PERK 3 | Commando |
| DEATHSTREAK | Final Stand |

## MODE: CAPTURE THE FLAG

TERRAIN: MINOR ELEVATION CHANGES, MULTI-LEVEL STRUCTURES • FACTIONS: MILITIA/TF 141 • WEATHER/T.O.D.: HEAVY RAINSTORM/AFTERNOON

**INTELLIGENCE**
- ☐ UNPLAYABLE
- ☐ UNDERGROUND
- ☐ OVERHEAD
- ▬ WINDOW
- ⋮ LADDER
- ↑ UP
- ⚑ SPAWN POINT
- ⚑ FLAG

HOUSE 2ND LEVEL
CHICKEN SHACK ROOF
STORAGE WAREHOUSE 2ND LEVEL
SHANTY TOWN ROOF
TRAINYARD
DRAINAGE DITCH
INDUSTRIAL YARD
CONTAINERS
VILLAGE
UNDERPASS
TRAILER
CHICKEN SHACK
BRIDGE
BUILDING 57
EAST PATH
JUNKYARD PATH
SHANTY TOWN
OVERPASS
STORAGE WAREHOUSE
PARKING LOT
COURTYARD
HOUSE
SHELF

This is an all-purpose loadout. The highly accurate and powerful FAMAS is deadly as-is, but on this map, a few extra goodies come in handy, making this gun your trusty sidekick. The pouring rain homogenous colors hinder visual acuity, so the Thermal Scope makes a big difference. Combined with the FAMAS's accuracy and damage, you should be able to drop anyone you can see, but always aim for the head. In addition to the Thermal Scope, you have an under-barrel shotgun for close encounters. Switch to this when you clear buildings or tight spaces. A few blasts from this bad boy can knock enemies backward, giving you time to finish them off.

For your backup weapon, take the PP200 machine pistol. It has good range for a machine pistol, and it delivers more damage than the TMP. With the attached Red Dot Scope and silencer, this makes a great weapon for close- to medium-range encounters where you want to stay off radar. If you find someone crossing ahead of you, use the PP2000 rather than your unsilenced assault rifle. With its damage rate, you should be able to kill the enemy.

## MODE: DOMINATION

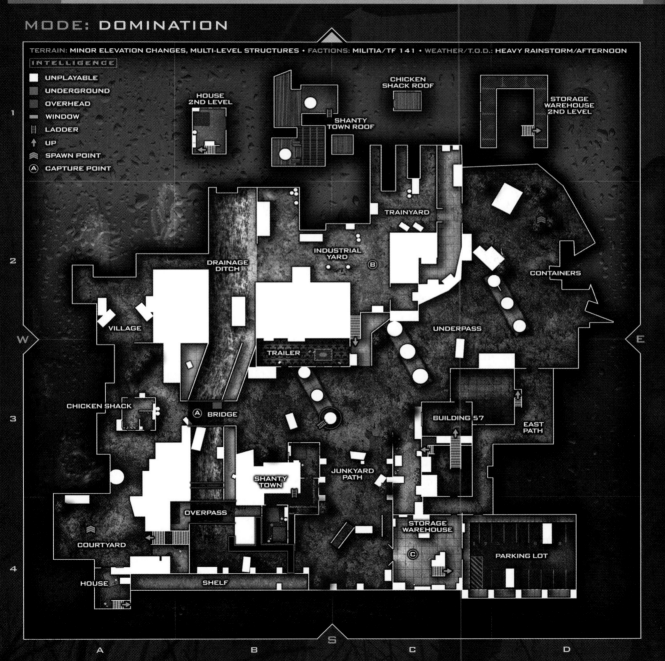

TERRAIN: MINOR ELEVATION CHANGES, MULTI-LEVEL STRUCTURES • FACTIONS: MILITIA/TF 141 • WEATHER/T.O.D.: HEAVY RAINSTORM/AFTERNOON

**INTELLIGENCE**
- UNPLAYABLE
- UNDERGROUND
- OVERHEAD
- WINDOW
- LADDER
- UP
- SPAWN POINT
- Ⓐ CAPTURE POINT

Given that visibility isn't the best on this map, take Claymores in your equipment slot. Place them in bushes, near burned-out vehicles, around corners, or inside doorways. Players look down about as often as they look up, so you're bound to get someone rounding a corner without looking! Also, you can set these to watch your back when you're sniping, which you can do with the FAMAS. You may get pinned down by another sniper and have to bug out. Pop a smoke between you and the enemy, making sure it's high or low enough to mask your movement, and then relocate quickly. Don't forget to use your smoke tactically in modes like Search & Destroy. To distract enemies, smoke the plant site opposite the one you intend to plant. Toss in a few grenades to further sell the bluff. Just don't use this ruse too often, or your enemies will get wise to it.

Your Perks are Bling, Lightweight, and Commando. Chose Bling so you can roll with a shotgun and a Thermal Scope. Select Lightweight to get in and out of areas faster than the enemy expects, and to aim more quickly out of a sprint (Pro version). Commando increases your melee distance so you don't have to go loud, and the Pro version eliminates falling damage. This can come in handy when you chase down or escape from enemies.

# MODE: HEADQUARTERS

TERRAIN: MINOR ELEVATION CHANGES, MULTI-LEVEL STRUCTURES • FACTIONS: MILITIA/TF 141 • WEATHER/T.O.D.: HEAVY RAINSTORM/AFTERNOON

INTELLIGENCE
- ☐ UNPLAYABLE
- ☐ UNDERGROUND
- ☐ OVERHEAD
- ▬ WINDOW
- ▯ LADDER
- ↑ UP
- ⛰ SPAWN POINT
- 🏛 HEADQUARTERS

HOUSE 2ND LEVEL

CHICKEN SHACK ROOF

SHANTY TOWN ROOF

STORAGE WAREHOUSE 2ND LEVEL

TRAINYARD

CONTAINERS

INDUSTRIAL YARD

DRAINAGE DITCH

VILLAGE

UNDERPASS

TRAILER

CHICKEN SHACK

BRIDGE

BUILDING 57

EAST PATH

SHANTY TOWN

JUNKYARD PATH

OVERPASS

COURTYARD

STORAGE WAREHOUSE

PARKING LOT

HOUSE

SHELF

## MODE: SABOTAGE

TERRAIN: MINOR ELEVATION CHANGES, MULTI-LEVEL STRUCTURES • FACTIONS: MILITIA/TF 141 • WEATHER/T.O.D.: HEAVY RAINSTORM/AFTERNOON

**INTELLIGENCE**

- ⬜ UNPLAYABLE
- ⬛ UNDERGROUND
- ⬛ OVERHEAD
- ▬ WINDOW
- ☷ LADDER
- ↑ UP
- ⩘ SPAWN POINT
- ▬ BOMB
- ☀ BOMB PLANT

Be careful on roofs if you don't have Commando Pro, as falling from them inflicts major damage, if not death.

If you spawn in the Parking Lot at the map's southeast corner, take your Thermal-Scoped FAMAS up to the Storage Warehouse's second floor. Immediately zoom in and hunt for enemies down toward the Courtyard or on elevated parts of the Shanty Town. If you don't see any enemies coming that way for a few seconds, relocate to where the Shelf meets the Junkyard path. This corner gives you a nice view to the spot that hosts much of the action, just under the highway. Watch up the hill for enemies trying to cross over to the ditch or meet you at your spawn.

Building 57 offers an elevated window from which you can see across the Bridge spanning the Drainage Ditch. This is a decent vista, but don't move too much, as enemies frequently snipe this window. The east path adjacent to that building offers a great avenue to circumnavigate enemies. Hug the perimeter and keep to the trees. When you get to the Trainyard, take the fight inside to the Trailer and move south from there.

# MODE: SEARCH & DESTROY / DEMOLITION

TERRAIN: MINOR ELEVATION CHANGES, MULTI-LEVEL STRUCTURES • FACTIONS: MILITIA/TF 141 • WEATHER/T.O.D.: HEAVY RAINSTORM/AFTERNOON

**INTELLIGENCE**

- □ UNPLAYABLE
- ■ UNDERGROUND
- ■ OVERHEAD
- ▬ WINDOW
- ▦ LADDER
- ↑ UP
- ⫷ SPAWN POINT
- ● BOMB
- ✳ BOMB PLANT

HOUSE 2ND LEVEL

CHICKEN SHACK ROOF

SHANTY TOWN ROOF

STORAGE WAREHOUSE 2ND LEVEL

TRAINYARD

DRAINAGE DITCH

INDUSTRIAL YARD

CONTAINERS

VILLAGE

TRAILER

UNDERPASS

CHICKEN SHACK

BRIDGE

BUILDING 57

EAST PATH

SHANTY TOWN

JUNKYARD PATH

OVERPASS

STORAGE WAREHOUSE

PARKING LOT

COURTYARD

HOUSE

SHELF

1  2  W  3  4

A  B  S  C  D

Things get a little jumbled once you hit the Shanty Town, so keep to cover as best you can. If you end up on the town's south edge, watch your left and right for sniper crossfire. Long-range gunners poach this lane.

The House in the southwestern corner is a great place to snipe north up to the Village. However, this part of the map doesn't always see a lot of play. But it does connect to the Shelf, which is a good place to see a good chunk of the map. From the Shelf, you can move across to the Shanty Town rooftops and maneuver to almost anywhere on the map from there; you can even drop down a level. Watch for mines in the weeds. If you move north through the town, you soon hit the Trailer. This is a great spot for sniping down the Junkyard Path, but again, many other players look for heads in its windows. Other loadout options include a silencer and radar-jamming Perks, but otherwise, this template's weapons should serve you well.

# MODE: TEAM DEATHMATCH

TERRAIN: MINOR ELEVATION CHANGES, MULTI-LEVEL STRUCTURES • FACTIONS: MILITIA/TF 141 • WEATHER/T.O.D.: HEAVY RAINSTORM/AFTERNOON

## INTELLIGENCE

- ☐ UNPLAYABLE
- ☐ UNDERGROUND
- ☐ OVERHEAD
- ▬ WINDOW
- ▤ LADDER
- ↑ UP
- ⟰ SPAWN POINT

HOUSE 2ND LEVEL

CHICKEN SHACK ROOF

STORAGE WAREHOUSE 2ND LEVEL

SHANTY TOWN ROOF

TRAINYARD

INDUSTRIAL YARD

DRAINAGE DITCH

CONTAINERS

VILLAGE

UNDERPASS

TRAILER

CHICKEN SHACK

BRIDGE

BUILDING 57

EAST PATH

SHANTY TOWN

JUNKYARD PATH

OVERPASS

STORAGE WAREHOUSE

PARKING LOT

COURTYARD

HOUSE

SHELF

A · B · S · C · D · E

# WASTELAND

Two major radiation zones line the east and west sides, so watch for the signs and the sounds of radiation. Whenever you hear it, back out as fast as you can to avoid getting fully irradiated and dying. To the west, you find a junkyard full of broken-down vehicles, as well as a Cemetery and Grave Diggers' Quarters. A church and statue occupy the northeast area, and a massive trench/cave system runs almost the entire length of the map from north to south, stretching east to the Tanks and west to the House. A long Ridge runs north to south, almost splitting the map in half.

## GRAVEDIGGER

| PRIMARY/ATTACHMENT | WA2000 / Thermal | |
|---|---|---|
| SECONDARY/ATTACHMENT | M93 Raffica / Silencer | |
| EQUIPMENT | Claymore | |
| SPECIAL GRENADE | Smoke | |
| PERK 1 | Marathon | |
| PERK 2 | Cold Blooded | |
| PERK 3 | Scrambler | |
| DEATHSTREAK | Final Stand | |

## MODE: CAPTURE THE FLAG

TERRAIN: ROLLING HILLS, GRASSY, SCATTERED RUN DOWN STRUCTURES • FACTIONS: OP FOR/TF 141 • WEATHER/T.O.D.: FOGGY/MORNING

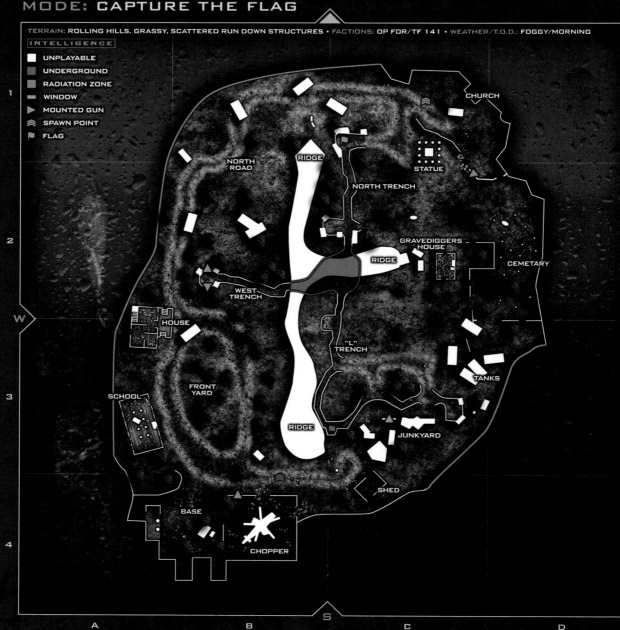

**INTELLIGENCE**
- UNPLAYABLE
- UNDERGROUND
- RADIATION ZONE
- WINDOW
- MOUNTED GUN
- SPAWN POINT
- FLAG

CHURCH
STATUE
NORTH ROAD
RIDGE
NORTH TRENCH
GRAVEDIGGERS HOUSE
RIDGE
CEMETARY
WEST TRENCH
HOUSE
"L" TRENCH
TANKS
FRONT YARD
SCHOOL
RIDGE
JUNKYARD
SHED
BASE
CHOPPER

This class gives you the option of hunting enemies through a Thermal Scope and being loud, or sneaking through the trenches and being silent. You can do both if you like. The WA2000 rifle with the Thermal Scope is a good choice. You can see enemies hiding in the bushes or heads peeking just above the trenches. The Thermal Scope allows you to you see foes when they think they're hidden—they appear white hot. Find a good spot to shoot long distances, because once you fire, you light up the enemy's radar. If you're far enough away, their radar can't detect you.

The M93 Raffica has good power, accuracy, and damage, but offers only a three-round burst. If you need to move from your sniper spot, break out this weapon in transit. It keeps you off radar. A lot of the activity occurs on the map's eastern side. You can find some great hiding spots in the Junkyard. Make your shots count and aim for the head when you use this machine pistol.

Take Claymores and Smoke Grenades into this level, as there are plenty of hiding spots for mines. Pretty much anywhere along the Ridge is a good place for them, because players often hug that area when they move.

# MODE: DOMINATION

TERRAIN: ROLLING HILLS, GRASSY, SCATTERED RUN DOWN STRUCTURES • FACTIONS: OP FOR/TF 141 • WEATHER/T.O.D.: FOGGY/MORNING

**INTELLIGENCE**

- ☐ UNPLAYABLE
- ◻ UNDERGROUND
- ◼ RADIATION ZONE
- ☐ WINDOW
- ► MOUNTED GUN
- 🪶 SPAWN POINT
- Ⓐ CAPTURE POINT

CHURCH

RIDGE

NORTH ROAD

Ⓐ

STATUE

NORTH TRENCH

GRAVEDIGGERS HOUSE

RIDGE

CEMETARY

Ⓑ

WEST TRENCH

HOUSE

"L" TRENCH

FRONT YARD

TANKS

SCHOOL

RIDGE

Ⓒ

JUNKYARD

SHED

BASE

CHOPPER

Also, you can place your mines at the map's outer edge or spots along the road. Another option is to place them inside doorways, and rig some down in the trenches, which are frequent hot spots. Just set and forget one each time you spawn.

Marathon, Cold Blooded, and Scrambler are your Perks. Marathon gets you wherever you have to go in a hurry. Cold Blooded makes you invisible to enemies on radar and UAV sweeps, so you can stay hidden and snipe a little longer. Scrambler helps by jamming enemy radar near you. Just remember that enemies can deduce that you're nearby when their radar jams. You can use this to your advantage by luring enemies. If you have a good vantage point, watch and wait as they try to flush you out of hiding. When they come looking for you, pick them off.

While this map features a few rolling hills, it doesn't have any structural second stories. You can gain elevation on the Ridge's edges and on other hills, like the Front Yard, but they don't offer much advantage. Try to stay low and motionless. Watch for enemies slowly crawling through the grass and weeds. Use your machine pistol if you see something move nearby.

## MODE: HEADQUARTERS

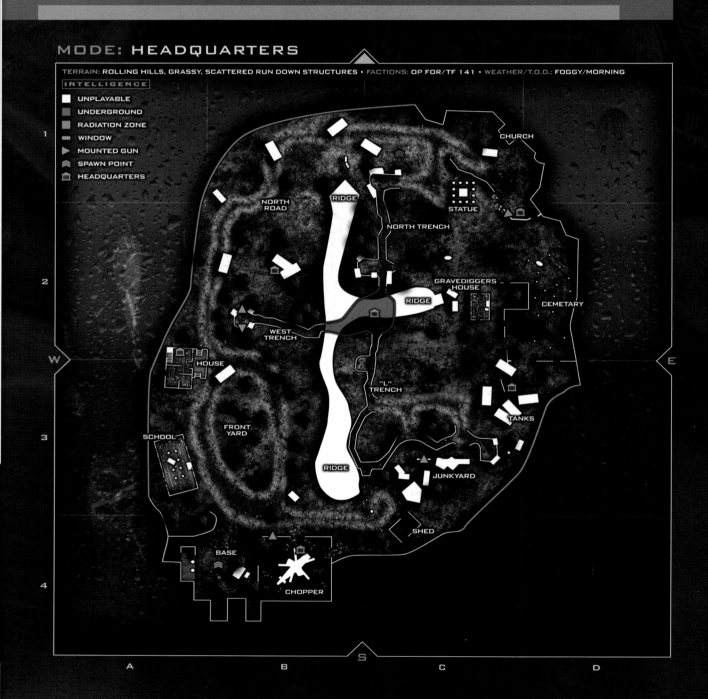

TERRAIN: ROLLING HILLS, GRASSY, SCATTERED RUN DOWN STRUCTURES • FACTIONS: OP FOR/TF 141 • WEATHER/T.O.D.: FOGGY/MORNING

INTELLIGENCE

UNPLAYABLE
UNDERGROUND
RADIATION ZONE
WINDOW
MOUNTED GUN
SPAWN POINT
HEADQUARTERS

# MODE: SABOTAGE

TERRAIN: ROLLING HILLS, GRASSY, SCATTERED RUN DOWN STRUCTURES • FACTIONS: OP FOR/TF 141 • WEATHER/T.O.D.: FOGGY/MORNING

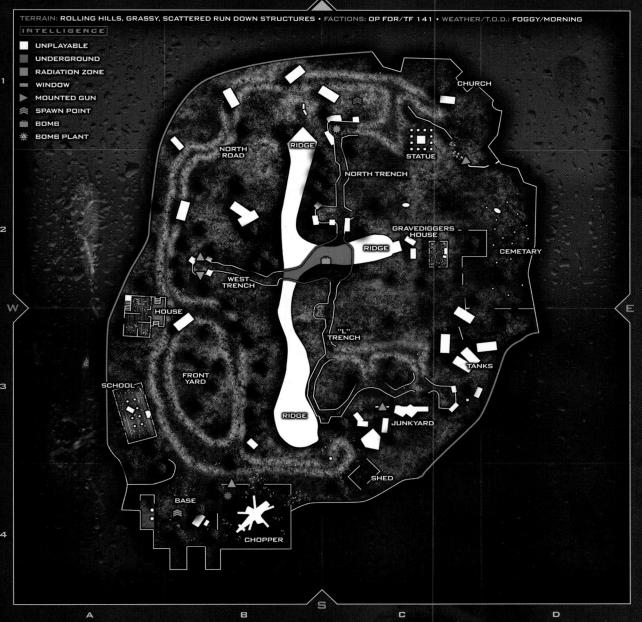

**INTELLIGENCE**

- ☐ UNPLAYABLE
- ☐ UNDERGROUND
- ☐ RADIATION ZONE
- ▬ WINDOW
- ▶ MOUNTED GUN
- ⧓ SPAWN POINT
- 🎒 BOMB
- ☀ BOMB PLANT

Put your crosshairs on suspicious areas to see if you get an "X." If you do, pull out the WA2000 and fire away. You don't always have to give up your position if you carry a loud and a silenced weapon.

The trenches see a lot of action. It ranges from close quarters and ambush action to medium-range scoped fire. Claymores are obviously great in here, and if you can spare some grenades, even better. Try setting up an ambush in the trenches with a buddy or a Claymore, waiting for players to run through. Everyone tries to use the trenches to get across the map, because the area is thick with snipers. Move slowly when you traverse the trenches. If your head pops up, it could get shot off. They are generally deep enough for you to crouch-walk; just be careful.

A great sniping line runs from the Junkyard looking north to the Statue, and vice versa. Another is on the other side of the Ridge in the west. Take up a window in the School, and you can watch north and east while your back remains covered. This is a good spot to wait for enemies to pass; just set a Claymore at the back door.

## MODE: SEARCH & DESTROY / DEMOLITION

TERRAIN: ROLLING HILLS, GRASSY, SCATTERED RUN DOWN STRUCTURES • FACTIONS: OP FOR/TF 141 • WEATHER/T.O.D.: FOGGY/MORNING

**INTELLIGENCE**

- ■ UNPLAYABLE
- ■ UNDERGROUND
- ■ RADIATION ZONE
- ▬ WINDOW
- ▶ MOUNTED GUN
- ⚐ SPAWN POINT
- ⬕ BOMB
- ✳ BOMB PLANT

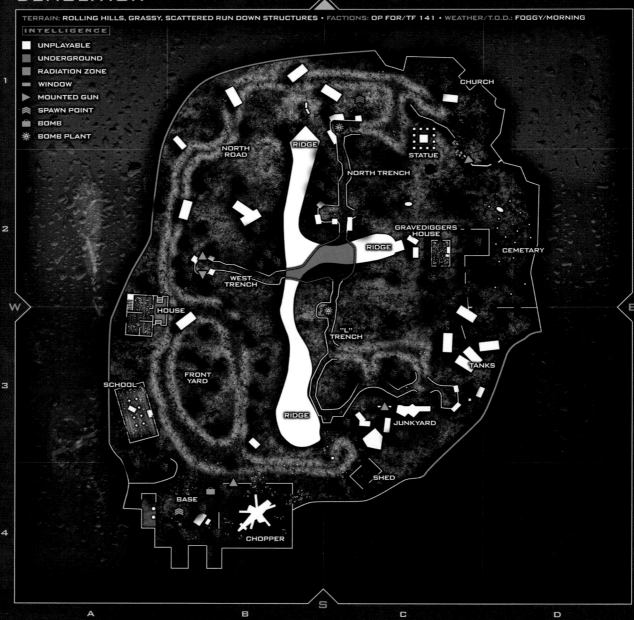

A nice hill and some trees for cover are between the north road and the Ridge's north edge. You can snipe south toward the Base, and you can even get some good lines from the Cemetery looking at the "L" Trench exits.

You encounter much sniper fire here, as much as silenced fire. Take this map slowly. If you run out there like an idiot, you'll end up buried in the Graveyard. If you're feeling brave, you can try one of five mounted guns: one in the Base looking north, two in the West Trench looking both north and south, one in the Junkyard looking north, and one next to the statue looking southwest. These are high-caliber, loud weapons. If you're completely out of ammo, these are great options. Otherwise, you're just begging to get sniped. Use your Thermal Scope and your silencer, and you and your team can prevail.

# MODE: TEAM DEATHMATCH

TERRAIN: ROLLING HILLS, GRASSY, SCATTERED RUN DOWN STRUCTURES • FACTIONS: OP FOR/TF 141 • WEATHER/T.O.D.: FOGGY/MORNING

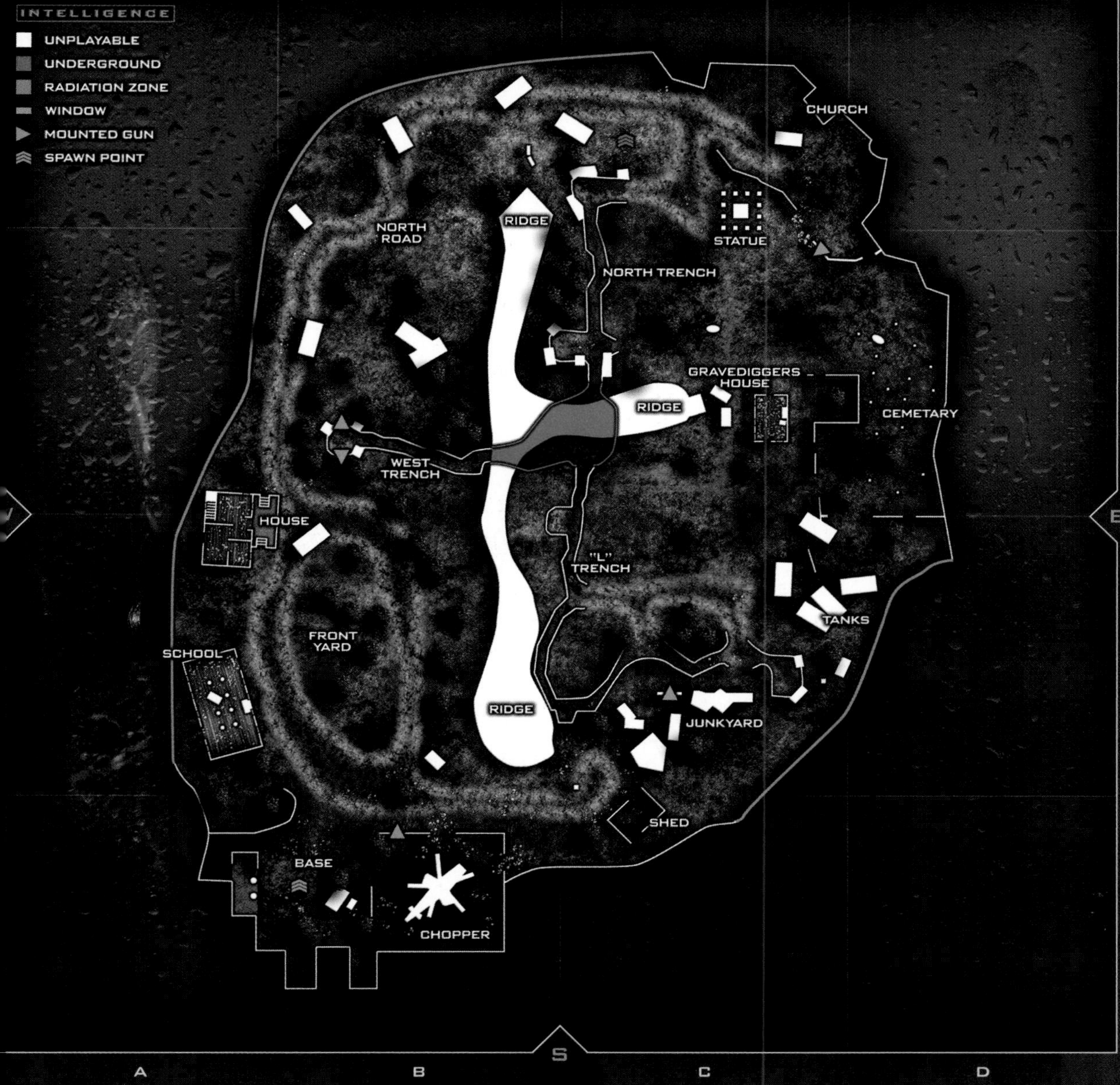

## INTELLIGENCE

- ⬜ UNPLAYABLE
- ⬛ UNDERGROUND
- ◼ RADIATION ZONE
- ▬ WINDOW
- ▶ MOUNTED GUN
- ≫ SPAWN POINT

CHURCH

STATUE

NORTH ROAD

RIDGE

NORTH TRENCH

GRAVEDIGGERS HOUSE

RIDGE

CEMETARY

WEST TRENCH

HOUSE

"L" TRENCH

FRONT YARD

TANKS

SCHOOL

RIDGE

JUNKYARD

SHED

BASE

CHOPPER

E

A    B    S    C    D

# ACHIEVEMENTS & TROPHIES

## ACHIEVEMENTS AND TROPHIES

| NAME | CONDITIONS | GAMERSCORE (XBOX 360) | TROPHY COLOR (PS3) |
|---|---|---|---|
| Is That All You Got? | Earn all available Trophies for *Call of Duty: Modern Warfare 2* | N/A | Platinum |
| Back in the Saddle | Help train the local militia. Finish Mission 1, S.S.D.D. | 15 | Bronze |
| Danger Close | Get hand picked for Shepherd's elite squad. Finish Mission 2, Team Player. | 15 | Bronze |
| Cold Shoulder | Infiltrate the snowy mountainside base. Finish Mission 3, Cliffhanger. | 15 | Bronze |
| Tag 'Em and Bag 'Em | Find Rojas in the Favelas. Finish Mission 5, Takedown. | 15 | Bronze |
| Royale with Cheese | Defend Burger Town. Finish Mission 6, Wolverines! | 15 | Bronze |
| Soap on a Rope | Storm the Gulag. Finish Mission 10, The Gulag. | 15 | Bronze |
| Desperate Times | Execute the plan to help the Americans. Finish Mission 12, Contingency. | 15 | Bronze |
| Whiskey Hotel | Take back Whiskey Hotel. Finish Mission 14, Whiskey Hotel. | 15 | Bronze |
| The Pawn | Assault Makarov's safe house. Finish Mission 15, Loose Ends. | 15 | Bronze |
| Out of the Frying Pan… | Complete the mission in the airplane graveyard. Finish Mission 16, The Enemy of My Enemy. | 15 | Bronze |
| For the Record | Complete the single-player campaign on any difficulty. | 35 | Silver |
| The Price of War | Complete the single-player campaign on Hardened or Veteran Difficulty. | 90 | Gold |
| First Day of School | Complete S.S.D.D. and Team Player on Veteran Difficulty. | 25 | Bronze |
| Black Diamond | Complete Cliffhanger on Veteran Difficulty. | 25 | Bronze |
| Turistas | Complete Takedown and The Hornet's Nest on Veteran Difficulty. | 25 | Silver |
| Red Dawn | Complete Wolverine! and Exodus on Veteran Difficulty. | 25 | Silver |
| Prisoner #627 | Complete The Only Easy Day…Was Yesterday and The Gulag on Veteran Difficulty. | 25 | Silver |
| Ends Justify the Means | Complete Contingency on Veteran Difficulty | 25 | Bronze |
| Homecoming | Complete Of Their Own Accord, Second Sun, and Whiskey Hotel on Veteran Difficulty. | 25 | Silver |
| Queen Takes Rook | Complete Loose Ends and The Enemy of My Enemy on Veteran Difficulty. | 25 | Silver |
| Off the Grid | Complete Just Like Old Times and End Game on Veteran Difficulty. | 25 | Bronze |
| Pit Boss | Run The Pit in S.S.D.D and finish with a final time under 30 seconds. | 10 | Bronze |
| Ghost | Plant the C4 in Cliffhanger without alerting or injuring anyone in the blizzard. | 10 | Bronze |
| Colonel Sanderson | Kill 7 chickens in under 10 seconds in The Hornet's Nest. | 10 | Bronze |

## ACHIEVEMENTS AND TROPHIES CONT.

| NAME | CONDITIONS | GAMERSCORE (XBOX 360) | TROPHY COLOR (PS3) |
|---|---|---|---|
| Gold Star | Earn 1 star in Special Ops. | 20 | Bronze |
| Hotel Bravo | Earn 4 stars in Special Ops. | 20 | Bronze |
| Charlie On Our Six | Earn 8 stars in Special Ops. | 20 | Bronze |
| It Goes to Eleven | Earn at least 1 star in 11 different Special Op missions. | 20 | Bronze |
| Operational Asset | Earn all 3 stars in at least 5 different Special Op missions. | 20 | Bronze |
| Blackjack | Earn 21 stars in Special Ops. | 20 | Bronze |
| Honor Roll | Earn at least 1 star in each Special Op mission. | 20 | Silver |
| Operative | Earn all 3 stars in at least 10 different Special Op missions. | 30 | Silver |
| Specialist | Earn 30 stars in Special Ops. | 30 | Silver |
| Professional | Earn all 3 stars in at least 15 different Special Op missions. | 30 | Silver |
| Star 69 | Earn 69 stars in Special Ops. | 90 | Gold |
| Downed but Not Out | Kill 4 enemies in a row while downed in Special Ops. | 10 | Bronze |
| Ten Plus Foot-Mobiles | Kill at least 10 enemies with one Predator missile in single-player or Special Ops. | 10 | Bronze |
| Unnecessary Roughness | Use a Riot Shield to beat down an enemy in single-player or Special Ops. | 10 | Bronze |
| Knock-Knock | Kill 4 enemies with 4 shots during a slow-mo breach in single-player or Special Ops. | 10 | Bronze |
| The Road Less Traveled | Collect 22 enemy Intel items. | 10 | Bronze |
| Leave No Stone Unturned | Collect 45 enemy Intel items. | 10 | Bronze |
| Drive By | Kill 20 enemies in a row while driving a vehicle in single-player or Special Ops. | 10 | Bronze |
| Desperado | Kill 5 enemies in a row using 5 different weapons or attachments in single-player or Special Ops. | 10 | Bronze |
| I'm the Juggernaut… | Kill a Juggernaut in Special Ops | 10 | Bronze |
| No Rest For the Wary | Knife an enemy without him ever knowing you were there in single-player or Special Ops. | 10 | Bronze |
| Some Like it Hot | Kill 6 enemies in a row using a Thermal weapon in single-player or Special Ops. | 10 | Bronze |
| Look Ma Two Hands | Kill 10 enemies in a row using Akimbo weapons in single-player or Special Ops. | 10 | Bronze |
| Three-some | Kill at least 3 enemies with a single shot from a Grenade Launcher in single-player or Special Ops. | 10 | Bronze |
| Two Birds with One Stone | Kill 2 enemies with a single bullet in single-player or Special Ops. | 10 | Bronze |
| The Harder They Fall | Kill 2 rappelling enemies in a row before they land on their feet in single-player or Special Ops. | 10 | Bronze |

# CALL OF DUTY MODERN WARFARE 2

By Phillip Marcus and the Sea Snipers

© 2009 DK/BradyGAMES, a division of Penguin Group (USA) Inc. BradyGAMES® is a registered trademark of Penguin Group (USA) Inc. All rights reserved, including the right of reproduction in whole or in part in any form.

DK/BradyGames, a division of Penguin Group (USA) Inc.
800 East 96th Street, 3rd Floor
Indianapolis, IN 46240

© 2009 Activision Publishing, Inc. Activision, Call of Duty and Modern Warfare are trademarks or registered trademarks of Activision Publishing, Inc. All rights reserved. The ratings icon is a registered trademark of the Entertainment Software Association. All other trademarks and trade names are the properties of their respective owners..

Please be advised that the ESRB ratings icons, "EC", "E", "E10+", "T", "M", "AO", and "RP" are trademarks owned by the Entertainment Software Association, and may only be used with their permission and authority. For information regarding whether a product has been rated by the ESRB, please visit www.esrb.org. For permission to use the ratings icons, please contact the ESA at esrblicenseinfo@theesa.com.

ISBN-10: 0-7440-1164-7

ISBN-13: 978-0-7440-1164-7

Printing Code: The rightmost double-digit number is the year of the book's printing; the rightmost single-digit number is the number of the book's printing. For example, 09-1 shows that the first printing of the book occurred in 2009.

12 11 10                                        4 3

Printed in the USA.

## CREDITS

**Title Manager**
Tim Fitzpatrick

**Screenshot Editor**
Michael Owen

**Lead Designer**
Keith Lowe

**Designer**
Tim Amrhein

**Map Foldout Designer**
Dan Caparo

**Production Designer**
Tracy Wehmeyer

All map illustrations by Rich Hunsinger (generatorstudios.com).

This guide's multiplayer section was created by the Sea Snipers (seasnipers.net).

## BRADYGAMES STAFF

**Publisher**
David Waybright

**Editor-In-Chief**
H. Leigh Davis

**Licensing Director**
Mike Degler

**Marketing Director**
Debby Neubauer

**International Translations**
Brian Saliba

## ACKNOWLEDGMENTS

BradyGAMES sincerely thanks everyone at Activision and Infinity Ward for their gracious support from the very beginning of this project, and for another uncompromising installment in the *Call of Duty: Modern Warfare* series. Very special thanks to Vince Zampella, Mark Rubin, Pete Blumel, Robert Bowling, Zied Rieke, David Wang, Letam Biira, Byron Beede, Kap Kang, and Amanda O'Keeffe for opening your doors to us and making this guide possible. A thousand thanks for your hospitality and for all your hard work during an incredibly busy time—thank you!

**Phillip Marcus:** Like so many others out there, I spent many long nights with friends online in *Call of Duty 4: Modern Warfare*. When I was asked to work on the sequel, the answer was rather obvious.

To Pete Blumel at Infinity Ward, a big thank you for being both friendly and welcoming to us during a busy time, and quickly providing us with any details or access we needed—it was a pleasure to work with you. Thanks as well to Candice Capen and Anthony Rubin for sharing their expertise on all matters single-player and co-op, and for sanity-checking our work. Finally, a special thanks to Jason Fox, a good friend who took a week off from life to help with Spec Ops, and Rich Hunsinger, who created the other half of this tome.

*Call of Duty: Modern Warfare 2* is an excellent game, and I hope this guide enhances your enjoyment of it in some small way!

**Jason Fox:** I would like to thank Tim and Leigh from BradyGAMES for giving me the opportunity to help with this guide, and Phil for comforting me at every moment of transformation from simple game controller to angry projectile. I'd also like to thank Rich for helping on a few of the more challenging missions. Most importantly, a huge thank you to my wife Lindsey and my son Jake for letting me do crazy things like this all the time.

**Rich Hunsinger:** Special thanks to the S.T.R.A.D.T. team (Sea Snipers Tactical Research And Development Team), consisting of following Sea Snipers, for their tireless efforts in helping to create the content for this guide. Without their help, I would never have gotten this guide done on time or to this level of quality. I worked them almost to death, and one of them to the emergency room!

[SS]Rator a.k.a. Rich Hunsinger
[SS]SportoFu a.k.a. Jordan Evans
[SS]Grifter a.k.a. Ian Bardecki
[SS]Midnight a.k.a. Ammon Terpening
[SS]Wally a.k.a. Jon Toney

Since we started writing and illustrating strategy guides, we have always tried to make each guide better than the last. We try to give players what you want, because we want it too. If it's in the game, we will do everything in our power to bring it to you in the guide.

The Sea Snipers would like to thank BradyGAMES for this awesome opportunity, specifically Leigh Davis, Tim Fitzpatrick, Debby Neubauer, and the rest of the BradyGAMES staff. Big thanks to all of the guys at Infinity Ward. Every time we get the privilege to work at your studio, you make us feel like part of your team, and we really appreciate that. Thank you to Producers Mark Rubin and Pete Blumel for taking care of us while we were there. You guys got us everything we needed on top of trying to finish your game. Very cool. I'd sincerely like to thank CEO Vince Zampella and 402, a.k.a. Robert Bowling, who had everyone who worked on *Call of Duty 4: Modern Warfare* sign my guide for me—wow, thank you guys! Todd Alderman, Geoff Smith, Royce, Brad Allen, and Soupy: thank you guys for all your help. I hope we didn't bug you too much that week. Thanks to [SS]Chief, a.k.a. Michael Fry, who is currently serving in the U.S. Navy, for getting us the opportunities we have now. Thanks to all our families for putting up with us while we were working on this guide, and to the S.T.R.A.D.T. team who worked at Infinity Ward with me. I worked you guys hard and you never complained—you just passed out. That's hardcore. You all did what was asked of you within the deadline. Without all your help, I'd still be marking objectives on the maps. Finally, thank you to my beautiful wife Kate, who always stops whatever she's doing to make sure everything I need is taken care of, so I can concentrate on these guides. I love you, baby girl.